UP NORTH

A Guide to Ontario's Wilderness from Blackflies to the Northern Lights

Doug Bennet
Tim Tiner

Illustrations by Marta Lynne Scythes

REED
BOOKS
CANADA

First published in Canada by
Reed Books Canada
75 Clegg Road
Markham, Ontario
L6G 1A1

Canadian Cataloguing in Publication Data

Bennet, Doug
  Up North : a guide to Ontario's wilderness
from blackflies to the northern lights

  Includes bibliographical references and index.
  ISBN 0-409-91101-1

  1. Natural history – Ontario, Northern. 2. Natural
history – Ontario, Northern – Miscellanea.
3. Natural history – Outdoor books. 4. Ontario,
Northern – Miscellanea. I. Tiner, Tim. II. Title.

  QH106. 2. 05B45 1993   508.9713   C93–093961–1

Edited by Charis Wahl/Ex Libris
Jacket and interior design by Danielle Koch
Line illustrations by Marta Lynne Scythes
Interior photographs by Doug Bennet and Tim Tiner, except as indicated

Cover photograph by Peter D'Angelo, Tony Stone Images
Author photograph by Steve Livingston

Printed and bound in Canada

Table of Contents

PLANT KINGDOM
PLANTS

TREES

HEAVENS
DAY SKY

NIGHT SKY

MOTHER EARTH

F ROM THE TIME we are children, there are hundreds of questions swirling around in our minds prompted by experiences in the woods and wilderness when we go "up north." Such experiences make fresh the sense of wonder with which the pre-technological human mind must have viewed the natural world, with all of its sublime and spectacular phenomena. The intent of this book is to answer, from that sense of wonder, a good number of those common questions and relate some of the amusing bits of stories, history and ideas that surround them.

As much as possible, *Up North* aims to incorporate the whole outdoor experience— the bugs that pester, the wind which scatters them, the trees the wind sways, the life within the soil beneath the trees, the birds in the air, animals in the night, and the stars, moon and northern lights that dance across the night sky. We have concentrated on the most commonly seen or experienced species and things in central Ontario, since they are what occupy your immediate attention most of the time when camping or visiting the cottage.

By central Ontario, we refer to the vast, mixed-forest hinterland from the Rideau Lakes, Kawarthas and Bruce Peninsula, on to the rocky Canadian Shield as far as the Temagami and Mississagi Provincial Park areas—the "up north" of millions of Ontarians. Although much of the guide's information applies as well to other parts of the country, including far northern Ontario and much of Quebec, we have sought, by concentrating on this specific region, to give as complete a picture as possible within the space of the book.

We have arranged the entries in a way that we hope is useful to readers. There are four main chapters: Animal Kingdom, Plant Kingdom, The Heavens and Mother Earth. Subsections within the chapters are arranged alphabetically; thus, amphibians come before birds in the Animal Kingdom. Finally, within each subsection, individual entries are arranged alphabetically by common name: hawk (broad-winged) before owl (barred), and so on. An index is also included.

Being journalists ourselves, rather than biologists, we have endeavoured to be accurate while straying from a strict scientific or academic tone in these pages. Our intent is to answer the many questions of campers and cottagers in the same spirit in which they are asked. If we anthropomorphize, it is because that is indeed what campers and people naturally tend to do when they talk about and relate to nature around them. We have striven, however, to ensure that a sense of fun does not distort the true nature of the subject.

Doug Bennet

Tim Tiner

ANIMAL KINGDOM

AMPHIBIANS

FOR MANY, *our earliest experiences with wildlife involve catching frogs at local ponds or creeks. Through our lives, the spring and summer night choruses of many and varied froggy voices speak of tranquillity and refuge from busy urban lives. From thumbnail-sized spring peepers to fat, bellowing bullfrogs, they clamour for attention in the business of propagating their species each year.*

By contrast, salamanders and newts scurry in the leaf litter, or glide through aquatic habitats, in a silence that masks their immense numbers. Rarely seen, they are the modern representatives of the first vertebrates to crawl onto dry land hundreds of millions of years ago.

In a world increasingly under threat, it is the amphibians that are among the first to suffer. Creatures of both water and land, literally breathing through their permeable, moist skins, they are especially susceptible to environmental adversities of all kinds. As night choruses fall silent in many areas, amphibians are being recognized as early-warning signals of what could be in store for their fellow creatures on Earth.

BULLFROG
Big, Hungry and Loud

IN THE AMPHIB-
ian world, the bull-
frog is king. Larger
than any other green hop-
per in Ontario and a big
eater, a bullfrog will
devour just about any-
thing it can subdue,
including, on occasion,
bats and small birds flying
too close to the water,
other frogs and even its
own kind. But mostly it
nibbles on insect finger
food.

Bullfrogs were named for their deep calls, so like the distant bellowing of a bull. The French name, *oua-oua-ron*, imi-
tates the repeated drone of amorous males. The bigger the
frog, the deeper its voice and brighter yellow its chin. If not
dissuaded by the sight and sound of each other, males will
fight for territory, wrestling until one is dunked and sent
packing.

Bullfrogs are more aquatic than most other frogs, and are
seldom seen on land. They emerge from hibernation in the
muddy sediments of lake bottoms in May. The ancient
Greeks believed frogs were spontaneously formed from mud
and could dissolve back into it, making them symbols of
both fertility and resurrection. Their sudden appearance
with life-giving rain also gave them status as rainmakers the
world over. The Hurons said all the world's water was held
inside a giant frog until the creation hero Iosheha stabbed it.

Water temperatures have to rise a fair bit to rouse bullfrogs from their winter sluggishness and get them in the
mood for breeding. Males establish territories several metres
wide by June, calling loudly to keep rivals away and to
advertise for mates. Females usually choose the best mating

Maximum jumping distance:
2.5–3 m (8–10 ft)

World's record frog jump:
6.2 m (20.3 ft)

**U.S. professional-jumping-frog
school:** Croaker's College,
Sacramento, California

**Average adult bullfrog body
length:** 10–15 cm (4–6 in)

Maximum length: 23 cm (9 in)

Weight: 100–350 g
(4–13 oz)

Markings: Green or greenish
brown back, with black
blotches on younger frogs;
grey-white or pale yellow
undersides; chin, brightest
on mature males; large
brown or grey eardrum circles,
on mature males bigger
than the eye

Alias: Giant bullfrog, jumbo,
mammoth jumbo, jug-o'rum,
l'oua-oua-ron, *Rana
catesbeiana*

BULLFROG

Call: Male mating call a deep, hoarse drone, usually lasting about a second and repeated in contagious choruses; loud, deep croak when startled

Preferred habitat: Marshy bays with lily pads; fens and large ponds

Average breeding territory: 1–6 m (3–20 ft) wide

Incubation period: 4–20 days, depending on temperature

Tadpole: Black-spotted green back, white belly, up to 12 cm (5 in) long

Mortality among newly emerged frogs: More than 80% annually

Age at sexual maturity: 4–6 years old

Lifespan: Few more than 5 years; up to 16 years in captivity

Predators: Fish, dragonfly nymphs, giant water bugs, leeches eat tadpoles; minks, raccoons, skunks, great blue herons, water snakes, pike, bass, snapping turtles eat adults

Average number of bullfrogs per ha (2.5 acres) on suitable lakes: About 30 in June, 200 in July, 100 in August

Range: Southern Ontario north to about Temagami and the southeast shore of Lake Superior; also found in Quebec, New Brunswick, Nova Scotia and Southwest British Columbia

Famous frogs: Kermit, Jeremy Fisher, Jeremiah, Dan'l Webster, Davey Crockett, Grandfather Frog

Number of frogs used for science or entrées in North America: More than 15 million annually

Also see: Lakes, Leopard Frog

territory—cool, deep water with abundant underwater vegetation for hatching eggs—rather than the best male. When they've found it, they check in with the proprietor, who obligingly hops on the back of all comers. Up to six females may use the same nursery site, if it's a good one. They come already bloated with eggs, which are chemically attracted to the male's sperm as both are released simultaneously into the water. The process can take hours, yielding gooey rafts of up to one metre square (three square feet), containing as many as 20,000 floating eggs. Each egg is a tiny incubator, with a clear, porous membrane that swells like a balloon on contact with the water.

In warm weather the eggs hatch quickly. The bullfrog's breeding season extends well into July because, unlike most smaller species, its tadpoles do not need to transform into adults before winter. Bullfrog pollywogs hibernate beneath the ice as their parents do, and take two years, sometimes even three, to sprout legs and begin to hop. After emerging in frog form in July, they take another two or three years to reach breeding age.

Perhaps more than other frog species, the king is in trouble in Ontario. Their big, meaty legs have long been prized in fancy restaurants, though they can no longer be collected without a licence. Poaching, habitat destruction, pesticide poisoning, acid rain, global warming and the thinning ozone layer are also cited as possible causes of their decline in many areas. Because they breathe through their permeable skin, which is protected only by gland secretions, amphibians easily absorb impurities. High acidity in lakes and ponds in spring kills eggs and tadpoles. Because they are so sensitive both on land and in water, amphibians are increasingly regarded as vital indicators of ecosystem health. A world without them would mean lean times for many predators, lakes and ponds choked with algae and skies darkened with swarming insects.

LEOPARD FROG
Denizen of Pond and Meadow

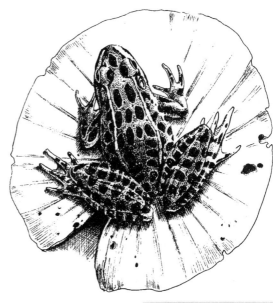

EOPARD FROGS are probably the most-often-seen frogs because they are common both on land and in water. (In the latter they lie stretched out, their eyes just breaking the surface.) They are, in fact, the most widespread frog species in North America. With their attractive, spotted markings, they blend well with the green grass and shadows of summer meadows or with algae beneath the water. Their main defence is in sitting still, hopping only a short distance to a new hiding spot when chased. But since frogs are better at perceiving movement than focusing on objects, a slow-moving heron may easily sneak up on one. Leopard frogs especially are set upon by all manner of predators, from bullfrogs and cruel little boys to fishermen and companies supplying high-school biology classes.

In late April or early May, rising water temperatures stir leopard frogs from their muddy winter beds deep beneath the water, where they draw oxygen through their skins. They soon join the choir of spring peepers, wood and chorus frogs already singing. Males, calling from under the water as well as above, make a snoring or chuckling noise to attract females, followed by grunts to warn other suitors to back off. By late May, most have mated and spread out to summer hunting grounds in and around their streams, ponds and wetlands.

Their eggs hatch 10 to 20 days after being laid, yielding tadpoles that are like pieces of clay, constantly being remoulded by metamorphoses to become something completely different. The temperature of the water controls the speed of their changes. At first tadpoles are tiny sluglike lar-

Average time between skin sheddings for amphibians: 1 month

First appearance of frogs on Earth: 190–150 million years ago

Average adult leopard frog length: 5–10 cm (2–4 in)

Markings: Black, irregular, raisin-shaped spots on bright-green or sometimes light brown or grey back. White undersides

Alias: Northern leopard frog, meadow frog, grass frog, *la grenouille léopard, Rana pipiens*

Food: Algae and decaying vegetation when a tadpole; grasshoppers, crickets, beetles, flies, spiders, snails, smaller frogs when an adult

Call: Deep staccato snore or chuckle about 1–3 seconds long, (often described as the

LEOPARD FROG

sound made by rubbing a balloon) usually followed by grunts; a piercing scream when attacked

Haydn's impression of a croaking frog: 2 violins, 1 viola and 1 cello in Quartet No. 49 in D Major, Op. 5, No. 6

Habitat: Ponds, slow rivers, lakes, swamps, marshes and moist meadows near water

Average clutch: 2,000 eggs, in spherical globs of jelly, about 15 cm (6 in) long and 5 cm (2 in) wide, often stuck to stems or twigs in shallow water

Tadpole: Up to 9 cm long (5.5 in), speckled olive back, white belly

Tadpole mortality in the first 6 weeks: 95–99%

Maximum lifespan: At least 3 years in wild, 9 years in captivity

Predators: Dragonfly larvae, fish, aquatic insects, leeches eat tadpoles; raccoons, minks, weasels, otters, garter snakes, water snakes, bullfrogs, great blue herons, kingfishers, bitterns, hawks, turtles, trout, pike, bass, and many more species eat adults

Range: All of Ontario to tree line; also found in all other provinces except the island of Newfoundland

Pickeral frog range: Southern Ontario to southern Georgian Bay and Algonquin Park

Number of Ontario frog species: 9

Number of frog species worldwide: 2,770–3,500

Also see: Bullfrog, Great Blue Heron, Spring Peeper

vae, blind and with no mouth, hanging on to their egg jelly or to vegetation by sticky structures under their heads. They are nourished by absorbing their egg yolk. Gills filter oxygen from the water. Soon the pollywog's eyes clear, a mouth breaks open on its head and it grows a tail, enabling it to swim and scrape up algae and decaying plant material to eat. All frog or toad tadpoles are strict vegetarians.

Males call from under, as well as above, the water

Over time, tiny hind legs begin to sprout and flaps of skin grow over the gills as lungs form. Front legs develop inside the covered gill chambers, breaking through the skin about a week before the amphibian uses them to crawl onto land. During the last stages of rapid change, the pollywog is like an awkward adolescent and cannot eat. Instead, it lives off the re-absorbed tissue of its shrinking tail, losing about 25 percent of its tadpole weight. Bones harden, true teeth form, eyes rise up from the head, a long tongue develops and the intestine shortens to that of a meat eater. Nine to 13 weeks after hatching, the once fishlike creature has become a tiny froglet. Before it goes into hibernation with the first cold days of fall, it may have doubled its weight again.

Leopard frogs have a close cousin in the bog- and creek-dwelling pickerel frog, which has a similar speckled pattern. Pickerel frogs, however, have straight rows of squarer spots on a light brown background. Their skin secretions are poisonous to other frogs and snakes. The slightly smaller mink frog has splotchy, less distinct markings on its olive green back. It sports a yellow chin. Mink frogs are a more northern species, inhabiting still rivers and bays to just south of Algonquin Park. They are named for the musky smell they produce if captured. Their hollow call, sounding like two large sticks being struck together, can be heard well into August.

6

RED-SPOTTED NEWT
Amphibians with Triple Lives

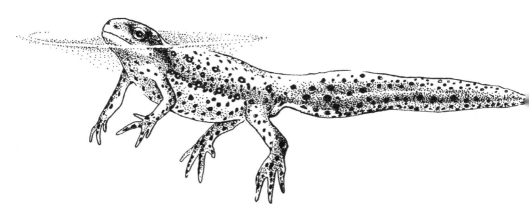

MASTERS OF CHANGE, newts take metamorphosis one step further than other amphibians. After spending two to five years completely on land, newts change colour, regrow finned tails and return to breed and spend the rest of their active lives in ponds. Newts can also regenerate severed tails or legs. When threatened, they lift their tails high above their heads, ready to escape when a predator snatches their expendable appendage. Normally, though, slow-moving newts are less harassed by predators than other salamanders are because of poison glands on their backs. The bright red colour they sport during their terrestrial "eft" stage serves to warn would-be assassins of the unpleasant taste in store for them if they bite, allowing newts to wander about in daylight, in rainy weather, far more often than most salamanders.

After spending the first two or three months of their lives in the water, newts lose their finned tail edges and gills, and develop lungs. Their moist brown skin becomes rough, dry and spotted with red as they crawl onto dry ground in August or September. These red efts are land-loving, carefree, prepubescent newts. They live under rotting logs during the day and are believed to navigate by magnetic fields actually visible to their eyes at night.

Average adult length: 10–12 cm (4–5 in), including tail

Eft length: 3–10 cm (1–4 in)

Hatchling length: About 1 cm (0.4 in)

Markings: Efts have rows of black-bordered vermilion spots on their orange-red backs and pale undersides with black spots. Aquatic adults have olive green, yellow or brown backs and yellow undersides

Alias: Eastern newt, red eft, pond newt, *le triton vert, Notophthalmus viridescens*

Food: Insects and larvae, frog eggs, tadpoles, snails, worms

Habitat: Shallow ponds, bays and swamps with abundant vegetation and few predatory fish; moist, mature forests in eft stage

Clutch: Up to 375 eggs, laid singly on submerged stems and leaves

Incubation period: 20–35 days

Lifespan: Up to 15 years

Predators: Insects, leeches eat eggs;dragonfly nymphs, diving beetles eat larvae; fish and amphibian blood leeches eat adults

Winter whereabouts: Under rocks, logs, and in banks below the frost line, or beneath ice in ponds

Range: Southern Ontario to New Liskeard and Wawa; and southeast of Lake Nipigon to Marathon; also found in Nova Scotia, Prince Edward Island, New Brunswick and Quebec. The central newt, a subspecies, is found southwest of Lake Nipigon.

Number of newt species native to Ontario: 1

Number of newt species worldwide: 43

Also see: Beaver, Redback Salamander

Unlike frogs, toads and other salamanders, the newt's instinct does not draw it back to its ancestral pond to breed. Red efts may travel overland to new ponds, promoting cross-breeding between populations. They are also well adapted to survive changing conditions where beaver ponds are started or left to drain.

Red efts are land-loving, carefree, prepubescent newts

When efts become sexually mature adult newts, their skin becomes soft and moist again and changes to olive green. Fins reemerge on their tails and they head back into the water. For the all-important mating dance, males retain very rough skin on their inner forelegs, used to clasp the backs of females and hold them tightly for almost an hour. All the while the male ritually waves his tail over his mate. Finally, he lets go, moves ahead of her and drops a capsule of sperm for her to pick up in her cloaca. Females can either fertilize their eggs immediately or store the sperm sack, along with those of several other males, for future fertilization. They lay their eggs in early spring.

Adults remain in the water for the rest of the summer, returning to land only occasionally to hibernate. If their pond dries up, newts turn brown again and either go searching for a new pool or wait several days in hope that their old waterhole fills up once more.

REDBACK SALAMANDER

Seldom Seen, but Everywhere

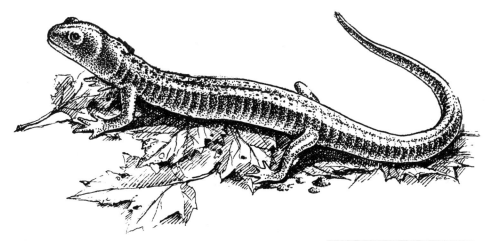

SALAMANDERS ARE THE oldest vertebrates on dry ground, closely resembling the first amphibians that evolved from fish and crawled out of the water almost 400 million years ago. Every summer, that moment in evolution is played out in the greatest historical reenactment on Earth, as amphibians emerge from their youthful aquatic stage to actually breathe air. With one foot in the water and the other on land, amphibians have lived through four planetary cataclysms, each causing the extinction of between 50 and 95 percent of all species on Earth.

Even today, amphibians are by far the most numerous of all land animals with backbones, comprising up to 75 percent of the vertebrate biomass in temperate forests. In moist Ontario forests redback salamanders are more numerous than any other vertebrate, often outnumbering all the birds put together. But they are seldom seen and never heard, being completely mute. They spend almost their entire lives under the soil, rocks and debris of the forest floor. Only in damp earth can they maintain the coating of moisture essential to their survival. So mysterious were salamanders to the ancients that the Greeks gave them their name, which means "fire animal," because they believed their moist skin allowed them to crawl through flames unscathed.

Without moist skin, salamanders would, in fact, be unable to breathe. Redback salamanders do not even have lungs.

Average adult length: 5–10 cm (2–4 in), including tail; hatchlings 2 cm (¾ in) long

Markings: Reddish brown back, dark grey sides, mottled with light grey near salt-and-pepper belly; rarely solid dark back and sides

Alias: *La salamandre rayée, Plethodon cinereus*

Food: Insects, spiders, mites, snails, slugs, worms, spiders

Habitat: Moist deciduous, white pine or hemlock forests

Territory: Less than 1 m² (1 sq yd)

Incubation period: 2 months

Average clutch: 6–10 white eggs, hanging in bunches like grapes

Age at sexual maturity: 2 years old

Lifespan: Up to 30 years

Predators: Snakes (especially ring-necked), owls, shrews, herons, thrushes and other birds

Range: Southern Ontario to Chapleau, Kirkland Lake and around Lake Superior; also found in Nova Scotia, Prince Edward Island, New Brunswick and Quebec

Age of oldest amphibian fossils: 370 million years

Cloaca: All-purpose excretory opening at base of tail in most non-mammalian animals

Number of salamander species in Ontario: 12

Number of salamander species worldwide: About 350

Also see: Red-spotted Newt, Humus

They use their skin and the roof of their mouths to filter oxygen from the air and to release carbon dioxide. Biologists speculate that they evolved in fast-flowing, cold streams. Without lungs, they were less buoyant and sank to the rocky bottom rather than being carried away with the current.

Naming them "fire-animals," the Greeks believed salamanders could crawl through fire unscathed

Evolution, however, has taken redbacks out of the water entirely. They go through their aquatic stage, with gills, inside the fluid of their egg cases, which the mother salamander hangs in bunches from the ceiling of her nest cavity, usually in a rotting log, in June or early July. A mother stays with her eggs for two months. She wraps her body around the bunch, guarding it and keeping it moist but not mouldy with their skin secretions. The young look like miniature versions of adults when they hatch. They may stay with their mother for a few weeks before heading out on their own in early autumn.

Females breed once every two years. Those not busy with young seek out mates on rainy days in September or early October. Male salamanders court by doing intricate dances, each species with its own unique style. Males release their sperm on the ground in a small capsule of jelly, which the female picks up with the muscles of her cloaca. During the winter salamanders crawl down rock crevices or passages left by decayed roots to hibernate below the frost line, at least 40 centimetres (16 inches) beneath the surface. They also move deep down if summer heat dries out the earth's upper layers. Only on moist nights, or very rarely on rainy days, do salamanders chance open-air adventures.

SPRING PEEPER

The Loudest Animal on Earth

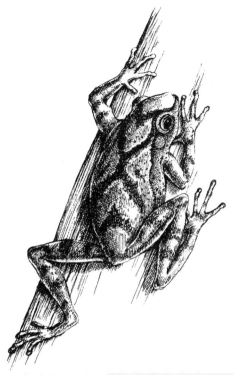

GRAM FOR GRAM, the spring peeper is probably the loudest animal on earth. Small enough to fit easily on a loonie and rarely actually seen, peepers make themselves very conspicuous on April nights, when their high, musical calls join together in a resonating din. Choruses of untold numbers sound to some ears like distant sleigh bells. To sing, males squeeze air over their vocal chords and amplify the sound by inflating their throats into balloonlike bubbles, producing a springy note that can carry for almost two kilometres (1.2 miles).

Together with the larger wood frog, which sports a black mask and quacks like a duck, spring peepers are the first frogs to sing in spring. Awakened by the thawing of the earth around their winter beds beneath the leaf litter, they rise en masse on the first rainy nights of the season. In rare cases when conditions are ideal, the ground crawls with thousands of peepers, wood frogs and blue- or yellow-spotted salamanders, drawn to their ancestral ponds like zombies, entranced by the urge to breed. Often migrating with patches of snow still on the ground, they slip in under the ice at the edge of ponds.

Males immediately take up positions around the pond, about a week before the opposite sex will be drawn by their serenades. Floating free or clinging to bits of debris and the previous year's dried vegetation, male peepers belt it out mid- to late April and into May. Chorus frogs, another tiny member of the tree-frog family, sometimes join in, with a call that sounds like the teeth of a comb being flicked. During cold snaps they quieten down. Female peepers gravitate toward the singers with the fastest tempo. If a balladeer can attract an admirer plump with eggs, he jumps on her back

Sound level of spring peeper call: 110–120 decibels

Sound level of an airport runway: 120 decibels

Sound level of average conversation: 60 decibels

Conspiratorial, subdued conversation: 40 decibels

Adult spring peeper length: 2–3 cm (0.8–1.2 in)

Markings: Tan, greenish-brown or grey back with a dark X; black bands on legs; white throat and belly

Alias: *La rainette crucifer, Pseudacris crucifer*

Call: Shrill, piercing "peeeep" with a rising pitch, lasting about a second, constantly repeated

Food: Algae when a tadpole; mosquitoes, gnats, ants, beetles and other small insects, sometimes worms and snails, when an adult

Habitat: Wetlands, small, temporary ponds in spring; damp forests and bushes near marshes in summer and fall

Breeding territory: 10–45 cm (4–18 in) wide

Average clutch: about 200 eggs laid singly or in small clusters

Incubation period: 5–15 days

Tadpoles: Up to 2.5 cm (1 in) long; green back speckled with gold; white belly

Age at sexual maturity: 3–4 years old

Predators: Fish, other frogs, turtles, snakes, birds; salamanders, dragonfly nymphs, diving beetles, giant water bugs eat tadpoles and eggs

Winter whereabouts: Hibernate beneath ground or leaf litter

Range: All of Ontario to James Bay; also found in Nova Scotia, New Brunswick, Prince Edward Island, Quebec and Manitoba

First appearance of tree frogs in evolution: 26 million years ago

Number of tree frog species native to Ontario: 3

Number of tree frog species worldwide: 630

and hugs her closely as they simultaneously release eggs and sperm into the water.

Peepers rise en masse on the first rainy nights of the season

Peeper choruses fall silent by the end of May, though a few individualists sometimes call before retiring for the season in October. While risking fatal late freezes, the spring peepers' early breeding allows their tadpoles to mature into tiny, bee-sized frogs by June or July, before summer's heat dries up their small nursery ponds. They spread out over wide areas and spend the rest of the year on land, hunting for insects at night, resting during the day under logs, rocks and leaves. Though they are tree frogs, clinging to vertical surfaces with sticky, bubbly pads at the end of each toe, spring peepers rarely climb higher than low bushes and shrubs. In addition to projecting their voices great distances, they can leap more than 17 times their own body length when moving from branch to branch.

AMERICAN TOAD
Land-loving Warty Wonder

Toad, that under cold stone
Days and nights has thirty-one
Sweltered venom sleeping got,
Boil thou first i' the charmed pot.

SHAKESPEARE'S WITCHES in *Macbeth* were not the first to employ toad poison for dark deeds. England's King John was rumoured to have been poisoned in 1216 via a cup of ale spiked with toad venom by a monk who had overheard the unpopular monarch's plans to raise the price of bread. The poison in question is a bitter white liquid that toads, when molested, exude from their "warts" and the parotid glands behind their heads. The secretion irritates the mucous membranes in the mouth, eyes and nose of predators. The substance does not cause warts, however. Toads can also puff up their bodies with air to nearly twice their normal size, a defence especially handy for convincing snakes that they are too big to be swallowed.

With their relatively thick, dry skin and terrestrial lifestyle, toads appear to be closer to reptiles than any other amphibian. Their hind legs are smaller than frogs' legs, limiting them to shorter hops or outright walking. Their colour-

Average adult length: 5–9 cm (2–3.5 in)

Maximum length: 20 cm (8 in)

Markings: Mottled brown, tan, rust or green on back and sides, with "warts," grey-white underside, large eardrums; males' throats darker than females

Alias: *Le crapaud d'Amérique, Bufo americanus*

Name for a group: A knot of toads

Call: High, musical trill in 15–20-second bursts

Food: Beetles, moths, grasshoppers, flies, larvae, slugs, worms

Estimated number of insects a toad eats in 3 months: 10,000

Habitat: Forests, meadows; shallow ponds and marshes in spring

Clutch: 4,000–7,000 eggs, like strings of beads around submerged vegetation, rocks or sticks

Egg-development period: 3–12 days

Tadpoles: Fat, black, with tiny wiggling tails

Age at sexual maturity: 2 years old

Lifespan: Few live past 3–4 years in wild, up to 36 years in captivity

Predators: Skunks, raccoons, hognose snakes, garter snakes, crows, hawks, owls

Winter whereabouts: Up to 1.3 m (4.3 ft) deep in sandy soil on land

Range: All of Ontario except extreme northwest; also found in Nova Scotia, New Brunswick, Prince Edward Island, Quebec, Labrador, Manitoba, Saskatchewan and Alberta

ing blends with the leaves and needles on the forest floor, and can change slightly with their surroundings, becoming darker when they are in moist, brown earth. Moisture requirements keep toads mainly in soft dirt depressions or under debris during the day. They can dig with their back feet quite quickly.

After hibernating below the frost line, toads retrace their steps in May to almost the exact spot where they first emerged from the ponds of their youth. They migrate to the ponds in large numbers, the males calling out in slow trills at first, speeding up with their metabolism as the weather grows warmer. The breeding season can be very brief in any one pond, with females leaving as soon as they lay their eggs. Toad tadpoles take about nine weeks to develop legs. Toadlets, about a centimetre (0.4 inch) long, crawl onto land in July or early August and remain around water's edge. On rainy nights they move farther, some travelling more than a kilometre as they become acclimatized to dry land.

Virtually all toads seen in Ontario are the common American toad. The majority are the small, two-to-three-centimetre (0.8 to 1.2 inches) variety, in their troubled-youth stage, through which few survive. Those that do, continue to grow throughout their lives and may reach the size of bullfrogs. Ontario's only other toad species, Fowler's or Woodhouse's toad, is restricted to the sandy shores of Lake Erie, especially around Long Point. Wood frogs, which can be up to five centimetres (two inches) long, look like toads because they are tan to reddish brown and are usually found on land, in damp forests. But they have dark masks and, like most frogs, smooth skin. Grey tree frogs are also often mistaken for toads because they have fairly rough skin and can be brown. They can also be green or grey, because they change colour within an hour or two to match the surface they're resting on. Tree frogs are mostly nocturnal and call up to 700 times an hour in one-to-two-second- long, high staccato trills, sounding like a bird, during their breeding season on June evenings.

BIRDS

BIRDS ARE *the most conspicuous variety of wildlife in the wilderness. At least 444 species of birds have been confirmed sighted in the wild in Ontario. About 300 of them nest in the province. Most species fly primarily by day, adding music and bright splashes of colour to the forest and waterfront.*

The majority of birds—more than 75 percent of all North American species—are migratory. An estimated five billion fly south from Canada and the northern U.S. every fall. Hardy chickadees, ravens, gray jays and ruffed grouse remain behind to tough it out through the winter. But before the snows are even melted, a parade of migrants begins, heralding the return of spring, reaching a crescendo with waves of wood warblers in mid-May. Some come all the way from South America to raise a new generation on the bugs, berries and seeds of a Canadian summer.

RED-WINGED BLACKBIRD

Flash of Scarlet Signals Spring

Length: 17–25 cm (7–10 in)

Wingspan: 30–36 cm (1–1.2 in)

Average weight: Males 66 g (2.4 oz), females 45 g (1.6 oz)

Markings: Males black with scarlet-and-yellow wing epaulets; females streaked brown and beige, with yellowish orange tints around head; males in first breeding season brownish with slight red wing patches

Alias: Red-wing, marsh blackbird, *le carouge à épaulettes, Agelaius phoeniceus*

Call: Variety of loud clicks, clacks, high whistles, chirps, chatters and staccato noises; song a gurgling "conk-a-ree," rolling at the end like a referee's whistle

Food: Caterpillars, dragonflies and other insects, invertebrates, seeds, small fruits

Preferred habitat: Marshes, swamps, meadows, fields

Average territory: 0.1 ha (0.25 acre) in marshes, much bigger in fields

Nest: Small, deep, tightly woven basket of grasses and strips of cattail leaves in cattails, reeds, small trees or shrubs, usually less than 2 m (6.6 ft) above the water or ground

Average clutch: 3–5 black-and-purple-speckled or streaked light blue-green eggs, about the size of grapes

Incubation period: 10–12 days

Fledging age: 10–13 days

A DOMINANT MALE red-winged blackbird in his prime is an iron-fisted patriarch commanding the best and biggest stretch of marsh, a harem of several mates and the fear and respect of his colony. He is a warrior troubadour who, many bird experts believe, has learned more songs than any of his rivals, warding them off with his virtuosity. While he sings, he flashes his bright scarlet epaulets, badges of age and experience that similarly convince others not to challenge him.

The flickering of red wing patches in flight, like technicolour strobe lights, is one of the earliest signs of spring. Male red-wings come first, arriving in flocks mixed with grackles and cowbirds, often when marshes are still frozen. They find food by scouring fields for crop and weed seeds, and by tearing into the fluffy tops of the previous year's cattails, snapping up tiny caterpillars of the cattail worm moth, which live in the seedheads all winter. Though they forage and roost together for a few weeks, males spend gradually more time each day staking out their turf in the marsh, singing boldly from prominent perches and chasing and fighting each other in a never-ending game of border encroachment. Less successful males are crowded out of prime marsh real estate and forced to establish territories in meadows or thickets.

Females, who arrive two or three weeks after the males, do not marry for love. They look for the richest, safest patch of marsh for raising a family, and mate with whatever lug happens to occupy it. After the initial formalities, and even hostilities, of establishing a relationship with the bellicose lord of the manor, they usually mate in May. Males will mate with and defend as many females as are interested in settling in their domain. Each female maintains her own nesting zone within her mate's territory, driving away potential new concubines. Four wives is usually the maximum for a well-situated male.

Female red-wings are certainly not stand-by-your-man

types. Although they may return to the same territory to mate every year, they show no qualms about having flings with interloping scoundrels when hubby's away feeding. Carleton University professor Patrick Weatherhead's studies suggest almost 30 percent of hatchlings are fathered through extramarital affairs, usually involving next-door neighbours.

Female red-wings are often not recognized as blackbirds because they look like big brown-streaked sparrows, coloration that effectively camouflages them in the nest. If predators are close by, the bright males try to distract or drive them away, exploding from the cattails with a loud burst and splash of colour. Males have even been known to strike humans that come too close to a nest. Red-wings also

Average annual adult mortality: 40–50 %

Lifespan: 2–2.5 years on average, up to 9 years

Predators: Raccoons, weasels, sharp-shinned and other hawks, crows, black rat snakes, water snakes

Average population density: 1–10 pairs per km^2 (0.4 sq. mi)

Average first arrival in central Ontario: Late Mar.

Average last departure from central Ontario: Late Oct.

Range: All of Ontario except far northwest. Also found in all provinces and the Northwest Territories

Winter whereabouts: Ontario population overwinters from extreme southern Ontario to northern Florida

Number of blackbird-family species breeding in Ontario: 10

Also see: Cattail, Wetlands

commonly band together to mob owls, crows, hawks, foxes and weasels. Despite all the vigilance, predators often make suppers of the contents of about half of all red-wing nests started in some areas each year.

Studies suggest almost 30 percent of hatchlings are fathered through extramarital affairs, usually involving next-door neighbours

Young red-wings that survive to fledge leave their parents about a week afterwards and form foraging flocks. Juvenile males are brownish until their third year. Later in the summer, after the last batch of young have fledged, adults moult, join large flocks and move out of marshes and into dry upland areas where they find seeds and berries during the day. Flocks gradually gravitate to traditional migration staging areas, such as Holland Marsh and Long Point, where hundreds of thousands may roost together between late August and September. Some roosts in the U.S. include millions. Indeed, red-wings are believed to be the most numerous single species of land bird in North America, with an estimated fall population of 400 million. Their giant flocks are considered a plague in some agricultural areas, but efforts to reduce their numbers by spraying and other means, mainly in the U.S., have had little effect. Red-wings are a tough bunch.

BLUE JAY
Smart, Loud, Bold and Brash

AMONG OTHER BIRDS, blue jays are not nearly the favourites they are to humans. Jays have a nasty habit of eating other birds' eggs and even their nestlings. Nest robbing is really only a rare treat for them, making up less than one percent of their diet, but it's enough to make them terrors. Small birds often gang up and mob a jay to drive it away, noisily diving at and sometimes striking it in the air. For their part, jays mob hawks, owls, crows, weasels and foxes, which can threaten them or their offspring. The jay's loud, harsh alarm call also commonly warns other birds and animals that a potential predator is entering the area.

Blue jays in general are considered bold, brash, alert and intelligent. They can adapt quickly to a wide variety of habitats, though they favour evergreen trees for nesting and roosting, and oak trees for feasting on acorns. When oaks have a major acorn crop, once every four to 10 years, blue jay populations increase significantly. In turn, jays spend much time burying and hiding small caches of acorns and other seeds in tree crevices for later use, helping to spread new vegetation via those they forget about.

In early spring, loose winter-feeding parties of jays begin to break up. Males fight, establish territories and, despite their reputations as raucous brigands, sing softly to their mates. In mid-April, when the Toronto Blue Jays come out to play, their feathered namesakes become unusally quiet and inconspicuous as they begin nesting, quite the opposite of most male songbirds. Females do most of the building of their well-hidden nests over the period of about a week. As with many species, her mate concentrates on fetching food and feeding her like a nestling. This "baby" behaviour helps

Name for a group: A party of jays

Origin of name: Old German *gahi*, meaning "quick"

Average flying speed: 33 km/h (20 mph)

Length: 26–32 cm (10–12 in)

Wingspan: 41–42 cm (16–17 in)

Weight: 92 g (3.3 oz)

Markings: Blue back, white underside, black necklace, blue crest

Alias: *Le geai bleu, Cyanocitta cristata*

19

BLUE JAY

bond the pair and provides extra energy and protein for developing eggs.

Blue-jay young, like many other birds, hatch featherless, blind and unable to generate enough heat to warm their blood to normal survival temperatures. For their first two or three days, they are closely brooded and not fed, instead living off the yoke absorbed from their eggs. After those first critical days, their circulatory systems rev up, their blood warms and they acquire downy insulation. Their bright red, opened mouths trigger an automatic feeding response in their parents, who nourish them with a rich soup of regurgitated caterpillars and other juicy insects. By late May or June, four-week-old fledglings accompany their parents in regrouping flocks of foraging jays.

Jays mob hawks, owls, crows, weasels and foxes

In the fall, especially September, blue jays gather in larger flocks, sometimes in the hundreds, and migrate south. Up to 30,000 a day have been counted in steady flights past the Holiday Beach hawk watch on Lake Erie in late September and early October. While some stay in Ontario to tough it out all winter, they vanish from certain areas in severe years.

A close relative, the gray jay, generally stays in northern Ontario all winter, rarely travelling farther south than about Perry Sound or Petawawa. Gray jays survive by building up winter food stores starting in June, chewing seeds to coat them with saliva, which acts as a preservative, and then sticking them beneath bark and moss. Their beaverlike endeavours allow 83 percent of territorial gray jays to live through winter, a much higher survival rate than migrant species enjoy. Unlike their southern cousin, the smaller, uncrested grey birds, also called whisky-jacks, are renowned for their friendliness, often taking food from campers. Their tame demeanour may have led to an old superstition that gray jays were the ghosts of dead lumberjacks.

BLACK-CAPPED CHICKADEE
Mating Song a Harbinger of Spring

PATROLLING THE WOODS in their grey, black and white uniforms, tame chickadee troops communicate with a rudimentary kind of language, one of the first to be discovered among wildlife. Named for their familiar, buzzy "chick-a-dee-dee-dee" call, they combine its four notes in innumerable ways and shift from one key to another to produce different messages. Repetiton may intensify or clarify the communication. They also have a wide repertoire of tweets, twitters, gargles and even hisses used in love, war and other social interactions.

The chickadee phrase humans most long to hear begins in midwinter, when males start laying claim to breeding territories by whistling their high, lingering mating song. Though the song may be heard into early summer, its first echo through the cold, still woods is taken as a promise that spring is around the corner. After spending the early winter in small foraging flocks, chickadees disperse over a wider area. The top one or two males of the flock take territories in the winter foraging area, often pairing up with their previous year's mate. The other, usually younger, chickadees are pushed out to less favourable sites. On average, only one couple per flock survives from one breeding season to the next, usually the dominant pairs with the best feeding and sheltering sites.

In place of chocolates, courting male chickadees offer females large insects, which have lots of protein to help in egg production. Couples are paired off by mid-April. If they can't find an unoccupied woodpecker hole or other tree cavity to call their own, they spend a week or two pecking one out, usually one to four metres (three to 13 feet) above the ground. Lower-ranking female chickadees sometimes fly to the territory of a dominant male for an illicit liasion, then return to their nests on the wrong side of the tracks to have their cuckolded husbands help raise their blueblooded brood.

From the time the eggs are laid, usually one a day, until

Length: 12–14 cm (4.5–5.5 in)

Wingspan:15–22 cm (6–8.6 in)

Weight: 11–12 g (about 0.4 oz)

Markings: Both sexes have a black cap and beard, white cheeks and belly, grey wings and tail, deep black eyes

Alias: Common chickadee, black-capped titmouse, long-tailed chickadee, *la mésange à tête noire, Parus atricapillus*

Call: Nasal, buzzing "chic-a-dee-dee;" whistled song is like the first notes of a white-throated sparrow, but with the first note much higher than the second, commonly written as "fee-bee" or "fee-bee-ee"

Food: Insects, insect eggs, caterpillars, spiders, invertebrates, conifer seeds, bayberries, poison ivy berries and blueberries, acorns, carrion

Preferred habitat: Mixed and deciduous forests, swamps

Average breeding territory: 5 ha (12.5 acres)

Average flock territory: About 10 ha (25 acres)

Average flock size: 6–10 birds

Nest: Cavities in trees or stumps, especially birch, lined with moss, grass, pine needles, feathers and fur, with the entrance about 2.5 cm (1 in) wide

Average clutch: 6–8 reddish brown-spotted, dull white eggs, about the size of pistachio-nut shells

Incubation period: 11–13 days

Average annual adult mortality rate: 40%

Maximum lifespan: 12 years

Predators: Sharp-shinned hawks, northern shrikes, long-tailed weasels, owls

Annual mortality rate for songbirds after their first year: 55%

Body temperature: 40°C (104°F)

Number of heartbeats per minute: 500

Approximate number of body feathers: 2,000

Average population density: 1–100 pairs per 10 km² (4 sq. mi)

Often seen with: White-breasted nuthatchs, brown creepers, downy woodpeckers in winter flocks, and vireos, warblers, ruby- and golden-crowned kinglets in autumn flocks

Range: All of Ontario, except far northwest. Also found in all other provinces and territories

Number of chickadee species breeding in Ontario: 2

the young are fledged, chickadee parents become quiet and secretive. Fathers bring food while mothers incubate. Like most songbirds, chickadee chicks hatch helpless and blind. But stoked with a super rich protein diet of insects, they increase their weight by 50 to 75 percent in the first 24 hours. They are 10 times their birth weight after 10 days and fledge when two to three weeks old. Families fly together for another week or so, until parents cut off the free food and the young disperse.

In late summer and fall, chickadees form small, inquisitive flocks again, often accompanied by migrating species also foraging for seeds, insects and bug eggs. Chickadees specialize in searching through the bark crevices of low outer branches, hanging upside-down from the tips and hovering under leaves. First-year immatures that join the flock are usually from other areas, not the offspring of the resident dominant pairs, ensuring the gene pool is mixed. Each troop maintains and defends its borders from neighbouring chickadee bands. Being inveterate hoarders, they always seem to be busy. The stakes can be high, since chickadees may cache hundreds or even thousands of seeds and other pieces of food in hollow stumps, beneath bark, inside dead, curled leaves and under moss for use in lean times.

Chickadees sometimes move south in large migrant flocks from mid-September to November, though in many years they seem to stay put for the winter. In "irruption years," when food is short in northern areas, they fly through by the hundreds, sometimes mixed with boreal chickadees, their northern cousins.

AMERICAN CROW
A Crafty Team Player

MODERN SCIENCE verifies the folk wisdom that crows are most intelligent birds. Their brain size, adaptability and longevity place them high on the evolutionary scale. Studies show crows can be taught to count to at least four or five. Some naturalists suggest they already know how to count. Crows also have a large variety of communication calls—ranging from 20 to 300 according to various authorities—forming "dialects" that vary from one region to another. Ernest Thompson Seton, writing in 1898 of a wise old Don Valley crow leader he called Silverspot, described a whole range of specific warning calls, alerts, directions and greetings. Crows can yell, gurgle and even mimic human laughter and words. Some people swear they can be taught to talk.

Crows are known for sticking up for one another, often coming to the aid of injured or distressed members of the flock when they call

---

One crow call, a long, constant cawing, is said to be summons for the flock to gather. There are many accounts of crows holding councils and even trials, with accused individuals standing aside silently while the rest of the flock caws, sometimes for hours. Finally, they all either fly away, with the accused off the hook, or suddenly attack and peck it to death. Ornithologists are dubious about such an interpretation of events.

But crows are known for sticking up for one another, often coming to the aid of injured or distressed members of the flock when they call. They cooperate closely, keeping one or two sentries posted while a flock forages, and joining togeth-

Length: 43–53 cm (17–21 in)

Wingspan: 84–100 cm (2.7–3.3 ft)

Weight: 440–570 g (1–1.2 lb)

Markings: Males, females and immatures all completely black

Call: Loud caw, many variations

Alias: Common crow, eastern crow, corn thief, *la corneille américaine, Corvus brachyrhynchos*

Food: Crows are omnivores, known to eat hundreds of different kinds of food, including seeds, berries, insects, snakes, young birds, eggs, frogs, squirrels, carrion and french fries

Preferred habitat: Forests, marshes, lakes, meadows

Nest: Large jumble of sticks and bark, lined with grass, moss, roots, fur

Average clutch: 4–6 dark brown spotted, green eggs, about as big as golf balls

Incubation period: 18 days

Fledging age: About 35 days

Lifespan: 7–13 years in wild, more than 20 years in captivity

Predators: Great horned owls, goshawks, red-tailed hawks, foxes, bobcats

Flying speed: 40–53 km/h (24–32 mph)

Name for a group: A murder of crows, an unkindness of ravens

Name origin: Imitation of call

Average first arrival in central Ontario: Early Mar.

Average last departure from central Ontario: Late Oct.

er to mob potential predators such as hawks or owls. A flock of crows kicking up a ruckus during the day can lead to a roosting owl. At the nest, a crow hatched the previous year often helps its parents feed a new batch of siblings.

Despite their intelligence, crows also have a somewhat unsavoury reputation among humans. Along with ravens, the closely related European carrion crow was long associated with death and misfortune in Britain and other countries. Farmers have been engaged in a timeless battle of wits with pillaging crows, trying everything from scarecrows to shotguns to get rid of them. Crows are said to recognize a shotgun on sight and take off long before a human can try it out on them. Crows are also known as jewel thieves, snatching up shiny, colourful doodads, including watches and eyeglasses, whenever they get the chance. Seton tells of discovering Silverspot's buried treasure trove of shells, white pebbles, bits of tin and a china cup handle. While ready explanations for such behaviour are lacking, the crow family, which includes jays, is closely related to birds of paradise and bowerbirds, which collect bright objects for their nests or courting sites.

Crows begin their wooing a few weeks after returning to the Canadian Shield in early March. Flocks break up as couples pair off. Males fly in courtship displays, diving and driving off competitors. Landing beside females, they bow repeatedly and utter soft, melodious sweet nothings. They usually build large nests at least five metres (16 feet) up, in a crotch of an evergreen. Their young hatch and become boisterous by May. By the time they clumsily begin to fledge,

Range: All of Ontario. Also found in all other provinces and the Northwest Territories

Winter home: South of Canadian Shield to Gulf of Mexico

Average population density: 1–10 pairs per 10 km² (4 sq. mi)

Length of raven: 55–68 cm (22–27 in)

Wingspan of raven: 120–132 cm (4–4.5 ft)

Also see: Barred Owl, Snowshoe Hare, Wolf

young crows are already black and adult sized, though with higher voices and bluish eyes. They are not the much-smaller black birds often seen close on the heels of crows, erroneously taken by many people to be babies following their mother. The little followers are red-winged blackbirds, angrily mobbing crows, which make regular snacking raids on other species' nests.

Crows begin flocking together again in late June, bringing their fledglings with them to learn the ways of society. They fly south in November to traditional roosting spots. Canada's largest winter roost, outside Essex, Ontario, hosts about 50,000 crows. American winter roosts can swell to Hitchcockian numbers of up to four million.

Ravens, also found throughout much of the Canadian Shield, stick around for the winter. They are almost identical to crows, but are larger by about a third, and utter a harsher croak or squawk instead of a caw. The back edge of a raven's tail is paddle shaped, not cut straight across like a crow's, its neck feathers more shaggy and its beak heavier. Ravens seem to have a greater love of flying than do crows, and take more to acrobatics and gliding, tending to flap their wings slowly and smoothly, like other larger birds. The two closely related species don't seem to get along and often chase each other. Crows have proven more adaptable, increasing in numbers in southern Ontario after the wary raven was pushed out of the region with the clearing of the forests for farmland in the 1800s.

CANADA GOOSE
Migrant Honker Across Shield Skies

Flying speed: 65–85 km/h
(39–51 mph)

Migrating altitude: 300–900 m
(1,000–3,000 ft)

Wing beats per second: 2

Length: 56–114 cm (1.8–3.7 ft)

Average height: 63–102 cm
(2–3.3 ft)

Wingspan: 1.1–1.8 m (3.7–6 ft)

Weight: 1–9 kg (2.2–20 lb),
depending on stock or race

Markings: Both sexes have black
neck and head, white chin
strap, light brown back, off-
white breast and tail

Alias: Honker, wild goose,
Canada, grey goose, *la
bernache canadienne, Branta
canadensis*

Call: Honk

EVERY HITCHHIKER ever stuck in Wawa knows the wanderlust symbolized by the fabled giant Wawa goose. It is an emotion stirred in human hearts all across the Canadian Shield each fall and spring by the enormous, shifting V formations of honking Canadas passing over in migration. When the geese drop down to rest and refuel, the deep, steady sound of rushing air from each wing beat betrays the essence of power in flight.

Geese fly in a V formation because it cuts wind resistance, and the suction created by the powerful downstrokes of one bird helps carry the one following it, like a bicycle behind a truck. Migrating flocks are made up of several family groups that merge in the air, with adults, according to some experts, taking turns leading the way, since they're the strongest and they know the route.

They keep track of each other by honking, but young making their first migration south are especially noisy. They have not had time in their four months of life to build up as much fortifying fat as adults have and are generally ravenous, nagging constantly, like kids in the back seat on a long car trip, for their parents to land for refreshments below. After flying continuously for 300 kilometres (180 miles) or more, geese commonly land in small lakes or large old beaver ponds near the southern edge of forested areas, where they can rest and spread out into nearby fields to forage.

Geese mate for life, although adultery is common

Though Canada geese nest in many urban and rural areas in southern Ontario, they are drifters in Shield country, passing through in April to May and September to October. Lakes and wetlands in the Canadian Shield are largely too deep, rocky and sterile to compete with the rich summer breeding grounds of the Hudson Bay lowlands for the affections of hundreds of thousands of migrant geese.

While Canadas may migrate during the day, they also take advantage of clear nights to fly by the light of the moon. Winds often drop after sunset, making progress easier. Impending winter weather sends each group south towards its traditional wintering ground. It is said their passing generally forecasts snow up to two weeks in advance. Biologists theorize that geese may be acutely sensitive to air currents, barometric pressure or weather-activated biochemical changes in their food.

The Cree and Inuit called the full moon of late April or early May the Goose Moon, for that was when the big birds returned to their nesting grounds around Hudson Bay. It was salvation on the wing for northern hunters, ending the leanest, hardest time of the year, when winter food supplies were running out and other game was scarce. Adult pairs return with their previous season's offspring, but send them off to form adolescent bands while preparations are made at the usual nest site to raise a new batch of young.

Geese mate for life, though adultery is common. After

Food: Sedges, grass, willow buds, grain, aquatic vegetation and insects

Preferred habitat: Marshes, ponds, lakes, rivers, fields

Nest: Sticks, reeds and down, lining a ground depression 75–90 cm (2.5–3 ft) wide, near water, sometimes on beaver or muskrat lodges

Average clutch: 4–6 dull white eggs, about the size of average potatoes

Incubation period: About 28 days

Fledging age: About 10 weeks

Age at sexual maturity: 2–3 years

Maximum lifespan: 25 years

Predators: Foxes, ravens, crows, gulls raid nests

Name origin: From proto-Indo-European word *ghans*, probably an imitation of the honking call

Name of a group: Gaggle

Place in Canadian monetary system: Back of $100 bill

Famous geese: Mother Goose, goose that laid the golden egg

Range: Southern Ontario and Hudson Bay lowlands. Also found in all the Western provinces, Quebec, Newfoundland and the Northwest Territories

Winter whereabouts: Southern Ontario to northern Mexico

Hudson Bay lowlands fall population: About 1.25 million

Number shot annually in Ontario: About 100,000

Number of people hunting waterfowl annually in Ontario: About 115,000

CANADA GOOSE

mating, females build a nest and stay on it, while ganders aggressively stand guard. Geese have been known to lunge at humans that come too close to nests.

Naturally, the downy yellow goslings assume the first living thing they see when they hatch in May or June is their parent, and follow it anywhere. Ontario sculptor Bill Lishman used this knowledge to convince goose hatchlings he was their mother and eventually taught them to follow his ultralight plane in formation in the air. Dominant geese pairs sometimes also kidnap goslings from other weak-willed parents. Adoptees may sometimes be used as decoys by foster parents trying to save their natural offspring from predators. Large families also tend to hog the best grazing sites.

Overall, eastern North America's honker population is strong and growing, owing to tight hunting controls and conservation measures. Like many game animals, overhunting pushed them towards the brink within living memory. In the mid-1940s there were an estimated 50,000 geese migrating along the Mississippi flyway, less than five percent of the present number. Southern Ontario's breeding population almost disappeared by the 1920s, except for remnants on Lake St. Clair. Geese later released from captivity, including one upwardly mobile flock on the Toronto Islands, gradually propagated under protected conditions. Today there are 125,000 to 150,000 geese nesting on islands, peninsulas, marsh hummocks, muskrat lodges and city parks throughout southern Ontario. About 30,000 remain through the winter.

RUFFED GROUSE
Drummer of the Forest

THE ABUNDANCE of ruffed grouse, the chickens of the forest, made them vitally important to the Ojibway and Cree, especially in winter. One Ojibway creation story tells of the grouse being the first-born of the world's primal mother, Spirit Woman. The grouse stayed behind with her after all her other bird children flew off. Similarly, the hare and the whitefish remained when the rest of her animal and fish offspring ran, swam and waddled away. Like the grouse, the other two faithful children were important staple foods for woodland hunters, and so became totem animals of large Ojibway clans.

With only limited powers of flight, ruffed grouse are secretive birds. Yet they overwhelm observers when flushed from their hiding places, exploding out of nowhere so suddenly that they are out of view before the shock of their thunderous flapping wears off. Flushed grouse usually fly straight up with their tails fanned out and then arch swiftly, flying up to 100 metres (110 yards) to another well-concealed spot. In the winter they might burst out from beneath powdery snow, where they take shelter during extreme cold spells. Grouse can actually fly quite silently if they wish to, but by stirring up a commotion, they throw potential predators off guard and warn others of their kind to flee.

In the spring, male grouse actively broadcast their locations in hopes of attracting a mate or two. Starting in late March, they climb onto carefully chosen fallen logs in forest clearings, preferably on slopes or ridges, where branch cover

Length: 40–48 cm (16–19 in)

Average wingspan: 60 cm (2 ft)

Average weight: Males 600 g (1.3 lb), females 460 g (1 lb)

Markings: Brown back and crested head, grey breast, black band at end of square-edged tail; black, iridescent neck ruffs; bare skin over eyes usually orangish on males

Alias: Woods pheasant, birch partridge, pine hen, drumming grouse, drummer, tippet, long-tailed grouse, white flesher, wood grouse, *la gelinotte huppée*, *Bonasa umbellus*

Brain size: 2 cm³ (0.1 cu. in)

Human brain size: 1,300 cm³ (79 cu. in)

RUFFED GROUSE

Call: Clucks, alarm whistles, hisses

Food: Hundreds of species of seeds, nuts, berries, fruits, buds, mushrooms and insects, occasionally snakes and frogs; relies heavily on aspen, birch, alder and hazel buds and twigs in winter

Habitat: Forest understory, ravines, stream edges, especially with aspen trees and saplings; roosts in hemlocks and other evergreens in fall and winter

Grouse explode out of nowhere so suddenly that they are out of view before the shock of their thunderous flapping wears off

Territory: 2–25 ha (5–62 acres) for individuals, about 20 ha (950 acres) for families

Nest: A ground depression lined with leaves and feathers

Average clutch: About 11 buff-coloured, walnut-sized eggs

Average incubation period: 23–24 days

Fledging age: 10–12 days

Chick mortality in the first 6 weeks: About 60%

Annual adult survival rate: 50%

Maximum lifespan: About 9 years

Predators: Skunks, weasels, mink, fishers, foxes, raccoons, lynx, great horned owls, Cooper's hawks, goshawks

will obscure them from raptors. They then "drum" by flapping their wings, starting slowly and accelerating into a high-speed whir for about 10 seconds, like a motor being started. The low, deep thumping, almost felt as a vibration in the listener's stomach, is caused by the sound of air popping back into the vacuum created beneath the grouse's wings with each rapid, blurred beat he takes. Males repeat the drumming about once every five minutes, and may signal back and forth to each other from up to a kilometre away, marking off their breeding territories. Like songbirds, their sessions are especially persistent at dusk and dawn, though they sometimes jam through the night.

When a female shows up, her drummer boy goes into a song-and-dance routine as well, strutting in front of her with tail spread, comb erect, wings hung low and fanning his long neck feathers so they look like an Elizabethan ruff. All the while he chortles softly. The attraction, at least for the female, ends soon after mating. She steals off to lay her eggs and raise the young on her own, while the father resumes his drumming, soliciting the attention of other unmated females well into May. In September, when the angle of the sun is the same as in spring, some males may resume drumming briefly, just as songbirds sing a fleeting reprise.

Expectant mother grouse usually select well-hidden nest sites at the base of trees or under logs. A female takes two weeks or more to lay all her eggs, waiting until they're all laid before she starts incubating so that they will hatch simultaneously. Unlike most naked newborn tree-nesting birds, the wide-eyed, downy grouse hatchlings leave the nest and follow their mother as soon as they are dry, within a few hours of emerging from their shells. They come into the world alert and instinctively knowing how to obey their mother's command calls to freeze, hide, come out or run.

In Ernest Thompson Seton's story, "Redruff," from *Wild Animals I Have Known*, perhaps the best-selling Canadian book ever, he tells of how a mother grouse, taking the newly hatched chicks on their first trip, resorts to the classic broken-wing distraction display when a fox shows up to spoil the parade. With a quick, clucked signal from the mother, her hatchlings immediately hide in the ground litter while

30

she lures the fox away, keeping just out of his jaws, for half a kilometre. Then she flies up and circles back to the exact spot where the chicks remain in silent hiding until she gives the "all-clear."

Chicks stay close to their mother, always on the move, in a circuit of sites they visit through the spring and summmer. After fledging, they roost together in trees at night. Those that survive to autumn are suddenly gripped with a crazed wanderlust that sends them off to establish their own individual territories, serving to disperse the population and avoid inbreeding. They usually go a few kilometres. Seton described the movement, known as the fall shuffle, as a strange kind of madness that makes them frantic and clumsy, travelling at night and flying into things.

As far back as 1721, closed hunting seasons were imposed in Canada for ruffed grouse because of sudden scarcity. Like snowshoe hares, grouse on the Canadian Shield are subject to cyclical population crashes, especially in northern areas, about every 10 years. The reasons are still not known for sure, though hunting apparently has little to do with it. Some authorities speculate that heavy-seed-crop years may drain much of the nutrients from trees, leaving too little in buds and stems to support high grouse population in winter. Over-browsed vegetation, such as aspen, birch and jack pine, may also produce less-tasty, less-nutritious foliage as a defence measure. Overcrowded grouse themselves probably become stressed. Parasites and disease spread easily in close company. The population then suddenly plummets to a tiny fraction of what it was. Though grouse are largely sedentary, such catastrophies can sometimes lead to mass migrations on broad fronts.

Scats: Curved, grey-white droppings 2–4 cm (0.8–1.8 in) long

Average number of droppings per hour: 4

Famous individuals: Redruff

Range: All of Ontario, except most of Hudson Bay lowlands. Also found in all other provinces and territories

Population density: Often 1–10 breeding pairs per 10 km^2 (4 sq. mi)

Estimated number of grouse shot annually in Ontario: About 1 million

Grouse-hunting season: Mid-Sept. to mid-Dec. in central Ontario, late Sept. to late Jan. in southern Ontario

Number of species of grouse in Ontario: 3

Also see: Trembling Aspen, Hemlock, Snowshoe Hare

HERRING GULL
Sublime Flight Over Northern Lakes

Average adult's lifespan:
10–25 years

Maximum lifespan: 31 years in wild, 50 years in captivity

Name origin: *Gullan*, Cornish for "wailer"

Length: 58–66 cm (1.9–2.2 ft)

Wingspan: 1.3–1.5 m (4.3–5 ft)

Weight: 1–1.4 kg (2.2–3 lb)

Markings: White head, tail and under-parts; black-tipped grey wings, pink legs, red spot on lower yellow bill; immatures brownish

Alias: Sea gull, common gull, lake gull, winter gull, harbour gull, *le goéland argenté, Larus argentatus*

Call: Wide variety of loud squeals, wails and clucks

Food: Omnivorous, preferring small fish, mollusks, crayfish, also mice, insects, wild berries, carrion and Kentucky Fried Chicken bones

Preferred habitat: Lakes, rivers, wetlands

Nest: Grass and other vegetation often laid in bare rock depressions, 35–90 cm (14 in–3 ft) wide, at least 2 m (6.5 ft) from the nearest nest in the colony, usually on small, rocky islands or inaccessible points

Average clutch size: 3 spotted, olive-coloured eggs, a little larger than chicken eggs

Incubation period: About 28 days

Fledging age: About 6 weeks

Age at first breeding season:
4 years

HERRING GULLS and human beings have similar relationships with the Canadian Shield: while there are fewer opportunies for individuals to support themselves, those that are fortunate enough to live there enjoy the serenity away from the rat race to the south. Life in large gull colonies around the Great Lakes and urban areas can be brutal and vicious from start to finish, with constant fighting over food and territory, violation of spouses and cannibalistic neighbours eating unattended nestlings.

In contrast, the less-abundant food sources to the north support only small colonies or single nesting pairs. Though they're the same species as many of the gulls in the crowded south, northern herring gulls seem a different breed, beautiful and serene as they fly alone above wilderness lakes.

Herring gulls frequent many different habitats because they are generalists—not specially adapted for any one thing, but taking advantage of opportunities wherever they find them. Despite their seemingly effortless wide-winged glides, they are not the strongest fliers, depending instead on updrafts and thermals. But few other birds are as well rounded, walking, swimming and flying with equal ability. Gulls can eat just about anything, but are mainly scavengers of dead fish, preferring to scoop them from the surface in their bills rather than dive. When the eating's good, herring gulls can wolf down equal to one-third their own weight in a single gorging. They will also eat the eggs and young of other birds, making them unpopular among both their feathered peers and some humans. Mormons, however, honour gulls, because a great flock of California gulls once miraculously saved their Utah settlement by feasting on a plague of locusts.

When they return in spring, herring gulls embark on one of the most complex and prolonged courtships in the bird world. Over a period of two months or more, males strut, call out, stretch their necks and offer gifts to passive debutantes to prove they'll be good providers. Among couples going steady, there is prolonged rubbing of bills, contorting of bodies and mutual preening. Finally, if the female decides

she's found Mr. Right, she initiates copulation by pecking at his breast and then bending over to allow his cloaca—an all-purpose digestive, urinary and sexual opening for both sexes—to rub against hers. They mate up to 12 times a day for about six days before she lays her first egg, usually in June.

Both females and males make and aggressively defend the nests. Males also feed their mates and help incubate the eggs. For the first few crucial days after they hatch, the downy young live mainly off their egg yolk, while their parents concentrate on guarding them. Chicks can walk within a few days, and begin venturing outside the nest two or three days after hatching. Mortality is high among the young, but with each passing year, survival becomes easier.

Gull numbers have increased greatly since the beginning of the twentieth century, when egg collecting as well as feather plucking for women's hats brought them close to extinction. They became protected by law in 1916, but pesticides in the aquatic food chain in the 1960s and 1970s caused thin eggshells, deformities and hormone inbalances among gulls around the Great Lakes. The banning of DDT and other controls has since improved conditions.

Predators: Mink, foxes, hawks, falcons, eagles and coyotes eat adults. Raccoons, skunks, snakes and other gulls raid nests

Flying speed: 25–67 km/h (16–49 mph)

Range: All of Ontario. Also found in all other provinces and territories

Winter whereabouts: Adults on Great Lakes, most immatures fly to Florida or Gulf Coast states

Ontario population: 150,000 on lower Great Lakes in early 1980s

Population density in central Ontario: Usually 2–10 pairs per 100 km² (39 sq. mi)

Average first arrival in central Ontario: Early Mar. to early Apr.

Average last departure from central Ontario: Late Nov. to Dec.

Age of gull-like ichthyornis fossils: 85 million years

Famous individuals: Jonathan Livingston Seagull, Gertrude and Heathcliffe; the slain gull of Chekhov's *The Sea Gull*, symbol of the destructive force of human whims

Number of breeding gull species in Ontario: 6

Number of gull species worldwide: 45

Also see: Canadian Shield, Lakes, Minnows

BROAD-WINGED HAWK

Secretive Predator from the Tropics

AS BIRDS OF PREY, hawks have the advantages of size, deadly striking power and remarkable eyesight. They peer downwards with eyes that can make out long-distance details up to eight times smaller than human beings could distinguish. On their breeding grounds, crow-sized broad-winged hawks use their powers of vision to detect minute moving prey from hunting perches near the top of the forest. Transparent, side-closing lids let them moisten their eyes without blinking so they won't miss a thing.

On the fresh, windy days of mid-September, eagle-eyed hawk watchers at strategic locations scan billowy white clouds and deep blue skies for large flights of migrating broad-wings. The raptors they admire so much face a daunting task when migration time comes around. Their winter homes are in the dense rain forests of the Amazon and Central America. Broad-wings must conserve their energy as much as possible because they have little time or opportunity for eating along the way and because their bodies are heavier in proportion to their wings than smaller migrants'.

To make it, broad-wings harness the energy of the sun on clear days, soaring upwards in tight circles on rising columns of warm air, called thermals. Because patches of open ground and rock faces heat up more quickly than the atmosphere, the air just above them expands and rises like a bubble as it warms. Broad-wings rise hundreds of metres before the thermal weakens, its moisture condensing into droplets, forming small cumulus clouds. Then, soaring off on wind currents, they may travel for kilometres, losing altitude slowly until reaching the next thermal, marked by groups of other hawks circling upwards. The amount of flapping required throughout is kept to a bare minimum.

Because they have farther to migrate than most other hawks, broad-wings return to Ontario later and head south earlier, when the sun is high and yields eight or nine hours of good thermals. Their predominantly cold-blooded prey is abundant only during the year's three or four warmest months, anyway. Draining from forests across the province, broad-wings pour into southern Ontario in mid- to late September, bunching up along the Great Lakes, which they can't cross for lack of thermals over water. Cold fronts of north-west winds can pepper the skies with huge kettles of broad-wings over hawk watches near Windsor and Port Stanley. Flights of 30,000 in a single day sometimes occur. Up into the 1930s, large numbers of hawks were shot at well-known migration spots because they were considered vermin.

Although broad-wings appear to migrate in flocks, they are really travelling as individuals following the same highway. Even mates, which may return to the same nest site every year, travel separately and remain single in their winter resorts. Their lifelong relationship is purely seasonal, bound by a common nesting site. Some ornithologists believe that they may not even recognize each other in the spring. They engage in courtship flights and mating calls as soon as they return.

Nest: Loose sticks lined with leaves, moss and bark, 30–60 cm (1–2 ft) wide, usually 6–12 m (20–40 ft) up in crotch of deciduous trees, especially birch or aspen, sometimes in an old crow, hawk or squirrel nest

Average time required to build a nest: 3–5 weeks

Average clutch: 2–4 spotted white eggs, about the size of small chicken eggs

Incubation period: 31 days

Fledging age: 35–42 days

Average number of nestlings that fledge: 1.5

Mortality rate in first 6 months: 50–75%

Maximum lifespan: 18 years

Predators: Great horned owls, raccoons, crows raid nests

Population density: Usually 2–10 pairs per 100 km² (39 sq. mi)

Range: Most of Ontario, except Hudson Bay lowlands. Also found in the forest regions of all other provinces except British Columbia, Prince Edward Island and Newfoundland

Winter whereabouts: Southern Florida to the Amazon jungle

Average first arrival in central Ontario: Mid- to late Apr.

Average last departure from central Ontario: Mid-Sept.

Number of day-hunting birds of prey nesting in Ontario: 14

Number of day-hunting birds of prey worldwide: About 292

Also see: Barred Owl, Sun, Thunder & Lightning, Turkey Vulture

GREAT BLUE HERON
Motionless Giant in the Shallows

LIKE THE FLINTSTONES' air bus rising out of the primordial past, a great blue heron lifts high into the air with just a few slow, heavy flaps of its huge pinions. With long legs dangling and neck folded back in an S, herons in flight do evoke images of extinct pterodactyls. It is widely accepted, in fact, that birds evolved directly from dinosaurs, though pterodactyls were not dinosaurs and the first birds probably did not fly. Feathers are thought to be modified scales that first evolved for insulation rather than flight. Many paleontologists are convinced that dinosaurs themselves were feathered and, like birds, warm-blooded.

Herons are a tad more subtle than the dinosaurs of popular conception, but they are every bit as terrifying to just about anything that moves and will fit down their throats. Patience is everything to hunting herons. Starting early in the morning, they wade along the edges of marshes and streams and wait statue-still until a fish or frog comes within range of their lightning-quick bills. After spearing a fish, they may flip it into the air to catch and eat it headfirst. Given the chance, blue herons will snap up small shorebirds, rodents and snakes, sometimes hunting on land or fishing at night if the light is good.

Though they hunt alone and defend fishing holes from each other—sometimes in aerial combat—all is forgotten when herons congregate in colonies in their off-hours. Heron rookeries are generally densely packed, noisy, foul-smelling places in remote, hard-to-reach swamps, marshes, islands or uplands. White, acidic bird droppings cover the trunks and lower branches of nesting trees, often killing them after years of use. Huge stick nests teeter on flimsy branches, helping to keep raccoons away, but making landings difficult. Sometimes eggs or chicks are even flung to the ground.

After laying their eggs in late April or May, at least one parent remains at the nest until the little ones are about a month old. Baby herons look like gawky little punk rockers with frizzy Mohawk hairdos. Life is not easy for them, with all the commotion in the nest, and even after they fledge,

Average population density: 23 breeding pairs per 1,000 km² (386 sq. mi)

Number of colonies in Ontario: At least 1,600

Average number of nests per colony: 35

Largest Ontario colony: 389 nests

Average colony age: 9 years

Oldest Ontario colony: 92 years

Bird species that live in colonies: About 12%

Average first spring arrival in central Ontario: Early Apr.

Average last fall departure from central Ontario: Early Nov.

Range: Most of Ontario north to boreal forest. Also found in all other provinces except Newfoundland

Winter whereabouts: North shore of Lake Erie to northern South America

Age of oldest bird fossils: 140 million years

Age of the long-necked ancestor of herons, storks and flamingos: 40–50 million years

Number of heron species nesting in Ontario: 6

Number of heron and related bittern species worldwide: 59

Also see: Leopard Frog, Osprey, Wetlands

the odds are stacked against them. Many do not learn the skill and patience needed for hunting and end up starving. Two-thirds of fledglings die in their first year and only about 10 percent survive to mate.

Herons have been hurt by development, water pollution, acid rain, wetland drainage, woodlot cutting and nest-site disturbance. After protection efforts in Ontario, however, their population is again increasing. The greatest concentration of colonies is along the southern edge of the Canadian Shield, where rich wetlands and isolated woodlots are common, and from eastern Ontario to Algonquin Park. Before migrating south, hundreds of herons gather in some spots in August. A few may linger in marshes near Lake Ontario into late November.

RUBY-THROATED HUMMINGBIRD

Tiny Wonder Fueled on Nectar

Average number of wingbeats per second: 40–80; males in courtship dives reach up to 200

Flying speed: 45 km/h (27 mph)

Heartbeats per minute: 1,260 when excited, 50–180 in torpor

Respiratory rate: 250 breaths a minute

Daytime body temperature: About 40°C (104°F)

Number of calories expended per minute of hovering: 11

Length: 7–9 cm (2.8–3.5 in)

Wingspan: 10–13 cm (4–5.2 in)

Weight: 3 g (0.1 oz)

Name of a hummingbird aviary: Jewel room

Markings: Iridescent green backs, grey-white bellies; males have bright iridescent red throats and forked tails

Average number of feathers: 940

Alias: Common hummingbird, *le colibri à gorge rubis*, *Archilochus colubris*

Call: High-pitched, twittering squeaks

Food: Nectar, sap, aphids, small insects, spiders

Preferred habitat: Mixed and deciduous forest edges, clearings, river and lakeshores, islands, swamps, beaver-pond fringes

Nest: Neat, deep, thick-walled cup of moss, lichens, grass, bud scales and plant down, bound tightly together with spiders' silk, about 4–5 cm (1.5–2 in) wide

THOUGH HUMMINGBIRDS are usually seen at sugar-water feeders throughout cottage country, they are a lot more common in the wilderness than most people imagine. In the wild, they're usually heard before they're seen, their whirring hum too deep a sound for a bee or other insect to produce. Ever on the lookout for nectar meals in colourful flowers, hummingbirds are often attracted by bright nylon tents or orange and red plastic tarps. Zipping through on wings moving too quickly to be seen, they may at first appear to be large dragonflies, but when hovering, they hold their tiny bodies vertical in flight. Their wings actually move in curving figure eights, allowing hummingbirds to fly straight up, down, backwards and even upside down. They can veer sideways on a dime or stop instantly, to hover while feeding.

Both sexes will aggressively fend off much larger brutes, from chickadees to turkey vultures

---

One thing hummingbirds can't do is soar. To stay aloft, these smallest of all birds must keep their wings in perpetual hyperflap. The feat takes incredible strength and energy. A hummingbird's Herculean chest muscles—comprising 30 percent of its body—and its atomic-speed heart are both proportionally larger than those of any other bird. Nectar provides sugar that can be burned immediately as energy in the hummingbird's high-octane engine. Insects lapped up with the nectar offer protein for building body tissue. Still, to keep going, hummers refill their bellies about every seven to 12 minutes. They may consume and burn food equal to half their weight every day. To sustain their metabolic rate, an 80-kilogram (176-pound) man would have to pack away 45 kilograms (100 pounds) of Smarties a day and drink five cases of beer to keep his skin from catching fire.

Hummingbirds are especially active just before dusk and after dawn, storing up or replenishing vital fuel. On most nights, they conserve energy by slowing down their heart and breathing rates by 90 percent, dropping their body temperature to half the daytime average. In the cold highlands of their wintering grounds in Mexico and points south, hummingbirds go into a prolonged torpor. Their ability to revive from this deathlike state made them sacred to the Aztecs, who considered hummingbirds to be the spirits of dead warriors. Inca women roused the tiny hummers from their deep sleep by warming them between their breasts. In British Columbia, hummingbirds were depicted on totem poles as messengers of the dead.

One quite erroneous belief people once held was that hummers and other small birds migrated by hitching rides on the backs of larger birds such as geese. In truth, ruby-throated hummingbirds, the one species to summer in eastern North America, can fly 800 kilometres (500 miles) non-stop across the Gulf of Mexico in 26 hours, fueled on two grams (0.07 ounce) of fat, which makes up about half their body weight before starting out. Ruby-throats spend a couple of days rebuilding their fat supplies between each 170- to 340-kilometre (105- to 21-mile) leg of their journey overland. They migrate during the day, close to the ground.

When hummingbirds arrive in central Ontario in mid-

Average clutch: 2 pea-sized oblong white eggs

Incubation period: About 16 days

Fledging age: 20–22 days

Lifespan: Up to 12 years

Predators: Sharp-shinned hawks, kestrels, bullfrogs, bass and other large fish sometimes capture adults; weasels, chipmunks, crows, preying mantises, yellow jackets and snakes eat eggs or young

Number of licks per second: 13

Hummingbird-pollinated flowers: Cardinal flower, fireweed, jewelweed, pink wintergreen, thistles, purple asters

Number of hummingbirds killed annually in the tropics for fashion accessories in late 1800s: About 5 million

Population density: 2–100 pairs per 100 km² (39 sq. mi)

Average first arrival in central Ontario: Mid-May

Average last departure from central Ontario: Early to mid-Sept.

Range: North to about Timmins. Also found in all other provinces except British Columbia and Newfoundland

Winter whereabouts: South Florida and Texas to Costa Rica

Number of hummingbird species breeding in Ontario: 1

Number of hummingbird species in the Americas: 319–338

Number of hummers elsewhere in the world: 0

Lookalikes: 3 species of large clear-wing sphinx moths hover at flowers in daytime like hummingbirds

Also see: Speckled Alder, Yellow-bellied Sapsucker

May, many flowers they depend on are not yet open, while rain and bad weather limit access to others. For about a month they turn instead to the plentiful sweet sap oozing from rows of holes drilled into tree trunks by yellow-bellied sapsuckers, which return north a little earlier than hummers. As the weather warms, hummingbirds are especially attracted to red flowers, which often have no scent but more nectar than others. Many long, tubular blossoms, such as the cardinal flower, can be fertilized only by the hummingbird, which picks up pollen on its head while probing each bloom with its needlelike bill and lapping nectar from the bottom of the flower cup with its long, brushy tongue.

Ontario's abundance of summer flowers provides a rich breeding ground for hummers, but they don't stick around for long. Males arrive first, establish territories in dense forests and wetlands and defend them against each other, calling out in high squeaks. Females also establish territories, and both sexes will aggressively fend off much larger brutes, from chickadees to turkey vultures, using their darting speed to advantage. Males impress potential mates by flying in wide, exact arches, about four metres (4.4 yards) in diameter, as if suspended on a string. Actual mating lasts for three to five seconds, then couples split for good. After breeding with several partners, many males head back to Mexico in July, while females are busy nesting.

Mothers spend several days building their nests before looking for swinging bachelors to father their broods. Nests are well camouflaged, three to six metres (one to two yards) above the ground on the outer horizontal branches of small deciduous trees and shrubs, often alders, in meadows or near stream edges. Bee-sized, blind, naked babies usually hatch in early summer and are fed regurgitated nectar and insects. When they fledge, they are good fliers right off the mark, their wings buzzing away like wind-up toys. Their landings, though, are not so accomplished.

After flying with their mothers for another 10 to 30 days, young hummers are sent off on their own, or are abandoned by mothers setting off for their tropical retreats. Most leave by late August.

BELTED KINGFISHER
Author of the Riverside Rattle

WHAT DO Wilfrid Laurier and halcyon days have in common? Sharing the $5 bill with the past PM is a colourful crested bird, the belted kingfisher, whose Mediterranean relative was granted the gift of calm weather for its nesting period, according to Greek legend. The tale involves the distraught queen Alcyone, who jumped into the sea in grief after learning of her husband's loss in a shipwreck. The gods took pity, turned both husband and wife into kingfishers and stilled the winds for two weeks around the winter solstice each year—a time still known as the halcyon days—so that they could build a floating nest of fish bones. Kingfishers don't really nest in the water, but their scientific name, *alcyone*, pays tribute to the story.

In Ontario, pigeon-sized kingfishers nest, amazingly enough, in burrows dug into high banks on or near lake and river shores. Both cartoonlike mates spend about three weeks chiselling with their great long beaks and kicking out sand with their tiny feet. Kingfishers' bills make them so top-heavy that sailors and fishermen used to hang their bodies on boats to serve as weather vanes. Their oversized headgear is designed to take the impact of hitting the water beak-first as they dive for fish.

Kingfishers hunt over shallow, clear water from a favourite perch, often on dead trees in standing water. Flying up with a distinctive rattling call and uneven wing beats, they may

Length: 28–37 cm (11–15 in)

Wingspan: 56–58 cm (22–23 in)

Weight: 127–175 g (4.5–6.2 oz)

Markings: Grey-blue bushy crest, breast band and back; white undersides; very long, sharp, heavy beak; short tail; red stomach band on females

Alias: Lazy bird, alcyon, *le martin pêcheur, Megaceryle alcyon*

Call: Loud, harsh rattle

Food: Minnows, perch and other young fish, frogs, tadpoles, crayfish, salamanders, insects and mice

Preferred habitat: Lakeshores, eroded stream banks, marshes

Average breeding territory: 800–1,200 m (880–1,320 yd) of shoreline

Average non-breeding territory: 300–500 m (330–550 yd) of shoreline

Nest: Burrows, 1–2 m (3.3–6.6 ft) long, in the sides of sand, clay and gravel banks, about 25 cm (10 in) wide

Average clutch: 5–8 glossy white eggs, about the size of large chestnuts

Incubation period: 23–24 days

Fledging age: About 5 weeks

Predators: Sharp-shinned hawks, Cooper's hawks, peregrine falcons

Flying speed: Up to 60 km/h (36 mph)

Average population density: 2–10 pairs per 100 km^2 (39 sq. mi)

Average first arrival in central Ontario: Early to mid-Apr.

Average last departure from central Ontario: Late Oct. to mid-Nov.

Range: All of Ontario. Also found in all other provinces, the southwestern Northwest Territories and the Yukon

Winter whereabouts: Southern Ontario to Cental America and the West Indies

Number of kingfisher species in Ontario: 1

Number of kingfisher species worldwide: 87

Also see: Crayfish, Minnows

hover briefly before dropping straight down with their wings fixed, like a little fighter jet. Captured fish are brought back to the perch, stabbed, flipped in the air and swallowed. If one is too big, it may stick out of a kingfisher's mouth while the bird's digestive juices go to work on the swallowed end. A pile of regurgitated bones and scales on the ground usually marks a regular kingfisher hunting perch.

Kingfishers nest in burrows dug in high banks on or near lake and river shores

Males arrive in April, about a month before females, and pick the nest sites. They stake out closely guarded territories along shorelines, keeping out other kingfishers and even escorting canoes along its length. Females later join in shore patrols. The availability of territory and nest sites limits their numbers.

After laying their eggs in May or early June, females do most of the incubating. The young hatch featherless, and about a week later sprout tiny pinfeathers in sheaths, making them look like porcupines more than birds. Full feathers explode from the sheaths all at once about two weeks later. Parents teach their fledglings to hunt by dropping fish into the water for them when they are hungry. Families break up when the young are about six weeks old. Many kingfishers remain in autumn as long as the fishing's good and the water hasn't iced over.

COMMON LOON
Spirit of the North Woods

MINTED IN NICKEL, plated in bronze and indelibly embossed on the imaginations of generations of wilderness seekers, the loon is a quintessentially Canadian symbol. Human reverence for the bird is documented by the 5,000-year-old loon pictographs on cliffs scattered around the Great Lakes region. Loons, in fact, are sacred birds, bridging the material and spiritual worlds in a continuum of ancient lore from eastern North America all the way to central Siberia. In many remarkably similar versions of the creation story on both continents, it is the loon that retrieves mud from the bottom of primordial seas to form the Earth.

In addition to the loon's ability to journey both in the sky and in the watery depths, the almost-human quality its long, soulful call probably earned the awe of northern peoples. The familiar, modulating wail, sometimes heard in choruses on still nights or after a rain, is actually just one of four distinct types of loon call, each rising in pitch according to the intensity of emotion. The wail is used to summon mates and offspring, or as a territorial declaration to neighbours.

Each male also has his own distinctive yodel for territorial defence. Neighbouring loons can recognize each other's

Average time underwater: 40–45 sec

Maximum time underwater: More than 3 min

Average depth of hunting grounds: 2–5 m (6.6–16 ft)

Deepest dives: 70 m (230 ft)

Average flying speed: About 120 km/h (72 mph)

Wing beats per second: 2.6–2.7

Migrating altitude: 1,500–2,700 m (5,000–9,000 ft)

Ontario Canadian Shield population: About 65,000 breeding pairs

Population density: Usually 1 pair or fewer per 10 km² (4 sq. mi)

Accolades: Official bird of Ontario and numerous outdoors organizations; bird on the $1 "loonie" coin

Length: 70–90 cm (2.3–3 ft)

Wingspan: 1.3–1.5 m (3.6–5 ft)

43

Weight: 2.7–6.3 kg (6–14 lb)

Loon weight/cm² (0.15 sq. in) of wing: 2.5 g (0.09 oz)

Mallard duck weight/cm² of wing: 1.4 g (0.05 oz)

Markings: Both sexes have iridescent black head and neck, white necklace around neck, checkered black-and-white back, white breast and belly, long, pointy black bill, red eyes; juveniles younger than 3 years old, and adults in fall and winter, have dark grey backs and white bellies

Alias: Great northern diver, *le huart à collier, Gavia immer*

Food: Perch, young bass, sunfish, minnows, crayfish, frogs, mollusks, leeches, aquatic insects, water-lily roots and other aquatic plants

Preferred habitat: Deep, clear lakes, large rivers

Breeding territory: 5–170 ha (22.5–425 acres)

Nest: Simple low pile of vegetation, often on the lee side of small islands, points, old muskrat lodges, or in a cove, just above waterline

Average clutch: 2 olive-coloured eggs with dark spots, about the size of an average potato

Incubation period: 28–29 days

Loonling mortality: 15–30 %

Fledging age: 11–12 weeks

Age at first breeding season: 4 years old

Lifespan: Up to 30 years

Predators: Crows, ravens, gulls, eagles, raccoons, skunks, snapping turtles and large fish such as pike eat chicks or eggs

Pests: Blackflies

yodels from those of interlopers. Males sometimes yodel at low-flying planes. When they sense danger, loons blurt out a staccato phrase, like the laugh of a mad scientist. The call probably inspired the saying "crazy as a loon," as well as the goofy laughter of Daffy Duck, himself a confused amalgam of black duck and loon. A fourth type of call consists of hoots made by pairs, families or groups of loons as a kind of random small talk.

Most of the communication between loons, however, is actually by body language. American biologist William Barklow studied loons up close for 15 years, infiltrating their ranks by snorkelling among them with a goose decoy painted to look like a loon on top of his head. He noted more than 25 regular communication body postures. Among them, loons greet each other by gracefully stretching out their wings, show submission by hunching low and indicate peaceful or amorous intentions by pointing their beaks downwards.

Normally, a breeding pair of loons maintains an entire lake, or a bay in a large lake, as their exclusive territory. In the rush to secure the best waters, loons return to their breeding grounds as soon as the ice breaks up in April or early May.

They are often the first birds swimming on the lake in spring and the last to leave in fall. Most are thought to mate for life, though they overwinter separately, renewing their relationship with an elegant, quiet, diving courtship waltz when they return to their original honeymoon lake each spring.

Loons mate and nest on land, within a metre of the shore. That's about as far as they ever venture on dry ground because their legs are placed so far back under their bodies that they can walk only by using their wings as crutches, though flapping enables them to run. The word *loon* itself comes from the Scandinavian *lom*, which in English means "lame." Their torpedolike bodies are built more for swimming and diving than flying. Many of their bones are solid, rather than honeycombed with air spaces like most birds'. Depending on the wind, they need 20- to 400-metre- (21- to 437-yard-) long takeoffs on the water to gain enough lift from their relatively small thrashing wings to fly. Takeoffs are impossible from land. Beneath the water, though, they pivot like otters and outswim most fish.

Even baby loons are in the water swimming within hours of hatching, usually in June. They paddle very close behind their parents, often riding on their backs during the first two or three weeks of their lives when they are tired, cold or in potential danger from underwater predators. Both parents take turns attending the loonlings, teaching them to fish when they are about four weeks old. In August, parents begin spending a few hours each day with growing groups of younger, non-mating loons for ritualized social gatherings on larger lakes, leaving their unfledged young at home. The visits grow longer until the young can totally feed themselves, by September or early October, when they are left for good. Fledglings soon form migratory flocks of up to 100 or more birds and follow their elders south, well spaced apart in long lines. Most young loons are believed to spend their second summer in the Maritimes, not returning to Ontario until they are two years old.

Their heavy dependence on fish, and their need for clear, undisturbed water to find them, has imperilled loons in areas under pressure from development. They have already been almost totally pushed out of summer breeding lakes in southern Ontario. Sudden water-level fluctuations from dams and motorboat wakes can flood out nests. Acid rain has cut down their fish supply in some lakes, while fish contaminated with mercury, aluminum, chlorinated hydrocarbons and other pollutants cause reproductive failure and nervous-system dysfunctions. Thousands of wintering loons wash up on Florida beaches some years, starved because they can no longer coordinate their muscles while trying to catch fish. So far, loon numbers in Ontario, which hosts about one-fifth of the summer North American population, appear to be stable. It is illegal to hunt them.

Range: All of Ontario, except far south. Also found throughout Canada except on the prairies, parts of the Arctic and built-up areas

Winter whereabouts: Ontario loons go to Atlantic coast, a few in Great Lakes

Average first spring arrival in Central Ontario: Mid- to late Apr.

Average last departure from central Ontario: Late Nov.

Oldest loon fossils: 40–50 million years

Number of breeding loon species in Ontario: 3

Number of loon species worldwide: 5

Also see: Blackflies, Common Merganser, Lakes, Perch

COMMON MERGANSER
Tree-nesting Shield Duck

Top flying speed: 70–85 km/h (42–51 mph)

Top migrating speed of any bird: 113 km/h (69 mph), by canvasback ducks

Number of merganser wing beats per second: 4.6

Length: 55–68 cm (1.8–2.2 ft)

Wingspan: 86–91 cm (2.8–3 ft)

Weight: Males 1.2–2.2 kg (2.7–5 lb), females 0.9–1.8 kg (1–2 lb)

Markings: Reddish brown head and crest, grey back, white breast, throat and square wing patches on female; green-black head, black back, white breast, neck and sides on males; orange-red feet and saw-edged bill on both

Alias: Goosander, fish duck, American merganser, flapper, saw-bill, sheldrake, *le bec-scie commun, Mergus merganser*

Call: Though usually silent, males make low, raspy croaks, females a guttural call

Food: Minnows, suckers, sculpin, sticklebacks and other small or slow-moving fish; aquatic insects, fish eggs

Preferred habitat: Forest lakes, ponds, rivers

Usual depth of hunting grounds: Less than 2 m (6.6 ft)

Deepest dives: 10 m (33 ft)

Nest: Usually a down-lined tree cavity with a 12-cm- (4.7-in-) wide opening, sometimes in a crevice, beneath rocks, stumps, roots or bushes; within 180 m (200 yd) of shorelines

OMPARED TO THE weedy waters of other climes, the Canadian Shield can be a rather duckless place. Despite its wealth of lakes, most are too deep, rocky and sterile to support the abundant aquatic plants eaten by mallards and other dabbling ducks. One duck that actually prefers the Shield's clear waters—the diving, fish-eating common merganser—has been pushed back in southern areas by cottage development, powerboats, overfishing and water pollution. Though not considered tasty hunting prizes, mergansers were once persecuted by cottagers who, after fishing out and fouling lakes, concluded the long-time resident mergansers must be responsible for the disappearance of fish.

In truth, mergansers are usually too thinly spread out to have a significant impact on fish populations. They concentrate on slow-moving species rather than sport fish. Loons also occasionally baulk at their competition, especially in small, secluded bays used for loonling nurseries. Irate loons sometimes speed underwater like torpedoes, their long beaks trained on trespassing mergansers.

In April, mergansers gather in large flocks on sheltered bays along the Great Lakes as they wait for the ice to break up on smaller lakes farther north. They often begin their air- and water-courtship chases at those sites and are already paired up when they arrive at the breeding grounds. Male

COMMON MERGANSER

mergansers, along with other ducks, geese and swans, have the distinction of being among the few birds with penises. Most birds merely have cloacas, an orifice combining all excretory functions, which are rubbed together during mating in what's known as a "cloacal kiss." Male ducks, however, inflate a fold of skin from the cloaca to do the job.

Male usefulness in continuence of the species does not extend far beyond their penises. Though they defend nesting territories for a time, soon after the last eggs are laid, males drift away from the breeding grounds. They are a very rare sight on the Shield in summer. No one seems to be too sure where they all go, though some return to wintering grounds on the Atlantic coast. Others may go farther north.

Soon after hatching, usually in June, merganser ducklings bail out of their tree cavity-nests like tiny paratroopers one after another, their light bodies fluttering to the ground without injury. Hatchlings waddle behind their mother to the water, and swim and dive immediately. They also hitch rides on their mother's back. But the most common summer merganser sight is a hen with a long line of paddling ducklings behind her, tracing the indentations of the shore. Often there may be 20 ducklings or more in tow, which could not possibly be all from one brood. Some authorities suggest mothers take turns baby-sitting each other's combined broods, while others say aggressive mothers may kidnap another's babies. Ducklings, apparently, are easily mixed up and bond readily with whatever group they end up with. They often form larger groups after their mothers go off to moult and abandon them for good, though they are still unfledged. Adults are also flightless for about a month while moulting.

Female mergansers can be recognized in flight by flashing square white patches on their wings. The body, bill and neck are stretched out in a straight line in flight. Like all ducks, mergansers are built for strong, steady flapping rather than gliding, and are among the fastest fliers in the bird world. And like loons, their feet are placed far back on the body for maximum diving propulsion, which makes walking on land difficult.

Average clutch: 8–12 light brown eggs, about the size of large chicken eggs

Incubation period: About 32 days

Fledging age: 60–70 days

Predators: Mink, martens, raccoons, skunks, snakes eat eggs; barred owls, pike, muskies, pickerel prey on young

Ontario Canadian Shield population: About 75,000 breeding pairs

Average population density: 8–10 pairs per 100 km^2 (39 sq. mi)

Name origin: Latin *mergus anser*, meaning "diving goose"

Oldest waterfowl fossils: 80 million years old

Range: All of Ontario. Also found in the forest regions of all other provinces and territories

Winter whereabouts: Great Lakes to southern U.S.

Average first arrival in central Ontario: Early Apr.

Average last departure from central Ontario: Late Nov.

Number of ducks shot annually in Ontario: 685,000

Number of common mergansers shot annually in Ontario: 2,500–5,000

Duck-hunting season: Mid-Sept. to late Dec.

Number of duck species nesting in Ontario: 26

Number of duck-family species worldwide: 148

Also see: Common Loon, Lakes

OSPREY
Crooked-winged Fishing Master

Length: 53–66 cm (1.7–2.2 ft)

Wingspan: 1.4–1.8 m (4.6–6 ft)

Weight: Females 1.6–2 kg (3.5–4.4 lb), males 1.2–1.6 kg (2.6–3.5 lb)

Markings: Black mask, white head and undersides, dark brown back, brown patches at front crook of white under-wing, short fan-shaped tail with light and dark bars, hooked beak

Alias: Fish hawk, *le balbuzard*, *Pandion haliaetus*

Call: Short, sharp, repeated whistle

Food: 99% bullheads, sunfish, bass, perch, pike, suckers and other fish, occasionally frogs, crayfish, snakes, rodents

Preferred habitat: Shallow lakes, rivers, marshes, swamps, bogs

Average defended territory: About 0.5–1.5 ha (1.2–3.7 acres) of shallow water

Nest: Usually 1 m (3.3 ft) wide and 30 cm (1 ft) deep, of woven sticks, cattails and other aquatic plants, 9–19 m (30–66 ft) above wetlands or shorelines in the crowns of broken-topped, dead trees

Average clutch: 3 mottled white or tan eggs, the size of large chicken eggs

Incubation period: 35–42 days

Fledging age: 49–61 days

Age at first breeding season: 3 or more years

Annual mortality rate: 40–60% for fledglings, 15–20% for adults

THE BANNING OF DDT may have come just in time for the osprey. At the top of the aquatic food chain, ospreys are the ultimate recipients of pesticides flushed by rain from farm fields into rivers and lakes and collected in the fish they eat. DDT interferes with estrogen, the hormone that regulates calcium, leading to thin eggshells and nesting failure. Breeding ospreys nearly disappeared from the lower Great Lakes in the 1960s. The Canadian Wildlife Federation listed them as endangered in 1973. After DDT was banned, offspring survival rates slowly increased in the late 1970s and 1980s, and osprey finally prospered again in Ontario, with the highest concentration, about 85 known occupied nests, in the Kawarthas.

Ospreys are the most widespread birds of prey in both Ontario and the world. They fly over every continent except Antarctica. They are also one of Ontario's largest raptors, and the only one, save for the bald eagle, that catches fish. They usually hover 10 to 30 metres (or yards) above shallow water, head hanging as they look for fish. When they see one, they tuck in their wings and drop straight down, braking as they snatch up their hapless prey. Their talons have sharp spines and a reversible toe to hold slippery fish, as pictured on the back of the $10 bill. There are many accounts of bald eagles, which are often more scavengers than hunters, accosting ospreys in the air and forcing them to drop their catch, which the eagle retrieves. Ospreys themselves are sometimes mistaken for eagles because of their large size and white heads. Crooked wings, looking like elbows, are the mark of osprey.

Unlike many hawks, ospreys can cross over large bodies of water in migration, rather than depending on warm air rising from sun-baked clearings to give them lift. They have more wing relative to their bodies than do other hawks, allowing them to flap long and hard instead of needing to glide to conserve energy. Sometimes they migrate carrying a fish; hawk watchers call this "packing a lunch." Radar has picked up migrants at almost 1,000 metres (1,094 yards) above the ground, far beyond binocular range. Most Ontario

ospreys migrate south in early to mid-September, following the Mississippi Valley south. They return in April, travelling alone, but following the same routes till they spread out on their breeding territories.

For about two weeks after they return, osprey males swoop and dive in courtship flights, calling out loudly. They return to the same nest, or aerie, every year, repairing and adding to it, sometimes for generations. Nests can sometimes weigh hundreds of kilograms. Occasionally, ospreys nest in the middle of heron colonies, which may prompt the herons to abandon the site. If they stay or return, however, the osprey presence ultimately benefits herons by keeping away nest raiders, such as great horned owls.

Females lay their clutch in late-April or May. After the eggs hatch, males must provide enough fish to double the weight of their offspring about each week. Mothers stay with the young constantly for their first month. Parents continue to feed them for up to several weeks after they fledge. Then they're on their own, though they remain in the area for a while afterwards. After they migrate, young ospreys enjoy a tropical adolescence, hanging out in the jungle and not returning to Ontario until they are two years old.

Lifespan: Up to 25 years, but rarely more than 12 years

Predators: Raccoons, crows, ravens raid nests; great horned owls may kill adults or young

Fishing success rate: 25–50% of all dives

Population density: Usually 1 pair per 100 km² (39 sq. mi), though more numerous in good fishing areas. An osprey colony at Lindsay has nests only 250 m (273 yd) apart

Range: All of Ontario except southwest. Also found in forest regions throughout Canada

Winter whereabouts: Florida to Argentina, mainly around the Caribbean and Gulf of Mexico

Average first arrival in central Ontario: Mid-to-late Apr.

Average last departure from central Ontario: Late Sept. to early Oct.

Also see: Bass, Broad-winged Hawk, Great Blue Heron

BARRED OWL
Voice in the Night on Silent Wings

Call: Slightly muffled, hollow, rapid hoots sound like "Who cooks for you, who cooks for you all" or "hoohoo-hoohoo, hoohoo-hoohooaw," rolling at the end, very resonant; also screams, barks

Name origin: Anglo-Saxon *ule*, meaning "howler"

Name for a group: A parliament of owls

Length: 34–58 cm (13.4–23 in)

Wingspan: 1–1.2 m (3.3–4 ft)

Weight: Females 610–1,000 g (1.3–2.2 lb), males 470–770 g (1–1.7 lb)

Markings: Both sexes grey-brown; vertical light and dark bars on whitish chest, white spots on back; round, puffy, ghostly looking head with grey facial disc around dark brown eyes; feathered legs

Alias: Northern barred owl, wood owl, crazy owl, *la chouette rayée*, *Strix varia*

Food: Mice, voles, squirrels, chipmunks, young hares, shrews, frogs, snakes, salamanders, smaller owls and other birds, crayfish, fish, insects, spiders

Preferred habitat: Dense, moist coniferous and mixed forests, especially in swamps and near marshes, rivers or lakes

Home range: 0.9–2.3 km^2 (0.3–1 sq. mi)

Nest: Usually in tree cavity with 50–70 cm (20–27.5 in) wide opening, an average of 5–10 m (16–33 ft) high, sometimes in an old crow or hawk nest

"WHO COOKS FOR YOU?" is probably the most persistent question of central Ontario's woodlands at night. The phrase, when hooted through cupped hands, is the approximate sound of the barred owl's call, which may be heard throughout the year. Though infrequently seen, the barred owl is one of the loudest and noisiest of Ontario's hooters. Its March-to-April mating season is known as the months of madness, for hoots, hisses, screams, barks and cackles are all part of the owl's courtship repertoire. Later, when they are nesting and their eggs or young are vulnerable to predators, barred owls enter their quietest period.

Each ear slit is in a slightly different position, enabling the owl's brain to detect noises at two different angles at once

---

To many eastern woodland peoples, owls represented the female moon spirit. It was thought to have beneficial, healing powers, and to be a messenger between living and dead relatives. Owl feathers were hung from tobacco pipes as prayer offerings to the Earth and moon. Owls were similarly associated with the moon and with female deities in the Old World. Athena, the Greek goddess of wisdom and war, was usually depicted with an owl at her side. Sometimes, though, the owl's persona was more ambiguous. To the Chinese, it was both a thunderbird and a stealer of souls. It was a symbol of death in ancient Rome and an evil night hag, a witch in bird form, in the Christian world. When her husband bumps off the king of Scotland, Shakespeare's Lady Macbeth hears an owl call and says:

"It was the owl that shriek'd. The fatal bellman,

Which gives the stern'st good night."

But to be as wise as an owl is an axiom that has survived from ancient Greek times. The image was probably fostered by the bird's huge, serious eyes, with lids that close downward like humans', rather than with the bottom lids rising up, as with most birds. Owl eyes are also set flat on their face like humans', giving the binocular vision—each eye's view overlaps to enhance depth perception and far-away details. A large number of light-sensitive retinal rods at the back of their eyes make owls see small objects in the dark up to six times more accurately than do humans. Their eyes are so large that owls can barely move them up, down or sideways in their sockets, while their broad face narrows their view to 110°, compared with 180° for humans. They make up for it by being able to turn their neck 270°, sometimes so quickly that their heads appear to turn completely around.

Despite their sharp, long-range sight, owls do not see as well close up. They don't give a hoot about farsightedness because highly specialized hearing allows them to pinpoint small prey exactly. In experiments conducted in absolute darkness, they have no trouble catching mice.

An owl's ear openings are long slits even bigger than its eyes, hidden by large flaps of skin and feathers at the sides of its head. The ear slits are at the edge of rings of feathers spreading from around the eyes, forming a facial disc that

Average clutch: 2–3 spherical, white eggs

Incubation period: 28–33 days

Fledging age: About 6 weeks

Lifespan: More than 10 years in wild

Maximum lifespan in captivity: 23

Predators: Great horned owls, crows, hawks may eat young

Droppings: Like melted candle wax

acts like a radar dish in picking up sounds. The disc feathers move to help direct the sound, and the skin flaps over the ears can be raised to deflect noises coming from behind the head. Each ear slit is in a slightly different position, enabling the owl's brain to detect noises at two different angles at the same time—high-tech stereophonics. The two sound lines target the prey precisely, with the owl snatching it up where they meet. Owls can hear and locate prey even beneath the snow. Deep or crusted snow makes hunting difficult, leading to good times and population explosions for mice.

Even while it is using noise as its meal ticket, the owl itself is silent, swooping down without warning, on fluffy, serrated-edged wing feathers that make no sound. Their puffy feathers always make owls look bigger than their real size. A light body, in relation to their large wings, makes them particularly buoyant, with less need of flapping. Owls usually hunt from perches on dead trees. Since they eat small animals whole, pellets of regurgitated bones, fur, feathers, claws and beaks often mark the spot beneath a regular perch or nest.

Though they are mainly nocturnal, barred owls sometimes hunt during the day, like moonlighting humans, when they're raising families. They're a settled lot, and from one generation to the next often use the same nest for one or two decades.

Unlike smaller birds, the downy white young hatch separately, a couple of days apart, because their mother starts incubating each egg as she lays it in April or May, rather than waiting till all are together. If food is in short supply, only the oldest—the biggest and first to eat—will survive. When they are four or five weeks old, usually in June, the young begin hanging around on branches outside the nest, though it is several more weeks before they fledge, and they continue to live off the folks until about four months old. In late summer or fall they set out in the world to establish their own territories and make something of themselves.

ROBIN
First Songster of the Morning

THE SIGHT OF A ROBIN bob-bob-bobbing along on freshly thawed ground is one of the most fabled first signs of spring. But south of the Canadian Shield, many hardy, resourceful robins never actually leave during winter. Instead they band together in small flocks and retire to sheltered areas, such as thickly wooded ravines with lots of durable berries and fruits to last them the season. Sometimes, if their supplies run out, they roam in search of new sources and may then be seen more easily in the middle of winter.

Forest-dwelling robins of the Canadian Shield, though, migrate out of the province. Unlike their outgoing, settled cousins to the south, forest robins are shy and reclusive, keeping well away from humans. Migrant males usually start their mating songs as soon as they arrive back in spring, when the overwintering robins are still largely silent. An Ojibway legend says robins sing to cheer people because they are descended from a boy who became a bird to escape the suffering of a too-difficult vision quest—an initiation rite involving fasting and dreaming—set by his father.

Robins are usually the first to sing reveille in the morning, leading off well before daybreak. The hours around dawn are

Length: 23–28 cm (9–11 in)

Wingspan: 38–42 cm (15–16.3 in)

Weight: 80 g (3 oz)

Markings: Males have a brick red breast and a dark, sooty grey back. Females have a duller orange-red breast and grey-brown back. Spotted breast on immatures

Alias: American robin, *le merle américain, Turdus migratorius*

Call: Repeated high, loud, rising and falling whistled phrases of several syllables, each very musical, commonly described as "cheer up, cheerily, cherry"

Food: Berries, fruit, caterpillars, earthworms, beetles, snails, insects, spiders

Preferred habitat: Forest edges and openings, open woodlands, fens, bogs and fire-regenerated areas

Nest: Round cup of grass and mud, 2–5 m (6.6–16.5 ft) above ground in crotch or branches of understory trees and shrubs, with branches above for concealment and shelter

Average breeding territory: 0.2 ha (0.5 acres)

Average clutch: 4 light blue-green eggs, about the size of peach pits

Incubation period: 12–13 days

Fledging age: About 14 days

Lifespan: Up to 12 years, but rarely more than 4 years

Predators: Cooper's hawks prey on adults; nests raided by crows, blue jays, grackles, red squirrels, chipmunks, flying squirrels, garter snakes

Average forest population density: 1–10 pairs per 10 km² (4 sq. mi)

Average first arrival in central Ontario: Mid-to late Mar.

Average last departure from central Ontario: Early Nov.

Range: All of Ontario. Also found throughout Canada south of the tree line

Winter whereabouts: Most Ontario migrants go to southeastern U.S.

Name origin: From English robin, a different species. Robin Old French for "Robert"

Name for a group: A nest of robins

Number of thrush species worldwide: About 310

Also see: Big Dipper, Red-eyed Vireo, Yellow-rumped Warbler

generally the busiest for breeding birds, for it's then that territories are most vigorously defined through song and defended, and it's often the time when mates first pair up. A second peak of activity comes before sunset. Male robins are very territorial, chasing each other away as they carve out their turf. Their songs, by serving as a proprietary proclamation and warning, help to minimize combat, which costs them a lot in energy.

Unlike their outgoing, settled cousins to the south, forest robins are shy and reclusive, keeping well away from humans

Couples often return to the same nesting spot from one year to the next, but the nest itself usually lasts for only one brood. By moving, parents avoid nest parasites. Heavy storms sometimes melt and obliterate the muddy structure. Females build the nest up by dropping grass on top of mud and moulding it into place by sitting, pushing with their wings and stamping their feet for up to 10 seconds. Then they turn several degrees and repeat the process, sometimes turning completely around several times.

With their first eggs laid in April and the young growing up quickly, robin parents may mate again in June, while their first fledglings are still begging for food. Females do all the incubating, but fathers stick around to feed the babies. Robins are usually aware enough to throw out parasitic cowbird eggs from their nests. Migrants gather in flocks in September and fly south at night, resting and foraging during the day.

SPOTTED SANDPIPER
Teeter-tail of the Shoreline

Length: 18–20 cm (7–8 in)

Wingspan: 33–36 cm (13–14 in)

Weight: 42–56 g (1.5–2 oz)

Markings: Greyish brown back and dark round spots on white breast and belly in spring and summer, females more heavily spotted than males

Call: Sharp, ringing whistle, commonly described as "peet" or "peet-weet"

Alias: Gutter snipe, teeter, teeter-tail, tip-up, sand lark, peep, spottie, seesaw, sand snipe, peet-weet, sand lark, river snipe, chevalier branle-queue, *Actitis macularia*

Preferred habitat: Shores of lakes, ponds, rivers, marshes, mud flats

Food: Worms, beetles, grubs, grasshoppers, small crustaceans, fish fry, aquatic insects

Nest: Grass or moss-lined ground depression hidden amid long grass, rocks or rotting logs on or near shorelines

Average clutch: 4 brown-spotted, walnut-sized eggs

Incubation period: 20–24 days

Fledging age: 13–16 days

Lifespan: About 3 years, maximum 8 years

Predators: Mink, merlin

Flying speed: 30–50 km/h (18–30 mph)

Range: All of Ontario. Also found in other provinces and territories

Winter whereabouts: Coastal US from South Carolina to South America

Also see: Mink

AMONG SPOTTED SANDPIPERS, it is the females that love 'em and leave 'em. A female may breed with up to four males in a season. After most amorous liaisons, she drops her eggs and moves on, leaving the males to incubate them and raise the young.

Female sandpipers begin the role reversal by arriving first on the breeding grounds, establishing and defending territories from each other. Within minutes of the males coming back, the larger, more aggressive females woo them with aerial displays, singing, strutting and ruffling their neck feathers. Couples stay together for about 10 days until all the eggs are laid, though a female usually helps incubate her last clutch of the year. Multiple clutches may have evolved to offset the high predation of sandpiper eggs, laid on the ground in relatively open areas. Only about half of all eggs hatch successfully. If their clutch is lost, males may also mate again.

Sandpiper eggs are large and take longer to hatch than the eggs of many other species. But the young pop out of their shells fully feathered and able to run and get food for themselves within an hour. They can swim when a few hours old. Fathers guard their broods until they fledge, reportedly sometimes squeezing a chick between their legs and flying away to escape danger.

Sandpipers spend most of their time probing shorelines with their long beaks for insects, especially at dawn and dusk, their tails constantly bobbing or teetering up and down.

YELLOW-BELLIED SAPSUCKER
The Tidy Woodpecker

Length of sapsucker: 19 cm (8–9 in)

Wingspan: 22–25 cm (9–10 in)

Weight: 43–55 g (1.5–2 oz)

Markings: Black-and-white-lined back, faint yellowish belly, white wing patch, red forehead, red throat on males, white throat on females; immatures brownish

Alias: Yellow-belly, *le pic maculé*, *Sphyrapicus varius*

Call: Piercing, harsh, nasal whine, descending, slurred squeal, squeaks; generally silent

Food: Wasps, flies, tent caterpillars, ants, beetles, other insects, sap, berries

Preferred habitat: Dry, young, open deciduous or mixed forests with clearings, especially aspens

Territory: 2–3 ha (5–7.5 acres)

Nest: Tree cavity with entrance about 4 cm (1.5 in) wide, usually 3–15 m (10–50 ft) up in a poplar, sometimes birch or maple

Clutch: 4–6 shiny white, olive-sized eggs

Incubation period: 12–13 days

Fledging age: About 4 weeks

Lifespan: Up to 6 years

Predators: Sharp-shinned hawks, Cooper's hawks, raccoons, red squirrels

Name for a group of woodpeckers: A descent

THE RED HEAD-PATCH sported by yellow-bellied sapsuckers and most male woodpeckers in Ontario was a symbol of bravery to the Ojibway, who hung it from their tobacco pipes. They said the patch was a gift from the trickster deity Nanabush, who had tried to copy the tree-knocking skill of his friend, the giant woodpecker, by placing two wooden pins in his nostrils and hammering away at a trunk. Instead, Nanabush knocked himself out and received a nasty wound. The giant woodpecker rescued him, stopped the bleeding and in return was dabbed with the blood of Nanabush to wear as a symbol of honour.

Woodpeckers were venerated in Europe and Asia, where they were associated with rain, thunder gods and agriculture

---

Woodpeckers were similarly venerated in Europe and Asia, where they were closely associated with rain, thunder gods and agriculture. The name for woodpeckers in many languages was "rain bird." They received their reputation both because they produced thundering sounds when knocking and because they frequented oaks, the sacred tree of Zeus, Mars, Thor and other thunder and agriculture deities of various cultures. The European green woodpecker, which, like the North American flicker, also probes the earth with its beak for ants, was in Greek and other Indo-European mythologies the father of the inventor of the plough or hoe.

One of the most common and fascinating woodpeckers in central Ontario is the much ballyhooed yellow-bellied sapsucker. With their long, brushy tongues, sapsuckers lap up wasps and flies that are attracted to the sweet sap oozing from the rows of evenly spaced holes they drill into trees. Birch and aspen are favourites for the job. Hummingbirds, yellow-rumped warblers, red squirrels and other creatures are also attracted by the sap or insects around the holes. The bounty is so plentiful that sapsuckers don't seem to mind the freeloaders. Sometimes, when the sap ferments, the whole party can get a little woozy.

Sapsuckers also invest in their future housing needs, or at least that of future generations, when they drill holes in trees. The holes invite fungi into trees, rotting and sometimes eventually killing them, making sapsuckers important agents of forest change. Sapsuckers spend about three weeks excavating nest sites in rotted trees.

Their favourite sites are in poplar trees that have been infected by *Fomes igniarius* fungus, which rots the centre of the trunk but leaves the outer sapwood alive. The availability of such trees is the biggest limiting factor on their population. Many other species also depend on old woodpecker holes for nesting or shelter.

Sapsuckers also seek out dead, dry trees that will reverberate well for courtship drumming. Their love code, much louder than their regular tapping, usually features a few fast knocks followed by a slow, rhythmical pounding. As with all woodpeckers, their strong head bones and neck muscles act as shock absorbers. Females also drum in territorial defence

Range: Most of Ontario south of the Hudson Bay lowlands. Also found in all other provinces and territories

Winter whereabouts: Central U.S. to West Indies and Panama

Population density: 2–100 pairs per 100 sq. km (39 sq. mi)

Average first arrival in central Ontario: Mid-Apr.

Average last departure from central Ontario: Late Sept. to early Oct.

57

Famous woodpecker: Woody

Number of Ontario bird species that nest in tree cavities: More than 30

Number of Ontario mammal species that den in trees: At least 7

Number of woodpecker species breeding in Ontario: 9

Number of woodpecker species worldwide: About 200

Also see: Fungi, Ruby-throated Hummingbird, Red Oak, Red Squirrel, Trembling Aspen

while their spouses spend about three weeks digging out their nest site. After the nest is built they reach the throes of passion for about two weeks before the first egg is laid. Males take the night shift incubating.

All woodpeckers can be identified by the way they perch, with their bodies parallel to a tree trunk, looking up. Their parrotlike claws, most with two toes stretching backwards instead of one like most birds, and stiff tails propped against the tree hold them in place (three-toed and black-backed woodpeckers are the exceptions).

The small downy woodpecker is another common Ontario species, foraging in deciduous forest canopies, while the almost identical, but larger, hairy woodpecker works closer to the trunk. Because they stay put all year long, downies and hairies escape the perils of migration and generally live longer than sapsuckers. The similarly abundant, blue-jay-sized flicker spends much of its time on the ground, foraging for ants. Flickers are noisier than most woodpeckers, uttering a loud, ratcheting cry, like the sound of a starter motor or a car engine trying unsuccessfully to turn over.

The king of the woodpeckers is unfortunately the most elusive. As big as a crow and sporting a great long beak and red plume that probably inspired Woody Woodpecker's hairstyle, the pileated woodpecker is an unforgettable sight. The species is limited, however, to mature forests covering at least 40 hectares (100 acres), usually remaining out of sight in the interior, where they nest in oblong cavities with openings 15 to 20 centimetres (six to eight inches) wide. They are very loud, both when calling and when hammering against trees.

WHITE-THROATED SPARROW
Clear Call of the Northern Wild

PATRIOTIC CANADIAN birders swear that the white-throated sparrow sings, "O, sweet Canada, Canada, Canada," while Americans contend the song goes, "Old Sam Peabody, Peabody, Peabody," or "oh, sweet poverty, poverty, poverty." While white-throats may vary their song slightly from one side of the border to the other, birds do not actually pronounce letters of the alphabet. Fanciful phrases attributed to them are merely human lyrics to their music, memory aids that fit the rhythms of their songs.

Whatever the interpretation, the song is one virtually everyone hears up north in summer, hanging in the air and carrying over other wild sounds like a naval whistle calling order on the deck. Archibald Lampman, nineteenth-century Canadian poet and wilderness enthusiast, described them this way:

The white-throat's distant descant with slow stress.
Note after note upon the noonday falls,
Filling the leisured air at intervals
With his own mood of piercing pensiveness.

Like other songbirds, white-throated sparrows call to proclaim their turf and keep out intruders of the same species. They sing especially at sunrise and into evening, in late spring and the first half of summer, sometimes even peeling off a few bars in the dead of night. They usually whistle from a low exposed branch where they can be easily seen, letting their rivals know who they are. Each recognizes the others

Call: Song a high, clear, lingering whistle, usually in 6 notes, lasting 4 or 5 seconds; single "tseet" call notes, loud clicks when frightened

Name origin of *sparrow:* Anglo-Saxon *spearwa,* "a flutterer"

Length: 15–18 cm (6–7 in)

Wingspan: 23–25 cm (9–10 in)

Weight: 26 g (1 oz)

Markings: White throat, grey breast, white or tan head stripes, tiny yellow patch between eye and bill, reddish brown back, grey undersides

Alias: Canada bird, Canadian song sparrow, whistlebird, nightingale, poor Sam Peabody, *le pinson à gorge blanche, Zonotrichia albicollis*

Food: Weed seeds, berries,

insects and their larvae, buds

Preferred habitat: Partly open coniferous and mixed forest understory, thickets, clearings, wetlands

Average territory: 0.2–0.6 ha (0.5–1.5 acres)

Nests: Cup-shaped, made of grasses, twigs, roots, pine needles and lichens

Average clutch: 4–6 olive-sized, light green, grey or bluish eggs with numerous brown spots

Incubation period: 12–14 days

Fledging age: About 12 days

Mortality rate for songbirds in their first year: 80%

Average songbird lifespan: 2–3 years

Maximum recorded songbird lifespan: 16 years (barn swallow, grackle and starling)

Predators: Sharp-shinned hawks, foxes, kestrels, owls

Average first arrival in central Ontario: Mid-to late Apr.

Average last departure from central Ontario: Mid-to late Oct.

Average population density: 1–10 pairs per 10 km² (4 sq. mi)

Range: All of Ontario, but rare south of Shield. Also throughout Canada to northwestern British Columbia and the southern Northwest Territories

Winter whereabouts: Eastern U.S. and extreme southern Ontario

Number of sparrow species breeding in Ontario: 18

Number of New World sparrow and related Old World bunting species: 284

Also see: Cedar Waxwing, Yellow-rumped Warbler

by their individual calls. Once they establish their borders and neighbours get used to each other, squabbles diminish. White-throats respond much more strongly if they detect a strange voice in the neighbourhood. Less-dominant males, usually one-year-olds, cannot establish their own territories and do not breed. Instead they become "floaters," silently stealing through the bush, ready to take over a piece of real estate if something should happen to the proprietor. They often fill the vacant niche within hours of the other bird's disappearance.

In contrast to the floaters, some female white-throats actually join in the mating chorus, normally an exclusively male rite among songbirds. It's a phenomenon of colour-coded personalities. Singing females have white head stripes and are more aggressive than their tan-striped sisters. They join their mates in chasing away intruders from their territories until they begin nesting. Males prefer the feisty white stripes as mates, while females are partial to the less aggressive, easygoing tan-striped males. Since the brassy white-striped amazons usually snap up all the shy tan guys first, tan-striped females and white-striped males are left stuck with each other in the dating game.

White-throats often build their nests in the same spot every year, well hidden on or near the ground in mats of blueberries, bunchberries or other shrubs in clearings or forest edges. The expectant mother remains on the nest almost constantly. While white-throats are normally vegetarian, both parents switch to insects when their young hatch. Insect outbreaks make for easy hunting and many more hatchlings survive.

After the young fledge, white-throats roost in evergreens and join roaming mixed flocks during the day. They scour the leaf litter, scratching and kicking with both feet at the same time, while other species specialize in trunks and the outer or inner branches of trees at various levels. Thousands of white-throats may migrate together at night, often mixed with yellow-rumped warblers, which have a similar range. Studies show sparrows may have better night vision than other small night migrants.

TREE SWALLOW
Almost Constantly in Flight

SPRING, BLESSings and fertility were long believed, from ancient Greece to China, to arrive on the wings of swallows. So high was their repute that killing a swallow or destroying its nest was considered ill luck, even a sin, in some cultures. Folk stories even told of benevolent swallows comforting Jesus at the crucifixion, from which their name *svalow*, old Scandinavian for "console," comes. Because they return so suddenly in early spring, swirling down from high in the air to skim the surface of the water for emerging insects, people also believed swallows hibernated in the mud beneath lakes or the sea. Others suggested that they wintered on the moon or in the heavens.

Modern bird-banding projects have established that tree swallows come from winter homes spread around the Caribbean Sea. They migrate during the day, flying too swiftly for most raptor predators to catch them, feeding on tiny flies transformed from larvae by early warm spells. They are thought to use the sun as a compass, gauging it by an internal clock that compensates for its changing place in the sky. Tree swallows arrive earlier than any other swallow species in a race for unoccupied nesting cavities in Ontario. They are the only swallows that have the ability to switch to berries when insects disappear during cold snaps.

Often returning to the same sites every year, tree swallows nest in early May, using tree cavities as close as 15 metres (50 feet) from each other. Unable with their tiny beaks to dig their own homes, they rely on old woodpecker holes or natural cavities. Dead, flooded trees in beaver ponds provide ideal sites, but the high demand by many species for such

Length: 13–16 cm (5–7.3 in)

Wingspan: 30–35 cm (12–14 in)

Weight: 18–24 gm (0.6–0.8 oz)

Markings: Like a uniform, with metallic, iridescent dark blue backs and heads, contrasting strongly with bright, clean white chin and undersides; very pointy wings; immatures and first-year females greyish brown on top

Alias: White-bellied swallow, *l'hirondelle bicolore*, *Tachycineta bicolor*

Call: Thin, liquid twitter, single little notes, or a "weet, trit, weet" song ending in a liquid warble

Food: 90% aphids, midges, blackflies, beetles, ants and gnats; also moths, bees, other flying insects, bayberries, seeds

Preferred habitat: Wetlands, beaver ponds, meadows, lakes, rivers

TREE SWALLOW

prime, sheltered housing limits the tree-swallow population. Some even resort to nesting in floating hollow logs and stumps. A high percentage of tree swallows don't get to nest, creating a wild-west atmosphere of fighting among both females and males as birds try to wrest nesting cavities from each other.

But tree swallows do have their fun side. They are often seen collecting feathers to line their nest cavities, playfully bobbing them in air. Though males arrive on the breeding grounds first and secure the nest sites, females do the renovations inside their quarters. Both take turns incubating the eggs.

After the young hatch, they are fed every two or three minutes. Spending more time aloft than any other songbird, swallows are in almost constant flight, swooping gracefully to snap insects from the air. They glide in circles, then flap quickly three or four times to gain altitude. Sometimes they dart close to a canoeist's or boater's head, veering off at the last second in their dogged pursuit of bugs. Because they fly just above water or ground, chasing insects that keep low when the pressure drops and rain is on the way, swallows are traditional weather portents.

When nesting is finished and the young fledged, swallows seem to acquire a festive spirit that brings them together in huge numbers at traditional roosts. In Ontario, the place to be in late July and early August is downtown Pembroke, where up to 175,000 swallows of every species roost in a small grove of willow trees on a sandbar in the Muskrat River. The enormous flock darkens the sky in spectacular swirlings as they disperse in the morning to forage and return again at dusk. Pembroke honours the gathering with a swallow festival every summer. Another flock of about 100,000 swallows gathers in Kingston's marshes. The birds migrate en masse in late August, forming even larger flocks when they land in the Florida Everglades. These can number into the millions.

WOOD THRUSH
Resident Forest Flautist

TESTOSTERONE, the hormone that fuels machismo among humans, cues birds to start singing. In the springtime, lengthening daylight stimulates testosterone production in male birds, putting them into breeding, serenading mode. Of all the avian melodies, the wood thrush's fluted, resonant tones, carrying far through the forest, are considered by many to be the most beautiful. The spotted songster, in fact, is a close relative of the celebrated European nightingale, long a favourite of poets and writers.

The wood thrush achieves its virtuosity by using its bronchial tubes, which branch off from the windpipe into the lungs, to sing two notes at the same time. Unlike a human, whose voicebox is located at the top of the windpipe, or trachea, a bird produces sounds from the bottom of its trachea. The more muscles attached to the voicebox, the greater the range of sounds it can produce.

For wood thrushes, Ontario is a good place to raise a family, but becomes much too cold in the winter. They spend most of the year in the tropics—therefore, in much more

Average first arrival in central Ontario: Mid-May

Average last departure from central Ontario: Late Aug. to early Sept.

Range: Mostly restricted to south and central Ontario. Also found in southern Quebec

Winter home: Mexico, Central America and northern Colombia

Number of pairs of muscles attached to the voicebox of songbirds: 5–9

Number of pairs of muscles attached to the voicebox of turkey vultures: 0

Number of pairs of muscles attached to the voicebox of geese: 1

Name origin: Old German *thruskjon*

Number of thrush species breeding in Ontario: 7

Number of thrush species world-wide: 30

Also see: Robin, Red-eyed Vireo, Yellow-rumped Warbler

crowded conditions. Warmer regions support greater abundance and variety of life-forms than do northern temperate areas. Migrating songbirds probably evolved from tropical species that gradually extended their ranges northward. They retreated with each renewal of winter, but learned to return to the vast nesting opportunities and superabundance of insects available in a northern spring. Longer northern days also afford more hunting time and faster nestling growth.

Migrating at night, wood thrushes fly across the Gulf of Mexico and up the Mississippi Valley, returning to the same Ontario nest site each May or June. Males arrive first, females two to six days later. They are secretive, hopping around and foraging for insects on the ground, well hidden beneath low understory vegetation deep in the forest. Males visit the nest just long enough to feed their incubating mates. Both parents feed the young until they are about three weeks old.

Sadly, fewer wood thrushes return from the tropics each year because of habitat destruction, both north and south. The 1990 Ontario population was only a quarter of what it had been 30 years earlier. In some areas, where they have been forced into shrinking pockets of forest, virtually every nest is parasitized by cowbirds. Although wood thrushes are increasing in some parts of eastern Ontario where farmland is being allowed to revert to bush, some predict the species could become extinct within 40 years. This might seem like a far-off crisis in a world of pressing environmental woes, unless you've ever heard the haunting, beautiful call of a wood thrush in the forest.

A close relative, the hermit thrush, nests in coniferous forest all the way to Hudson Bay, but overlaps with the wood thrush's range in central Ontario. The two species look and sound similar, though the hermit thrush is a bit smaller and sports a reddish tail. Its song features a long first note and varying pitches.

RED-EYED VIREO
Seldom Seen, Always Heard

LIKE A TV EVANGELIST—"Do you believe? Do you repent?"—the red-eyed vireo, or preacher bird, seems to sermonize with an endless stream of rhetorical questions, its voice rising up and down in couplets all day long. Though difficult to see, male red-eyes make their presence known by belting out up to 3,000 songs an hour from the tree tops, from May till mid-summer, even on hot days when most other birds are taking a siesta. They're known to sing with their mouths full of insects.

While males call attention to themselves high in the canopy, female red-eyed vireos nest silently in the understory below. The nest usually hangs between thin, forked, outer branches, which will not support raccoons or skunks and other predators. Dangers increase if forest fragmentation brings edge habitat closer. The sleek, sparrow-sized birds need at least half a hectare (1.2 acres) of unbroken forest with heavy undergrowth to nest successfully.

Among the greatest dangers to red-eyes are brown-headed cowbirds, parasitic denizens of open areas and forest edge. Cowbirds lay single eggs in the nests of other species, for them to raise. Most hosts do not recognize their own eggs or young, only the location of the nest. An impostor cowbird hatches first, grows faster and aggressively elbows its foster siblings out of the way at feeding time, sometimes pushing them from the nest, usually becoming the only survivor.

Call: Short, up-and-down whistled phrases of 2–5 notes, similar to robin, but slower and always the same, repeated sometimes 30–60 times a minute; also makes sharp, high single notes

Most vireo songs recorded in 1 day: 22,197

Length: 12–15 cm (5–6 in)

Wingspan: 15 cm (6 in)

Weight: 18 g (0.6 oz)

Markings: Greenish brown back, grey cap, white streak over red eyes, white undersides

Alias: Preacher bird, greenlet, teacher, *le viréo aux yeux rouges*, *Vireo olivaceus*

Food: Wide variety of insects; berries if insects are scarce

Preferred habitat: Deciduous and mixed forests, especially among aspens or maple, with understory shrubs and saplings

Nest: Neat, deep, thin-walled cup of bark strips, usually birch, grass, wasp-nest paper and cobwebs, 6–9 cm (2.4–3.5 in) wide, camouflaged with lichens

Average clutch: 3–4 olive-sized white eggs with dark brown marks; sometimes 2 broods a year

Predators: Sharp-shinned hawks, raccoons, skunks, red squirrels, chipmunks

Average first arrival in central Ontario: Mid-May

Average last departure from central Ontario: Late Sept.

Range: All of Ontario except extreme northwest. Also found in all provinces except Newfoundland

TURKEY VULTURE
The Graceful, Soaring Scavenger

Length: 65–80 cm (26–32 in)

Wingspan: 1.7–2 m (5.8–6.6 ft)

Weight: 1.6–2 kg (3.5–4.4 lb)

Alias: Turkey buzzard, *l'urubu à tête rouge, Cathartes aura*

Markings: Underside of wings have distinctive grey-black pattern. Red, featherless heads

Food: Carrion, though may kill defenceless animals such as newborn rabbits

Preferred habitat: Over open areas, large lakes, islands, swamps, cliffs

Mating season: Mid-Apr. to mid-May

Nests: No nests made, but lays eggs in hollow logs and stumps, caves, often in swamps and other hidden, undisturbed sites

Clutch: Usually 2 eggs

Incubation period: 30–41 days

Fledging age: 8–11 weeks

Predators: Foxes, skunks, snakes, other birds of prey may raid nests

Heartbeats per minute: 301

Body temperature: 40°C (104°F)

Number counted migrating along lower Great Lakes in fall: Up to 9,000

Range: North to Sudbury. Also found in the 4 western provinces, southern Quebec and occasionally in Nova Scotia

Winter whereabouts: New Jersey to South America

Average first arrival in Central Ontario: Early Apr.

Average last departure from Central Ontario: Late Oct.

SOMETIMES MISTAKEN for hawks, turkey vultures are actually much larger, second only to eagles in Ontario's raptor pantheon. They are expanding their range and have become increasingly common in south-central Ontario since the 1970s.

Turkey vultures are usually seen drifting or circling over fields, roads, cliffs or lakes near nesting sites. They hold their two-metre-wide wings in a shallow V, slowly tilting from side to side on wind currents, almost never flapping. The two-tone underside of their wings is the chief distinguishing feature.

Tibetans and Zoroastrians left their dead at sacred sites to be eaten by vultures

---

Because vultures evoke images of slow, parched death in the desert, there's a perception that they are the lowlifes of the bird world. These scavengers live on rotting carcasses, don't take the time to make real nests and even pee on their own legs to keep cool. When cornered, they vomit foul-smelling, half-decayed flesh and then hide their heads, ostrichlike, rather than fight. Turkey vultures don't sing, just hiss or growl on occasion. And their featherless, gnarled red heads (black on younger birds) do nothing for their standing in avian beauty contests.

But it's captivating to watch turkey vultures soar almost effortlessly overhead. Vultures are also notable as highly skilled specialists, with an acute sense of smell not possessed by other birds. They may forage all day over many kilometres before detecting the sweet scent of something dead. Then they home in with their keen eyes. In the U.S., one resourceful maintenance crew checking for gas-pipeline leaks turned to turkey vultures for help. The crew pumped a gas that reeks of rotten egg through the 70-kilometre (43-

mile) line, then, to find the leaks, simply looked for circling vultures.

From their communal roosts and nest sites in remote woods and swamps and on cliffs and small islands, turkey vultures set off when the morning mists have cleared and the sun has warmed the land enough to create thermals—the columns of warm, rising air that vultures ride upwards in circles. Their wings are too cumbersome to flap for very long. Though they usually forage alone, the sight of one vulture circling a find usually brings more. They'll eat anything from large mammals to fish and grasshoppers, as long as it isn't moving. Starting with the eyeballs, they'll strip the carcass to the bone. Vultures were respected by people of past cultures as mythic figures connected with the mysteries of death. Tibetans and Zoroastrians left their dead at sacred sites to be eaten by vultures. The vulture's scientific name, *Cathartes*, of Greek origin, means "purifier." Ornithologists speculate that the vulture's bald head allows it to dig deep into a corpse without soiling feathers.

As March warms, turkey vultures arrive in southern Ontario from their winter haunts in the southeastern U.S. Up to 700 in a single day have been seen near Grimsby on their Niagara Escarpment migration route, flying as high as 1,520 metres (5,000 feet) on high-pressure fronts. They often return to old nesting sites, where they pair off and devote spring and summer to raising a new family, with Mom and Dad taking turns incubating the eggs and feeding the young. Baby turkey vultures are cute, covered in a cottony white down. They spend much of their first two months stretching out their wings to bask in the sun. This classic vulture stance can often be seen among perching adults as well. It enables nature's purifiers to conserve energy for their long flights in search of the deceased.

Closest relative: Black Vulture
Also see: Broad-winged Hawk, Wind

YELLOW-RUMPED WARBLER
Outgoing Bundle of Energy

Length: 12–15 cm (5.3–6 in)

Wingspan: 20–23 cm (8–9 in)

Weight: 10–19 g (0.35–0.6 oz)

Markings: Yellow patches on top of head, in front of wings and above base of tail; males have black-streaked bluish grey back, black mask and chest and white throat and belly. Females have grey-brown back, streaked breast and white belly. Male's colours fade to resemble female's in fall

Alias: Myrtle warbler, *la fauvette à croupion jaune, Dendroica coronata*

Call: Loud, sharp "chip;" song a gentle trill

Food: Caterpillars, larvae, leaf beetles, ants, grasshoppers, mosquitoes, flies, insect eggs, bayberries, poison ivy and other berries, seeds, sap

Preferred habitat: Dry fir and spruce forest edges; also found in pine, cedar, hemlock, tamarack and mixed forests

Nest: Deep cup, 7–15 cm (3–6 in) wide, of twigs and grass, lined with feathers, usually 1.5–6 m (5–20 ft) up in evergreens

Average clutch: 3–5 grey-and-brown-speckled-and-blotched white eggs, the size of marbles

Incubation period: 11–13 days

Fledging age: About 2 weeks old

Population density: Up to 25–100 pairs per km² (0.4 sq. mi) in coniferous forests

T HERE ARE MORE brightly coloured summer wood warblers in the forest than any other group of birds. Roger Tory Peterson, North America's high sage of avian lore, calls them the butterflies of the bird world. Unfortunately for people who delight in seeing them, many of these tiny, hyperactive insect-eaters are "skulkers" of the thick, tangled undergrowth. Or they frequent high, dense foliage, avoiding the gaze of all but the most dogged birders. Yellow-rumped warblers, probably the most common of all, break the mould, being exceedingly outgoing as they forage in small groups among lower branches. "I've got a great view of a yellow-rump!" is the somewhat embarrassing cry of the birder who spots one.

Yellow-rumps also spend more time in Ontario than any other warbler because they are generalists and can live on berries, seeds and even sap longer than the rest. They begin arriving on warm fronts in late April, initiating a parade of migrant warblers that continues for two months. Although some yellow-rumped warblers winter in the U.S. Midwest, many species come from roosts in the tropics and take four to five weeks to reach Canada. They migrate at night, when there's less turbulence and the air cools feverishly working muscles. In ideal conditions, on clear nights, advancing waves of up to two million migrating songbirds have been detected by radar. Most fly 150 to 600 metres (500 to 2,000 feet) high. They rest and catch insects to rebuild their fat supplies for several days between flights.

Night migrants follow the stars. Heavy cloud or rain at night grounds them. In studies conducted inside planetariums in spring, white-throated sparrows, indigo buntings and other species flutter and orient themselves towards the North Star in night-sky projections. Other studies reveal most learn the skill rather than genetically inheriting it. Some species may also navigate using the Earth's magnetic field, the pressure shifts of weather fronts or low-frequency background sounds, such as ocean waves or winds thousands of kilometres away.

Spring warbler migration peaks in mid- to late May, when insect populations are exploding in Ontario. It's often an all-you-can-eat bonanza, the reason they fly so far north to raise families. Populations of many warbler species go up dramatically with outbreaks of spruce budworm and other insects. Baby warblers, fed by their parents about every 10 minutes, are stuffed with their own weight in insects each day. The high-protein diet turns hatchlings into fledglings in about two weeks.

After a fairly quiet nesting period, with both parents attending, yellow-rumped warblers return to their noisy ways when the young fledge in July. They forage in flocks, hunting flying insects from perches in the lower branches of trees. In the fall they turn up at shorelines, open areas and thickets. Switching to seeds and berries in cooler weather when insects become scarce, most yellow-rumps put off their return migration till late September. Some remain until mid-October.

Another warbler that, though a skulker, can be quite conspicuous in Ontario forests is the ovenbird. Wintering in the tropics as far south as Venezuela, it evokes an exotic jungle feel in Ontario's forests with its loud call, rising in volume to the rhythm of "teacher, teacher, teacher, teacher." Nesting and spending most of its time on the forest floor beneath thick undergrowth, the sparrow-sized, orange-crowned, olive-and-white bird is seldom seen. Its call is becoming less common as the large tracts of mature forests it needs shrink, both in its winter and summer homes and along migration routes.

Average annual survival rate for most adult warblers: Less than 50%

Maximum lifespan: At least 7 years

Predators: Sharp-shinned hawks, raccoons, skunks, snakes

Percentage of yellow-rump nests parasitized by cowbirds: About 30%

Range: From the Hudson Bay tree line to the southern edge of the Canadian Shield and Bruce Peninsula, with scattered nesting populations south of the Shield. Also found throughout Canada south of the tree line, except on the prairies

Winter whereabouts: Southern Michigan to Central America and West Indies

Average first arrival in central Ontario: Late Apr.

Average last departure from central Ontario: Mid-Oct.

Normal warbler body temperature: 38°C (100°F)

Average warbler body temperature during migration: 46°C (115°F)

Number of days a blackpoll warbler takes to fly from Nova Scotia to South America: 4

Amount of body weight a blackpoll warber loses in southward migration: 50%

Amount of tropical rain forest destroyed every day worldwide: 300 km² (116 sq. mi)

Number of warbler species nesting in Ontario: 36

Number of warbler species worldwide: 115

Also see: North Star, Poison Ivy, Red-eyed Vireo, Wind, Yellow-bellied Sapsucker

CEDAR WAXWING
Impeccably Mannered Team Players

CEDAR WAX-wings are just about the nicest, most congenial birds known in avian circles. They are well-mannered nomads that wander in groups in search of berries and other foods. A waxwing is almost never seen alone. They are so polite that they're often seen perched in a row, passing berries up and down the line to each other. When courting, couples also daintily pass flower petals back and forth. Even when nesting they have no territorial-exclusion zone, other than guarding the space immediately around their nest.

Their easygoing nature often brings small foraging waxwing flocks within ready view of people. In the nineteenth century, they were valued for more than their genteel manners. "They fatten, and become so tender and juicy as to be sought by every epicure for the table," wrote the patron saint of ornithology, John James Audubon, in 1842. Audubon himself employed the standard method of bird study of his era, the days before binoculars: shooting his subjects so that they could be viewed up close and made to sit still for painted portraits.

Although tightly packed flocks usually begin arriving in central Ontario in mid-May, waxwings are late nesters, taking up housekeeping from late June to the end of August, when most berries ripen. Their nests are usually wedged in the fork of a branch high in the tree canopy. Females almost never leave the nest while incubating eggs, their mates feeding them all the while. Since they do not defend a real terri-

Length: 17–20 cm (6.5–8 in)
Wingspan: 30–31 cm (1 ft)
Weight: 25–40 g (0.8–1.4 oz)
Markings: Both sexes have a black mask, brown breast, back and head crest, yellow bar at tip of black tail, waxy red tips on secondary feathers of black wings
Alias: Cedarbird, cherry bird, Carolina waxwing, cankerbird, *le jaseur des cèdres*, *Bombycilla cedrorum*
Call: High, dry, quiet "zeee," slightly vibrating, frequently repeated

tory, males continue to hang out with the boys, travelling up to two kilometres (1.2 miles) from their nests to find food. At first, nestlings are fed regurgitated insects, high-protein meals that allow them to grow very quickly, and their parents can be seen hunting from tree perches, snatching insects from the air like flycatchers. Several days after hatching they're weaned to berries.

> *Waxwings are often seen perched in a row, passing berries up and down the line to one another*

When the young have fledged, flocks resume their nomadic ways. Some groups begin flying south in mid- to late September, amalgamating into larger loose flocks as they go. If they can find enough food, many choose to stay behind, eating low-quality fruits, berries and cedar cones that remain on the branches of some trees and shrubs. Sometimes they have an unplanned winter bash, when fermented fruits, such as clusters of black pokeweed berries, actually make them drunk, causing them to sway and even topple from their perches. A sloshed waxwing may remain nearly oblivious, even to the point of being picked up. They usually sleep it off.

Food: Berries, especially mountain ash and dogwood, cherries, wild grapes, hawthorn fruits, cedar cones, sumac and alder seeds, caterpillars, insects

Preferred habitat: Open woods, forest fringe, above shorelines and wetlands, among trees with fruit or berries

Average flock: 30–60 birds

Nest: Bulky cup of grasses, twigs, rootlets, bark and lichens, 10–13 cm (4–5 in) wide

Average clutch: 3–5 olive-sized blue, grey or greenish eggs with black spots

Incubation period: 12–14 days

Fledging age: About 18 days

Lifespan: About 4–6 years in wild, 8–14 in captivity

Predators: Sharp-shinned hawks, red-tailed hawks; red squirrels and raccoons raid nests

Average population density: 1–10 pairs per 10 km² (4 sq. mi)

Average first arrival of migrant flocks in central Ontario: Late May

Average last departure of migrant flocks from central Ontario: Mid-to late Sept.

Range: All of Ontario to the tree line. Also found in all other provinces

Winter whereabouts: From about Sudbury and Sault Ste. Marie south to Central America

Also see: Cedar, Hawthorns, Yellow-rumped Warbler

CREEPY CRAWLIES

THERE ARE MORE than one million animal species on Earth. By some estimates, 73 percent are insects. Other tiny invertebrates, such as spiders, mites, worms, snails and springtails, make up the most of the balance. Mammals account for just 0.04 percent of the total. Among the insects themselves, one-third are beetle species, of whom fireflies are Ontario's flashiest representatives.

As anyone acquainted with the outdoors in spring and summer knows, Ontario has its share of creepy crawlies, with some 50,000 known invertebrates. The Canadian Shield is legendary for its profusions of blackflies, mosquitoes and other irrepressible flying insects. The same insects are also one of the main reasons the wilderness has so many beautiful insectivorous birds. There are plenty of striking dragonflies and spiders keeping bug numbers in check as well. Indeed, invertebrates are a vital link in the food chain, feeding fish, amphibians, many reptiles, bats, shrews, even bears.

The very process of decomposition, from which all new plant life springs, depends heavily on countless armies of springtails, termites, beetles, mites, ants, worms, centipedes and many others living above and beneath the ground. And without beautiful butterflies, moths and above all bees to pollinate flowers, many species of plants and trees would perish. A world without insects would be virtually unrecognizable.

BEES, WASPS & HORNETS
Societies of Heavily Armed Females

I T'S TRUE THAT only female bees, wasps and hornets have stingers. They're actually modified ovipositors, or abdominal egg-laying tubes, used by most insects to deposit eggs with accuracy. A stinger moves up and down to saw into the skin with tiny barbs, while injecting venom through its hollow tube. While bee stingers are often so barbed that they break off in tough skin, leading to the death of the bee, wasps can sting repeatedly. Bald-faced hornets are reputed to be the most painful, though yellow jackets are more aggressive and likely to administer multiple stings.

Having evolved their uniquely female instruments into awesome weapons, bees and their kin not surprisingly form solidly matriarchal societies. The first hardy bee usually seen in April or early May is the husky, densely furred bumblebee queen (illustrated). Her insulation allows her to be active in temperatures too cool for other species, though she oftens avoids the midday heat. After hibernating alone beneath the ground all winter, bumblebee queens search out early flowers for high-protein pollen needed to produce eggs. Having mated and obtained a year's worth of sperm the previous fall, the queen builds a small wax-chambered nest in the ground, often in abandoned mouse burrows or under tree stumps, and lays eight to 10 eggs. Some 20 to 30 days later, they have hatched, grown, pupated and become working adults. These infertile female workers take over the job of collecting nectar and pollen,

Lifespan of honeybee queen: Usually 2–3 years, up to 5 years

Average lifespan of a honeybee worker (from hatching as a larva): 6–8 weeks

Number of calories burned by a flying bumblebee per minute: 0.5

Maximum lifetime distance a honeybee worker travels before she burns out: 800 km (500 mi)

Distance of a bumblebee foraging trip: Up to 10 km (6 mi)

Foraging trips required to make
1 g (0.03 oz) of honey:
About 60

Annual honey production of a
commercial beehive: More than
50 kg (110 lb)

*Over millions
of years, bees
and flowering
plants have
evolved in tan-
dem, forming
one of the most
vital links
in nature*

Amount of honey needed by an
average honeybee colony to
get through the winter: 25 kg
(55 lb)

Bee food: Nectar, pollen

Honeybee markings: Striped
black or brown and yellow
abdomen, mostly black head
and thorax

Average honeybee length:
1–1.6 cm (0.4–0.6 in)

Bumblebee markings: Hairy
yellow and black, with smoky
wings

Bumblebee length: 1.3–2.3 cm
(0.5–0.9 in)

Bald-faced hornet markings:
Black body with white markings on abdomen and head

Bald-faced hornet length:
2 cm (0.8 in)

Only true hornet species in
Canada: European hornet,
3 cm (1.2 in) long

enlarging the nest and raising successive generations of young. The queen concentrates on laying more eggs.

Towards the end of summer the bumblebee queen lays a batch of unfertilized eggs that hatch into male drones. Still another set of eggs, given large chambers, extra food and special care, become new queens. The sole job of the drones is to leave the nest, establish territories and mate with young queens that come their way. They die soon afterwards. The workers in the colony, along with the old queen, also perish with the killing frosts of fall. Only young, fertilized queens, after loading up on nectar from late-blooming goldenrods and asters, survive by crawling beneath the ground for the winter, with the future of a whole new colony resting with them.

The only other true colonial nesting bee species in Ontario is the honeybee. Its large colonies in tree cavities and crevices are like permanent cities, persisting through the winter, often lasting for years or even decades. Honeybees transform nectar into large stores of honey for the cold months. Huddling together for warmth, wintering bees conserve their energy and live longer than quickly burnt out summer workers.

Until sugar became widely available in the past few centuries, honey was Europe's main sweetener. Indo-European peoples learned the art of domestic beekeeping, or apiculture, more than 4,000 years ago, and brought the first honeybee colonies with them to North America in the early 1600s. Native peoples called honeybees the white man's flies. The bees spread quickly into the wild, since queens frequently lead swarms from crowded nests to start new colonies in late spring or early summer. Soon after the queen mother leaves, her heir emerges from pupation to assume the throne of the old colony. If an old queen does not leave the nest, a princess may sting her to death, along with her royal siblings still in their pupal shrouds.

Some wasps are also colonial. Bald-faced hornets and yellow jackets, both wasps, follow life cycles very similar to bumblebees. They are the original paper producers, chewing wood fibre into sheets of saliva-soaked pulp that dries into the fine, grey paper walls of their nest. Starting out small, the nest grows in progressive layers as the colony grows through the summer. Hornets build in trees and bushes, where their irregularly shaped homes often have small branches running through them for support. Spherical yellow jacket nests are found in underground cavities or hanging by a single stalk from a tree branch. Yellow jackets often become pests to humans in late summer and early fall after their colonies begin to fall apart and the workers fan out looking for food in garbage or anywhere else they can find it.

Entomologists—bug experts—liken the selfless individuals of insect colonies to a single cell of an organism. There are innumerable species of bees and wasps, however, that are rugged individualists, hunting or foraging alone. Many wasps dig holes in the ground for their eggs and stock them with flies, spiders or caterpillars they have paralyzed with their stings. When the larvae hatch, their food is laid out in front of them, fresh, alive and immobile. Many of these species aren't readily recognizable as wasps, being small, black and white or all black. At the same time, there are many species of flies and moths that look like bees or wasps, evolving to imitate the bright colours that warn birds and animals to stay away from stinging insects.

Over millions of years, bees and flowering plants have evolved in tandem, forming one of the most vital links in nature. Flowers produce nectar solely for the purpose of attracting bees and like-minded creatures. Bees lap up nectar with their tongues and pack it onto their hairy legs and bodies for transporting back to the nest. In the process, they also pick up and spread pollen as they buzz from blossom to blossom. Both the sweet fragrance and bright colours of flowers are designed to advertise their wares to pollinators. Plants have helped ensure their own survival by taking turns—blooming in succession, one species after another throughout the year—allowing the bees and others to stay fed and get around to them all.

Yellow-jacket markings: Smooth, bright yellow-and-black bodies

Yellow-jacket length: 1 cm (0.4 in)

Paper-wasp markings: Black, brown and amber body, with a very thin waist and long legs

Paper-wasp length: 1.5–2 cm (0.6–0.8 in)

Length of wasp and yellow-jacket stingers: About 4 mm (0.016 in)

Wasp food: Insects, spiders, insect eggs, nectar, plant juices, honeydew

Humans with severe allergic reactions to insect bites or stings: 0.4% of population

Predators: Spiders, bee flies, robber flies, flycatchers, skunks, bears

Range of bees and wasps: All of Ontario to the tree line. Also found throughout Canada below the tree line

Number of species of bees, wasps, ants and sawflies worldwide: At least 108,000

Also see: Moccasin Flower, Oak, Trillium

BLACKFLIES
'The Worst Martyrdom I Suffered'

And the blackflies, the little blackflies
Always the blackfly no matter where you go,
I'll die with the blackflies a-picken' my bones
In North Ontario, i-o
In North Ontario
WADE HEMSWORTH,
Song about a survey crew on the White River

JUST AS THE FIRST fine days of May come along, the sun and warmth give rise to swarms of biting blackflies. Though they mass around the face, they are like commandos, landing silently behind ears, on necks, or burrowing under clothes. Their bite is quite unlike the precise pinprick of a mosquito. Instead, they rip into the flesh with jagged, scissorlike jaws and slurp from a blood-filled bowl in the open wound. The blood-encrusted, swollen ring of purple skin they leave behind is generally bigger and more itchy than the work of mosquitoes. A French Recollet brother travelling up the Ottawa River in the early 1620s wrote of his blackfly tormentors, "I confess that this is the worst martyrdom I suffered in this country."

Only female blackflies bite. It takes them three to five minutes of feeding to get enough blood to nourish their developing eggs. Fully tanked up, they are double their original size and must stagger away and lie low for one or two hours while they filter the blood's protein and drain its water content.

The Canadian Shield is prime blackfly country, perhaps the world's most notorious, because it courses with the fast, clear waterways needed by their young. Females stick eggs to rocks, plants and other debris in or beside rivers. Groups of blackfly larvae are easy to see, forming dense, greenish masses that look like moss on rocks. The larvae anchor themselves by secreting a silky goo onto surfaces and sinking tiny hooks at the end of their abdomens into it. As they sway in the current, they filter plankton—microscopic plants and animals—from the water with the bristles of two long brushes projecting from their mouths. If one loses its grip and is swept into the current, it releases a silk safety line, attached to the gooey base on the rock, from its abdomen. If it reaches a calm spot in the water, the larva uses its head and hooks to slowly winch itself back to its original spot.

The species that attack in early May are blackfies that hatch in the fall and grow slowly beneath the ice through the winter, moulting six to eight times. As rivers warm in spring, they spin cocoons and take several days to metamorphose into adults. When the cocoon opens, the blackfly floats up to the surface inside an air bubble and flies away. Building to peaks in mid-May and June, depending on the weather, they die off quickly after five or six hot days straight, their tiny bodies drying out.

Most species of blackflies hatch from eggs in spring and do not become biting adults until June or July. Their numbers are not as great as the early-spring hordes. Most species, in fact, specialize in blood from birds, or from mammals other than man. One preys solely on loons. Parasites spread by some are a major cause of duckling mortality. In agricultural areas, masses of blackflies can sometimes kill cattle. Luckily for nocturnal animals, most varieties restrict their feeding frenzies to daylight, though they become meaner and more numerous in the hours before sunset. They rest on plants and shrubs at night.

Though universally reviled, blackflies play a vital role in the ecosystem. Their swarms draw tropical birds from as far away as South America to feast and raise their young on blackfly protein. Blackflies themselves live primarily off plant nectar and are one of the most important pollinators of blueberries. Even purveyors of pain have a hand in creating sweetness and beauty.

First appearance of blackflies in evolution: At least 30 million years ago

Number of blackfly species in Ontario: About 50

Number of blackfly species worldwide: 12,000–13,000

Also see: Dragonflies, Lowbrush Blueberry, Mosquitoes, Yellow-rumped Warbler

DEER FLIES
& HORSE FLIES
Swimmers a Favourite Target

DEER AND HORSE flies are the brutes of the biting-insect crowd, lacking the daintiness of mosquitoes or the stealth of blackflies. Instead, they zoom in and quickly take a good-sized chunk of you. The sensation is akin to having a burning ember alight on your skin.

Although more painful than a black-fly's or a mosquito's, bites from the bigger flies do not swell or itch so much afterwards, probably because their quick work does not require a heavy injection of saliva, used by the smaller biters to keep blood from clotting while they suck.

Like most other biting insects, only female deer flies and horse flies strike, using the blood to produce eggs. As their name implies, deer flies, which are a little larger and fatter than house flies, probably evolved to prey mainly on medium-sized animals such as deer. Most species attack both deer and humans high up on the body, circling around the head as they scout for a good place to land. They often follow a moving target with dogged tenacity and constant buzzing, less deterred by insect repellent than are mosquitoes and blackflies.

Horse flies, for their part, are gargantuan moose feeders, usually hitting low on the legs. A moose can lose up to a cup of blood a day to the little vampires. Humans are usually too puny for horse flies' liking, and are less often attacked by them than by the smaller deer flies.

Both horse flies and deer flies have very good long-distance vision. They are especially attracted to swimmers by the shimmer of wet skin in the sunlight. It may take many long dives underwater to get one off your trail. They are extremely partial to hot, sunny days, and usually disappear quickly when the sun goes behind the clouds. They keep out

Species illustrated above:
The deer fly *Crysops callidas*

Fastest clocked flying speed of a horsefly: 112 km/h (67 mph)

Wind speed at which they usually become inactive: 10 km/h (6 mph)

Deer-fly wing markings: Most have a large black dot on each, or black patterns

Horse-fly wing markings: Usually clear

Deer-fly length: 8–15 mm (0.3–0.6 in)

Horse-fly length: 10–25 mm (0.4–1 in)

Markings: Various species can have black, brown, grey, orangish or yellow markings. Colourful eyes often iridescent green or purple stripes or patterns

---

They often follow a moving target with dogged tenacity and constant buzzing, less deterred by insect repellant than are mosquitoes and blackflies

---

of sight in temperatures below 13°C (55°F).

Four to eight days after getting their blood meal, horse flies and deer flies lay their eggs in various watery habitats, often on stems or beneath leaves just above the surface. When they hatch, the larvae drop into the water or wet soil and become predators of aquatic insects and other invertebrates. They spend eight to nine months as larvae, hunting beneath the ice through the winter. In midspring, they begin crawling onto dry ground and spend about one to three weeks pupating into adults. They take wing in late May or early June. Each species has its own emergence period through the summer. Males come out first, forming groups and waiting for the females to follow. Once mating is done, it's curtains for the males within a few days. Females live on for another couple of weeks, searching for blood for their eggs and tormenting their victims in the process.

Horse-fly aliases: Gadflies, green-headed monsters, breeze flies, ear flies, *les taons*, family *Tabanidae*

Food: Larvae eat aquatic and soil insects, worms and other invertebrates; adults mostly feed on nectar and honeydew

Clutch: In clusters of 100 to more than 1,000 long, flat, black, overlapping eggs

Eggs destroyed by other insects: 50%

Egg-development period: Usually 4–6 days

Number of larval stages: 5–11

Full lifespan: A little more than a year

Predators: Birds, dragonflies, wasps, robber flies

Range: Various species found throughout Ontario and all other provinces and territories

Number of deer- and horse-fly species in Ontario: 98

Number of deer- and horse-fly species worldwide: 3,750

Also see: Mosquito, Pegasus & Andromeda

DRAGONFLIES
Fearsome Insect Predators

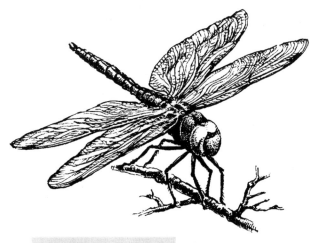

DRAGONFLIES are among the deadliest friends a human can have. They may look scary, but they do not harm people. Rather, they're like helicopter gunships coming to the rescue, striking fear into the hearts of marauding mosquitoes and blackflies. Little wonder the Japanese considered them symbols of victory in war. A single bug-eating dragonfly in a clearing or meadow on a sunny day can quickly clear swarms of biting insects away from a suffering human. A New England entrepreneur has even marketed dragonflies on tiny leashes, with one end clipped on to clothing, for summer walks in bug country.

From the moment they hatch in the water, dragonflies are fearsome predators. Dragonfly larvae, called nymphs, are stocky, crablike creatures that prowl the bottom of small ponds and slow streams. Like a living nightmare from the movie *Alien*, they have projectile jaws that spring out in a fraction of a second to snatch prey. Usually after sunset in late spring and summer, fully grown nymphs crawl out of the water and spend a couple of hours wiggling out of their juvenile skin, while keeping rectal gills at the tip of the abdomen in the water until their air-breathing equipment kicks in. The newly emerged dragonfly spends up to six more hours drying off and pumping fluid into the veins of its two pairs of wings. Finally, it lifts off on its maiden flight.

In central Ontario, dragonflies begin appearing in May. The first to show up is usually the green darner (illustrated), one of the largest, fastest and most common species. Though most species overwinter as nymphs beneath the ice, a portion of the green darner population migrates, flying south after cold fronts in late summer, often in squadrons of thousands. No one knows where they travel, though they are known as far south as Central America. Like monarch but-

Flying speed: Up to 30 km/h (18 mph)

Green darner length: 7–8 cm (2.8–3.1 in)

Green darner wingspan: 10–11 cm (4–4.4 in)

Darner species markings: Shiny green, blue, black, grey or purplish, sometimes with yellow

Skimmer species markings: Usually red, black, blue or green bodies with spotted, barred or unmarked wings

Alias: Mosquito hawks, horse singers, darning needles, snake charmers, snake doctors, *les libellules*, order *Odonata*. Larvae called "nymphs" or "bass bugs"

Food: Adults eat mosquitoes, blackflies, deer flies, horse flies, midges, butterflies. Larvae eat tadpoles, tiny fish, midges, butterflies, worms, larvae

Average number of mosquito larvae eaten during nymph stage: 3,000

terflies, only their descendants return in spring.

Male dragonflies establish and defend mating territories over bodies of water, where females will lay their eggs. Pond species known as skimmers are among the most territorial and aggressive. One male's domain may cover an entire small pond, or many may occupy a larger water body. He engages in frequent but brief aerial dogfights.

Dragonfly larvae have projectile jaws that spring out in a fraction of a second to snatch prey

Before mating, a male doubles over to deposit sperm from the tip of his tail into a special storage hold beneath the base of his abdomen. When a receptive female arrives in his territory, they form an acrobatic circle with their two bodies, the male holding her head by the tip of his tail while the female's tail swings forward to take the sperm from his cargo hold. The act takes only a few seconds. Females can store the sperm for a long time and go on to mate with other males. Since the last male to mate with her usually has the biggest share of offspring, males often jealously guard their partner after mating, remaining attached to her or flying just above, driving off other males until she lays her eggs. Ambitious males may try guarding two mates at once.

Female skimmers take four or five minutes to drop their eggs, which sink to the bottom of the pond to hatch. Darners, however, use the tip of their abdomens to slice open stems just beneath the surface of the water, to lay their eggs in. Club-tail dragonflies deposit their eggs in streams or along lakeshores.

Damselflies are similar to dragonflies, but are more slender and fluttery as they fly. When resting, they hold their wings upwards, folded together or half spread, while the speedier dragonflies hold their wings horizontally.

Habitat: Ponds, lakes, streams, wetlands, meadows

Egg-development period: 1–2 weeks for green darners, a few days to 9 months for other species

Nymphs: 2–50 mm (0.08–2 in) long, various shades of brown, green or yellow, plain or heavily patterned

Period spent as an adult: Up to 10 weeks

Winter whereabouts: Most species overwinter as inactive nymphs at the bottom of ponds, lakes and streams. Green darners may migrate south. Some leave eggs for the winter

Predators: Red-winged blackbirds, hawks, swallows, ducks eat adult. Larvae eaten by other aquatic insects, frogs, fish, turtles and birds

First appearance of dragonflies on Earth: 200–300 million years ago

Wingspans of early dragonflies: Up to 75 cm (2.5 ft)

Parasites: Aquatic mites; tiny wasps

Range: All of Ontario and throughout Canada to the tree line

Number of Ontario dragonfly and damselfly species: 153

Number of dragonfly and damselfly species worldwide: About 5,000

Also see: Mosquito

FIREFLIES
Sex Flashers of the Wilderness

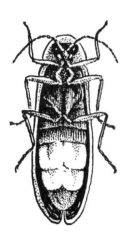

COMPARED TO OUR own crude attempts at illumination, fireflies are far more efficient. Only two percent of their bioluminescent energy is lost as heat, compared with about 97 percent for most household light bulbs. These high-tech beetles with the power of light confounded ancient philosophers, and even modern scientists have been unable to copy the wonder of "cold light" economically. We do know that the chemical luciferin and the enzyme luciferase react with oxygen in fireflies' abdomens to make them appear, as to the ancients, like sparks from a fire coming to life.

Species illustrated: *Photinus pyralis* (above) *Pyractomena angulata* (opposite)

Number of fireflies needed to match the light output of a 60-watt bulb: 25,000

Average length: 0.5—2 cm (0.2—0.8 in)

Full-grown larvae: 1—1.5 cm (0.4—0.6 in)

Alias: Lightning bug, glowworms, family *Lampyridae*

Habitat: Moist ground beneath debris, bark, decaying vegetation. In meadows, wetlands, moist open forests

Food: Worms, snails, insect larvae, and especially slugs, mites, each other

Egg-development period: About 1 month

Pupal stage: About 2 weeks

Lifespan: Up to 2 years

Predators: Frogs, toads, spiders

Even modern scientists have been unable to copy the wonder of "cold light" economically

---

On clear, early summer nights, choruses of bellowing bullfrogs and brilliant flashes of countless fireflies, seeming to multiply the stars, perform a mystical sound-and-light show over still lakes. An Ojibway story traces firefly origins to a ferocious, celestial lacrosse game between young Thunderbirds, the supernatural raptors responsible for rain, thunder and lightning. The ball, made from the lightning of a great storm, was thrown far past the goal towards the earth below. Its impact created Hudson Bay and caused stars to fall from the sky, breaking into thousands of blinking pieces that became fireflies.

Though greenish or yellow firefly flashes seem most noticeable in June, there are many species occupying various habitats, each flashing at a different time of the summer and of the night. Each variety has its own signal, a sexual Morse code ensuring the rendezvous of two bugs made for each other. This also makes it possible to flirt with fireflies by mimicking their blinking patterns with a flashlight, to which they respond. Females of some species are able to fake the flash of smaller species. Once seduced, the poor male fireflies are eaten.

Even as youngsters, fireflies are spindle-shaped, goo-sucking, killer glowworms. Already glowing in their eggs, they hatch beneath moist debris in midsummer and spend most of their lives as carnivorous larvae, using poisonous jaws to paralyze, liquify and suck the insides from worms, snails, slugs and other larvae. To top off their powers of alchemy, fireflies contain steroids called bufodienolides that make birds puke. Birds learn quickly to pass up meals that blink.

Larvae hibernate in soil chambers until late spring and emerge metamorphosed as adults, though some females remain wormlike with little or no wings. Their long, tank-like bodies are usually dark with yellow, red or orange trim. Adults live only a few weeks and most do not eat at all. They have but one purpose left in the love-lit climax of their lives.

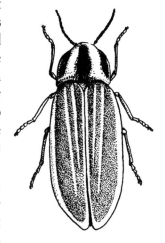

Number of species in Canada:
  At least 26
Also see: Falling Stars

MONARCH BUTTERFLY

Amazing Migrant Bound for Mexico

Average distance covered by one generation migrating north: 1,700 km (1,000 mi)

Distance covered by one generation migrating south: Up to 4,000 km (2,400 mi)

Duration of trip from Ontario to Mexico: 6–8 weeks

Cruising speed: 5 m/s (16.5 ft/sec)

Gliding speed: 3 m/s (10 ft/sec)

Time from hatching to emergence as an adult: 3–4 weeks

Average number of days adult monarchs emerging in spring and early summer survive: 34

Average number of months adults emerging in late summer survive: 7–8

Name origin of *butterfly*: From the butter yellow colour of European brimstone butterflies

Markings: Bright orange wings with black lines, white spots on black border around wings. Black body also marked with white. Caterpillars are yellowish green after hatching, turning to bands of bright yellow, black and white

Alias: Milkweed butterfly, King Billy, *Danaus plexippus*

Food: Milkweed and dogbane leaves for caterpillars, nectar for adults

Habitat: Meadow, forest edge

Average clutch: About 300 pinhead-sized green eggs attached beneath milkweed leaves

Egg-development period: 3–12 days

OF ALL BUTTERFLIES that flutter and glide, the monarch, for its beauty, familiarity and extraordinary migrational feats, flies supreme in the imagination. Faced with the prospect of winter, most other butterflies and moths spin cocoons beneath bark or lay eggs before they die. Monarchs fill up on nectar, convert it into fat, and gather on hilltops, fields and the north shores of the Great Lakes in August and September, and head south. They employ the same migration strategy as hawks, spiralling upwards on warm columns of rising air, called thermals, climbing to at least 1,200 metres (3,900 feet), then gliding in the wind until they hook on to another thermal. At night, or on days when temperatures dip below 12°C (54°F), they rest, often roosting in trees en masse.

Milkweed toxins stored in the monarch's body make both the caterpillars and adults unpalatable to vertebrate predators

By November, hundreds of millions of monarchs from all over eastern North America converge on a small area in the Sierra Madre mountains of central Mexico. They gather in about a dozen two- or three-hectare (five- to 7.4-acre) stands of fir trees 2,700 metres (9,000 feet) above sea level. Yet none have ever made the trip before in their lives. Turning the sky and landscape orange, butterflies crowd onto tree limbs and go into semidormancy for several months, the cool mountain temperatures allowing them to conserve energy. The whereabouts of the Mexican rendezvous was a mystery to the world until it was finally discovered in 1975, the culmination of a lifetime of work and

wing-tagging by the University of Toronto's Fred and Norah Urquhart.

While just one monarch generation flies all the way from its northern birthplace to Mexico and lives through winter, it takes several generations to make it all the way back in spring. Overwintering monarchs may live far longer than previous generations because they remain chaste until longer days and temperatures above 21°C (70°F) stir them from their Mexican siesta. Then the delayed hormones kick in and they hold a mass love-in before setting off.

Having sexually matured, the Mexican migrants are at the end of their life cycle and burn out quickly as they race to be the first to lay eggs on milkweeds emerging from the soil in the northward march of spring. Their offspring hatch, grow, transform into adults and continue the trip north until they too expire and leave the journey to their own progeny to complete.

Predators: Birds, shrews, mice, ants, spiders

Range: Southern Ontario to as far north as James Bay. Also found in all other provinces

Population cycle: Peaks about every 11 years

Lookalikes: Viceroy butterfly smaller, with 2 white spots on the front of its forewings

Number of other butterflies that migrate south: At least 12

Also see: Broad-winged Hawk, Moths

Though adult monarchs feed from and pollinate many different kinds of flowers, only the leaves of milkweed and dogbane can nourish their young. Growing in meadows and fields, most species of milkweed produce toxins in their milky sap that protect them from most foraging animals and insects.

Monarchs find milkweeds a safe haven to lay their eggs on, and have evolved a tolerance for their poisonous tissues. In fact, milkweed toxins stored in the monarch's body make both caterpillars and adults unpalatable to vertebrate predators. After vomiting once from a monarch meal, birds steer clear of the butterfly's bright colours. The unpleasant reputation allows monarchs to flutter lazily about with relative impunity. The smaller viceroy butterfly, which looks so much like the monarch, also packs toxins, though not from milkweeds.

Starting off about two millimetres (0.08 inch) long, monarch caterpillars eat constantly for about two weeks, go through five skin sheddings and grow to 2,700 times their hatching weight. In human terms, it would be like a three-kilogram (6.6-pound) infant putting on eight tonnes. The caterpillar then transforms into a turquoise pupa and suspends itself from a silk pad stuck to a branch or leaf. The pupal covering gradually becomes transparent and, after about 10 days, a butterfly emerges. It spends about an hour inflating its wings with fluid, then flys away. Several generations of monarchs are born in Ontario after the first migrants return in mid- or late May.

MOSQUITOES
Straw-nosed Marauders

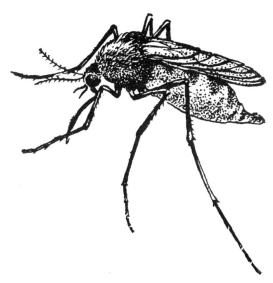

MOSQUITOES OWE their survival to warm-hearted individuals—mammals and birds whose bodies course with warm blood. Female mosquitoes are straw-nosed marauders that produce their eggs from the protein of a warm-blood soda. Their tracking systems lock on to the carbon dioxide exhaled by animals and humans and follow increasing concentrations to the source. As they get closer, body heat, odour and sight also guide them. They are especially attracted by dark colours, such as brown, grey and navy blue. Mosquitoes and blackflies also seem partial to some people's sweat more than others, and are usually more attracted to women than men.

Upon landing, a mosquito drills into the flesh with several razor-thin stylets held within its long proboscis snout. As it sinks its sucking tube into a tiny blood vessel, it injects saliva containing an anticoagulant into the wound to keep the blood coming. The body responds to foreign compounds from insect bites or stings by surrounding the wound with histamine, a chemical that marshals natural defences such as white blood cells to sweep away and destroy toxins. Swelling, itching and redness around the bite are all part of the allergic defence reaction. Reactions are worst with the first bites of early spring. Outdoors types, though, often build up a resistance to the saliva of biting insects and are liberated from much scratching.

A mosquito needs a few minutes of uninterrupted siphoning to get a full tank. If brushed away before finishing, it tries biting again until it has the blood it needs. Females can double or triple their weight in a single feeding, their abdomens ballooning red with blood. If the weather is warm, the acquired protein yields a batch of eggs a few days afterwards. Both mosquitoes and blackflies may lay several

Alias: Scitters, *les moustiques*, family *Culicidae*

Most common biters in central Ontario: *Aedes punctor* and *Aedes communis* (illustrated) in late spring, *Aedes vexans* in summer

Flying speed: 5 km/h (3 mph) in calm air

Wingbeats per second: 300–600

Wind speed at which mosquitoes take cover: 15 km/h (9 mph)

Food: Nectar, honeydew, blood

Maximum number of full blood meals *Aedes vexans* **able to take in a lifetime:** 8

Average clutch: 60–300

Larvae: Beige, 1–2 mm (0.04–0.08 in) long after hatching, grow to 7–15 mm (0.3–0.6 in)

Number of larvae per ha (2.5 acres): Up to 80 million

Lifespan: Up to 1 year

MOSQUITOES

Predators: Flycatchers, swallows, warblers and other birds, bats, dragonflies, wasps; dytiscid beetles eat larvae

Annual amount spent fighting mosquitoes and biting flies in Canada: More than $200 million

Range: All of Ontario and throughout Canada

Name origin: Spanish *mosca,* meaning "fly"

Age of oldest-known mosquito fossil: 35 million years

First appearance of winged insects on Earth: 350 million years ago

Number of mosquito species native to Ontario: About 60

Number of mosquito species worldwide: About 3,000

Also see: Blackflies, Dragonflies

clutches of eggs in their lifetimes, returning for blood each time. They need mate only once, storing the sperm internally for all future needs.

Most mosquito species go through just one generation in a year. Early-hatching varieties come alive en masse in temporary pools of snowmelt in April and early May. Wormlike mosquito larvae are called wrigglers because they squirm rapidly from the surface to the bottom of the water to feed, then float vertically back up again to get air through a long tube at the end of their abdomens. They filter algae, particles of decaying vegetation, protozoa and bacteria from the water with long hairlike fans near their mouths. After shedding their skin four times over one to four weeks, depending on water temperatures, they metamorphose into adults in curved, brown pupal casings. After a few days, the shell opens and becomes a floating launch pad for the winged adult.

An especially rainy April and warm May are ideal conditions for multitudes of mosquito larvae to hatch and survive into adulthood. The emergence of the first flying adults in spring usually comes within a few days of the blooming of pin cherry and chokecherry trees, two of their favourite food sources. Males, which don't bite, and females feed primarily on the nectar of flowering trees and shrubs, as well as honeydew—drops excreted by insects that suck plant juices. Once satiated on sweet nectar, a day or so after emerging, female mosquitoes go looking for the boys, who hang out in thick, harmless swarms on spring and summer evenings. Like blackflies, each species tends to swarm over a particular kind of landmark, such as spruce trees, pond edges or moss clumps. Males use their brushy antennae to detect the distinct buzz of female wingbeats. Both sexes may mate several times. A few days later, females are out for blood.

Starting about mid-May, biting mosquitoes usually build to a peak around mid-June, when most species are emerging. Adults live only a few weeks, and their eggs, laid in shallow puddles or on damp ground likely to flood again the following spring, cannot hatch until first being frozen by winter. A few species, however, go through several generations throughout the summer. One breeds only in pitcher plants but does not suck blood. Some in the *Culex* genus hibernate as adults, using a blood meal in the fall to sustain them through winter. Two species found south of the Canadian Shield are known to spread diseases such as malaria, encephalitis and dengue fever in warmer parts of the world. Malaria, brought in by workers from tropical areas, was spread by the two species in several southern Ontario epidemics in the nineteenth century, including one that stopped construction of the Rideau Canal. Luckily, the AIDS virus is too fragile to survive in the harsh biochemical environment inside a mosquito.

> *A mosquito needs a few minutes of uninterrupted siphoning to get a full tank*

Though each species of mosquito may have its own niche, most are stirred by rising and falling light levels, making them most annoying at dusk and dawn. During the heat of the day, they rest in the shade on plants and trees. Being slow fliers, they also take cover even in light wind. Camping in breezy locations, such as the east side of lakes, where prevailing winds have room to sweep in, is one of best ways to avoid bugs.

Humans have experimented with many other devices to rid themselves of mosquitoes and biting flies. Some native North Americans smeared themselves with animal grease and red ochre, prompting John Cabot to speak of seeing "red Indians" in the new land. Homespun bug defences such as eating garlic and vitamin B, or not washing, have been discredited. A modern folk remedy, Avon's Skin-So-Soft bath oil, does help keep mosquitoes away for 15 to 20 minutes because it contains the oil of citronella grass, a natural repellent. The main ingredient of most repellents now in use, Deet, or Diethyl-m-toluamide, was developed in the 1940s by the U.S military—still the biggest funder of insect-repellent research in the world. No one is sure how it works, though it may block sensors in the mosquito's antennae, mouth and legs from detecting the lactic acid vapours given off by the skin, which stimulate mosquito feeding.

MOTHS
Pollinators of the Night

Biggest Ontario moth: *Cecropia* (illustrated), with wingspan up to 17 cm (7 in)

Maximum caterpillar length: 9 cm (3.5 in)

Only fully domesticated insect: Silkworm moth, which, unlike honeybees, cannot survive in the wild. Domesticated in China thousands of years ago

Purpose of antennae: Used by males to detect chemical scent of female. Each species has a unique scent, except those that use no scent at all

Greatest distance a male moth (the European emperor moth) can smell a female: 11 km (7 mi)

Lifespan: Most species about a year

Alias: *Les mites*, order *Lepidoptera*

Time spent in adult stage: Several days to several months

Average period between tent-caterpillar outbreaks: 11 years

Moth food: Nectar, honeydew, overripe fruit, carrion as adults; leaves, acorns, other vegetation as caterpillars

Predators: Bats, birds, mice, predatory beetles, wasps, ants, spiders

Winter whereabouts: Usually as eggs or cocoons beneath bark, in the ground, in galls, wrapped in pine needles or amid other debris

Earliest moth seen in spring and last in fall: Pale-coloured geometrids, which hibernate as adults

WHEN DARKNESS DESCENDS on summer nights, the air around campfires, lanterns and cottage windows becomes filled with swirling moths seemingly intent on self-destruction. The suicide fliers are drawn to the flames and light because they normally navigate a straight course by keeping constant the angle of moonlight or sunbeams falling on their eyes. Night lights created by humans disorient moths, causing them to flutter round and round the source without being able to get their bearings.

Moths take over from butterflies at night in pollinating a wide array of flowers as they suck up nectar with their long, coiled tongues. Nocturnally blooming flowers, such as jimsonweed and evening primrose, are usually white or light toned, making them easier to see in the darkness than the deeply coloured flowers butterflies visit by day. Still, if some flowers are fragrant enough, they can attract pollinators around the clock.

Butterflies are actually only a small section of the much-larger moth-dominated order *Lepidoptera*. Unlike their relatives, butterflies have large knobs at the end of their antennae. Some moth species are also active during the day and can even be as brightly patterned as butterflies. Most, however, have dull wings, which they keep outspread to blend with tree bark while resting. Butterflies, in contrast, usually rest with their wings folded together, except when catching the sun's warm rays to increase their metabolic rates.

Some moths, when they lift their wings to fly away, flash a pair of large spots on their wing undersides that look like eyes, which may startle an attacking predator. Others have thin membranes stretched over tiny air cavities on their abdomen or thorax for picking up ultrasonic sound waves screeched by bats for their sonar tracking of flying prey.

Though most noticeable as adults, moths have the greatest impact on the ecosystem when they are caterpillars. Some species do not even eat as adults, remaining alive only long enough to mate and lay eggs. Their offspring, though, are protein factories, eating up incredible quantities of vegetation and concentrating nutrients into their plump, juicy, bite-sized bodies for birds and other animals. Even seed- and fruit-eating birds depend heavily on the high-protein caterpillar meals that allow their nestlings to reach adult size in a matter of weeks. Outbreaks of spruce budworm—a moth caterpillar —cause population explosions of many birds species as well as defoliate large tracts of evergreens, leading to more forest diversity.

Moth caterpillars have a very wide range of eating habits. Many hatch from eggs laid in plant tissues and cause the bulging galls common in goldenrod stems and oak trees. Often overwintering as eggs, gall caterpillars hatch in the spring and eat away at a stem or acorn from the inside, causing the plant to surround the area with hard, tumorlike gall tissue. The hidden munchers eat a hole out of the gall before transforming into adults and flying away in late summer.

Other species, such as tent caterpillars, live communally, spinning large silk nests for refuge when they are not outside, grazing on leaves. Caterpillars also use strands of silk as safety lines if they fall or get blown off their perch. Some use silk to pull the edges of leaves to curl up around them, or tie together coniferous needles, for protection. While most moths use their silk spinnerets to make cocoons, butterflies almost always make their transformations inside a skin covering as a pupa chrysalis.

Name origin: Old English *moththe*

Oldest moth fossil: 180 million years old

Number of species whose caterpillars eat clothes, fur and feathers: 2

Number of Ontario moth species: About 2,000

Number of Ontario butterfly species: About 150

Number of moth and butterfly species worldwide: At least 150,000

Number of species of foreign moths released in Canada: At least 15

Ontario moths that are daytime fliers: 2–5%

Also see: Little Brown Bat, Monarch Butterfly, Red Oak, White Spruce

SNAILS & SLUGS
Stomach-footed Hermaphrodites

SLIME. There's no doubt about it, snails and slugs have plenty of it. Slime protects them from fatally drying out. Endowed with limbless, almost formless, soft bodies, the nocturnal crawlers also excrete slime to help pull themselves along at a proverbial snail's pace. Aquatic snails can crawl upside down, clinging to the underside of the water's surface film. Snails and slugs are called gastropods, from the Greek for "stomach foot," because muscular movements in the lower portion of their bodies push them forward.

Crawling speed: 1–6 m (3.3–20 ft) an hour

Maximum length in Ontario: snails 5 cm (2 in); slugs 7.5 cm (3 in)

Shell length of the Australian trumpet sea snail: 60 cm (2 ft)

Age of oldest sea snail fossils: 570–590 million years

Age of oldest land snail fossils: 230 million years

Food: Algae, diatoms, fungi, live and rotting vegetation, carrion

Habitat: Terrestrial species in moist soil, litter layer, beneath logs and in low vegetation in forests, meadows; aquatic species in almost all types of water

Lifespan: 1–6 years

Name origin of *snail*: From ancient Germanic *snahhan,* meaning "to creep"

Name origin of *slug*: From *sluggard,* a slow or lazy person

Number of Ontario land-snail species: About 90

Number of snail and slug species worldwide: About 130,000

Being as slow as they are, gastropods don't cross paths too often. Accordingly, they maximize their breeding opportunities by being hermaphrodites—every individual has both male and female parts and can lay eggs. Whenever snails or slugs of the same species do meet, they can mate. Some species prick each other's interest by exchanging stabs of "love darts"—hard little spikes that, like Cupid's arrows, inject a chemical that stimulates mating. Other species may first circle around each other, softly touching tentacles or mouth parts. True to their nature, copulation is drawn out, with partners exchanging packets of sperm. Since the meeting may not take place near a good egg-laying site, sperm can be stored internally and used much later for fertilization. Some species of pond snails (illustrated) fertilize their own eggs.

Having no shells, slugs are even more vulnerable to drying out than snails. They die within a few minutes when exposed to dry air. Slugs can squeeze into almost any moist space, though, stretching up to 11 times their normal length. While snails are found both in soil and water, slugs are strictly terrestrial.

1. Sometimes called grass frogs, leopard frogs need their camouflage to escape predators, from bullfrogs to high-school biology-class suppliers.
See page 5.

2. A male red-winged blackbird flashes his red badge of courage to assert his supremacy over rivals in love and war. Cocks holding prime marshland breeding grounds may have as many as four mates.
See page 16. Photo © Bill Ivy

3. With its huge ears, sensitive nostrils and long legs, the high-strung deer is ready to "high-tail it" up to 70 km/h at the first whiff of danger. See page 123.

4. Its sturdy wings enable the green darner to be one of the few dragonflies to cruise south and escape Ontario's insect-unfriendly winters. See page 80.

5. Painted turtles bask in the sun to speed up their solar-powered metabolisms, so they can eat more and grow faster. See page 158.

6. Gifted with an acute sense of smell rare among birds, the turkey vulture uses its enlarged nostrils to detect dead delicacies as it soars high above the ground. See page 66. Photo © Bill Ivy

7. Ontario's most common serpent, the garter snake, was named for its colour pattern, which resembles that of the old-fashioned garters men wore to hold up their socks. See page 155.

8. The razor-sharp teeth of a beaver can bring down a tree 12-cm (5-inch) thick in three minutes flat. See page 117.

9. Like those of all rodents, the beaver's front teeth never stop growing. If the chompers are not worn down by constant gnawing they curl back, making it impossible for the beaver to eat.

10. Beavers form matriarchal societies, settling down in lodges of five to nine family members. The home is abandoned if the mother dies or the local supply of accessible trees runs out.

11. Beavers, like people, are driven by the urge and ability to control their environment. The buck-toothed engineers build dams to create deep, safe reservoirs that will not freeze to the bottom in winter and can be used for logging operations.

12. Like its relatives, the sacred floating lotuses of Egypt and India, the water lily of Ontario was highly regarded. In one Ojibway story, the fragrant flower was the embodiment of a star maiden come to Earth. See page 195.

13. Lobster mushrooms, which are common in evergreen forests, illustrate fungi's differing roles. They are actually two fungi in one—a white mycorrhizal fungus, which transfers nutrients to tree roots, encrusted by the orange Hypomyces lactifuorum, a parasite fungus that preys upon it. See page 176.

14. The curved petals of the voluptuous moccasin flower entice bumblebees into its enfolded chamber. There the bees find not nectar but frustration. At the exit their backs are brushed with pollen. See page 187. Photo © Bill Ivy

15. Plush carpets of vibrant moss on the rough edges of moist forests grow thicker each spring, before tree leaves unfold and block out the sun. See page 189.

16. Vegetating open areas like miniature bushes, fruticose lichens are crispy when dry, but become spongy delights to bare feet after a rain. See page 183.

17. Stands of hemlock are inviting, gentle havens from thick forest undergrowth. They make ideal human campsites in summer, and deer check in for shelter from winter storms. See page 211.

SPIDERS
Spinners of Insect Fate

SPIDERS are the very essence of "creepy" in the popular mind, the mere sight of one giving countless Miss Muffets the willies. Freud contended that spider phobias rise from a primal fear of a cannibal witch or ogre with long, pointy, bending fingers, subconsciously identified with the arachnid's pointy, bending legs. Despite the immense importance they have in controlling insect populations, spiders have long been associated with witches and Halloween. Both Greek and Hindu goddesses were represented as spiders, spinners of fate, while flies were often regarded as the souls in transition from one life to the next. The image of a fly caught in a spider's web represented, to the ancients, the helplessness of humanity in the web of fate.

Not all spiders spin webs, but all have spinneret glands at the rear underside of their abdomens that produce silk. Jumping spiders, which stalk and leap upon their prey, remain anchored to a silk safety line in case they fall. Nocturnal wolf spiders run down their prey, but use silk to tie their shelters together. Silk is made of protein strands. The strands are coated in fungicides and bactericides to protect them from other hungry organisms. The antibiotic qualities of spider webs have made them in many cultures a common folk remedy for wounds. Layers of webs from large spiders have also been used for fishing nets by the natives of New Guinea.

Though a silk strand may be 1/100 the diameter of a human hair, it is twice as strong, for its size, as steel. Web

Estimated weight of insects eaten annually by spiders in Canada: Equal to the weight of the country's entire human population

Name origin: Old English *spinthron*, meaning "spinner"

Name of a group: A smother of spiders

Alias: *Les araignées*, Arachnids

Number of eyes: 8

Food: Insects, mites, daddy longlegs, tadpoles, tiny fish, other spiders

Average clutch: 2 to several thousand eggs, depending on species

Lifespan: Most species less than a year, a few live up to several years

Predators: Birds, toads, frogs, salamanders, shrews, snakes, centipedes, spider wasps, other spiders; insects eat eggs

SPIDERS

Winter whereabouts: Most
  species in eggs or egg sacks;
  a few hibernate, in logs,
  beneath bark, under dead
  leaves and grass
Largest Ontario spider: Carolina
  wolf spider, up to 8 cm (3 in)
  wide, including legs
Black-widow range: Lake Erie
  hinterlands and Barrie to
  Gravenhurst
First appearance of spiders on
  Earth: Probably at least 180
  million years ago
Famous individuals: Inky
  Beanky, Charlotte, Boris,
  Shelob, The Spiders from Mars
Number of Ontario spider
  species: About 1,500
Number of spider species world-
  wide: More than 33,000
Spider relatives: Daddy longlegs,
  mites, ticks, scorpions, pseudo-
  scorpions, horseshoe crabs
Also see: Fungi

strands are also incredibly elastic, stretching up to 30 percent before breaking. In the industrialized world, spider silk is used mostly for the cross hairs of optical equipment; but researchers are reproducing the genes of spider webs with the aim of creating building materials with the same diverse qualities.

Spiders can spin different types of silk from different glands for their varying needs. There are seven different kinds of silk in all, though no one species has all seven brands. The spider adjusts its spinneret valves to control the thickness, elasticity and strength of the silk as it spins. Orb-web spiders join strong strands, like girders, to a central point across a vertical space, then thread concentric rings through them with a special sticky silk that catches flying insects. A thick zigzag strand is woven through the webs of some species to make it visible to birds and mammals, which can see the big picture better than insects can. Spiders are always busy, usually building a new web every few days. Their work is best seen glistening with morning dew.

All spiders also have venom, which they inject into their victims through small, fanglike appendages. The paralyzing poison gives spiders the option of consuming their catch right away or wrapping it up and keeping it fresh and alive for later snacking. Spiders actually drink, rather than eat, sucking out their victim's bodily juices through a pump in their digestive system. They bite humans only in self-defence, though they can leave an irritating, swollen red mark. In Ontario, only the very rare black widow spider presents any kind of a threat to humans. Its poison usually causes fever, breathing trouble and paralysis for one or two days, though it can be fatal to very small children or sick people.

Female black widows are also synonymous with the femme fatale because of their habit of devouring their mates after the males have served their purpose. The practice is actually common to most spiders. Mating usually in late summer or fall, when insects are becoming scarce, the much-larger female finds in an ex-lover's body a quick protein meal to nourish the eggs. To avoid being eaten even before mating, a male may strum love notes on a strand of a potential mate's web, signal to her with his legs in a kind of sexual semaphore or send a chemical message. If she appears receptive, the male rushes in and fertilizes her. If he's lucky, he can beat a quick retreat as soon as he's finished, before she becomes peckish. Males often wrap their mates in silk to keep them tied down during their escape.

Females wrap their eggs in yellowish cocoons. Some, such as the *Dolomedes tenebrosus* nursery web spider (illustrated), carry their egg sack with them for a time. In most cases, the eggs are timed to hatch in spring,

---

A male may strum love notes on a strand of a potential mate's web

---

when insect-prey populations are exploding. Tiny, newly hatched spiderlings swarm to the highest point of the vegetation where they find themselves and spin a thin strand of silk, which catches in the breeze and lifts them up into the air, sometimes thousands of metres. This "ballooning" spreads them out over wide distances, keeping their populations from becoming too concentrated in one area. Ballooning spiders can sometimes cover bushes or shrubs with silk.

The ranks of eight-legged arachnids are swelled by many other species that are not true spiders. Daddy longlegs, or harvestmen,

unlike spiders, have only two simple eyes on a single "turret" and can neither spin silk nor inject venom. Instead, they chase small insects and mites, surround them with their legs and sit on them. Some also scavenge dead insects. If they are themselves captured, their detachable limbs continue to quiver after being severed, distracting the predator and giving daddy longlegs a chance to escape. Unlike spiders and mites, however, they cannot regrow lost legs. Also unique among arachnids, male daddy longlegs have a penis.

The most abundant of the eight-leggers—more numerous even than any group of insects—are mites, spherical, often brightly coloured beasts ranging from a quarter of a millimeter to half a centimetre (0.2 inches) in diameter. They are a diverse group, found in every type of soil and aquatic environment, and have been around for more than 400 million years. Some are predators of tiny invertebrates and microorganisms, some eat vegetation, while others play vital roles in breaking down decaying vegetation and spreading fungal spores.

SPRINGTAILS
Tiny Specks That Leap to Life

Population density: Up to millions per cubic metre

Length: 0.25–6 mm (0.001– 0.25 in)

Jumping distance: Up to 10 cm (4 in)

Markings: Most dark grey, black or brown, some yellow, orange, green, blue or violet

Alias: Snowfleas, order *Collembola*

Food: Decaying leaves and other vegetation, live plants, pollen grains, spores, fungal strands, soil algae, bacteria, carrion, animal droppings, insect eggs, microscopic invertebrates

Habitat: Soil and litter layers almost everywhere

Mating techniques: Females pick up sperm capsules left on the ground or water by males. Males of some species use their long antennae to waltz females towards their seed. Others surround females with circle of sperm cases or pool their capsules together into a large sperm mine field, called a "garden of love"

Clutch: 5–100 eggs

Ability to live in torpor: Up to 18 months if soil dries out and takes away the moisture they need to remain active

Predators: Water striders, beetles, mites, pseudo-scorpions

Lifespan: Up to 3 years

Range: All of Ontario and throughout Canada

Number of Ontario springtail species: About 200

Number of springtail species worldwide: About 6,000

FEW PEOPLE HAVE heard of springtails, yet the tiny jumpers are everywhere, among the most abundant of animals. Tiny specks of dirt on dead leaves may, on closer inspection, prove to be herds of grazing springtails moving about the surface. They sport stiff, forked tails that hook beneath their bodies and, when released, catapult them forward in great leaps. Though they have six legs, they are not insects, instead forming their own order.

Crawling and jumping in the trillions, springtails feast on dead organic matter, and are an integral part of the complex decomposition process that must take place for all life to spring from death. Springtails nibble and transform leaves, bits of twigs and other debris into fine tailings, which bacteria and fungi break down into basic elements that can be reabsorbed by living things. Because they have no excretory tailpipe, they jettison their high-nitrogen waste with their old exoskeletons when they moult.

For such minuscule creatures, springtails are remarkably hardy and long-lived. Large numbers of some species, commonly referred to as snowfleas (illustrated), appear like specks of soot or dirt in wet snow on warm, sunny days in mid- to late winter. Though cold-blooded like almost all invertebrates, they react to low temperatures by producing a sugar alcohol called glycerol, a natural antifreeze that protects them in temperatures as low as -22°C (-8°F). They even live in Antarctica. Springtails scramble to the surface in late winter because they breed in puddles of snowmelt. The frigid deluge allows different populations to mix and interbreed.

WATER STRIDERS
Staying Afloat on Tippytoes

THE WATER strider is a miracle bug, walking on water with seemingly the greatest of ease. It accomplishes the feat by spreading its weight out in a sprawled stance. Each leg is tipped with many tiny waterproof hairs, which form a soft crust or film of closely packed molecules, and prevent the insect from breaking the water's surface tension. If a solid object punctures the thin film, it falls through into the water.

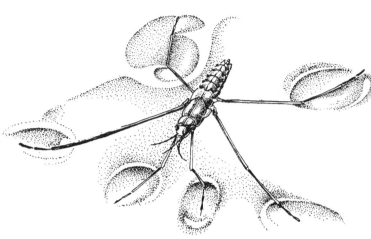

Lying still, water striders are almost invisible. When they move, with their long, jointed legs acting like oars, their shadows glide across the shallow bottom of their pools. They often congregate in large groups in calm channels, the water surface coming alive with their activity. They move quickly towards any small surface disturbance, looking for a meal that has dropped in—often another insect that has fallen into the water. Using their two short forelegs to grab their victims, water striders then pierce their prey with their needlelike mouth parts and suck out their life juices.

Water striders appear as soon as the ice melts, and mate through spring and early summer. A couple may cling together in a love embrace for more than an hour. Females lay creamy white, waterproof eggs on floating objects. Young water striders look like small versions of their parents. They grow and moult five times within 40 to 60 days and are then ready to mate. The summer's second generation usually seeks shelter beneath rocks or other debris on dry land near the water to hibernate in October.

Lifespan: About 6 months

Markings: Various species may be black, dark grey or yellow on top, with brown or grey markings, and white beneath. Middle legs longer than body. Some species, especially those in temporary ponds, have a winged stage and most often fly at night, sometimes attracted, like moths, to lights

Body length: 2–12 mm (0.1–0.5 in)

Alias: *Gerridae*

Food: Springtails, mites, spiders, insects

Habitat: Calm water in streams, ponds, swamps

Egg-development period: About 2 weeks

Predators: Fish

Number of Ontario water-strider species: 11

WORMS & LEECHES
The Intestines of the Earth

Maximum earthworm density in Ontario: 60 per m² (sq. yd) may be found in isolated spots, but not over continuous wide area

Maximum potworm density in Ontario: 100,000 per m² (sq. yd), but only in isolated pockets

Number of earthworms collected annually in Ontario for bait and research: More than 1 billion

Earthworm lifespan: Most live less than 1 year. Some live up to 10 years in captivity

Length of smallest Ontario earthworm species: Less than 2 cm (1 in)

Maximum Ontario earthworm length: 30 cm (1 ft)

Longest earthworms in world: 3.3 m (11 ft)

Potworm length: 3–30 mm (0.1–1.2 in)

Number of hearts in an earthworm: 5

Alias: *Les vers, Annelids*

Colours of most common earthworms: Pink, red, grey, green or whitish

Food: Decaying leaves and other vegetable and animal matter

Average earthworm clutch: 6–10 eggs in a rubbery, yellow-brown case the size of a small pea

Egg-development period: 30–100 days, depending on temperature, moisture and species

Average number of hatchlings that emerge from egg cases: 1–3

D O EARTHWORMS feel pain when they are pierced with a fish hook? Well, they certainly feel something, as indicated by the sudden stiffening and contraction of their bodies. Worms aren't much for brains, but those they do have consist primarily of a ring of nerve cells around their digestive tract near their mouths. In most animals, nerves register pain basically as an alarm system for bodily preservation.

Earthworms are not nearly as durable as popular myth would have it. Two new worms do not crawl away when an individual is severed. Nor do a male and female exist at either end. Besides mouth and brain, the front end contains the worms' vital organs, and light-sensitive cells, though not true eyes, that tell them to take cover from the light of day. The tail end features only the anus.

Each individual, however, does have both male and female parts. Spending most of their lives in dark soil, worms need the adaptation to take every opportunity for mating. Two individuals mate by exchanging sperm, keeping the gene pool varied. Some species can reproduce without mating at all.

Aristotle called worms the "intestines of the Earth."

Darwin dubbed them "nature's ploughmen." He estimated they could turn over up to 10 tonnes of soil a year per hectare, ultimately replacing the top three centimetres (one inch) of soil every 10 years. Through digesting grains of sand and any organic matter small enough to fit into their mouths as they move, earthworms excrete castings of soil compounds high in nitrogen, calcium, potassium and phosphorus, all vital to plant growth. They can even transform human waste into fertile soil and are being used in several sewage and compost pilot projects across the country.

Earthworm tunnels also loosen and aerate the soil. They open up passages for rootlets and fungal strands and increase the soil's ability to retain water. In longtime agricultural areas, the constant work of earthworms gradually smooths out fields, making them flat. Archeologists have worms to thank for the burial of many ancient ruins. If not for the efforts of British custodians, Stonehenge would be covered over by the ceaseless work of earthworms at the rate of 18 centimetres (seven inches) a century.

In acidic, coniferous forest soils, earthworms become rare. Instead, they are replaced by smaller, whitish, segmented potworms and millipedes, which play similar roles in digesting and decomposing vegetation and fungi.

The most infamous of wormy creatures, though only distantly related to true worms, are leeches, or bloodsuckers. Most types of leeches specialize in a particular kind of vertebrate blood. Only three or four common species attach themselves to humans with their sucker tails. They hold on tenaciously, but can be easily removed with salt or by burning them. In the days when "bleeding" was a commonly prescribed remedy for a wide range of ailments, well into the 1850s, doctors attached leeches to their patients. As barbaric as it sounds, the practice may have had some beneficial effects. Today, medical researchers are studying many leech chemicals that could have a bearing on circulation and cancer treatments. Some surgeons are even now applying leeches after operations for skin grafts and for reattaching severed body parts. The leeches drain off congested blood, giving capillaries time to grow back together without becoming deluged.

Earthworm age at sexual maturity: About 1 year

Predators: Red-bellied snakes, red-necked snakes, garter and other snakes, woodcocks, robins and other birds, moles, shrews, voles, salamanders, flatworms

Winter whereabouts: Hibernate curled in tight circle in soil, or can remain active if soil isn't frozen beneath the snow

Earthworm immigration: Leading biologists believe past ice ages swept away any indigenous Ontario earthworms with the soil. All present species probably arrived over the past 500 years with potted plants or agricultural supplies from Europe or the south

Earthworm range: Few species found north of Lake Nipissing. Also found in southern regions of other provinces

Name origin of *worm*: From proto-Indo-European *wrmi*, meaning "snake," possibly from the word *wer*, meaning "twist"or "turn"

Name origin of *leech*: From Old English *laece*, meaning "physician"

Number of Ontario earthworm species in the wild: 16–19

Number of earthworm species worldwide: More than 8,000

Number of leech species worldwide: 650

Also see: Humus, Soil

FISH

ONTARIO HAS long been considered an angler's paradise, but rod and reel are not prerequisites for experiencing the inhabitants of the deep. Fish can be viewed jumping out of the water at low-flying insects at dusk, spawning near shore or along creek beds in spring or fall, or flitting amid the weeds of a small stream. Crayfish, though not really fish but crustaceans, are easy to find hiding beneath rocks by day and lurking in the shallows at night. Most fun of all are Ontario's apparently numerous lake monsters, which offer anyone the opportunity of joining in the biggest fish stories of all.

SMALLMOUTH BASS
Maternal Males Watch Out for Fries

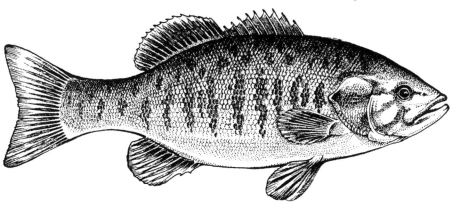

DESPITE THEIR REPUTATION among anglers as feisty fighters, male smallmouth bass are truly New Age, sensitive fish. Male bass assume most of the traditional maternal duties for their species. In late June or early July, they dig out a shallow nest in gravel, anywhere from 30 to 180 centimetres (one to six feet) wide, in water depths of one to six metres (three to 3.20 feet). After mates formally rub against and nip each other, the female lays her eggs in the nest, then leaves her mate to fertilize and care for them. Males guard and fan the eggs and remain with the young in the nest for up to three weeks after they hatch.

Young bass must eat well in their first months if they are to survive the winter, during which they fast and hide out amid the rocks beneath the ice. If spring and summer are cool, delaying their hatching and development, most are goners. Heavy storms also destroy nests, and bass fry are susceptible to acid rain. Bass are warm-water fish that spend most of their time motionless in the shadows near shore, waiting to suddenly dart at any prey that comes within reach. They are most active at dusk and dawn.

Smallmouth bass relatives, members of the sunfish family, also feature nest-building, fry-rearing males. The largemouth bass is almost identical, but prefers calmer, weedier waters. Rock bass are more squat, bony and homely, with blood red eyes.

Average adult length: 25–50 cm (8–15 in)

Average weight: 225–1,350 g (0.5–3 lb)

Weight of largest ever caught: 5.4 kg (11 lb)

Markings: Green back and sides, with dark hash marks along sides and dark spots on back, white belly

Alias: Black bass, green bass, l'achigan à petite bouche, *Micropterus dolomieui*

Food: Crayfish, minnows, small frogs, insects, leeches, baby fish

Preferred habitat: Near clear, rocky shores, up to 6 m (20 ft) deep

Winter whereabouts: Lying dormant at bottom of water

Maximum lifespan: 15 years

Name of a group: A shoal of bass

Range: Southern Ontario to Kapuskasing, Lake Nipigon and Sioux Lookout. Also found in all other provinces except Newfoundland, Prince Edward Island and Alberta

Number of lakes with smallmouth bass in Ontario: 2,400

101

CRAYFISH
Ontario's Biggest Invertebrates

Largest Ontario crayfish:
Up to 20 cm (8 in) long

Smallest Ontario crayfish:
Less than 4 cm (1.5 in) long

Alias: Crawfish, *les écrevisses*,
family *Astacidae*

Average lifespan: 2.5–3 years,
some live up to 5 years

Markings: Olive or grey-brown
back, mottled with dark
brown; bluish legs and
orange claw tips

Preferred habitat: Lakes,
streams, marshes, swamps

Food: Aquatic plants, algae,
insect larvae and other recently
moulted crayfish

Average clutch: 60–300 eggs,
depending on species

Range: Various species
throughout Ontario, except
far northwest

Number of crayfish species in
Ontario: 9 (7 native,
2 introduced)

Number of crayfish species
worldwide: 469

THE SHORELINES of many lakes are teeming with crayfish. Often only a few rocks need to be removed near shore to reveal the miniature lobster-like creatures hiding from the light of day. Crayfish are nocturnal crustaceans, preying on smaller invertebrate animals. They are themselves the largest invertebrates in Ontario. Their exoskeletons are made out of chitin, a fingernail-like armour that covers all insects. But unlike insects, crayfish have two sets of antennae, which they use to feel around and detect chemical scents in the water.

Despite their minimonster appearance, crayfish are devoted mothers to their clinging offspring. Most species mate from August to October or April to May. The following May, June or July, females lie on their backs and bend their tails forward to stick eggs to their undersides. Even after they hatch, the young hang on beneath their mother's tail for up to several months. As they grow, young crayfish, like insects, shed their old exoskeletons six to 10 times. Their new, softer skin is inflated before it hardens to give them space to grow inside the new shell. In this soft stage, crayfish are delectable morsels for fish, birds, mammals and Cajun-restaurant goers. To escape quickly, they flip their tails beneath them and catapult backwards at high speed.

MINNOWS
Populating Every Habitat

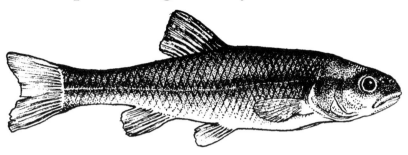

A MONG HIS MANY misadventures, the Ojibway culture hero and comic deity Nanabush takes a Jonah-like role by being swallowed by a giant sturgeon. Nanabush rescues himself by killing the behemoth from the inside and then cutting it into small pieces, which float off to become the small fish of the world.

Most tiny fish, including the babies of many large species, are commonly called minnows. Some, in fact, are adult fish belonging to a group called darters—actually pint-sized perch that dart sharply about on the bottom of fast-flowing headwater streams. Unlike darters, which have two fins on their backs, true minnows have just one, which is always soft, not spiny. Minnows also have teeth in their throats instead of in their jaws. They form the largest single family of fish in the world, and though most are five to eight centimetres (two to three inches) long, goldfish and carp—both imports from Eurasia—are included in their ranks. Some carp in the Great Lakes can weigh in at 14 kilograms (31 pounds).

Ontario's many minnow species occupy virtually every aquatic habitat, each finding its own niche. Creek chub (illustrated) are probably the most common stream minnow. Northern redbelly dace, which average five centimetres (1.9 inches) long, live in the tea-coloured, acidic waters of boggy lakes and beaver ponds. Other minnows are less tolerant of acid rain than any other Ontario fish. Lake chub, which are about twice as big, live in larger lakes, but move into rocky streams to breed. Golden shiners, inhabitants of the clear, weedy waters of quiet lakeshores, are probably the most popular bait used by anglers.

Maximum lifespan: 8 years

Average adult length: 5–13 cm (2–5 in)

Length of largest native minnow (fallfish): Up to 46 cm (18.4 in)

Biggest carp ever caught: 25 kg (55 lb)

Alias: *Les vairons, Cyprinids*

Food: Plankton, algae, aquatic insects, fish fry

Average clutch: Up to 500

Egg-development period: 4–10 days

Predators: Trout, bass, pike, many other large fish, kingfishers, mergansers, wading birds

Range: Some species found throughout Ontario. Also found in all provinces and territories except Newfoundland

Name origin: Old English *myne*, meaning "small fish"

Number of minnow species in Ontario: 28

Number of minnow species worldwide: More than 1,500

Number of native fish species in Ontario: 144

LAKE MONSTERS
Relics from Past Ages?

GIVEN THE NUMBER of deep lakes in Ontario, the province's abundance of lake monsters is not surprising at all. Lake Simcoe even has two, Kempenfelt Kelly and Igopogo. Generally, the lake leviathans are described as long, winding, serpentlike creatures, which, although fearsome looking, do not appear to be particularly nasty. The odd, no-doubt-accidental capsizing of a small motorboat in calm water seems to be the worst they can manage. In recent years, sport fishers have added high-tech detection to Ontario monster lore by picking up very large creatures on their sonar fish finders.

Lake monster sightings are no recent phenomenon created by wayward Scots nostalgic for Nessie. Native peoples told of both good and bad beings inhabiting the waters they paddled. The May-may-gway-siwuk were shy creatures resembling humans, but with strange faces and fishlike tails. Offerings of tobacco moved them to calm the waters and protect Ojibway travellers. When Champlain came up the Ottawa River in the early 1600s, the Algonquins told him of a large creature that dwelt in Muskrat Lake, near Petawawa. Great snaky beasts were first spotted in eastern Lake Erie in 1817 and in Lake Ontario in 1829. More sightings followed throughout the nineteenth century. Reports of a large serpent near Kingston in 1902 kept local sharpshooters posted on shore in hopes of bagging the prize of a lifetime.

As with all great mysteries, there is no hard and fast evidence supporting the existence of lake monsters. But crypto-zoologists—those who study reports of unknown animal species—are hot on the trail. Some believe the largest lake serpents could be rare, secretive descendents of giant, long-necked reptiles called plesiosaurs, which lived in the dinosaur era more than 65 million years ago. They cite the discovery of a living coelacanth, an ancient fish previously known only from fossils 70 to 320 million years old, off the coast of South Africa in 1938. Gorillas were similarly dismissed as primitive fantasies until white men encountered and, inevitably, started shooting them in the mid-nineteenth century.

Other theories propose that various lake monsters may be remnant populations of well-known marine animals, such as manatees, dolphins or walruses, stranded after the ancient Champlain Sea receded from the interior 11,500 years ago. Whale bones from that period have been found in the Ottawa Valley. Seals have been found in Siberia's Lake Baikal and dolphins in China's Lake Tung Ting, both deep in the interior of Asia.

The Muskrat Lake monster, christened Mussie, has been reported several times since 1968 and is described as being three to four metres (9.8 to 13 feet) long, with a large tusk. Ichthyologists, or fish experts, have also suggested that especially large sturgeons, known to live more than 150 years and exceed two metres (6.5 feet) in length, may be behind all the mysterious sightings. The Chamber of Commerce of Cobden, on Muskrat Lake, has not waited for scientific confirmation before putting up large billboards with cartoon images of their friendly monster welcoming tourists to the town. Two UFO landings have also been reported around Muskrat Lake.

Since 1906 there have also been repeated sightings of Ontario's own Sasquatch-type creature, dubbed Old Yellowtop or Precambrian Shield Man. It is described as apelike, with dark fur and a long, light-coloured mane. One time it was observed eating berries. All sightings were made in the Cobalt area, where it was last seen by a busload of miners in 1970.

PERCH
Schools Seeking Warm Currents

Average number in a school:
50–200

Average length: 10–25 cm
(4–10 in)

Maximum length: 36 cm (14 in)

Average adult weight:
100–300 g (4–11 oz)

Maximum weight: 1.8 kg (4 lb)

Markings: Green or yellow back
and sides, usually with 7 dark,
vertical stripes, white or grey
underside, 2 dark dorsal fins,
orange lower fins, yellow or
green eyes

Alias: Yellow perch, lake perch,
American perch, panfish, *la
perche, Perca flavescens*

Food: Animal plankton, aquatic
insects, small fish, fish eggs,
mollusks

Preferred habitat: Clear, open
waters of lakes and rivers

Maximum lifespan:
About 11 years

Range: All of Ontario to James
Bay. Also found in all
other provinces except
Newfoundland and Prince
Edward Island

PERCH FIND SAFETY in numbers, but chance encounters with their schools provide sudden bonanzas for anglers, who catch more perch than any other fish in Ontario. From the time they hatch, perch fry form schools, often mixing with minnows, near the shore. They find no protection from their parents, who remain in adult groups and could very well be disposed to devour their own children. Transparent at first, the five-millimetre- (quarter-inch-) long hatchlings grow more slowly in colder water, but live longer. In lakes with high population densities, adults may never exceed 15 centimetres (six inches), while perch in the Great Lakes can be twice that size.

Like herds of bison or caribou, perch schools travel in definite migration patterns. After spawning, they move farther offshore as waters warm towards the centre of lakes in summer. Preferring temperatures of between 20 and 24°C (68 to 75°F), perch generally stay in the warm, upper layer. They move into shallow water to feed at dusk and dawn, and rest at the bottom at night. In winter the schools become more dispersed, but continue to actively feed beneath the ice.

Male perch begin mating when they are three years old and females when they are four. They usually spawn at night and in early morning in weedy, shallow water near lakeshores or in rivers in mid-April to early May, when the water is 7 to 12°C (45 to 54°F).

BROOK TROUT
Keeping to Cold Waters

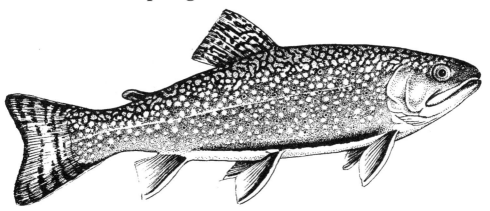

NEITHER BROOK TROUT nor their larger relatives, lake trout, are really trout at all. They're char. Early settlers named them for their resemblance to European brown trout, now an introduced species in Ontario. The other part of the brook trout's name comes from its preference for cold, clear headwater streams. It can stand rushing water much better than most other large fish. Brook trout are also common in the headwater lakes of highland areas, such as Algonquin Park.

The best time to see brook trout is after the ice breaks up in May, or when they are spawning from late September to November. During those periods they are near the shore, often jumping completely out of the water after flying insects. Brook trout have trouble living in water warmer than 20°C (68°F), and as the top layer on lakes and rivers warms up in June, the fish head for deep, cooler waters. Brook trout also need ample oxygen, which keeps them out of the deepest waters as summer wears on. These restrictions concentrate brook trout into a transition zone between the top and bottom layers of lakes, three to 12 metres (ten to 40 feet) beneath the surface.

As the top layer cools again in late September, brook trout move into shoreline waters to feed and spawn in gravel or sandy beds one to two metres (three to seven feet) deep. The beds must have springwater percolating up through them, which may protect brook-trout eggs from acid-rain meltwater in the spring. Male brook trout develop purplish

Average adult length: 25–30 cm (10–12 in)

Average weight: 200–900 g (0.4–2 lb)

Largest brook trout ever caught: 6.7 kg (14.5 lb), 80 cm (31.5 in) long, in the Nipigon River, Ontario

Largest lake trout ever caught: 28.6 kg (63.1 lb), in Lake Superior

Name of a group: A hover of trout

Markings: Dark olive green back with lighter green swirls, sides splattered with white spots and red dots bordered by light blue, white belly, reddish fins, tail squarish, with little indentation

Alias: Speckled trout, eastern brook trout, brookie, native trout, *l'omble de fontaine*, *Salvelinus fontinalis*

Time when most active: Early morning and late evening

Food: Minnows, perch, sculpins, stoneflies, mayflies, dragonfly nymphs, caddis fly larvae, crayfish, snails, clams, worms

Preferred habitat: Shallow, clear, cold headwater lakes and streams with rocks, logs, or beneath overhanging trees and bushes in fall, winter and spring; 3–12 m (9.8–39 ft) below the surface in summer

Preferred water temperature: 12–15°C (54–59°F)

Clutch: Up to 200 eggs

Egg-development period: 4-6 months

Average survival rate of eggs: 65–75%

Average size at end of first growing season: 7.5 cm (3 in)

Age at sexual maturity: 1–3 years

Lifespan: Few live longer than 4–5 years, some up to 8 years

Predators: Mink, otters, osprey, pike, sea lampreys; kingfishers, water snakes, snapping turtles, bass, pickerel may take small trout; crayfish, whitefish and brown bullheads eat eggs

Range: Most of Ontario except far south and west. Also found in all other provinces, though scattered in the west

Number of brook-trout lakes in Ontario: about 2,100

Number of brook-trout lakes with acid levels that can affect brook-trout reproduction: About 40

Number of lake-trout lakes in Ontario: About 2,300

Brook trout fishing season: Jan. 1 to Sept. 30 in most of central and eastern Ontario, Jan. 1 to Sept. 15 in much of northern Ontario, last Saturday in Apr. to Sept. 30 in most of southern Ontario

Also see: Lakes, Minnows

red stomachs during spawning season. They mate during the day, sometimes in the hundreds, with females pushing up gravel to establish a small nest, or redd. After she shakes and releases her eggs into the nest and the male fertilizes them with his sperm, the female covers the eggs with gravel. The transparent eggs hatch from February to April, and the fry stay put beneath the gravel for about a month, living off large yolk sacks attached to their undersides.

The best time to see brook trout is after the ice breaks up in May, or when they are spawning from late September to November

---

Because trout are less active in the frigid water beneath the ice, they do most of their growing in spring and fall, feeding in the rich, shallow waters. This is especially true of larger, greenish grey lake trout, which retreat to the coldest lower layer of lakes during the summer. Because of their deep-water needs, they are restricted to lakes that usually cover at least 25 hectares (62 acres). In the smaller lakes, they grow very slowly because they are restricted to algae, plankton and insect larvae during the summer. In larger lakes they can eat fish such as perch and whitefish that enter into their summer zone.

An artificially bred cross between brook and lake trout, called spake, can live in deep water but grow more quickly. Stocked widely since 1957, it is the first major genetically engineered fish species. Overall, it has not been regarded as a success and is no longer stocked by the Ministry of Natural Resources in Ontario.

MAMMALS

PERHAPS THE MOST *exciting wilderness experience of all is to encounter wild, free-roaming mammals. Partly it is because mammals are probably the most seldom-seen beasts, aside from ever-present and audible red squirrels and chipmunks. Not that other mammals are not around. There are often more mammals than birds in a forest, but most of them are tiny and hidden during the day. Ontario's nine species of mice and voles, eight varieties of bats, nine weasel relatives, four bunnies, raccoons, porcupines, beavers, foxes, coyotes, wolves, bobcats, lynx and others are all solely or primarily denizens of the dark. Others, such as the seven shrew species and several moles in the province, seldom emerge above the ground or leaf litter. In all, there are 69 different native terrestrial mammal species in Ontario, more than 50 of them in the central region of the province.*

Although mammals are elusive, their signatures are all around us: beaver lodges and dams, muskrat homes, bear-clawed trees, the rustling of mice scurrying in the night, paw and hoof prints in the mud, and a galaxy of droppings, or scats. At the right time and place, a moose may be watched in the flesh, neck deep in a quiet bay, feasting on water lilies. In fact, central Ontario is one of the best places in the world to view moose, bears and many other wild animals, or to hear the spine-tingling howls of a wolf pack at night.

LITTLE BROWN BAT
Symbol of Fortune and Fertility

Frequency of sonar calls:
40–100 kilohertz

Upper limit of human hearing:
20 kilohertz

Average frequency of human conversation: Less than 5 kilohertz

Adult little brown bat body length: 8–10 cm (3–4 in)

Wingspan: 22–27 cm (8.5–10.5 in)

Weight: About 8 g (0.3 oz)

Weight of a loonie: 7 g (0.25 oz)

Body temperature: 40°C (104°F) when active, same as surroundings in hibernation

Heartbeats per minute: More than 1,300 in flight, 100–200 when stationary, as low as 10–15 in hibernation

Weight loss during hibernation: Up to 25%

Markings: Mostly medium brown, darker on shoulders, ears, face; lighter on underside; dark brown wings and tail membrane almost hairless

Alias: Flittermouse, reremouse, *la chauve-souris, Vespertilion brun, Myotis lucifugus*

Food: Mosquitoes, mayflies, midges, moths, beetles, caddis flies and other flying insects 3–10 mm (0.1–0.4 in) long

Preferred habitat: Forests, meadows, lakes and streams

Gestation period: 50–60 days

Litter: 1 baby

Age at first flight: 18–21 days

Age at sexual maturity: 1–2 years

Lifespan: Average probably 10 years, up to 32 years

Predators: Owls, hawks, martens, skunks, raccoons, snakes

THE CRUSADING EFFORTS of Batman aside, bats remain enshrouded in myth and misconception, most of it bad. Little-seen denizens of the night, the only mammals to really fly have been looked on since the Middle Ages of Western culture as unnatural, the associates of witches and vampires or the incarnation of the devil himself. In other cultures, bats represent fertility, because they have exceptionally long penises, spanning two centimetres (0.8 inches) in the case of the little brown bat, nearly a quarter of its body length. The length is needed to get around the skin membrane that joins the female's legs together. In the mystic East, the Chinese greeted bats as omens of good luck. The Wu-fu charm, traditionally hung above the doors of Chinese homes, depicts five bats circling the tree of life, representing the five top human blessings—virtue, wealth, children, longevity and a contented death.

In a single night, the little brown bat can eat enough insects to equal half its weight

Without doubt, bats do descend like a blessing on warm summer nights to devour the hordes of flying insects that torment larger mammals such as humans. The little brown bat, Ontario's most common, can catch and is believed to eat more than 10 mosquitoes a minute on the wing, scooping them up in its wide tail membrane and flipping them into its mouth. In a single night, the little brown can eat enough insects to equal half its weight. For nursing females, it might be more than their entire weight. Extensive studies in the U.S. turn up fewer mosquito bites in areas with lots of bats. Little browns prefer hunting three to six metres (10 to 20 feet) above water, especially in the first two or three

hours after sunset, and before dawn.

While it is not true that bats are blind, hearing is certainly their most important sense for capturing large quantities of bugs. Using sonar, or echo location, little brown bats emit a steady stream of high-pitched squeaks that bounce off objects and insects within a range of two metres (6.6 feet). Their large ears and brain interpret the distance more accurately than human sonar devices. The sonar calls are too high for human hearing, though bats can make audible squeaks of fright if threatened.

Before engaging their sonar systems, bats depend on highly tuned internal temperature readings to tell them if it is worth going out to look for insects. Without temperatures high enough to guarantee plentiful insects, it is too dangerous for bats to gear up to full metabolism. Instead they go into semihibernation, even on cool nights in the summer, with their body temperature, heart and respiratory rates dropping to put their systems on slow burn until warm air rouses them.

Although three of Ontario's bat species migrate to the

Roosts: Beneath loose bark, in tree cavities, under rocks, in crevices as narrow as 1 cm (0.4 in), often used for decades

Winter whereabouts: Hibernate in caves and old mines in large groups

Average time food takes to go through a bat's system: 20 minutes

Number of times bats chew per second: 7

Range: All of Ontario, except far northwest. Also found in all other provinces and territories

Name origin: From Old Norse *bakke*, meaning "flutter"

Oldest bat fossils: 60 million years

Number of Ontario bat species: 8

Number of bat species worldwide: About 900

Also see: Barred Owl, Moths

southern U.S. for winter, flying as high as 3,000 metres (10,000 feet), little brown bats hibernate in colonies in caves or abandoned mine shafts. They travel up to 800 kilometres (480 miles) to return to traditional hibernaculas—group hibernating sites—starting to swarm around them in mid-July or August. They mate in late summer, with both males and females having more than one partner and forming no pair bonds in what York University bat-specialist Brock Fenton refers to as the "disco-mating system." By late September or October, they settle in for the winter, the males in tight clusters, the females hanging alone or in small groups. The biggest cause of death among little brown bats is usually lack of fat reserves among first-year young who were too inexperienced to catch enough insects before going into hibernation.

Females come out of hibernation first, in mid-April or May, and fly to nursery colonies to give birth and raise their young. Males and non-breeding females, lacking the food needs of expectant mothers, slumber until warmer temperatures arrive in mid-May, then spread out to smaller summer roosting sites. Newborns cling to their mothers' undersides during nightly hunting flights. When the babies get too big, they are left in the nursery, but can fly and hunt themselves when they are little more than three weeks old.

In flight, little brown bats are jerky and undulating as they outmanoeuvre insects in the air. Such a sight should not inspire fear. Contrary to myth, they do not become entangled in people's hair, and never carry rabies, although they are susceptible to the disease. Rabid bats die soon after contracting the virus. Little browns carry no other human disease, very few parasites and, in fact, are quite clean, spending a half hour at a time grooming and cleaning their all-important ears with twists of their tiny thumbs. To admirers, they are charming, intelligent, even cute, like downy little mice with wings. Biologists believe bats may be closely related to monkeys. Like primates, they have just two nipples for nursing their young. Though Ontario's species are insectivorous, fruit- and nectar-eating bats in the tropics are among the principal agents for propagating rain forests by pollinating plants and spreading seeds. Their numbers are rapidly decreasing because of habitat destruction and hunting.

BLACK BEAR
Big Sleeper with Special Powers

DOES A BEAR defecate in the woods? Well, not during hibernation. Neither does one urinate, eat or drink, though females do give birth in late January or early February, nursing and tending their young between intermittent deep slumbers.

Bears are considered true hibernators, although their body temperature drops only a few degrees Celsius in winter, and they can wake easily. Denning bears have a unique chemistry that achieves wonders beyond the ability of other true hibernators. If most animals went without urinating for more than a few days, backed-up waste would result in fatal urea poisoning. Even hibernating groundhogs must relieve themselves once in a while. Bears, however, recycle urine from their bladder into new proteins. Water from the recycled urine and from fat reserves prevent dehydration. Unlike other animals denied food or room to move for long periods, a bear lives off its fat without losing muscle or bone mass.

Adult body length: 1.2–1.8 m (4–6 ft)

Height at shoulder: 60–90 cm (2–3 ft)

Average weight: Females 45–70 kg (100–154 lb), males 70–150 kg (154–330 lb)

Biggest Ontario bear ever recorded: 330 kg (726 lb)

Biggest black bear ever found in Canada: 364 kg (800 lb), in Manitoba

Markings: Completely black, except for lighter-coloured snout; rarely reddish, brown or blond

Alias: American black bear, l'ours noir, Ursus americanus

113

Food: Berries, currants, nuts, cherries, grass, roots, leaves, coniferous inner bark, insects, fish, frogs, eggs, birds, small mammals, fawns, carrion

Daily calorie intake in late summer: 20,000

Average number of calories burned daily during hibernation: 4,000

Preferred habitat: Mixed-age forests with large patches of trees less than 90 years old

Home range: Females 10–40 km² (4–16 sq. mi), males 200–1,600 km² (77–618 sq. mi)

Distance travelled to fall foraging grounds: Up to 100 km (60 mi) or more

Winter whereabouts: Den beneath roots of trees, rock crevices or brush pile

Average litter: 2–3

Gestation period: 7 months, including 3–4 months delayed implantation

Age at sexual maturity: 4–5 years

Birth weight: 200–500 g (0.4–1.1 lb)

Fat content of bear milk: 25%

Fat content of human milk: 4%

Period cubs stay with mothers: About 17 months

Mortality of young in their first year on their own: 1 in 3

Lifespan of adults: Average 10-15 years, up to 41 years

Predators: Small cubs sometimes taken by adult male bears, wolves, lynx, eagles

Top running speed: About 50 km/h (30 mph)

The fat fuel causes winter cholesterol levels to double, without resultant cardiovascular problems.

The system works so well that while most other species are going through their most difficult and dangerous season, 99 percent of all bears survive comfortably through winter. Scientists are working diligently to isolate the bear chemicals that could help humans suffering from kidney and bone diseases to recycle urea and calcium.

> *While most other species are going through their most difficult and dangerous season, 99 percent of all bears survive comfortably through the winter*

Mother bruins carry recycling to the point of ingesting their babies' waste, recapturing the fluids lost through nursing. It also keeps the den clean. Although bears mate in June or early July, embryos don't start developing until 10 weeks before birth, when sows have stored enough nutrients needed to get them through winter. Newborns are little bigger than chipmunks, very lightly furred, deaf, toothless and blind. They are not, however, formless bits of mush sculpted by their mother's tongue, a folk belief responsible for the expression "licked into shape." Following only their sense of touch, they find their mother's nipples by moving towards the heat that can be felt from them.

Each year of a bear's life is like a big Viking feast. Although the black bear is central Ontario's largest carnivore, it concentrates on a changing smorgasbord of easily obtained food sources through the warm months. More than 90 percent of its diet is vegetarian.

After sleeping off the previous year's banquet, bears

emerge groggy, 20 to 40 percent lighter, but not yet peckish. It takes about two weeks to clear the head and shake off the hibernative state before eating resumes. They start off light, with a green salad of grasses, sedges, horsetails, wild leeks and skunk cabbage, most in abundance before other vegetation sprouts in early spring. Roots, rotting logs filled with ants and grubs and the occasional animal are important supplements. Late spring serves up fresh aspen leaves. Bears continue losing weight until they plunge into the main course with the ripening of berries in early July. Then they start gaining a kilogram (2.2 pounds) a day. From August to October, eating goes into overdrive, as the bear spends up to 20 hours a day devouring high-fat-and-protein acorns, beech and hazel nuts, mountain ash berries, cherries and more berries. Finally, between late September and early November, a great sleepiness comes over the stuffed bruins as the wind blows colder. They spend up to 10 days digging out a den before blissfully retiring.

The most famous bear of all was a Canadian from Ontario

Throughout its days of foraging, the black bear lumbers through forest and meadow with impunity, having few if any enemies to challenge it. Bears are generally shy of humans and scamper away from their presence. Before the advent of the gun, the only way native hunters could readily kill a bear was to find one in its winter den, or to set a pit or falling-log trap for it. Hunters asked permission from the spirits that presided over bears to kill it (as they did with other animals), and offered apologies afterwards. Bears were supremely respected as symbols of strength and courage, the primary Earth and healing spirits. Veneration of the bear, with remarkably similar lore, was also practised by hunting cultures from Eastern North America through Siberia to Scandinavia. The earliest evidence of religious thought on

Best senses: Smell, hearing

Tracks: Hind foot 18 cm (7 in) long, resembling a wide human foot; front foot 10 cm (4 in) long

Scats: Varying in size, shape and colour with food eaten; up to 5 cm (2 in) in diameter

Range: All of Ontario south to edge of Canadian Shield, as well as Manitoulin Island, Grey, Bruce and Simcoe counties. Also found in all other provinces and territories except Prince Edward Island

Population density in Algonquin Park: 1 per 3–4 km² (1–1.5 sq. mi)

Ontario bear population: 65,000–75,000

Number of bears shot annually in Ontario: 6,500

Number of people hunting bears annually in Ontario: 20,000–30,000

Bear-hunting seasons: Mid-Apr. to mid-June and Sept. to Nov.

Famous individuals: Yogi, Smokey, Winnie-the-Pooh, Fozzie Bear, Gentle Ben, The Three Bears, Baloo, Paddington, Artio, Brer Bear, Misha, Bruin

Name of a group: A sloth

Name origin: From proto-Indo-European *bheros*, meaning "brown"

Origin of a "bear market": From British proverb, "to sell the bearskin before catching the bear"

Number of Ontario bear species: 2

Number of bear species worldwide: 7

Also see: Beech, Big Dipper, Groundhog, Trembling Aspen

Earth is found in bear-cult cave shrines left by Neanderthals in central Europe at least 75,000 years ago.

In more recent times, bears have engendered widespread affection as cuddly, inanimate childhood companions and good-natured cartoon buffoons. The most famous bear of all, in fact, was a Canadian, from Ontario. Winnie-the-Pooh was actually a female cub named Winnipeg, bought on the railroad platform in White River, north of Lake Superior, by an army horse veterinarian on his way to the front in 1914. The vet gave Winnipeg to the London Zoo, where she captivated a boy named Christopher and inspired his father, A.A. Milne, to write the immortal tales of the bear of very little brain. South of the border, U.S. president Theodore Roosevelt's refusal in 1902 to shoot a bear that had been carefully leashed to a tree for his convenience captured the public's—and a toy manufacturer's—imagination and spawned the "teddy" bear.

Roosevelt's noble sentiments have not necessarily carried over to all modern hunters. The preferred bear-hunting method of many—especially a large overflow of big-game enthusiasts from American states where hunts are much more restricted—is to sit in trees and blast bears attracted to large quantities of rotting meat left below. Bears are the only game animal in Ontario targeted in a spring hunting season. Because Ontario bears have a lower reproductive rate than those in warmer, more biologically diverse areas, the shooting of females, some of them mothers, has raised great concern. As much as one-third of the population is taken in some areas. Black bears are also under increasing threat from poachers seeking parts to export to Asia. Bear gall bladders, considered a panacea in traditional Oriental medicine, can sell for as much as $30,000 in Taiwan or Korea. Bear-paw soup, said to bestow power and fertility, is served up at more than $1,000 a bowl.

BEAVER
Builder Laid Foundation of Nation

EUROPEAN EXPLORERS came to Canada looking for the Northwest Passage. Instead, they found the beaver, and for 200 years Canadian history revolved around the quest for its cherished pelt. The fur trade was Canada's biggest industry until logging overtook it in the 1800s, earning the beleaguered beaver acclamation as national mascot. Both the Canadian beaver's abundant numbers and the denseness of its soft, inner fur, needed for warmth in frigid waters, made it more important to humans than any other fur bearer. In the days before umbrellas, upper-class heads were kept fashionably dry with broad hats of beaver felt. Mercury, used to separate the fur from longer guard hairs and break it down into felt, frequently caused mental deterioration among the ranks of ungloved hatmakers, giving rise to the term "mad as a hatter."

Before the coming of the white traders, native bands followed sustainable economies, fine-tuned through millennia, with each family's traditional hunting and trapping territory defined by a watershed. Families rotated their activities from one river branch to another within the larger basin, ensuring that beavers and other animals they hunted could

Time it takes a beaver to cut a 12-cm (5-in)-thick tree: 3 minutes

Thickest tree ever recorded cut by a beaver: 1.2 m (4 ft)

Average annual number of trees cut by an adult: More than 200

Area of young aspen forest needed to support family for 1–2 years: 1.5 ha (4 acres)

Average area covered by a beaver pond: 4 ha (10 acres)

Biggest beaver dam ever recorded: 1,500 m (5,000 feet) long, 3 m (10 ft) high, in Saskatchewan

Longest measured beaver canal: 230 m (750 ft), in Colorado

Adult body length: 60–90 cm (2–3 ft)

Weight: 18–36 kg (40–80 lb)

Tail length: 23–33 cm (9–13 in)

Heaviest beaver ever found:
50 kg (110 lb)

Markings: Glossy chestnut brown body, scaly black tail

Alias: American beaver, *le castor*, *Castor canadensis*

Calls: Mumble, hiss or nasal blowing when angry, cry when frightened

Food: Water lilies, arrowhead, watercress, duckweed, yellow arum, cattails, grasses, sedges, leaves, berries and ferns in summer; bark and twigs of aspen, birch, poplar, mountain maple, willow in winter

Average daily food helping:
600–800 g (1.3–1.8 lb)

Preferred habitat: Small forest lakes, ponds, streams and marshes with stands of aspen and birch nearby

Colony territory: 0.6–2.2 km (0.3–1.8 mi) along a stream or shoreline

Home: Domed lodges of branches and mud, about 2 m (6.6 ft) high and 4–8 m (13.3–14.6 ft) wide above waterline, hollowed out from an underwater entrance; built at the centre of ponds or side of deep lakes; occasionally in bank burrows

Average number of beavers per lodge: 5–9

Average number of lodges per km² (0.4 sq. mi) in Algonquin Park: 0.4–1

Gestation period: 3½ months

Average litter: 2–4

Birth weight: 230–680 g (0.5–1.5 lb)

Age at which young beavers leave home: Usually 1 year; some stay for 2 years

rebuild their population in each area. They maintained intimate knowledge of the land rather than seeing it as a vast, unfathomable expanse.

The native system was disrupted by the steel-age goods and technology of Europeans. Metal pots, axes, guns and other trade items offered huge time-saving advantages and luxuries, but hooked natives into the European market system, while they lost their own complex survival technologies. Traditional family trapping grounds were quickly exhausted to satisfy the new demands for fur. Both natives and traders pushed farther west. The Iroquois, seeking control of the trade routes, nearly wiped out the Huron nation in Ontario as well as several other peoples. A chain reaction of disruption spread across the continent until, by the turn of the twentieth century, there were few beavers, but much dependency.

In the 1930s, Grey Owl captivated the world with the image of a native trapper from the forests of Canada turned wildlife crusader. Though after he died Grey Owl turned out to be a wayward Englishman named Archibald Belaney, he helped reinforce conservation efforts to save the beaver. In 1937, the animal was put on the back of the Canadian nickel. Going full circle, the government began assigning trapping territories on the basis of watersheds. In Ontario, the Ministry of Natural Resources restocked areas where beavers had been wiped out, with animals taken from the protected population in Algonquin Park. The beavers took quickly to prime, unused habitats, and became so abundant that they're now often considered pests in some agricultural, cottage and even urban-fringe areas.

Both beavers and people are driven by the urge and ability to change and control their environment. A native tradition holds that the Creator took the power of speech away from beavers to keep them from becoming superior to humans. The Ojibway said that beavers could change form, into birds or other animals. They were highly respected and an important food source, especially their rich, fleshy tail. It was taboo to throw a beaver's bones to the dogs, for fear of insulting its spirit.

Beavers form essentially matriarchal societies. According to some experts, when the young leave home for good, swimming downstream in search of new horizons, females choose their mate for life and determine where they will live. If her partner dies, the female recruits a replacement and life goes on. If a matriarch dies, the colony usually breaks up. After mating in the water, beneath the ice, in January or February, mothers give birth sometime between late April and early June. Newborns are fully furred, and their eyes are open. They are able to swim within hours. Unlike most mammals, they continue growing until late in life, when they are five or six years old.

A pair of beavers can build an incredibly solid dam in three or four days

---

Unlike the bear-sized sabre-toothed beaver that became extinct with the close of the ice age 10,000 years ago, the modern beaver survived climate change because it was an engineer. Beavers—still the largest rodents in North America—can go to work wherever there is a stream and an ample supply of deciduous trees, especially aspen. If the water is shallow or intermittent, they build a dam, creating a reservoir deep enough to swim and dive in safety, one that will not freeze to the bottom in winter. The inundated area, often covering several hectares, is like a farm, growing the succulent water plants beavers eat in the summer. As well, it's a conduit for reaching and transporting felled hardwoods. Wherever the ground is soft, beavers may dig thin, shallow canals and tunnels into the woods and across peninsulas.

By controlling the water level, beavers ensure their lodge will not be flooded out or left high and dry by seasonal watershed fluctuations. A pair of beavers can build an incredibly solid dam in three or four days, with branches stuck diagonally into the mud so that the wall slopes down-

Age at first breeding season: 21 months

Lifespan: Average 4–5 years, up to 16 years in wild and 23 years in captivity

Predators: Wolves, bears and rarely coyotes

Capacity to hold breath under water: Up to 15 minutes

Heart rate while underwater: As low as 20% of normal rate

Swimming speed: Usually about 4 km/h (2.4 mph), up to 10 km/h (6 mph)

Tracks: Front feet 6–10 cm (2.5–4 in) long, handlike, with 5 fingers; back feet webbed, 13–16 cm (5–6.3 in) long

Scats: Oval, dark brown, saw-dustlike pellets, at least 2 cm (0.8 in) long, usually in water

Number of beaver pelts traded for a musket from the Hudson's Bay Company in 1700s: 10–12

Number of beavers trapped annually in Ontario today: About 90,000

Famous beaver hot spot : Hochelaga (Montreal), Iroquoian for "where the beaver dams meet"

Age of oldest beaver fossils: 12 million years

Common beaver pond inhabitants or visitors: Muskrat, mink, otters, moose, great blue herons, mallards, black and wood ducks, hooded mergansers, three-toed woodpeckers, migrant geese, tree swallows, harriers, frogs, minnows

Estimated Ontario beaver population: 1.5–2 million

Range: All of Ontario, though rare in southwest. Also found in all other provinces and territories

Also see: Canadian Shield, Trembling Aspen, Wolf

stream, fully braced against the force of the constrained water. Beavers scoop up mud with their paws to fill in the structure once all the branches are woven in place. They often build a series of dams along a stream, sometimes reaching up to three metres (10 feet) high and 500 metres (1,640 feet) long.

Beavers in a well-established colony may not be busy at all during the relatively carefree days of spring and early summer. They are active mostly from dusk to dawn, occasionally warning each other to dive for safety with a loud tail slap on the water when danger approaches. From September until freeze-up, the colony works hard to build up a winter food supply of branches, extending their nocturnal toilings into the day. Old hands say the timing and severity of winter can be predicted by how hard beavers work and how early they start. (Biologists are not so sure.) Beavers are often on land in this period, standing on their hind feet, propped up by their tails, cutting down trees. They cannot control where a tree falls, but heavy growth on the tree's sunny side usually topples it towards the water. A winter's larder of tasty trunks and branches, piled and submerged beside the lodge, may equal more than 30 cubic metres (1,000 cubic feet), allowing beavers to remain holed up for most of the winter.

Flooded areas behind beaver dams become swampy, often creating rich habitat for a succession of plants and animals, in the water and in the dead and dying trees. As beavers cut down alder, birch and aspen near shore, they accelerate forest succession by eliminating shade over young evergreens. After perhaps several generations of beavers have used up all the young broad-leaved trees they can safely reach, they desert the area for greener pastures. The caretakers gone, their dams slowly deteriorate and the ponds drain, leaving behind rich, silty soil that becomes a meadow. Eventually, the forest reclaims the spot, and if enough early-succession aspen and birch grow up again, another colony of beavers searching for a new homestead may happen upon it and start the process all over.

EASTERN CHIPMUNK
Chip and Dale Are Frauds

CUTE, CUDDLY, tame, adorable by popular acclaim, chipmunks are, in fact, highly secretive, independent and aggressive animals. They usually don't enter the holes to their underground burrows while being watched. Though many will take food from campers' hands, chipmunks, unlike squirrels, never become dependent on humans. They spend most of their days, from the time they emerge from hibernation in March or April, filling their cheeks to bulging with food and carrying it back to their burrows, often storing away a lifetime's supply in a single season. Lawrence Wishner, the American dean of chipmunks, who spent six years living among the tiny beasts, says they are driven by an "obsessive genetic fear of starvation."

Their paranoid hoarding has helped establish one of the longest-standing niches of any mammal in the forest. Primordial chipmunks roamed the Earth 25 million years ago, their ancestors having split from proto-squirrels 15 million years earlier. One native legend holds that the chipmunk got its stripes from the swipe of a bear paw during an altercation at a council of animals near the beginning of time. The word *chipmunk* is Algonkian for "head first," after the manner they descend trees.

The smorgasbord of nuts, seeds, berries, cones, mushrooms and insects that forms most of their diet in Ontario forests supports up to 30 chipmunks per 0.4 hectare (1 acre). One of the biggest factors preventing an explosion of chipmunks is their extreme dislike for one another. They live alone, and when they meet, there are almost always strong words, scraps or chases. Chip and Dale could never have been pals. If there are too many chipmunks in one area, the population

Adult body length:
  14–16 cm (5.6–6.4 in)
Average weight: 80–105 g
  (3–4 oz)
Tail length: 6.5–11.5 cm
  (2.6–4.6 in)
Number of stripes: 9
Alias: Chipping squirrel, *le suisse*,
  Tamias striatus
Calls: "Chip," "chuck," trills,
  whistles or squeals, chatter
Preferred habitat: Dry uplands,
  hardwood-forest edge
Home: Underground burrow
Average home range:
  0.2–0.4 ha (0.5–1 acre)
Average litter: 4–5
Gestation period: 31 days
Average lifespan: 1.3 years
Maximum lifespan: 12 years

Age at reaching adult size:
2–3 months

Predators: Foxes, wolves, raccoons, weasels, rats, snakes, birds of prey

Top running speed:
12 km/h (7.4 mph)

Swimming speed:
11 km/h (6.8 mph)

Best sense: Hearing

Well-known individuals: Chip and Dale, Simon, Alvin and Theodore

Normal body temperature:
35–42°C (95–108°F)

Body temperature when hibernating: 5–7°C (41–45°F)

Enter hibernation: Sept.-Nov.

Winter whereabouts: In light hibernation beneath ground

Primarily active: Daytime

Range: All of south and central Ontario to the tip of James Bay, and south and west of Lake Nipigon. Also found in Manitoba, Quebec, New Brunswick, Nova Scotia and Prince Edward Island

Also see: Broad-winged Hawk, Mink, Red Pine, Red Squirrel, Soil

becomes stressed, mating drops off and miscarriages and maladies increase.

The constant discord explains much of the noisy chattering heard from chipmunks in the woods. The din peaks for about a week in June and another in September, when mother chipmunks drive their six- to eight-week-old youngsters off on their own. They may have two litters a year. The waifs scatter, chased by cantankerous adults, who proclaim their territory in treetop choruses. Most of the new chipmunks fan out until the chatter fades, indicating an area with fewer adults, and a likely place to dig a home. Many are eaten by predators before they get that far.

Chipmunks make their football-sized burrows about a metre (three feet) underground, finishing them off by ingeniously digging a new entrance tunnel and pushing the dirt from it to fill their original 10- to 15-metre-(32- to 50-foot-) long working shaft. The pile of excavations at the end of the first passage then no longer marks the entrance for enemies. Abandoned burrows are often taken over by young chipmunks. Over several generations a burrow may acquire up to 30 tunnels, with all but the main entrance sealed from beneath.

After a comfortable winter of intermittent sleep in leaf-lined chambers, male chipmunks resurface in March or April in a lustful state. They call on female burrows, only to be thrashed and rejected until she is ready. Then, love briefly conquers chipmunk belligerency and a couple will nuzzle, play, lounge and squeak together for hours before and after mating. After that, the relationship's over. If two or more males are present when the female emerges, a chase ensues that can last all day. The female accedes to the suitor who can stick with it the longest. The ritual is repeated during the second mating season in July.

WHITE-TAILED DEER
Alertness and Speed Are Everything

WHITE-TAILED DEER are all grace, beauty, tension and bounce. They are wound like a tightly coiled spring, their hooves kicking into the air after barely touching the ground. Watching deer leap over obstacles in the flash of an eye, covering up to six metres (20 feet) in a single bound, their white tails waving goodbye, you might find it impossible to imagine any predator ever catching one.

A deer's life, however, is one of almost constant stress, with its survival dependent on its powers of flight. Its chronic nervousness would send blood-pressure levels skyrocketing in humans. White-tails, in a sense, eat on the run, not fully digesting their food during early morning and evening grazings in clearings. Later, retreating to safe, sheltered spots in deep woods, they ruminate like cows, summoning the cud

Adult height at shoulder:
0.7–1.1 m (2.3–3.5 ft)

Adult body length: Females
1.6–2 m (5.3–6.6 ft), males
1.8–2.2 m (6–7.2 ft)

Average weight: Females
55–80 kg (120–175 lb),
males 90–135 kg
(200–300 lb)

Markings: Reddish brown back in
summer, dull grey brown in
winter, white undersides; fawns
with white-spotted backs in first
summer

Alias: Long-tailed deer, bannertail, Amerian fallow deer, *le cerf de Virginie, Odocoileus virginianus*

Call: Light squawk, snort; fawns bleat

Food: Grasses, sedges, seedlings, fresh shoots, especially aspen, yellow birch, mountain maple and chokecherry in spring; leaves, berries, water lilies, mosses and hair lichens in summer; acorns, mushrooms, berries in fall; buds, twigs, conifer needles and bark, especially cedar, maple, aspen, dogwood, spruce and hemlock in winter

Daily food helping: 2.5–3.5 kg (5.5–7.7 lb)

Preferred habitat: Forests mixed with abundant clearings and scrub

Male territory: About 13–17 km (8–10 mi) wide

Gestation period: 6 ½ months

Average litter: 1–2

Birth weight: 1.5–3 kg (3.3–6.6 lb)

Fawn mortality rate in their first 6 months: 40%

Lifespan of an adult: Usually 2–8 years, up to 13 years in wild

Maximum lifespan in captivity: 20 years

Predators: Wolves, bobcats, lynx, coyotes, bears, red foxes

Pests: Deer flies, blackflies, mosquitoes

Top running speed: About 70 km/h (42 mph)

Swimming speed: About 7 km/h (4 mph)

back up into their mouths to chew before swallowing it again for further processing in their four-chambered stomachs. All the while, their huge ears and sensitive nostrils scan far beyond the field of vision for every rustling or whiff of danger. When a threat is detected, a raised, waving tail of one deer is a flag to all the others, signalling them to flee. They're sneaky, and often circle around to get upwind of a predator. Normally only the young, sick or injured are caught. Rarely, a lynx or bobcat will ambush deer from a tree. As a last resort, a deer's sharp hooves can disembowel a predator.

In Ontario, the cold grip of winter is probably the greatest reaper of white-tailed deer. A third of the herd commonly perishes in the cold months. Alternatively, mild winters in the 1980s allowed southern Ontario's deer population to double or triple.

When snow piles up 40 or 50 centimetres (16 to 20 inches) deep, foraging over wide areas becomes too exhausting for deer. Small family groups and lone males migrate, sometimes as much as 90 kilometres (54 miles), to traditional deer yards. Near the tip of the Bruce Peninsula, up to 4,000 deer congregate in a yard covering less than 10 square kilometres (3.8 square miles). A series of yards in the Loring Valley south of Lake Nipissing attract up to 15,000. The refuges are in lowland hemlock, spruce and fir stands or cedar swamps, providing dense shelter from the wind and snow. Herds tramp down the snow and find some safety in numbers against predators. Food is limited. When the best food is all eaten, deer turn to less nutritious, harder-to-digest species, such as balsam fir, to stay alive.

The often haggard and hungry that survive winter double their numbers when fawns are born in May and June. Does find hidden, secluded spots in deep forests or grassy thickets to have their babies. The fawns, with almost no odour and their white-spotted backs blending in with their sun-dappled surroundings, remain well concealed for several weeks, until they can run fast enough to keep up with the herd.

While groups of a few does and their young travel together along regular deer trails throughout spring and summer, bucks lead more reclusive, solitary lives. Males start to grow antlers in mid-March—budding, horny manifestations of their rising testosterone levels. The largest, strongest deer in their prime, between four and seven years old, grow the biggest antlers, signifying their status to both potential mates and rivals. Native shamans often wore antlers in recognition of the power they represented. The Iroquois crowned their chiefs with antlers, saying they were like antennae, making them supersensitive to their surroundings. Male deer shorn of their antlers, in fact, quickly lose their aggression and sexual drive.

Testosterone continues to build in bucks even after their antlers stop growing in September and they've rubbed off the once-soft velvety linings. As the November rut approaches, their necks swell to twice their normal size and they become gripped with a mixture of lust and rage, marking out territories and seeking mates. After out-pushing their rivals in head-to-head matches, victorious bucks may strike up mating liaisons, each lasting a day or two, with a number of does, coupling with them frequently and passionately during their brief time together. Their antlers form a separation layer and break off in January or February, providing a source of vital calcium and salt for mice, rabbits, porcupines and other gnawing vegetarians.

In areas of deep, extensive forest that have few open patches with shrubs for browsing, deer are relatively rare. The earliest French explorers reported no white-tailed deer in their travels through the dense forests of central Ontario. But as Europeans denuded the wilds to the south of hundreds of thousands of deer a year for food and buckskins in subsequent centuries, farming and logging in Ontario gradually opened up vast new areas for white-tails. The North American white-tail population stood at a low point of fewer than 500,000 around the turn of the century, before strict game laws brought protection. Today, there are probably more than 30 million. In areas where no hunting is permitted, such as most provincial parks, deer often become much more tame and, driven by their own mammalian curiosity, can linger around and even be drawn near to patient observers.

Tracks: About 7 cm (2.8 in) long, double, curved, wedge-shaped hoof marks

Scats: Clumps of black pellets stuck together, in spring; lighter-cloured oval pellets, like large jelly beans, in piles of 20–30, in winter

Average number of times a deer defecates on a winter day: 13

The study of animal droppings: Microhistorlogical analysis

Range: Southern Ontario to about Kirkland Lake; absent north of Lake Nipigon. Also found in all other provinces except the island of Newfoundland

Famous deer: Bambi, Rudolph

Estimated fall Ontario deer population: 350,000–400,000

Number of deer shot in Ontario each fall: More than 50,000

Number of people hunting deer in Ontario each fall: 165,000

Closest Ontario relatives: Caribou, moose

Number of deer species worldwide: 40

First appearance of deer on Earth: 45 million years ago

Also see: Deer Flies, Hemlock, Moose, Trembling Aspen, Wolf

RED FOX
Crafty Reputation Well Deserved

Adult body length: 60–70 cm (2–2.3 ft)

Weight: 3–7 kg (6.6–15.4 lb)

Tail: Bushy, 30–46 cm (1–1.5 ft) long

Markings: Orange or yellow-red back and sides, white chin, chest and tail tip, black legs; all-black "silver foxes" or greyish brown "cross foxes" are less common colour forms of same species

Alias: *Le renard roux, Vulpes vulpes*

> *Occupying roughly the same niche as foxes, a coyote usually drives off the smaller canines from its territory*

Calls: A shrill, barking yelp

Food: Voles, mice, hares, rabbits, groundhogs, chipmunks, squirrels, grouse, ducks, gulls, small birds, eggs, snakes, grasshoppers, beetles, crickets, berries, nuts, grass, carrion

Average daily food helping: About 400 g (0.9 lb)

Preferred habitat: Forest edge

Home range: 5–20 km² (2–8 sq. mi)

Home: Dens in ground burrows up to 25 m (62 ft) long, often in dry, sandy, south-facing hillsides, in old groundhog burrows, with several entrances 25 cm (10 in) wide

FROM AESOP'S FABLES to native North American legends, from Chaucer and Dante to Kafka, the fox is cited for its beguiling cunning and intelligence. Not all the press is good. Machiavelli said rulers must have the deceit of a fox. At the heart of such tales is an animal that employs a broader range of strategies to fill its plate with a much greater variety of pickings than does its canine cousin, the wolf.

Foxes have a vegetarian bent, and will go to great lengths to get what they want. But their staple is meadow voles, which they capture by first listening with sensitive ears for scurrying in the long grass, and then they pounce. Similar catlike stealth is used to get as close as possible to larger prey before making a fast, deadly dash. When they accumulate more food than they need on their nightly hunting forays, foxes often store some away for the future.

Though normally silent, foxes let loose during the mating season, in late January or early February. Then competing males go nose to nose in screaming matches until one backs down. Fights are rare, though contestants may jump up and push each other with their forepaws. The winner of a vixen's heart stays with her after the young are born in March or April, and helps her raise them. Cubs remain in the den for about a month, nourished by a puppy chow of regurgitated meat. In the fall, the family breaks up, with the young males travelling an average of 75 kilometres (45 miles) away from their mother's home range. Vixens stay closer to home. Foxes often survive the winter by feeding on the remains of animals killed by wolf packs. At night, they wrap their bushy tails over their noses and feet to keep from freezing as they sleep.

Because they thrive around forest edges, foxes became more common with the opening of the countryside by European settlement. The British, in the interest of their much-loved equestrian hunts, bolstered numbers with red foxes from Europe, essentially the same species as in North America. In the twentieth century, coyotes from the prairies spread over the same rural countryside. Occupying roughly

Average litter: 4–7

Gestation period: 49–55 days

Age at sexual maturity:
10 months

Lifespan: Up to 12 years in wild,
19 years in captivity

Predators: Wolves, coyotes,
bobcats, lynx, bears; cubs
killed by fishers and great
horned owls

Average running speed: About
45 km/h (29 mph)

Swimming speed: 4–5 km/h
(2.4–3 mph)

Tracks: Front foot 4.5 cm (1.8 in)
wide and 5–6 cm (2–2.4 in)
long, with 4 toes

Scats: Like small dog droppings,
about 5–8 cm (2–3 in) long,
with bits of hair and bone chips

Name of a group: A skulk or den

Famous individuals: Reynard,
Brer Fox, Seminole Sam,
Russel, Mr. Todd

Average number of foxes per
km² (0.4 sq. mi) in southern
Ontario: 1

Average number of foxes per
km² (0.4 sq. mi) in the boreal
forest: 0.1

Range: All of Ontario and
throughout Canada as far
north as Baffin Island

Number of Ontario pelts sold a
year: About 6,000

Number of Ontario fox species: 3

Number of fox species
worldwide: 9

Also see: Wolf, Groundhog

the same niche as foxes, a coyote usually drives off the smaller canines from its territory.

Still, overcrowding in many areas spurs diseases such as distemper and encephalitis, which send fox populations falling in roughly eight- to 10-year cycles. Foxes are also very subsceptible to rabies, averaging 1,500 reported cases in Ontario every year, about 40 percent of the provincial total. Though the rabies virus, which attacks nerve cells, first spread to Ontario from the Arctic in 1954, the province now has the highest incidence in North America. The provincial government spreads bait laced with rabies vaccine over wide areas to combat outbreaks. Rabid foxes may wander aimlessly and appear unnaturally tame.

GROUNDHOG
Sleeping Through Its Greatest Moment

AWAY FROM THE bright lights and fanfare, almost all Ontario groundhogs are fast asleep on their one day of celebrity. Only in Wiarton, Ontario, does one rotund, grumpy, albino star bask in the limelight on Groundhog Day, coaxed in front of the cameras by formally attired civic officials. A lot is riding on Wiarton Willie. If he sees his shadow, it is supposed to mean six more weeks of winter— probably because February 2 is often a typically crisp, sunny, midwinter day that produces a good shadow. If he fails to find a shadow, spring is said to be imminent. The tradition is based on the old European folk belief that badgers and hedgehogs could predict the weather. February 2 used to be a holiday, called Candlemas in Christian times, though originally it was the pagan festival of Brigid, celebrating the first stirrings of spring. It was one of many days farmers gathered to, among other things, guess the weather for the coming growing season.

In a sense, groundhogs do forecast the weather, since they know Ontario winters rarely end even six weeks after February 2. They keep sleeping right on through. Groundhogs are true hibernators and remain curled tightly in a largely uninterrupted, deep sleep for six to seven months. Their body temperature drops to as low as 3°C (37°F), bringing their metabolism almost to a standstill, so they use just a trickle of their stored fat. When males emerge in late March or April, they still have enough fat to live off for several weeks longer, until new vegetation sprouts.

Heartbeats per minute when active: 80

Heartbeats per minute during hibernation: 4–5

Average time between breaths during hibernation: 6 minutes

Adult body length: 40–50 cm (16–20 in)

Weight: 1.8–5.5 kg (4–12 lb)

Tail length: 10–15 cm (4–6 in)

Markings: Varying shades of coarse brown fur, darkest on feet, face and tail

Alias: Woodchuck, chuck, whistle pig, bulldozer, *la marmotte*, *Marmota monax*

Males awake with romance rather than breakfast on their minds. They immediately look for a mate, fighting off similarly minded rivals who get in their way. This period of early spring groundhog activity, coming at the leanest point in the year for wildlife and humans, often provided a much-needed meal for native people in past times. A courting male enters the winter den of a female wagging his tail like a puppy. More often than not, he's chased right back out by the wakened, grouchy occupant.

When he finally finds an agreeable mate, he makes himself at home in her burrow for a month or so. It is the only time adult groundhogs shack up. When she is ready to give birth, in April or early May, the female terminates the honeymoon and kicks her loafing spouse out for good.

Young groundhogs begin viewing the surface world four to six weeks after they are born. About mid-June, when they are too big for their natal burrow, their mother puts some young ones in old dens nearby or digs new burrows for them. She's not out of their life and continues to visit them. But quarters are only temporary. About a month later, the young are gripped with wanderlust and drift away. They may go just a few hundred metres, or much farther before either finding an abandoned burrow or digging their own.

Groundhogs dig quickly, excavating up to 320 kilograms (700 pounds) of soil for a burrow. Their homes usually have two entrances, with additional escape holes that drop straight down into their tunnels. Burrows often start on hillsides or gullies, slope one to two metres (three to six feet) below the surface, then rise up to the main grass-lined sleeping chamber, protecting it from flooding. There are additional toilet chambers, which are cleaned out regularly. Older groundhogs may have both a summer burrow in an open area and a winter home in or at the edge of a forest.

In late summer, decreasing daylight triggers hormones that drive groundhogs to prepare for winter. Before turning in, they go on an eating binge to bulk up on the energy-rich brown fat that gets them through the winter. Finally, their affairs all in order, groundhogs block off their hibernating chambers, allowing other animals to use the rest of the burrow through the winter.

Calls: Loud, shrill warning whistle, like a sonic squeak, low churring when threatened, growls when fighting

Food: Grass, leaves, flowers, clover, seeds, berries, bark, insects, snails, rarely bird eggs or nestlings

Daily food helping: 700 g (1.5 lb)

Preferred habitat: Open woods, forest edges, meadows, fields

Home: Ground burrow, 4–5 m (13.2–16.5 ft) long

Territory: Up to 100 m (330 ft) wide

Gestation period: About 28 days

Average litter: 4–5

Birth weight: About 30 g (1 oz)

Age at sexual maturity: 2 years

Lifespan in captivity: Average 4–5 years, up to 9 years

Predators: Foxes, weasels, bears, wolves, coyotes, hawks

Origin of the name *woodchuck*: Derived from Algonkian language name for "groundhog," called *wejack* by Ojibway

Famous individuals: Wiarton Willie, Punxsutawney Phil

Closest Ontario relatives: Squirrels, chipmunks

Animals that use old groundhog burrows: Foxes, skunks, raccoons, rabbits, hares, minks, porcupines, snakes

Range: All of Ontario. Also found in all other provinces and territories except the islands of Newfoundland and Prince Edward Island

Also see: Clouds, Red Fox

SNOWSHOE HARE
Humour, Mystery and Procreation

Adult body length: 38–50 cm
(15–20 in)
Weight: 1.5–2.3 kg (3.3–5 lb)
Ear length: 6–7 cm (2.4–2.8 in)
Markings: Buffy, greyish or
dark brown in summer, white
in winter
Alias: Varying hare, snowshoe
rabbit, *le lièvre d'Amérique*,
Lepus americanus
Calls: Rarely, snorts, grunts,
low chips; deep groan when
fighting, loud bleat or scream
when frightened
Food: Herbs, grass, leaves,
ferns, fungi, almost any green
vegetation in summer, conifer
needles, twigs, bark, buds,

SILENT, INSCRUTABLE, yet somehow intrinsically funny, hares have always been subjects of fable and magic. Among the 500-year-old engravings in the marble rock face of Petroglyphs Provincial Park, near Peterborough, appears a hare-headed supernatural teacher common to most northern Algonkian-speaking peoples. The Ojibway called the spirit Nanabush. He is credited with remaking the world after a great flood, stocking it with game animals and giving humans fire, hunting weapons and the sacred pipe for communicating with the spirits. In innumerable humorous and moral tales and in both male and female manifestations, Nanabush, in the role of trickster, shows the pitfalls of improper social behaviour through the trouble he/she makes for him/herself.

American anthropologist Daniel Moerman theorizes that the hare's practice of eating its own droppings is at the root of its mystical status. After partial digestion and storage in its long appendix, a hare's food is excreted at night as soft, vitamin-rich, greenish pellets and is eaten again for full digestion. (Waste from food on its second time through is left as the familiar, berrylike rabbit pellets.) Like the carrion eaten by raven and coyote—culture heroes in other regions—the hare's food is a transitional substance, somewhere between living matter and dust.

The abundance of snowshoe hares was of vital importance for native people, especially where bigger game was scarce in the winter. Leaving large tracks with their oversized "snowshoe" feet, specially adapted for staying aloft in deep snow, hares were readily trapped along their regularly travelled paths. In peak years there might be more than 2,000 hares per square kilometre (0.4 square mile) in some areas. High densities quickly lead to overcrowding, depletion of food and cover and concentration of predators, bringing populations crashing down. These cycles, averaging nine to 10 years, are most pronounced in the less-diverse, more-fragile ecosystem of the far northern boreal forest. Densities may drop to one or two hares per square kilometre. The disappearance of hares caused extreme privation for northern hunters. Fear of cannibalism in times of famine helped give rise to stories of windigos, demons that ate humans who neglected their responsibilities or showed undesirable social behaviour.

With their famed procreative exuberance—undoubtedly at the heart of the Easter Bunny's pre-Christian fertility-symbol origins—hares can spring back from their cyclical lows. One promiscuous male, or buck, may mate with two dozen females. To do so, he may have to out-race and out-fight a number of other bucks chasing the does, jumping up and administering boots to the head with his great furry hind feet in bouts of bunny jousting. Before she pairs off, a female may perform a mating dance, thumping her own feet on the ground. From the start of mating in March, does may have two and sometimes more litters a year.

Most hares are very short-lived. On top of high baby-bunny mortality, at least 80 percent of the adult population dies each year. Less than two percent see their fifth birthday.

especially birch, aspen and jack pine in winter

Number of hare or rabbit taste buds: 17,000

Number of human taste buds: 9,000

Number of taste buds of average bird: 200

Hare habitat: Forests, thickets, coniferous swamps

Home: Several lairs in depressions of leaves and litter under bushes, low-hanging evergreen boughs, logs or old groundhog holes

Gestation period: About 36 days

Average litter: 2–4, with 2 or more litters a year

Birth weight: 70–80 g (2.5–2.9 oz)

Age at sexual maturity: About 1 year

Predators: Lynx, bobcats, weasels, martens, mink, fishers, wolves, coyotes, foxes, hawks, barred and great horned owls

Top running speed: 50 km/h (30 mph)

Maximum jumping distance: 4 m (13 ft)

Scats: Vary with diet and season, often round droppings the size of large berries

Tracks: 12–15 cm (5–6 in) hind feet land ahead of much smaller, circular front feet. Toes of hind feet may spread up to 12 cm (5 in) wide

Hunting season: Sept.1-June 15 in central and northern Ontario, with no bag limit

Number of people hunting small game in Ontario every year: 300,000

The hare's high reproductive rate provides a conveyer belt of little bunnies for a cafeteria full of predators. The rarely seen lynx, hunting at night in dense thickets and swamps, depends on snowshoe hares for 70 to 97 percent of its diet. For several years after hare populations crash, lynx mothers can't keep their litters alive unless they move to better, more distant hunting grounds.

One promiscuous male, or buck, may mate with two dozen females

Camouflage, stillness and silence are a hare's first line of defence against predators. It stays put beneath ground cover, dropping its heart and breathing rate, and runs only when it's sure it's been spotted. Much of a hare's time is spent sleeping or grooming in one of several ground or litter depressions, called forms, beneath thick bushes, low coniferous branches or piles of snow. It comes out to forage in the evening, and is most active around 11 o'clock at night.

The snowshoe hare was once Ontario's only bunny, but European settlement brought new breeds of long-ears. The eastern cottontail rabbit hopped north across the U.S. border in the mid-nineteenth century, occupying forest edges to a little past Algonquin Park. Unlike hares, which are born fully furred and able to run within hours, rabbits are slow starters, born helpless, naked and blind in hidden nests. Cottontails have greyish to reddish brown backs, white undersides and are about the same size as snowshoe hares. European hares, introduced from Germany in 1912, are much larger, weighing three to six kilograms (6.6 to 13.2 pounds) and sporting big donkey ears. They live mainly in agricultural areas. Unlike the snowshoe hare, the newcomers do not have the ability—vital to many northern mammals—to put on a white winter coat. The new growth, like many seasonal wildlife alterations, is triggered by the decreasing amount of daylight in fall.

MINK

Among the Smallest of Carnivores

A MINK'S RICH, luxurious coat, underlain by an inner layer of supersoft, dense fur, is ideally suited for its semiaquatic lifestyle in sometimes frigid waters. Body oils spread during grooming keep it glossy and waterproof. Together with the fur's streamlined lay, its qualities have long attracted humans and made mink one of the most highly prized pelts to grace the backs of the genteel. It takes about 70 to 80 minks to make a full-length coat. Fortunately for those in the wild, about 90 percent of the market today is supplied by commercially raised animals.

Mink are probably the most commonly seen species of Ontario's weasel family, other than skunks, because they frequent shorelines and other open areas. For savage killers, they are deceptively cute, with little pointy faces, small round ears and long, thin bodies on short legs. Mink usually walk or run with their backs gracefully arched. Chancing upon a non-threatening human, one may stop close by, stand up on its hind feet and curiously check out the scene. Although they are mainly nocturnal, relentless hunting often keeps them going through the day.

Weasels—mink included—are the smallest but among the fiercest and most agile of all carnivores. Mink often attack and eat animals larger than themselves, killing with a bite to the neck. Even muskrats—themselves ferocious—are attacked in their lodges and literally eaten out of house and

Adult body length: 43–47 cm (17–18.5 in)

Weight: Females 0.8–1.2 kg (1.8–2.6 lb) , males 1.7–2.3 kg (3.7–5 lb)

Tail length: 18–23 cm (7–9 in)

Markings: Light to dark brown or black, darkest on the back, with white chin patch, often a white chest spot, bushy tail

Alias: American mink, *le vison d'Amérique, Mustela vison*

Calls: Snarl, squeak, bark, hiss, purr

Food: Fish, frogs, crayfish, muskrats, mice, voles, hares, rabbits, squirrels, waterfowl, small birds, eggs, garter snakes, salamanders, clams, worms, snails, slugs, insects, grasses

Average daily food helping: About 100 g (4 oz)

Preferred habitat: Along forest streams, lakes and marshes

Average number per km² (0.4 sq. mi) in prime habitat: 3

133

Average territory: 0.5–3 km (0.3–1.8 mi) of shoreline for females, 2.5–5.5 km (1.5–3.3 mi) of shoreline for males

Home: Maintains a number of dens in bank burrows about 10 cm (4 in) wide, log cavities, under roots and rocks, sometimes old groundhog holes or muskrat lodges

Average litter: 4–6, born April to mid-May

Gestation period: 40–70 days, depending on delayed implantation

Lifespan: Up to 8 years in wild, 14 years in captivity

Predators: Lynx, bobcats, foxes, wolves, bears, great horned owls, snowy owls

Top running speed: 10–12 km/h (6–8 mph)

Swimming speed: 3–4 km/h (1.8–2.4 mph)

Maximum time underwater: 2 minutes

Tracks: Rounded, 2.5–3.5 cm (1–1.4 in) wide, with 4 toes

Scats: Dark, 1 cm (0.4 in) long, in piles, with bone chips and scales

Range: All of Ontario. Also found in all other provinces and territories

Mink trapped annually in Ontario: 15,000–30,000

Mink raised on farms worldwide: 20–60 million annually

Number of Ontario mustelid species: 10

Number of mustelid species worldwide: About 63

Also see: Muskrat, Porcupine, Striped Skunk

home, the mink gaining both a meal and a new den. When the tables are turned, larger predators have great difficulty catching and outfighting a mink. Adding insult to injury, minks produce a stench from their anal musk glands more rank than any member of the weasel family save the skunk. A mink cannot direct spray like a skunk, but it lets fly with its musky defence far more readily, at the slightest threat. *Mink* is, in fact, a Swedish word meaning "stinky animal."

Besides defence, musk glands are used by mink to communicate with each other and in seeking a mate. Indeed, the world of odours is everything to mink and other weasels. When hunting, even during a chase, mink use their nose more than their eyes, becoming so absorbed that they're known to run right over the feet of human spectators without seeming to notice them. Males hunt on long circuit routes that may take a week to complete, finding prey both at the bottom of deep, watery dives and on the forest floor. Overnight dens along the route are often stocked with carcasses for the mink's next trip through, especially in winter. Up to a month's supply of food has been found in some mink storehouses.

Throughout the mink's home range there are other weasel species that concentrate on different, though partly overlapping, habitats. The largest, the otter, weighing up to 14 kilograms (30 pounds), does almost all its hunting in the water. Its well-known playfulness on water slides and snowbanks is a characteristic some authorities also attribute to mink. Short-tailed weasels, which hunt mostly on the upland forest floor or in the tunnels of rodents, look very much like mink, but are only half the size. They also have white undersides, and in winter are the only native weasel species to turn completely white, except for a black-tipped tail. In their white coat they are known as ermines. Less common are fishers and martens, once nearly wiped out by trapping. Martens are slightly larger than mink, but with much larger, more pointed ears. They usually catch prey in coniferous trees. The bigger, more heavyset fisher hunts mostly on the ground in mixed forests.

MOOSE
A Gentle Giant Until the Rut

H UGE, STRONG, SILENT and a little funny looking, the moose is another quintessential Canadian symbol. It is by far the biggest animal in Ontario. Even tubby bears going into hibernation weigh much less than the lanky, stilted herbivore. Yet, for most of the year, the moose is like a towering, gentle farmhand. It is usually calm and benevolent even when awestruck canoeists drift close by as it feeds on succulent water lilies in the early morning or late afternoon.

Shakespeare was right when he wrote, "hell hath no fury like a lovesick moose" (the unpublished Stratford, Ontario, Folio). During the fall rut, which peaks in late September and early October, males become aggressive and unpredictable, even crazed. Their mood starts to change in late August when, after growing antlers for five months, they begin rubbing off the nourishing velvet lining on bushes and trees, colouring their huge racks orange-brown with dried blood and plant juices. Males challenge each other to estab-

Adult body length: Females 2–2.6 m (6.6–8.6 ft), males 2.4–3 m (7.9–10 ft)

Height at shoulders: 1.5–2 m (5–6.6 ft)

Weight: Females 375–550 kg (825–1,210 lb), males 400–600 kg (880–1,320 lb)

Average daily food helping: Up to 50 kg (110 lb) in summer

Markings: Completely dark brown, calves reddish brown

Size of 7-year-old bull's antlers: Up to 2 m (6.6 ft) across, weighing 38 kg (84 lb)

Alias: Elk (European name), l'orignal, Alces alces

135

Calls: Usually silent, but during rut, males make long, hoarse, guttural, 2-syllable grunt or loud roar. Females make a drawn-out bleat or moo

Food: In summer, water lilies, duckweed, duck potato, deciduous leaves, ferns, horsetails, asters, jewelweed, grass, blueberries; in winter, twigs, buds and bark of beaked hazel, red maple, birch, mountain ash, aspen, poplar, willow, dogwood, juneberry, cherry and twigs and needles of fir

Preferred habitat: Forests, lakes, marshes, meadows

Home range: 10–15 km² (4–6 sq. mi) for females, 20–40 km² (8–16 sq. mi) for males

Gestation period: 8 months

Average litter: Usually 1, sometimes 2

Birth weight: 12–17 kg (25–35 lb)

First-year calf mortality: More than 50%

Age of most females in first breeding season: 2.5 years

Maximum lifespan: At least 18 years in wild, 20 years in captivity; in prime when 6–10 years

Predators: Wolves; bears may attack young

Top running speed: About 60 km/h (36 mph)

Average time breath held underwater: 30 seconds

Maximum time able to hold breath: 50 seconds

Deepest dives: 6 m (20 ft)

Tracks: Cloven hoof prints 15 cm (6 in) long

lish their status for the breeding ahead. Antlers are the measure of a moose, and the less impressive of two contesting bulls usually backs down before a fight develops, left only with the psychological wounds of antler envy. Occasionally, they do drop the gloves, pushing head-to-head until one loses ground and retreats. Most younger males, lacking the rack dimensions and strength of their elders, don't get to mate.

In one celebrated Vermont love affair, a moose in 1986 wooed and occasionally nuzzled a brown-and-white Hereford named Jessica for 76 days

The biggest antlers also have the deepest, most impressive resonance for females listening to distant bulls thrashing them against branches. Females moan longingly for up to 40 hours straight to attract bulls through the dense forest to their breeding arenas in meadows and bog edges. Biologists in the role of female impersonators imitate the sound by squeezing their noses, cupping their hands and calling. The mooses' great, long donkey ears and acute sense of smell serve them well in locating each other during the rut. Males also kick up the ground, pee and then wallow in the depressions to perfume themselves.

Rutting moose seem to have trouble distinguishing their competitors from other things that are large and loud. In addition to chasing humans up trees, bulls have been known to demolish trucks in head-on collisions and even to challenge trains. On the other hand, males have also mistaken cattle for potential mates. In one celebrated Vermont love affair, a moose in 1986 wooed and occasionally nuzzled a brown-and-white Hereford named Jessica for 76 days. Like all moose, both his antlers and his interest finally dropped off in December and he slunk back into the woods.

Baby moose are similarly apt to follow humans or other species, mistaking them for their mothers. Mothers can be as dangerous as rutting males when guarding against such possibilities and generally seclude their offspring for as long as possible.

Females repair to islands, swamps or waterside alder thickets safe from wolves, in May or early June, to give birth. Newborn calves are about a metre (one yard) long. Moose milk—not to be confused with the Yukon rum-and-canned-milk drink of the same name—allows moose babies to grow faster than any other mammal in North America, gaining a kilogram (2.2 pounds) a day in their first month and up to three kilograms (6.6 pounds) daily afterwards. Yearlings may weigh more than 200 kilograms (440 pounds), over 15 times their birth weight, before their mothers shoo them off to make way for new babies.

During the summer, calves sometimes rest their heads or front legs over their mother's neck when they get tired of swimming. Moose escape the swarms of blackflies, mosquitoes and deer flies that follow them by taking to the water and feasting on water lilies and other sodium-rich aquatic plants. In the winter they switch to twigs, and occasionally bark after the sap starts to run. The name *moose* is derived from the Algonkian word *moosee*, meaning "bark or twig eater."

With their long legs, moose are much better suited to deep snow than are white-tailed deer. Where winter conditions are mild enough to allow high densities of deer, moose often become scarce because of a parasite commonly called brain worm. The parasite evolved over millions of years to live off white-tailed deer without harming them. Moose, however, are recent immigrants from Eurasia, arriving within the past 11,000 years, after the brain worm had already specialized in white-tailed deer.

In moose, it causes disorientation, blindness and eventually death. Snails feeding on deer dung spread the parasite when moose suck them up while browsing. Severe winters from the late 1950s to early 1970s caused a crash in Algonquin Park's deer population, leading to a ten-fold increase in moose.

Scats: Large piles of oblong, 2.5–4.5 cm (1–2 in) long, dark brown pellets in winter; less distinct, greenish piles, like cow pies, in summer; dried droppings can be burned as spruce-scented incense. They have also been varnished and sold as Christmas tree decorations in New Brunswick

Estimated Ontario moose population: About 120,000

Average population increase in spring: 20–25%

Estimated moose-carrying capacity of Ontario range: 150,000–200,000

Number of moose shot by hunters each fall in Ontario: 10,000–12,000

Hunting season: 5 days in late Oct. south of Lake Nipissing, mid-Oct. to mid-Nov. or Dec. elsewhere

Number of people hunting moose in Ontario in fall: 100,000

Number of moose hit annually on the Trans-Canada Highway: Hundreds

Range: Most of province, except southern and eastern Ontario and north of tree line. Also found in all other provinces and territories

Self-proclaimed moose capital of Canada: Hearst, Ontario

Famous individual: Bullwinkle

Also see: Deer Flies, Porcupine, White-tailed Deer, Water Lily, Wolf

DEER MOUSE
Coming Alive at Night

Population per km²
(0.4 sq. mi) of young forest:
Up to 10,000

Heartbeats per minute: 300–500

Average human heartbeats
per minute: 72

Number of naps per day:
Up to 20

Adult body length: 7–10 cm
(2.4–4 in)

Weight: 12–32 g (0.4–1.2 oz)

Tail length: 5–11 cm (2–4.4 in)

Markings: Grey to reddish brown
back and sides, white belly,
feet and chin

Alias: Vesper mouse, singing
mouse, *la souris sylvestre,*
Peromyscus maniculatus

WHEN THE SUN goes down, the meek inherit the earth, emerging from every crack, crevice and hole in the ground to skitter across their dark domains. Mice are usually the most numerous mammals in the forest, and have among the most profound influences on the ecosystem. Forests usually teem with several hundred per square kilometre, rivalling the total number of birds. Mice are far less conspicuous because they stick with the oldest of mammalian survival tactics, being tiny, nocturnal and partly subterranean. It was only after a giant meteorite, comet or some other shattering catastrophe struck the Earth 66 million years ago and ended the reign of the dinosaurs that furry animals began coming out into the light of day and putting on weight. Even today, rodents, which have sharp front gnawing teeth that grow throughout their lives, account for 40 percent of all mammal species worldwide.

Mice have long had a dubious reputation in western civilization, defamed as the creation of witches or the devil, and as omens of all four riders of the apocalypse. The very word *mouse* is evolved from a Sanskrit word meaning "thief."

But in native North American legends, the mouse is usually a good and trusted friend. Such respect may have been born out of an intrinsic understanding and reverence among hunting cultures of the food chain they were a part of. A host of larger predators are directly dependent on the droves of mice that sprout from the earth. The abundance of prey, contrary to popular myth, has far more control over the numbers of predators than vice versa.

The word mouse is evolved from the Sanskrit word meaning "thief"

Forest-mice populations rise and fall with the tree-seed cycles, which vary greatly from year to year to keep seedeaters in check. Mice, in turn, form the largest core of seed distributors in the forest, unwittingly planting trees in forgotten caches and spreading minute herb pits and mushroom spores in their droppings. Those droppings fertilize the soil, while mouse tunnels help air, water and roots spread through the ground. Together with shrews, mice eat up to 80 percent of the cocoons of the European sawfly, an insect that can do much damage to trees.

Deer mice are the most common mice in most Ontario forests. Their rustling in the leaves and even singing, described by Ontario naturalist R.D. Lawrence as "an incredibly high, yet soft, crooning," can be heard throughout much of the night. More laid-back than most of their relatives, deer mice rarely put up a fight against intruders into their territory. In winter, while occasionally scurrying beneath or above the snow, they mostly snuggle together for warmth in dens of up to 12 mice. They breed throughout the warmer months, with females inviting suitors into their love nests for several minutes of romance before kicking them out again and raising babies on their own. The young are weaned and scattered, or drift away, about three weeks

Calls: Loud, shrill, buzzing trill lasting up to 10 seconds a burst; squeak, chitter

Food: Mostly seeds, especially maple; also berries, some beetles, caterpillars, centipedes, grasshoppers, snails, spiders, moths, cocoons and carrion of birds and small animals

Preferred habitat: Forests, especially of maples, and meadows

Average territory: Males 1 ha (2.5 acres), females 0.6 ha (1.5 acres)

Distance travelled in lifetime from birthplace: Up to 500 m (1,640 ft)

Nest: Beneath ground, tree cavities, hollow logs, stumps, lined with shredded materials, usually 15 cm (6 cm) in diameter; moves frequently

Gestation period: 25–27 days

Average litter: 3–6

Average number of litters a year: 3–4

Inbred individuals: Up to 10%

Minimum age at sexual maturity: Females 29 days, males 39 days

Maximum lifespan: Probably 2–3 years in wild, 9 years in captivity

Predators: Owls, weasels, foxes, raccoons, skunks, coyotes, shrews, snakes, almost all other full or partial meateaters

Average number of mice eaten by a long-tailed weasel in one year: 1,300

Winter state: Reduced activity in tunnels beneath snow and ground, living off caches of seeds and nuts. Torpid for days at a time

Famous individuals: Mickey, Minnie, Mighty, Jerry, Speedy Gonzalez, Topo Gigio, Algernon

Greatest mouse achievement in space: In 1960, 3 lab mice, Sally, Amy and Moe, travelled 1,100 km (660 mi) above Cape Canaveral, higher than any other animal had gone, and returned alive

Past medicinal uses: Ingested for a wide range of ailments, especially for children, from bad breath to bed-wetting

Range: All of Ontario. Also found in all provinces and territories except the island of Newfoundland

Number of mouse species in Ontario: 6

Number of vole species in Ontario: 3

Number of shrew species in Ontario: 7

Number of rodent species worldwide: About 1,600

Also see: Barred Owl, Red Pine, Soil

after birth, allowing Mom to meet a batch of new fellows and raise another family.

Around campsites, deer mice can be quite tame, standing up on their hind feet, their large, beady black eyes searching hopefully for a discarded crumb or raisin. Unlike the "city mouse" image of the rather distantly related house mouse from Europe, the deer mouse is fastidious, carefully grooming and preening itself for up to 20 minutes at a time with its dexterous little paws.

A menagerie of other tiny creatures crosses paths with deer mice throughout the wilderness. The almost-identical white-footed mouse is more territorial than its amiable cousin, but becomes scarce towards the northern limits of its range in the deciduous forests of central Ontario. It spends much of its time in trees. The woodland jumping mouse, which unlike most other mice hibernates six or seven months of the year, frequents tangled debris along stream edges. In open areas, the grass-eating meadow vole, or meadow mouse, at the peak of its two- to four-year population cycle, lives in densities up to 10 times as high as its forest relatives. In captivity, they can produce up to 17 litters a year, more than any other mammal on Earth. Voles have shorter tails than mice and look more beaverlike. They eat and tramp down a labyrinth of regular paths beneath the tall grass of a meadow.

Barrelling along the same runways are also the smallest and among the most ferocious of all mammals. Ontario's seven species of shrews, weighing between 2.5 and 20 grams, (0.1 to 0.7 ounces) are almost constantly on the move, their meteoric metabolism demanding they eat every two hours, consuming up to three times their weight in food a day, or starve. Insects, slugs and other invertebrates are their mainstay, but shrews also kill and eat animals much larger than themselves, such as mice, voles, frogs, snakes, even baby rabbits. Poison from the short-tailed shrew's rows of simple, pointy teeth paralyzes its victims and can cause pain and swelling in human flesh. Shrews, with their long torpedo snouts and coats of dense, grey, velvety fur, are very rarely seen, spending most of their lives beneath the leaf litter or in other hidden locations.

MUSKRAT
Giant Mouse That Saved the World

USKRAT IS THE hero of many native re-creation stories. In an Ojibway version, after menacing water spirits flooded the world, the magical protagonist Nanabush sent diving animals to the bottom to fetch mud. Loon, Beaver and Otter all tried and failed before Muskrat finally emerged with wet muck in his paws. Nanabush used the material to create the new world. The Iroquois said the muskrat spread mud over the back of a turtle to form the Earth.

The muskrat was a natural for its role in the creation stories, since it spends most of its time in the water. If it needs to stay underwater a long time, it can, like beavers, drop its heart rate by half and reduce body temperature to burn less oxygen. The rodent's stiff eel-like tail is both a rudder and a propeller in the water. Dense fur traps air during underwater dives, providing buoyancy and insulation. Even in winter, muskrats remain active, foraging for water-plant roots beneath the ice.

The name *muskrat* is actually derived from the Algonkian word *musquosh*, though the English approximation fits well. A muskrat is essentially a giant mouse that produces musk, emitted by males in hope of attracting partners for fleeting muskrat love. The musk is used as a base for perfumes, keeping them from evaporating quickly on skin.

Adult body length: 23–36 cm (9–14 in)

Weight: 0.7–1.8 kg (1.5–4 lb)

Tail: 18-27 cm (7–10.5) in long, dark, scaly, flattened like an eel

Markings: Completely dark to reddish brown

Alias: Marsh rat, marsh hare, rat, *le rat musqué*, *Ondatra zibethica*

Food: Cattails and other water plants, grasses, some mussels, snails, crayfish, fish, frogs and carrion if vegetation scarce

Preferred habitat: Marshes, lakes, streams and swamps at 1 m (3.3 ft) deep or less

Home: Domed pile of cattails, reeds, grass, sticks and mud, up to 1 m (3.3 ft) high and 3 m (10 ft) wide, or bank burrow with underwater entrance

Female's territory: 20–40 m (65.5–131 ft) wide

Average litter: 4–7, born in spring

Average lifespan: 2 years; some live up to 4 years

Predators: Mink, red foxes, coyotes, red-tailed hawks, great horned owls, occasionally raccoons, bobcats and harriers; young sometimes eaten by snapping turtles and pike

Maximum time underwater: 12 minutes

Range: All of Ontario. Also found in all other provinces and territories

Number trapped annually in Ontario: 100,00–600,000

Also see: Cattail, Mink, Painted Turtle, Wetlands

PORCUPINE
Cute, but Not Quite Cuddly

Number of quills: About 30,000

Length of quills: Up to 10 cm (4 in)

Adult body length: 50–85 cm (1.6–2 ft)

Weight: 4.5–14 kg (10–30 lb)

Average height: 46 cm (18 in)

Tail length: 15–20 cm (6–8 in)

Markings: Black- or brown-tipped yellowish or grey-white quills, mixed with dark, dense underfur; black face

Alias: American porcupine, Canada porcupine, porky, quill pig, hedgehog (really another species), le porc-épic, Erithizon dorsatum

Calls: Snort, nasal cooing, wail, bark, sniff, teeth chattering

Food: Buds and catkins, especially of sugar maple and

SOMETIME WITHIN the past 15 million years, porcupines calmly waddled their way from South to North America after the two continents collided at the isthmus of Panama. Armed with a dense coat of formidable quills, they met with little resistance. Though porcupines will attempt to escape up a tree when threatened, they resort to their prickly defence if their slow-moving legs don't carry them away in time. The quills are modified hairs with hundreds of tiny, overlapping barbs. Porcupines don't actually shoot their quills, but cause them to stand on end, like bristling fur, when they are in danger. A swat from their tails can release hundreds on contact. Once embedded, the hollow quills swell, burn and work their way into the flesh every time a victim's muscles contract, digging a millimetre deeper each hour. Eventually they emerge through the skin again, though sometimes they spear right through the body. An animal with a mouthful of needles may starve.

A predator needs to learn only once to leave a porcupine alone. Bobcats, when extremely hungry and unable to catch anything else, may give it a try anyway. The fisher, however, is a skilled porcupine killer. It uses its speed and agility to snake around a porcupine's rearguard defence and viciously bite its face until it dies. Then, flipping the prickly corpse over, the fisher feasts on the soft, unprotected underbelly. In areas where overtrapping wiped out fishers, unchecked tree-eating porcupine populations caused considerable damage to large stretches of forest. Ontario's government reintroduced fishers in several regions in the 1950s to reestablish a balance.

At the moment of truth, the female flips her tail up over her back so that the male can rest on its quill-less underside with his similarly unarmed belly

---

A porcupine's quills were also of little help against native hunters. Because they are slow and about the only animal that can be killed simply with a large rock, porcupines were a godsend in times of scarce game. They were accordingly honoured, and like the beaver's, their bones were kept away from dogs out of respect. Natives also wove elaborate, dyed quillwork decorations into clothing, moccasins, belts, mats, necklaces, bracelets and bags. Because the work was so time-consuming and highly valued, quill embroideries were used as a medium of exchange before the coming of Europeans.

Of course, pincushion bodies seem a little impractical when it comes to sex. Porkies have it all figured out, however, when males go courting females on their territories in autumn. Couples dance in circles when they meet, admiring each other's cute brushcuts, rubbing noses and eliciting loud, high wails and low murmurings of lust. At the moment of

aspen in spring; leaves of aspen, basswood, beech, ash, yellow birch, water lilies, raspberry canes and other plants in summer; acorns, beechnuts, mushrooms in fall; buds, twigs and inner bark of pine, hemlock, fir, spruce, aspen, birch, beech and sugar maple in winter

Preferred habitat: Forests

Average territory: Females 12–80 ha (30–200 acres), males 30–150 ha (75–375 acres); average 7 ha (17.5 acres) in winter

Home: Rock outcrops, tree cavities, hollow logs, brush debris, ground burrows, caves and crevices

Gestation period: 7 months

Average litter: 1

Birth weight: About 490 g (1.1 lb)

Age at sexual maturity: Females 18 months, males 2 years

Lifespan: 10–30 years

Predators: Fishers, great horned owls, rarely bobcats, lynx, foxes, bears, wolves

Scats: Brown, fibrous, jelly-bean-sized, capsule-shaped pellets

Population density: Up to 30 per km² (0.4 sq.mi) in areas where fishers are scarce

Range: All Ontario south to about Hamilton. Also found in all other provinces except the islands of Newfoundland and Prince Edward Island

Date porcupines branched off from the ancestors of guinea pigs and chinchillas: About 40 million years ago

Number of porcupine species in Ontario: 1

Number of porcupine species worldwide: 23

Also see: Mink, Trembling Aspen, Water Lily, White-tailed Deer

truth, the female flips her tail up over her back so that the male can rest on its quill-less underside with his similarly unarmed belly. Later they return to their solitary lives, denning alone for the winter, coming out to eat buds and starch-rich inner tree bark on milder days.

Baby porcupines are born the following spring, about 25 centimetres (10 inches) long, with open eyes and soft quills that harden as they dry. They can climb trees when only a day old. Their ready defence makes juvenile mortality extremely low among porcupines, allowing the species to get by comfortably with just one baby a year. Four-month-old females leave home to establish their own territories. Males stay closer to Mom. Being slow, with a low-energy diet but with plenty to eat, porcupines usually don't travel too far. They spend most of their time in trees, as high as 20 metres (65 feet) up, sleeping during the day and eating at night. Because they often feast on and sometimes kill the most common tree species in an area, they are an important agent of forest diversity.

Though porcupines are consummate vegetarians, mineral imperatives in their diet also govern their behaviour. All animals must balance potassium inside their cells with sodium outside to conduct the electrical charges that make muscles move. Most plant tissues have much more potasium than sodium, except water lilies and some other aquatic plants, which porcupines swim out to, buoyed in the water by their hollow quills. They also get salt from mineral licks, such as high-sodium pockets of clay, or by gnawing discarded antlers or bones. The salt of human sweat is another big attraction, the reason porcupines chew unattended canoe paddles, axe handles and outhouses in the night. Road salt is largely responsible for the strong showing of porcupines in roadkill stats. Porkies even gnaw aluminum, probably to help wear down their teeth.

RACCOON
Thriving in City and Wilderness

AN OMNIVORE PAR excellence, the raccoon is so adaptable that it is more likely to be spotted at night in the city than in the wild. Metro Toronto's raccoon population is estimated at 50,000 to 80,000, with Rosedale boasting some of the biggest, best-fed bandits found anywhere. One created a stir in the city's financial district in the early 1980s when, at first mistaken for a suicide jumper, it was spotted halfway up the gold 40-storey Royal Bank tower. Even in the wild they often show up brazenly at campsites in the night, drawn by the irresistible aroma of food scraps and garbage.

Despite their ubiquitousness in Canada, raccoons are considered extremely exotic in England, where the Brits harbour a dizzy fascination for them. Cuddly as they may seem, raccoons are ferocious furries when cornered, and few predators will tangle with them.

Raccoons are extremely bright and, like humans, have a

Adult body length: 40–75 cm (1.3–2.5 ft)

Shoulder height: 23–26 cm (9–10 in)

Weight: 5.5–14 kg (12–31 lb)

Heaviest raccoon ever found: 28 kg (62 lb)

Tail: 20–33 cm (8–13 in)

Markings: Two-tone brown-and-tan fur, with black mask over eyes, black-and-tan striped tail

Alias: Coon, bandit, *le raton laveur*, *Procyon lotor*

Calls: Chatter, low, fierce growl, a hoarse, staccato call when afraid, babies purr when content

Food: Crayfish, frogs, clams, turtle and bird eggs, fish, birds, small rodents, snakes, snails, insect larvae, berries, nuts, grapes, cherries, seeds, carrion

Preferred habitat: Deciduous forests with lots of lakes and streams

Home: In cavities about 8 m (26 ft) high in trees, often facing south, or old groundhog or skunk burrows, large abandoned bird or squirrel nests and beneath large rocks

Gestation period: 63 days

Average litter: 4

Age at sexual maturity: Females 10 months, males 22 months

Maximum lifespan: 10 years in wild, 22 years in captivity

Predators: Wolves, fishers, lynx, bobcats, coyotes, large owls and eagles sometimes prey on cubs

Top running speed: 25 km/h (15 mph)

Swimming speed: 5 km/h (3 mph)

Tracks: Handlike, 6 cm by 11 cm (2.5 by 4.2 in)

Scats: Irregular shaped, 5 cm (2 in) long pellets, in piles

Number of raccoons per km² (0.4 sq. mi) in Toronto: 12–15, up to 100

Range: All of Ontario except far northeast. Also found in all other provinces except Newfoundland and Labrador

Raccoon hunting season: Oct. 15–Dec. 31

Number of raccoons shot or trapped a year in Ontario: 30,000–100,000

Also see: Black Bear, Crayfish

very sensitive sense of touch. Their front paws, in fact, have many thousands more nerve endings than do human hands. With dexterous fingers, raccoons reach under crevices in shallow water, feeling their way to crayfish and frogs without actually seeing them or even seeming to pay attention. Cubs can climb even before they can see or hear. Driven by a keen curiosity, raccoons explore the nocturnal world with their paws, constantly picking up objects and thoroughly feeling their food before eating. Biologists believe their sense of touch is actually enhanced by water. Raccoons are not really washing food when they wet it in a stream. Their scientific name, *lotor*, is Latin for "washer." The word *raccoon* itself is derived from the animal's Algonkian-language name, *aroughcon*, meaning "hand scratcher."

Driven by a keen curiosity, raccoons explore the nocturnal world with their paws

During cold snaps in winter, raccoons huddle in their dens and try to live off their fat. They are not adapted, however, to survive long without eating, and hard winters cause many to starve. On mild days, they come out to search for torpid frogs and crayfish beneath cracks in the ice. In February and early March, they also go looking for love. Males go calling on females and, if invited into their quarters, mate with them repeatedly before moving on.

Raccoon females, like most mammals, are single mothers. Their cubs are usually born in April. When they are a few months old they join their mother on nighttime marauding expeditions in her territory, which she marks, warning other raccoons to stay away, with piles of droppings on prominent branches, rocks and stream banks.

STRIPED SKUNK
The Sweet-faced Stinker

WHEN THE French first caught wind of the skunk in Canada, they dubbed it *l'enfant du diable*, "child of the devil." At first, the folks back in the old country couldn't believe the fantastical stories of the sweet-faced forest pussycat striking terror in the hearts of man and moose. The English adopted the Algonkian name *seganku*, simplified to *skunk*, and quickly learned to steer clear of it. Turn-of-the-century naturalist Ernest Thompson Seton described the skunk's smell as "a mixture of strong ammonia, essence of garlic, burning of sulphur, a volume of sewer gas, a vitriol of spray, a dash of perfume musk," all mixed together and intensified a thousand times.

A skunk has a double-barrelled spray that squirts from two little nozzlelike projections on its anus. To fire, the skunk tightens its sphincter, popping the nozzles out, and lets fly an oily, yellow-green fluid. About 30 centimetres (one foot) out, the two streams merge and turn into a fine misty spray. A skunk can shoot three to four metres (10 to 13.3 feet) with accuracy. The stream is usually directed at an enemy's eyes, where it causes blinding pain for 15 to 20 minutes unless washed out. The active ingredient, butylmercaptan, is a sulphide, bearing a stench that can carry for a kilometre. A skunk, however, stores only enough musk for four or five sprayings and takes several weeks to fully replenish an empty tank. The spray is used only as a defence of last resort. If

Adult body length: 35–51 cm (1.1–1.7 ft)

Adult tail length: 17–30 cm (7–12 in)

Weight: 1.8–4.5 kg (4–10 lb)

Markings: Black body with two wide white bands running down the back, joining at the bushy tail and top of the head; also thin white vertical line between the eyes

Alias: Canada skunk, wood pussy, big skunk, line-backed skunk, polecat (really a European animal), *la mouffette rayée*, *Mephitis mephitis*

Food: Mostly grasshoppers, beetles, bees, larvae and other insects; also spiders, worms, bird and turtle eggs, nestlings,

mice, rats, chipmunks, squirrels, frogs, salamanders, rabbits, snakes, snails, berries,
grapes, nuts, green vegetation,
roots, fungi, carrion

Preferred habitat: Forest edges,
thick brush, open areas

Home range: 2–6 km² (5–15 sq. mi)

Home: May have several dens
in hollow logs, under rock
piles, ground burrows about
60 cm (2 ft) deep; sometimes
old groundhog or fox holes

Gestation period: 59–77 days

Average litter: 6

First-year mortality: 50–70%

Age at sexual maturity:
About 1 year

Lifespan: Few live longer than
3 years in wild; up to 12 years
in captivity

Predators: Great horned owls,
rarely foxes, coyotes, wolves,
bobcats

Amount of spray in each
fully loaded scent gland:
About 15 ml (0.5 fl oz)

Top running speed: 16 km/h
(9.6 mph)

Ontario rabies cases accounted
for by skunks: 19%

Number per km² (0.4 mi): 0.5–
26 in the wild, up to 36 in
urban areas

Range: All of Ontario. Also found
in all other provinces and territories except Newfoundland
and Labrador

Famous individuals: Pépé Le Pew,
Flower, Miss Ma'm'selle
Hepzibah, Jimmy Skunk

Famous skunk hot spots: Chicago,
meaning "Place of the Skunk"

Number of skunk species
worldwide: 13

threatened, a skunk first lifts its tail, stamps its feet, arches its back and growls. Finally, it forms a horseshoe, face and bum towards the assailant, flips up the tip of its tail and squirts.

All members of the *Mustelidae*, or weasel, family have musk glands, used for marking territory and attracting mates. Skunk musk is so odious that it evolved as a perfect defence mechanism, allowing skunks to forgo the sleek, swift body of their weasel brethren. Instead, with their malodorous repu-tation preceding them, they waddle casually about, seldom running from anything. The white stripes are an advertise-ment so that none can mistake them in their nocturnal wanderings. In more recent times, the skunk's fearlessness, and its penchant for road-killed carrion, has made it one of the most common victims of the automobile.

Skunks are more generalists than other weasels, adapting to a wide range of habitats and food sources, including plants. They're more common in open areas than deep forest and are probably more often seen in the city than in the wild. In the winter, rather than slogging it out with lean hunting like other weasels, skunks usually find hollow logs, or groundhog holes, or dig burrows to nestle down in. They are not true hibernators because their body temperatures, heart and breathing rates are little altered. On mild days, they often wake and dig for sleeping snails, snakes, jumping mice or chipmunks.

In mid-February to mid-March skunks come out of their winter sleeps to mate. A male may have more than one part-ner, sometimes overwintering with harems. Young, called kits or skunklets, are born in May. Though their musk glands start working within about eight days, they must wait a couple more weeks for their eyes to open to take aim. After about two months they follow their mother, single file, on nightly food-gathering journeys. All have flown the coop by the fall, when they are about half grown. For all their negative reputation, skunks are said to make playful, affec-tionate pets and great mousers, although keeping them domestically is illegal in Ontario.

RED SQUIRREL
Loud, Hot-blooded Nut Hoarder

THE RED SQUIRREL lives in the fast lane. It's a high-strung, cantankerous bundle of energy, racing at hyperspeed along branches and around tree trunks during the day. Its specialized vision makes instant trigonomic computations using vertical objects, mainly trees, to judge leaping distances between limbs. Sensing hairs guide the squirrel to twist and contort its body around obstacles as it navigates through the forest canopy. Potential competitors, such as gray jays, flying squirrels, even the larger grey squirrel, are chased off or soundly thrashed. Roosting owls are harangued until they fly off to find peace. Even trespassing humans may be incessantly berated with loud, angry chirping, the protester stamping its feet and jerking its tail violently with each syllable.

Behind all the ill temper is the red squirrel's driving need to jealously guard from pilferers any of a number of well-stocked middens in its territory. A single cache many contain more then 50 litres (1.4 bushels) of cones and nuts. Altogether, thousands of cones may be stashed in tree cavities, hollow stumps, under logs or beneath the ground, where they stay moist and keep from opening and losing their seeds.

In late summer and fall, red squirrels tirelessly cut green cones from branches with their razor-sharp teeth and drop them to the ground for later collection. They also spread and dry mushrooms on sun-soaked bushes before storing them. These nonperishable supplies allow them to stay active throughout all but the coldest days of winter. They may eat more than 100 spruce cones a day, each with an average of 80 seeds. Piles of discarded cone scales beneath a prime feeding spot used by generations of squirrels sometimes rise more than a metre (three feet) high.

Adult body length: 18–23 cm (7–9 in)

Tail length: 10–15 cm (4–6 in)

Weight: 140–300 g (5–11 oz)

Markings: Reddish brown back and tail, brighter in winter; white underside and eye ring; flattened, bushy tail

Alias: American red squirrel, pine squirrel, chickaree, red robber, boomer, bummer, chatterbox, rusty squirrel, barking squirrel, *l'écureuil roux, Tamiasciurus hudsonicus*

Call: Loud, ratcheting cherr, sharp squeak, bark, squeal

Food: Mostly pine and spruce cones; also cherry pits, hazelnuts, acorns, berries, mushrooms, cedar, birch and aspen buds, bark, roots, maple sap, insects; occasionally carrion, bird eggs or nestlings

Preferred habitat: Coniferous and mixed forests, bogs, cedar swamps

Territory: 0.3–3 ha (0.75–7.5 acres)

Home: Nest, or "dray," made in tree cavities, often old pileated-woodpecker holes, twig, leaf and bark bundles in branches, or ground burrows, lined with shredded vegetation

Average litter: 3–7

Gestation period: 36–38 days

Birth weight: About 7 g (0.25 oz)

Mortality rate: 60–80% in first year, 20% in second year

Lifespan: Up to 7 years in wild, 10 years in captivity

Predators: Martens, fishers, mink, weasels, foxes, coyotes, hawks, owls, bobcats, lynx

Population per km² (0.4 sq. mi): 30–200

Top running speed: 25 km/h (15 mph)

Maximum jumping distance: 2.4 m (8 ft)

Best senses: Sight and smell

Name origin: From the Greek *skiouros*, meaning "shadow tail"; the Ojibway name, *adjidaumo*, means "tail in the air"

Range: All of Ontario. Also found in all other provinces and territories except the island of Newfoundland

Number of Ontario squirrel species: 5

Also see: Blue Jay, Eastern Chipmunk, Mink, Red Pine

The strong resins and tannins of raw nuts and seeds, even the poisons of many mushrooms, have no ill effects on squirrels. According to folk belief, squirrel meat may have psychedelic fallout. Woodlore traces the expression "squirrelly" to trappers and others who went a little funny eating too many squirrels, suggesting active ingredients remain potent within their flesh.

Sometimes it seems as if the squirrels are a little crazy themselves, chasing each other round and round tree trunks in a dizzying whirl. While usually this is part of their territorial squabbling, in late winter and early summer the chase involves males trying to outlast each other in pursuit of a receptive "cow" female. They split up after mating. After nursing for five to seven weeks, the young set off on their own. Without the security of home and family, many don't make it very far in a world of hungry squirrel-eaters. Those that manage to survive establish their own territories, where they learn every branch, perch and hideout along their regular foraging routes and become very difficult for any predator to catch.

In hardwood forests, grey squirrels are a little less tense, possibly because they don't carry all their nuts in a few baskets, like the hot-blooded reds do. Instead, greys bury their food a nut or two at a time, relying on a wide dispersal to stay fed. In central Ontario, most grey squirrels are actually black—a colour that absorbs more heat in winter—and don't range much farther north than Parry Sound and Algonquin Park. Northern flying squirrels, which compete with reds for nest cavities, live throughout most of the province and are probably as common as any squirrel. They're almost never seen because unlike their kin, they come out at night, sailing through the forest in descending glides 30 to 40 metres (100 to 130 feet) long.

WOLF
Respected, Feared and Slandered

PROBABLY NO OTHER animal has a more complex psychological relationship with humans than the wolf. Despite an ancient, deep-rooted fear of the great canine among humans, "man's best friend" is a wolf, domesticated as a dog. All dogs descended from wolves 10,000 to 20,000 years ago, and the two can still interbreed. Like all domesticated animals, dogs have proportionally smaller brains than their ancestor. Originally, they were probably lone wolves who learned to follow human bands, living off their scraps. Gradually, the stragglers were accepted into a human social and behavioural structure not unlike their own, forming perhaps the strongest bond between species in history.

Given the respect hunter-gatherer peoples in North America had for the wild wolf, which was regarded as wise and trustworthy, it is probable that modern animosity towards wolves evolved more with pasturalism. Reviled by shepherds, herders and farmers for preying on their stock, big bad wolves became the nemeses of the Little Red Riding Hoods and Three Little Pigs of folklore. The most cursed of individuals assumed the form of the hated beast, becoming

Adult body length: 1–1.5 m (3.3–5 ft)

Average weight: 20–27 kg (44–59 lb)

Shoulder height: 60–68 cm (2–2.2 ft)

German shepherd shoulder height: 71–74 cm (2.3–2.6 ft)

Crushing power of a wolf's jaws: About 100 kg/cm² (1400 lb/sq. in)

Crushing power of a German shepherd's jaws: About 50 kg/cm² (700 lb/sq. in)

Biggest wolf ever found in Ontario: 54 kg (119 lb)

Biggest wolf found anywhere: 89 kg (196 lb), in Alaska

Running speed: Can trot at 10 km/h (6 mph) for hours and sprint up to 70 km/h (42 mph)

Average distance travelled per night: 15–30 km (9–18 mi)

151

Distance wolves able to smell a
moose: Up to 2 km (1.2 mi)

Average number of wolves in
a pack: 5–10

Average pack territory: 120–240
km² (46–93 sq. mi)

Average population density in
Algonquin Park: 1 wolf per 26
km² (10 sq. mi)

Maximum population density:
1 wolf per 17 km²
(6.6 sq. mi)

Markings: Usually salt-and-
pepper grey or brown,
sometimes black or creamy;
amber or brown eyes

Alias: Timber wolf, grey wolf,
le loup, Canis lupus

Calls: Deep howl, growl, whine

Food: Beavers, hares, groundhogs, mice, voles, muskrats,
squirrels, grouse, insects in
summer; young, weak or old
deer and moose, rabbits,
hares, carrion in winter and
early spring

Daily food helping: 1–6 kg
(2.2–13 lb)

Attacks on deer or moose
successfully completed: 10%
or less

Preferred habitat: Forests;
beaver meadows and open bog
rendezvous sites for raising
young in summer

Den for cubs: In ground burrow,
sometimes an enlarged fox
burrow, hollow log or rock out-
crop, near water

Gestation period: 63 days

Average litter: 4–6

Age at sexual maturity: Females
2 years, males 2–3 years

Average first-year mortality:
About 60%

werewolves. At the end of the world, in Norse mythology, the ravenous Fenis-wolf would be let loose to wreak death and destruction.

On the arctic tundra, a sometimes-naked Farley Mowat studying wolves in the early 1960s concluded in *Never Cry Wolf!* that their fearsome reputation was "a palpable lie." In truth, documented true-wolf attacks on humans are extremely rare throughout history, and no serious injuries have ever been definitively recorded in North America. Even rabies is extremely uncommon in the species. Natives told of picking up and playing with wolf pups from their dens, while the parents merely backed away. Yet the tenth act passed by the first legislature of Upper Canada, in 1793, placed a price on the head of all wolves in the new colony. The bounty remained until 1972, and was continued by some counties long afterwards. Park rangers routinely killed wolves in Algonquin until 1959, and it is still legal to shoot or trap wolves anywhere else in the province outside provincial parks at any time of year.

The campaign of extermination and rampant habitat destruction drove wolves out of southern Ontario. In wilderness areas, agitation for their demise continues, largely by recreational hunters competing with wolves for moose and deer. The availability of browse and the severity of winters have a far greater influence on prey populations than do wolves. Studies show wolves usually taking less than two or three percent of deer in their winter yarding areas.

With longer legs, wider feet and a leaner build than dogs of comparable size, wolves are built for long-endurance running in snow. If they can stay within 100 metres (109 yards) of a fleeing deer or moose, they stick with it for up to 40 kilometres (25 miles) , running it down in deep snow, often on frozen lakes. A healthy adult moose standing its own ground can normally keep a pack at bay with its hooves. Most victims are young, old or weakened animals. By eliminating those individuals, wolves help isolate disease, ease pressure on limited browse from nonbreeding older deer and keep the weaker young from passing on their genes.

Wolves themselves carefully regulate their own numbers, through their social structure to ensure overhunting doesn't put their food supply in jeopardy. Packs usually consist of a dominant mating pair, their offspring from several generations and sometimes aunts, uncles or occasional lone wolves that are gradually accepted into the pack. Only the dominant female breeds, in late February or mid-March, and she may sometimes be the pack leader. When the cubs are born two months later they almost double the size of the pack. All members help in raising them, but the cubs are at the bottom of the totem pole. They are the last to eat, and during hard winters all may perish. If some adults leave the pack or die, there's room for more cubs to survive and the pack's number remains relatively constant.

Packs also keep population densities low by maintaining very large territories for their long-distance hunts and warning other wolves to stay away. In addition to marking their manor with urine and droppings, packs declare propriety over all the land within earshot of their howling, which on still nights can carry over 300 to 400 square kilometres (115 to 154 square miles). Wolves also howl to locate each other when individuals are hunting separately, as they often do in the summer. Each wolf has its own distinct voice that can be recognized by others in the pack. Often, usually before or after a nightly foray, all join in a group howl in excited anticipation of a feast. Next to actually eating, it is probably when wolves are happiest, tails wagging, joyously bonding like humans in the warm glow, or drunken revelry, of a singalong. The pack leader starts off with a deep, long howl, joined by the other adults at different pitches and the cubs with yips and whines. They are especially vocal in August and September, when cubs hone their singing abilities and howl at the drop of a hat.

In the rural and forest-fringe areas of southern and central Ontario, a higher-pitched howling usually belongs to the coyote. Taking advantage of the cleared rural lands vacated by timber wolves, the more omnivorous and adaptable coyotes moved into Ontario from the west in the early decades of the twentieth century and are now quite numerous in many areas. Ontario coyotes are bigger than their prairie relatives, owing to marriages of convenience between the first pioneer coyotes and remnant wolves.

Average adult mortality: 20%

Lifespan: Average 4-8 years in wild, up to 15 years in captivity

Predators: Bears, large hawks may attack cubs

Tracks: 11–13 cm (4.4–5 in) long, proportionally wider than a dog's foot

Scats: Like dog droppings, with fur and bone chips

Estimated number of wolves in Algonquin Park: About 250

Estimated number of wolves in Ontario: 5,000–8,000

Estimated portion of Ontario's wolf population killed by humans annually: About 20%

Range: All of Ontario, south almost to the edge of the Canadian Shield. Also found in Labrador, Quebec, all the western provinces and the territories

Famous individuals: The Big Bad Wolf, Akala, Lobo, Fenis-wolf

First appearance of canines: At least 25 million years ago

Animals that depend on wolf leftovers during the winter: Foxes, martens, fishers, ravens and eagles

Number of Ontario canine species: 5

Number of canine species worldwide: 30–35

Also see: Moose, Red Fox, White-tailed Deer

REPTILES

WITH ITS RELATIVELY cold winters, Ontario is not the most hospitable place for reptiles, cold-blooded creatures that, unlike mammals and birds, cannot produce their own body heat to keep from freezing when the temperature drops below zero. Only one lizard, the five-lined skink, dares to inhabit the province, eking out an existence in a few southern fringe areas. Similarly, just a handful of turtles make their portable homes in Ontario, and only painted and snapping turtles can be said to be common.

Among the 15 native snake species, the ubiquitous garter snake is the one seen by most people nine out of ten times. Unlike the world's tropical realms, which seem to have the same attraction to all things lethal as they do to sun-seeking tourists, Ontario has just one poisonous reptile, the massasauga rattlesnake. Another species, the timber rattler, hasn't been seen in the province in many decades.

Ironically, in the lands where the most dangerous species dwell, they are accorded a larger degree of respect and reverence. In this part of the world, reptiles' reputations as—in the words of Carl Linnaeus, the father of the modern biological classification system—"foul and loathsome creatures" has not served them well at the hands of humans. Many of Ontario's turtles, and particularly its snakes, are rare because of human persecution. Too often, fear and ignorance have won over the natural fascination and curiosity we have as children for these often colourful, limbless or shelled wonders. Most are now protected by law, though their futures remain far from certain.

GARTER SNAKE
Ontario's Most Successful Reptile

ARTER SNAKES are common and familiar just about everywhere, primarily because they are more adaptable than most other snake species, which are in retreat across the province. Garters are generalists, hunting anywhere and eating almost any prey they can get their expandable jaws around. Their horizontal black-and-yellow colour pattern—resembling the old-fashioned garters used to hold up socks—blends well with the grass, leaves and litter in many habitats, giving garter snakes the advantage of stealth when stalking, or when hiding from larger predators.

A foolproof reproductive system also allows garters to be quite fruitful. Both in October and in April, in group-hibernating spots, garters hold orgies, entwining in knots of many mating snakes for several hours. Males have a choice of two penises, which pop up from the base of their tails. As well as producing many young at a time, females can store sperm from a single mating in their bodies to fertilize future eggs for up to five years. Thus a single snake can slither far and wide to start a whole new population without needing to find a male.

Like several other snake species in Ontario, garters give birth to live young, usually around the end of August. Mothers may stay near their babies for several days afterwards, and siblings often stick together for a few weeks, growing by frequently shedding their skin, including the clear scales that protect their unblinking eyes. Even as adults, snakes continue to grow, though much more slowly.

All snakes lack apparent noses or ears, are near-sighted and probably do not have a sense of taste. Yet their senses are finely honed for survival. They smell by constantly dart-

Average adult length:
Male 30–50 cm (12–19 in),
females 40–75 cm (16–30 in)

Maximum length: 124 cm (4 ft)

Markings: Usually 3 yellow stripes on a black, brown or dark green background, sometimes with a reddish tint

Alias: Common garter snake, *la couleuvre rayée, Thamnophis sirtalis*

Number of times adults shed skin annually: 2–4

Food: Frogs, toads, earthworms, insects, salamanders, mice, voles, small birds, fish, tadpoles

Digestion: Large meals may take days, during which garters remain inactive, hiding beneath rocks or debris. Slow metabolism allows them to go weeks without food if necessary

Habitat: On ground almost anywhere, especially near water

Home range: Up to 0.8 ha (2 acres)

Home: Rests under rocks, logs

Average litter: 20–40

Length at birth: About 12 cm (5 in)

First-year mortality:70–80%

Age at sexual maturity: 2 years

Maximum lifespan: 20 years

Predators: Raccoons, skunks, weasels, hawks, owls, larger snakes

Winter whereabouts: Hibernate in large groups, often with other species, in rock piles, crevices, stumps and decayed root passages a metre or more beneath the ground

Largest known garter hibernaculum: Up to 10,000 snakes, in Manitoba

Range: All of Ontario to mid-boreal forest and almost James Bay; also found in all other provinces except Newfoundland

Also see: Draco, Water Snake

ing their tongues out to pick up odours from particles in the air or whatever they touch. When they withdraw their tongues, the forked tips touch a set of twin sensory sacks at the roof of the mouth, called Jacobson's glands, which transmit the odours to the brain for identification. Snakes are also extremely sensitive to vibrations, which are relayed via the jawbone to their inner ear. They can judge from an animal's vibration whether it's small enough to be eaten.

Anything more than about a metre away is a blur to a snake. To focus close up, it must move its head back and forth like a magnifying glass, because the lens of its eye cannot change shape. All of the retina, however, is sensitive to movement, which can be detected in a very wide field of view because the eyes sit on the sides of the head.

Snakes themselves betray almost no body scent, and their heads appear tiny and harmless when poking through the grass. They strike like lightning, lunging up to half the length of their bodies, and usually eat prey headfirst and whole, the easiest way to both restrain and swallow still-struggling food. A snake's loosely hinged jaws can open almost 180°. A garter has six rows of tiny, sharp, backwards-curving teeth for drawing its mouth over prey rather than for chewing. To keep themselves from being eaten by mammals, garters when caught release a bad-tasting, pale greenish brown liquid from a gland at the base of their tails. The defence is not as effective against birds, which usually have a poor sense of taste.

The less-common ribbon snake is related to and closely resembles the garter, with bright black-and-yellow stripes. But it's usually much smaller and more slender, with a more distinct "neck" between its head and body. It specializes in catching amphibians and usually frequents the edges of lakes, ponds, streams or wetlands.

MILK SNAKE
Victim of False Beliefs

MILK SNAKES, like so many others, are plagued by human myth and misconceptions. They are named for the completely erroneous belief that they attach themselves to cows' udders and suck their milk dry. The theory may have developed from frequent observations of the large snake in cow pastures and barns, where it hunts at night. Milk snakes are actually constrictors, coiling around their prey and tightening their grip until the unfortunate victim suffocates.

When threatened by a larger predator, milk snakes often vibrate their tails and bite aggressively. They do not have real rattles like a rattlesnake, but the quivering of their tail against dry leaves can sound like one. Similar imitations by even larger constrictors, the black rat and eastern fox snakes —mainly restricted to a few areas in southern or eastern Ontario—may have served them well against most predators, but prompted humans to strike them down. All three snakes are now legally protected.

So also is the large eastern hognose snake, which instills fear if cornered by raising its head, spreading the skin of its neck like a cobra and puffing itself up. It hisses loudly as it slowly exhales, giving rise to the belief that the "puff adder" releases a stream of poisoned air. It may also strike repeatedly, but doesn't actually bite. If all else fails, it rolls over, sticks out its tongue and plays dead.

Adult length: 50–90 cm (20 in–3 ft)

Markings: Back and sides have rusty blotches with black rims on a grey or creamy brown background, with a Y-shaped crest on the head and a checkered black-and-white underside; young shiny red and white

Alias: *La couleurve tachetée, Lampropeltis triangulum*

Food: Mainly other snakes; also mice, voles, chipmunks, small birds, fish, bird and snake eggs, slugs, insects

Habitat: Meadows, open forests

Average clutch: 8–16 capsule-shaped white eggs, about 4 cm (3.6 in) long; laid in June or July in rotting logs, hatch in Aug.–Sept.

Range: Southern Ontario to about Arnprior and Sault Ste. Marie; also found in southwestern Quebec

Also see: Draco, Garter Snake, Water Snake

PAINTED TURTLE

Basking by the Riverside

Average shell length:
14–18 cm (5.5–7 in)

Average weight: Males about
300 g (10.5 oz), females
400 g (14 oz)

Markings: Olive, black or brown
shell, with sections divided by
pale yellow lines; bright red
dabs around the edge of
shell, red-and-yellow streaks
on dark grey skin of head and
neck, red streaks on front legs;
yellow plastron (underside)

Alias: Midland painted turtle, *la
tortue peinte, Chrysemys picta*

Food: Aquatic plants, algae,
insects, snails, larvae, tadpoles,
crayfish, fish, fish eggs,
salamanders, carrion

Call: Squeak or sigh

Habitat: Small ponds, weedy
bays, marshes, bogs, slow
rivers

Average clutch: 5–8 oval,
cherry-tomato-sized white eggs

Incubation period: 60–100 days,
depending on the temperature

Nests usually lost to predators:
More than 90%

Age in first breeding season:
Males 3–5 years old, females
5–10 years old

Lifespan: Up to 40 years

Predators: Skunks, raccoons,
foxes, minks, weasels, crows,
bullfrogs, snakes, fish and
other turtles eat eggs or
hatchlings

Winter whereabouts: Up to 45 cm
(1.5 ft) deep in mud beneath
water

I N IROQUOIAN COSMOLOGY, the Earth rests on the back of a great turtle. The turtle had rescued the goddess Antaentsic after she fell from the sky into a vast ocean below. Mud scooped from bottom of the sea by a muskrat or toad was placed over the turtle's back, forming her new realm, the Earth, Turtle Island. In a similar Hindu story, the world was started on the back of Vishnu, transformed into a turtle after a great flood. Among some Algonkian-speaking peoples, who also had flood creation stories, the great turtle Makinak was the symbol of fertility.

During cold snaps, turtles' hearts and breathing stop and ice crystals form in the blood

---

Perhaps the best domed hero for the creation story would be the painted turtle, which spends much of its time sunning itself above the water, usually on rocks and logs. Basking is more than just California dreaming for turtles. Temperature is everything to these cold-blooded creatures, whose body temperature rises and falls with that of their surroundings. Most reptiles need temperatures of at least 10°C (50°F) to function. But because they don't need to stoke an internal furnace with food to heat their bodies, the way warm-blooded mammals and birds do, their food requirements are much less. Painted turtles can't eat if their body temperature falls below 15°C (59°F). With a sun-powered metabolism, the more they bask, the faster they digest and the more they can eat and store fat for the winter.

Temperature even determines turtle gender. After being buried by females on land, eggs that incubate under fairly steady temperatures of 22 to 26°C (72–79°F) yield male turtles. In central Ontario, however, about 85 percent of painted turtles hatch as females.

Regardless of their gender, many painted turtle hatchlings in Ontario have to wait till spring to see the light of day. To survive the winter, late-hatching September broods often remain in their subterranean birth nests, living off their egg yolk. During cold snaps they literally turn into turtcicles. Their heart and breathing stop and ice crystals form in their blood. The babies' temperature can drop to -8°C (18°F), and up to 59 percent of their body fluids freeze without harming them. Within shrunken blood and tissue cells a portion of unfrozen fluid remains. Though some frogs and insects have similar abilities, the painted turtle is the only reptile able to maintain this semi-freeze-dried state. Their little bodies, however, cannot remain so for long, and a prolonged deep-freeze is fatal.

Once spring does arrive, hatchlings head straight for the water and stay there for the rest of their lives, save for brief annual egg-laying missions by females. Painted turtles eat, sleep and hibernate underwater. Like all submerged turtles, they breathe by filtering water through special tissues in the cloaca, an all-purpose excretory and reproductive opening beneath the base of the tail. The water is held in two small sacs, like aquatic lungs, that draw oxygen from the water into the blood in exchange for the body's carbon dioxide waste.

Range: Southern Ontario to about North Bay and Sault Ste. Marie; also found in the southern portions of northwestern Ontario and in all other provinces except Prince Edward Island and Newfoundland

Name for a group: A bale of turtles

Famous turtles: Yertle, Michelangelo, Donatello, Churchy La Femme, Brer Tarrypin, Makinak, Kumaa

Also see: Algae, Milky Way, Snapping Turtle

RED-BELLY SNAKE
The Little Serpent

TINY DENIZENS of darkness, pencil-thin red-belly snakes are seen not nearly as often as their numbers warrant. They spend the day hidden under rocks and logs, surfacing later to prey on other small, crawling things that emerge under the cool cover of night. Smaller than any other snake in Ontario, red-bellies themselves appear to be little more than long worms with backbones and brilliantly coloured undersides. Variously described as timid and dainty when captured, they are apparently too small to bite, though they have been known to curl their upper lips in a nasty Elvis snarl. In contrast to its bright underside, the red-belly's rusty brown back blends with dead pine needles and other ground litter.

Red-bellies breed after emerging from hibernation in April, though some also mate in October, with the females storing sperm internally and fertilizing their eggs the following spring. Mothers give birth, rather than laying eggs, in late August or early September. Newborns, eight or nine centimetres (three to 3 ½ inches) long, are dark with white neck rings. Like most snakes, they shed their skins for the first time an hour or so after birth.

After spending much of the summer in meadows and clearings, red-belly snakes migrate in September and October, usually in rainy weather, back to forest hibernating spots. Slithering into the earth beneath rocks and stumps, they sometimes share their hibernacula with the similar, though slightly larger brown snake, which sports black spots down its dull brown back.

SNAPPING TURTLE
Relic of the Dinosaur Past

WITH THEIR LONG, jagged-ridged dragon's tails, snapping turtles are a living relic from the age of dinosaurs 70 million years ago. Effective, protective shells have given turtles little need to change through the ages. Snappers, though, are actually one of the few species of turtles that cannot fully retract their limbs into their dome when in danger. A small plastron, or underside shell, and very thick, meaty legs prevent the classic turtle defence. A razor-sharp beak and powerful jaws—some say capable of detaching a human finger—are instead the snapper's salvation.

Despite its fearsome reputation, the snapping turtle is mainly vegetarian. It is most carnivorous in the spring, before aquatic weeds are abundant, when it sucks up small fish or frogs. Larger prey is dragged down to the bottom to drown before being ripped apart by the turtle's huge claws. But a snapping turtle almost always retreats swiftly when a larger animal comes near in the water. Only when trapped on land will it lunge quickly and accurately, up to 20 centimetres (eight inches), with its long neck outstretched. Once they bite, snappers hang on tenaciously. Some have had to have their jaw muscles cut before they let go. They also ooze a foul-smelling, syrupy musk.

Lifespan: 30–90 years

Oldest definite recorded age of a turtle (eastern box turtle): 138 years

When turtles first appeared on Earth: 200–250 million years ago

Average adult snapping turtle shell length: 20–30 cm (8–12 in)

Record shell length: 47 cm (18.5 in)

Length from beak to tail tip: Up to 1 m (3.3 ft)

Average weight: 4.5–9 kg (10–20 lb)

Record Canadian snapper: 22.5 kg (50 lb)

Markings: Dark shell, often covered with algae; dark grey or brown skin; underside plastron can be dull yellow

Alias: Common snapping turtle, snapper, *chelydre serpentine*, *Chelydra serpentina*

Pests: Leeches

Call: Sometimes hisses when threatened

Food: Mostly algae, water-lily roots, other aquatic plants, and insects; occasionally fish, crayfish, frogs, ducklings, baby muskrats, snakes, snails, leeches, carrion

Habitat: Shallow, muddy ponds, lakes, marshes and slow-moving rivers and creeks with abundant vegetation

Average territory: About 3 ha (7.5 acres)

Mating season: Soon after emerging from winter torpor, when water temperature reaches 16°C (61°F), in late Apr. and May

Average clutch: 20–40 rubbery, round, white eggs

Incubation period: 55–125 days

Hatchling length: 3 cm (1.2 in)

Age at first breeding season: 16–18 years old

Predators: Skunks, foxes, minks, muskrats, raccoons and otters eat eggs; blue herons, crows, hawks, bullfrogs, snakes and fish eat hatchlings. Otters kill adults in winter

Winter whereabouts: Inactive beneath mud, vegetation or logs at bottom of water, or dug into banks, often in groups

Average population density in shallow lakes and rivers: 1 per hectare (2.5 acres)

Range: Southern Ontario to about Sault Ste. Marie and Lake Timiskaming; also found from Thunder Bay to Lake of the Woods, southern Manitoba, Saskatchewan, Quebec, New Brunswick and Nova Scotia

Also see: Algae, Painted Turtle

Normally, snapping turtles don't chance being trapped on land. They spend most of their time underwater at the muddy bottom, active mainly at night. Sometimes they sun themselves on rocks, logs or water's edge, a quick dive away from safety.

From June to early July, however, females seek out dry, sandy or gravelly sites for laying their eggs, travelling up to 20 metres (22 yards) from the water. Working most often in the morning, they dig holes 10 to 15 centimetres (four to six inches) deep in shore embankments or hillsides with their hind feet, deposit their eggs, cover them up and leave. The site must be in the open, where the sun can incubate the eggs. Under such exposed conditions, 50 to 90 percent of all nests are cleaned out by predators. Most of the tiny turtles that do hatch in September and early October have fairly soft shells and are soon eaten by birds and fish. To survive, they probably have to bury themselves in the mud quickly and go into hibernation before even having their first meal.

While very few snappers make it to adulthood, those that do are longer-lived than any other animal in the wild. Little wonder many cultures regarded turtles as symbols of longevity, tranquility and happiness. Their reproductive lives are far longer than those of humans. Females play the odds by producing a new clutch almost every spring till they are in their seventies. A few offspring are bound to make it through.

With a reproductive strategy based on longevity, snapping turtles can be threatened in areas where they are hunted by humans. They are the turtles in turtle soup and the only Ontario species allowed to be captured. Some 5,000 to 8,000 a year were taken until 1990, when commercial hunting was outlawed, but fishing-licence holders may still catch them. Near settled and agricultural areas, they've been found with PCB and pesticide levels up to five times the safety limit, resulting in deformed hatchlings and lower reproductive rates.

WATER SNAKE
Graceful Swimmer Demands Respect

THOUGH ALL ONTARIO snakes can swim, the northern water snake is an aquatic specialist. It glides quickly and smoothly through the water, swimming just below the surface, a huge, dark, waving serpent. When water snakes catch prey, however, they bring them out of the water to eat, then hide on shore for up to several days while they digest. On sunny days they bask on rocks, logs and old beaver lodges, or in tree branches overhanging the water. They also come out of water in May or early June to mate, entwining around each other on reeds or other vegetation. In late August or September, they give birth to live young.

Unless cornered near shore, water snakes seldom attack large mammals or people in the water. If captured or threatened, however, they can be very aggressive. They attempt to strike repeatedly and can inflict a painful bite. Water snakes have four rows of 30 to 40 very sharp teeth, curving inwards to hold their slippery aquatic prey. Unlike most other snakes, when they bite, they rip their victim's flesh as they remove their teeth. The bite injects an anticoagulant that makes bleeding hard to stop. Like many species, they also flatten themselves to appear bigger when threatened, and release a stinky fluid from their cloacal gland if caught.

The water snake's aggressive defence has brought much

Average adult length: 60–100 cm (2–3.3 in)

Maximum length: 135 cm (4.5 ft)

Diameter: Up to 5 cm (2 in)

Markings: Alternating bands of brown with black or grey; appears uniformly black when wet

Alias: Common water snake, *la couleuvre d'eau, Natrix sipedon*

Food: Minnows, perch and other fish, frogs, tadpoles, salamanders, toads, crayfish, occasionally mice or shrews

Habitat: Lakes, bays, slow-moving rivers, wetlands and rocky shorelines

Average litter: 20–25

Maximum lifespan: At least 7 years

Predators: Great blue herons, minks, raccoons, skunks, foxes, red-shouldered hawks, herring gulls, pike, bass and other large fish, turtles

Winter whereabouts: Hibernate in rock crevices or beneath water

The ancients viewed a snake shedding its skin as a symbol of rebirth

Mortality rate during hibernation: Up to 40%

Range: Southern Ontario to about North Bay and Sault Ste. Marie; also found in southwestern Quebec

Average adult Massasauga rattlesnake length: 50–70 cm (1.5–2.3 ft)

Rattler markings: Dark brown blotches on a light grey or tan background; more uniformly dark with age

Rattler whereabouts: Scattered in marshes and coniferous forests around Georgian Bay, Muskoka and a couple of spots in southern Ontario

Average number of people bitten by Massasauga rattlesnakes per year in Ontario: 1

Number of people who have died of Massasauga rattlesnake bites in Ontario: 2

Number of Ontario snake species: 15

Number of snake species protected in Ontario: 7

Number of snake species worldwide: About 2,500

Also see: Draco, Garter Snake, Lakes, Milk Snake, Minnows

persecution from humans. Fortunately it is now protected in Ontario, illegal to kill or capture. When swimming, it's often thought to be a water moccasin, a poisonous species found only in the southeastern U.S. On land, its blotchy appearance is often mistaken for the similarly patterned Massasauga rattlesnake, Ontario's only venomous serpent. Though once common, Massasaugas are now rare in Ontario. Rattlers prey mainly on frogs and rodents and do not bite people unless cornered or startled. Their poison causes swelling and discolouration within 15 minutes, but rarely death. Nonetheless, fearful humans almost invariably killed them whenever they were found. As a threatened species, rattlers were finally granted protected status in 1991.

Snakes have long inspired fear and loathing in Western cultures, from the appearance of the serpent, as evil incarnate, in the Garden of Eden. The Genesis story, however, is just one version of a very old tale involving an earth goddess and a fertilizing phallic snake, told by the earliest agricultural societies in Asia, Africa and Europe. The ancients viewed the wonder of a snake shedding its skin as a symbol of rebirth. The power of snake venom must also have engendered a strong reverence. Hindu, Norse and Egyptian cosmology all featured a great snake supporting or enfolding the world. The polar star, upon which the Earth's axis seems to spin, was said to be the eye of the serpent that fertilized the Earth. In China, snakelike dragons were powerful but beneficial beings that brought summer rains with their thunder. Zombie was a West African snake god.

In the Americas, snakes were everywhere regarded as important spirits. Quetzalcoatl, the great diety of the Aztecs and other Central American peoples, was a feathered snake. A vanished agricultural people that lived in large towns left a giant serpent-shaped earthern mound in Ohio. A much smaller version, probably made by the same people, overlooks Rice Lake at Serpent Mounds Provincial Park. Ojibway lore features both benevolent and dangerous snakes. Nanabush's enemies were the serpent people that lived beneath the water. But the creator, Kitche Manitou, gave snakes the job of protecting plants from overindulgent browsers.

WOOD TURTLE
The Forest's Domed Wanderer

UNLIKE OTHER TURTLES in Ontario, the wood turtle spends much of the warm months of the year on land, partially burying itself to the edge of its shell when resting. Its young, however, hatch in September from soft, leathery eggs, not the harder-shelled variety laid by terrestrial tortoises. Wood turtles are usually found near gravel-bedded rivers or creeks and spend most of the spring and fall in the water, where they also hibernate through winter till April.

A high-domed carapace, or upper shell, flared low at the edge, makes the wood turtle particularly distinctive. Each of the scutes, or sections of its shell, also have a pyramidal look formed by rising concentric rings of scaly ridges. The number of rings reveals the reptile's age, but they become faded and blurred on older turtles. The wood turtle's Latin name, *insculpta*, refers to the overall sculpted look of its shell.

Wood turtles also stand out among their kind for their personalities: they are bright, dancing—some say whistling—turtles, though the latter is disputed. Biologists have found that wood turtles, in the classic maze test, find their way through as quickly as do rats, one of the most intelligent of mammals. In June, courting wood turtles dance together by swinging from side to side for up to two

Adult shell length: 10–20 cm (4–8 in)

Weight: About 1 kg (2.2 lb)

Markings: Grey or brownish, deeply lined shell; yellow plastron with dark patches along the ridges; orange and yellow markings on light brown legs and neck

Alias: *La tortue des bois, Clemmys insculpta*

Call: Hiss and wheeze

Food: Blueberries and other berries, flowers, plants, insects, small fish, tadpoles, frogs, worms, carrion

Habitat: Open pine and poplar forests with sandy soil; floodplains, meadows

Average clutch: 6–8 oval, golf-ball-sized, pinkish white eggs

Hatchling size: About 3 cm (1.2 in) long

Age at sexual maturity: About 14 years old

Lifespan: Up to 58 years

Predators: Raccoons, minks; large fish, crows, blue herons, hawks eat hatchlings

Winter whereabouts: Inactive up to 90 cm (3 ft) deep in mud or under rocks and debris at river or creek bottoms or banks

Estimated Ontario population: About 1,000

Range: Sault Ste. Marie, Muskoka, Algonquin Park, upper Ottawa River, Frontenac County, east of Georgian Bay; also found in southwestern Quebec, New Brunswick and Nova Scotia

First turtles in space: In 1971 the Soviets sent several around the Moon and back to Earth

Number of turtle species native to Ontario: 8

Number of turtle species worldwide: 257

Also see: Jack Pine, Painted Turtle, Snapping Turtle

hours before jumping into the water to consummate their relationship.

Wood turtles are bright, dancing—some say, whistling—turtles

Except for Algonquin Park and the Sault Ste. Marie and Georgian Bay areas, the wood turtle is not very common, and it's listed as rare in the province. Most other turtle species are similarly hard to find. Stinkpot turtles lurk north to Georgian Bay, Haliburton and the Ottawa River, but they are so small and secretive that they are seldom seen. Blanding's turtle is a threatened species in Ontario, but is still found in the Ottawa valley, on the east side and south of Algonquin Park, Manitoulin Island and on the north shore of Lake Erie. A deep yellow chin and throat sets it apart from all others. Blanding's turtles also have a hinge running across the width of their plastron, allowing them to close their shell more completely than other species.

Like all the rest, the Blanding's turtle's neck folds into an S-shape when pulled into the shell. An air pump at the base of the neck allows turtles to breathe, since their rib cage is fused to their shells and unable to expand to draw air.

PLANT KINGDOM

PLANTS

I T IS SAID that the natives had no word for "wilderness." The bush was their home, their provider, a vast pharmacopoeia and treasure trove of life-giving substances, with each plant having its place and purpose, its secrets and mysteries. Many native peoples saw plant spirits as benevolent healers aiding them against diseases sent by offended animal spirits when hunters did not show them proper veneration. Recognition of the curative powers of plants and appreciation of their beauty stretch far back into humanity's prehistory. Soil studies of 60,000-year-old Neanderthal grave sites have revealed that the dead were laid to rest on beds of spring flowers, all known in more recent times as traditional folk remedies.

Native or folk medicines, such as those mentioned in this book, are not recommended for those unschooled in their preparation. The same active ingredients that give plants their curative powers are also often poisonous in large concentrations.

In addition to Ontario's many hundreds of species of flowering plants, including trees and grasses, there are many other kinds of vegetation in the province, such as spore-producing ferns and horsetails. Strictly speaking, some of the entries included in this section are not part of the plant kingdom at all, though they are popularly perceived as such. Fungi, algae and lichens are grouped into a third kingdom all their own. They predate the evolution of modern plants and reach back towards the origins of life.

ALGAE
At Work for Three Billion Years

POND SCUM and the green, slippery film coating submerged rocks, if thought of at all, usually provoke a certain queasiness in humans. Yet algae, and the photosynthetic bacteria known as blue-green algae—the primordial ooze—have dominated the Earth longer than any other life-forms. In fact, they made most other life and the air we breathe possible. Some three billion years ago in ancient seas, primitive, single-celled cyanobacteria, or blue-green algae, evolved the ability to release oxygen from the water as a waste product of its photosynthesis. At the time, there was no free oxygen in the atmosphere, which was composed mostly of deadly carbon dioxide and other gases such as methane, ammonia, nitrogen and hydrogen.

Gradually, blue-green algae pumped oxygen through the seas and into the atmosphere, at the same time drawing carbon—on which all life-forms are based—from the air. By 600–700 million years ago, there was enough oxygen in the atmosphere to support the higher metabolism of the first multi-cellular marine animals. By about 400–500 million years ago, oxygen finally formed a thick-enough ozone layer around the planet to allow plants to grow on land, shielded from the sun's deadly ultraviolet radiation.

Those plants probably evolved from algae. A missing link was recently discovered in one species of freshwater algae that has lignin, a substance that makes land plants stiff and erect.

Algae come in a wide variety of forms and are found in every type of aquatic habitat, as well as in soil and on moist wood and rocks. They form the base of the aquatic food chain. Many algal species are microscopic, single-celled organisms, while kelp, a brown seaweed, can be 30 metres (100 feet) long. Algae form smooth, surprisingly sensuous velvet mats covering submerged rock faces, and wispy green, translucent water clouds that enshroud canoe paddles near the shores of quiet streams.

LOWBRUSH BLUEBERRY
Carbohydrate Boost for Diners

BLUEBERRIES ARE the most common and best loved of a galaxy of summer berries. Their ripening is perfectly timed, through millions of years of natural selection, for just after the late spring/early summer bug-population peak, when birds are searching for new sources of food. Even most fruit- and seed-eating birds nest when insect numbers are highest, because bug meals, with up to 70 percent protein, are needed for their hatchlings to reach adult size in the space of a couple of weeks. After the young have flown the coop, many birds are happy to switch back to fruits and berries, which are three to 13 percent protein.

Like most other summer berries, blueberries are high in carbohydrates, or sugars, and low in fats. Fruits and berries ripening later in the year are higher in the easily stored, longer-burning fats needed by birds in migration. Blueberries' conspicuous colours advertise their presence to birds, while their sweet smell attracts many mammals, from mice to bears. Fluctuation in berry crops from year to year has a major effect on animal populations. By enticing wildlife with juicy flesh, blueberries and other fruit-produc-

Other names: Whortleberry, bilberry (really European varieties of blueberry), low sweet blueberry, deerberry, *le bleuet*, *Vaccinium angustifolium*

Height: Up to 30 cm (1 ft)

Leaves: 2.5 cm (1 in), rounded, smooth edged, leathery, turning reddish-purple in exposed areas, bright crimson in fall

Flowers: White, like tiny bells, up to 6 mm (0.2 in), in clusters

Berries: Green at first, turning pink, reddish purple and finally dark blue-purple when ripe in July in southern Shield areas and in Aug. towards Temagami

Average number of seeds per berry: More than 100

Preferred habitat: Dry, acidic soil, where light penetrates through forest canopies, along shorelines, rocky or sandy open areas, hillsides, islands, burnt-over areas

Range: All of Ontario. Also found in all eastern provinces, Manitoba and Saskatchewan

Closest relative: Canadian or highbrush blueberry grows up to 4 m (13 ft) high in swampy or dry open forests in southern or eastern Ontario.

Other common summer berries: Wild strawberries, raspberries, blackberries, mulberries, huckleberries

Also see: Bees, Black Bear, Blackflies, Granite, Moss

ing plants have their seeds spread and fertilized by way of bird and mammal droppings.

Most often, blueberry seeds take root and thrive in dry, rocky habitats, helping to hold down the thin layer of soil painstakingly built up by lichens, moss and grass. Once established, lowbrush blueberries spread out in dense, tangled colonies, sending forth underground stems that sprout new plants. As with many other heath or open-area shrubs, discarded blueberry leaves are slightly toxic to tree seedlings in the surrounding litter, keeping them from growing up and shading out the shrubs.

In May and June, blueberries produce tiny white flowers that hang downwards and are pollinated by small bees and blackflies. The insects dig deeply into the flowers to reach the nectar, at the same time inadvertently shaking sticky pollen onto themselves. They cross-pollinate by brushing their pollen-laden bodies against the female pistil near the opening of the next flower they visit. Widely varying amounts of nectar in each flower increase cross-pollination by keeping insects flitting from one to another until they finally hit a jackpot. Flowers that are pollinated only by their own male parts usually yield smaller berries that ripen later than the others.

In addition to nurturing countless numbers of bees, flies, birds and mammals, blueberries were also an important food source for peoples such as the Ojibway, who were primarily hunter-gatherers. Choice areas were often burnt to encourage the growth of blueberries, which flourish after fires. Dried or charred blueberries, added to rice, meat or bread, provided vital nutrient during the long winter. Crushed berries were also used to make a blue-grey dye, and both leaves and berries were brewed as a tea. Blueberry leaves contain the chemical myrtillin, which acts like insulin to reduce blood sugar, as well as other minerals that serve as blood purifiers and are used to treat kidney problems. These same ingredients can also be toxic in high concentrations.

> *Choice areas were often burned to encourage the growth of blueberries, which flourish after fires*

BUNCHBERRY
Hair-triggered Pollination

Height: 5–20 cm (1.2–8 in)

Alias: Pop flower, dwarf dogwood, dwarf cornel, cracker berry, plant of gluttony, *le cornouiller du Canada, Cornus canadensis*

Leaves: Dark green, smooth edged and pointed, with distinct parallel veins. All leaves at same level, meeting together at the stem; 4 leaves on plants without flowers, 6 leaves on plants with flowers or berries. Turn deep red in autumn and stay on plant till spring

Flower: 4 large, white petals (actually "bracts," or modified leaves), with about a dozen tiny, greenish white true flowers in the centre

Berries: Scarlet, in small clusters, 1 large seed in each berry, eaten by vireos, thrushes, sparrows and grouse. Ripen in mid- to late summer

Spare parts: Each underground stem has a dormant bud that shoots up if the main stem is killed

Preferred habitat: Moist, cool forests with rich, acidic soil

Companion plants: Wild lily-of-the-valley, bracken fern, beaked hazel, wintergreen, red osier dogwood

Range: All of Ontario to the tree line

Native uses: The Ojibway and Iroquois made tea from bunchberry roots for treating colic in infants, as well as coughs and fevers

Also see: White Trillium

CLUMPS OR MATS of shade-tolerant bunchberry spread their striking white flowers in June. The plant is actually a shrub, a member of the dogwood family. But since a woody stem or trunk does not give it any more chance of getting extra light beneath the trees, it conserves the little energy it receives by growing its stem horizontally beneath the ground, often for many metres. The bunchberry plants poking above the soil are actually branches attached to the same buried stem, or rhyzome. Because its root system can survive the winter, bunchberry can use its limited energy to grow slowly but steadily. It usually does not have enough energy to bloom every year, with those in deepest shade blooming the least.

Bunchberries use insects and other foreign agents for a unique method of pollination. They offer no nectar in return. The cluster at the centre of each flower is actually made up of many individual tiny flowers. They remain closed, their stamens tightly bound, until fully mature. Then, when an insect, animal or falling debris touches a millimetre-long spike sticking up from one of the closed petals, they pop open, springing the stamens forward and catapulting their pollen into the air in a faint spray.

BURDOCK
The Original Velcro

BURS ARE SO SUCCESSFUL at surreptitiously sticking to passersby that Europeans inadvertently brought them to North America, where burdock spread far and wide. By clinging to pants, socks and mittens, burs co-opt people into becoming agents of nature, spreading the sticky seeds according to plan. After his dog attracted a passel of burs while out for a walk in the late 1940s, Swiss inventor George De'Mestral put the dry but sticky balls under his microscope. Observing their tiny hooks, he got a great idea, and Velcro was born.

Burdock lives for two years and has just one shot at reproduction. In its first year, it can be mistaken for rhubarb, with very large leaves growing low to the ground. The leaves capture oodles of sunlight and use most of the energy to develop a deep taproot that can survive the winter. The following spring, the burdock root sends up a tall, branching stem, putting all its energy into reproduction. The plant dies as its seeds ripen in the fall, but remains standing through winter and beyond, passing out its still-potent seeds within clusters of faded brown burs on the fur of animals.

Though many people avoid and even destroy burdock, to others it has long been a valued health food. Burdock roots are higher in potassium, nitrogen and calcium than carrots. The ancient Greeks, who called the plant "Lover of Man" because of its seeds' cling, made wreaths of burdock to relieve headaches, a practice later adopted by the Iroquois. The new plant was thought to have magic powers by the Iroquois, who also carved voodoolike dolls out of the root to cast spells on enemies, or boiled the root to remove such spells. The Ojibway boiled roots and leaves as a tonic and to soothe upset stomachs.

Height: 60–180 cm (2–6 ft) in second year

Alias: Bur, bur bush, lesser burdock, wild burdock, clotbur, cocklebur, begger's buttons, wild rhubarb, *la petite bardane*, *Arctium minus*

Leaves: 30–50 cm (1–1.7 ft) long, 30 cm (1 ft) wide oval rosettes in first year, smaller pointed oval leaves in second year

Flowers: Purple hooked bristles with white tips growing from green burs, 1.5–3 cm (0.6–1.2 in) blooming from July to Sept., pollinated by insects

Preferred habitat: Fields, forest edge and open woods

Lifespan: 2 years

Name origin of Velcro: The combination of the French words *velours* and *crochet*, meaning "velvet" and "hook"

CATTAIL
Prolific Plants of the Marsh

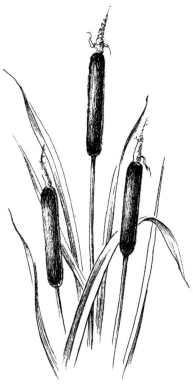

CATTAILS rise up in the richest habitats in the wilderness. Like other marsh plants, they are extremely efficient at filtering nutrients and even impurities from the water. Cattail roots have a nutrient content similar to rice and corn, but have a much higher yield. A Syracuse University project in the 1950s estimated cattails could provide up to 30 tonnes (33 tons) of dry flour per 0.4 hectares (one acre), far more than wheat, rye, oats or corn.

Fall cattail roots are especially nutritious, because as winter nears, the plants suck all their nutrients back into the roots. They continue to breathe air through dead, dry, hollow stalks sticking up through the ice and water. In spring, the nutrient stores are used to send up fresh green stalks, which rapidly overtake the previous year's pale, dead relics.

By June or July, spikes of male pollen heads form above the familiar dense, velvety female seed heads, which look like big hotdogs on roasting sticks. Wind blows yellow pollen to surrounding cattails. Seeds emerge in fall and winter on fluffy fibres that travel far on wind, water or an animal's fur. If a marsh or pond dries up, the seeds, like those of many water plants, can remain dormant for a long time and sprout when water returns. Cattails can also spread quickly by sending out underground stems that establish circular colonies of clones around a parent plant.

Height: 1–3 m (3.3–10 ft)

Alias: Broad-leaved cattail, swamp bullrush, cossack asparagus, reed mace, *la massette quenouille, Typha latifolia*

Flowers: Cylindrical, velvety female seed head, 10–15 cm (4–6 in) long, lime green at first, turns dark brown after pollination. Spiky male pollen head above, 8–12 cm (3–5 in) long, dark green at first, turns yellow

Leaves: 2 cm (0.8 in) wide, very long and pointed, like swords

Preferred habitat: Marshes, swamps, wet meadows, open ponds, lakeshores and bays

Number of seeds per cattail: Up to 250,000

Range: All of Ontario

Common nesters: Red-winged blackbirds, marsh wrens, swamp sparrows, sora rails, American coots, pied-billed grebes, common gallinules and bitterns

Cattail foods: The Iroquois dried and pounded autumn roots into a sweet flour for bread and puddings. Natural-food enthusiasts cook the white syrupy core of crisp spring shoots and use pollen heads in bread and cakes

Number of Ontario cattail species: 2

Number of cattail species worldwide: 10

Also see: Muskrat, Red-winged Blackbird, Wetlands

173

FERNS

Descendants of Giant Tropical Trees

Height: 30–120 cm (1–4 ft)
Width: 30–100 cm (1–1.3 ft)
Fronds: Split in three triangular branches, bright green in summer, yellow turning rust in fall
Alias: Eastern bracken, brake-fern, pasture-brake, eagle fern, pasture fern, fiddlehead, *fougère à l'aigle, Pteridium aquilinum*
Spore casings: In "fruitdots" lining underside edges of fronds, appearing in latter half of summer
Number of spores produced by a single frond: Millions
Roots: Long, dark brown, horizontal rhizomes; true roots reach 25 cm (10 in) deep
Preferred habitat: Dry, sandy soil in areas of scattered trees; also grows in moist forests and burnt-over sites
Range: Southern Ontario to the southern boreal forest
Fern remedies: The Ojibway boiled lady fern and sensitive fern, both found in moist areas, into a tea for relieving pain and helping nursing mothers to produce more milk. Fresh, moistened lady fern was also slapped onto scrapes and bruises to ease pain
Name origin of *fern*: From proto-Indo-European *porno*
Name for fern enthusiasts: Ferners
First appearance of vascular spore-producing plants: 400 million years ago
Number of fern species in Ontario: About 45

ONE PERSON'S FIDDLEHEAD is another's black gold—if they live hundreds of millions of years apart. Today's ferns are the diminutive remnants of the Carboniferous period 300 million years ago, when giant, tree-sized ferns and horsetails dominated the Earth's first steamy jungles. The buried, fossilized material of those jungles—preserved from rotting by the acidic conditions of vast bogs and swamps—forms today's coal deposits.

Ferns appeared long before plants had developed flowers or seeds, reproducing instead by spores, like mushrooms. Ferns, however, are more advanced than algae, lichens, mosses and fungi, which depend on the slow diffusion of water and nutrients through their tissues to grow. Vascular canals, like veins, transport a fern's supplies much more quickly, allowing it to grow both higher and faster.

Old European beliefs held that fern "seeds" had the power to make people invisible and to open locked doors

As the Earth's climate cooled, giant ferns perished in temperate zones, leaving behind only species that buried their woody trunks underground as horizontal stems, called rhizomes. The visible ferns that rise from the ground each spring are the plant's deciduous leaves, called fronds. There are still some tree ferns in the tropics that reach heights of 25 metres (80 feet) and are easily mistaken for palm trees.

Old European beliefs held that fern "seeds" had the power to make people invisible and to open locked doors. There does, indeed, seem to be something almost magical about fern spores and reproduction. Unlike a seed, which contains a tiny, inflatable, rolled-up plant and a supply of protein to nourish it, a spore is a single cell. It grows by dividing after it has landed in a suitable site. After several weeks, it produces a tiny, heart-shaped plant called a prothallus, usually less than a centimetre wide, lying flat and close to the ground.

The prothallus is short-lived and, unlike its parent, reproduces sexually. As with primitive water plants, sperm travels through a film of rain or moisture from male to female organs on the underside of prothallia. The fertilized egg grows into a tiny fern, drawing nutrients from the prothallus until it sinks its own roots. The rhizome that develops underground sends more fronds above the surface as it spreads.

Because of its versatility, bracken is the most common fern not only in Ontario, but in the world. It grows in clumps both in dry, open fields and in the shade of thick-canopied, moist forests. Its slightly extraterrestrial-looking, curled fiddleheads are among the first plants to emerge from the forest floor in April, grabbing maximum sunlight to fuel their rapid growth before tree-leaf buds open and cast them in shadow. They grow so fast that people who dine on newly emerged fiddleheads are supposed to pick them in the morning. By afternoon they may have already lost their succulence and become slightly toxic with defence chemicals produced to ward off grazers. By late May or early June, bracken ferns may be well over a metre (3.3 feet) high.

Number of fern species worldwide: Up to 10,000
Also see: Limestone, Wetlands

Eaten raw, bracken has an enzyme in its tannic acid that destroys vitamin B_1. Although the acid is traditionally removed by soaking fiddleheads in wood-ash water, authorities now recommend against eating them, because they have been found to cause cancer in cattle and lab animals. In past times, native peoples also roasted thick bracken fern rhizomes in the fall and ground them into flour, which was high in oils and starch.

FUNGI
Tying the Forest Together

Number of spores or microscopic fungal colonies in 1 g (0.03 oz) of soil: 300,000–3 million

Number of spores in a single mushroom: Billions

Average spore diameter: 0.015 mm (0.00059 in)

Length of time spores can remain dormant: Up to 20 years

Rate of growth: Under ideal warm, moist conditions, a new fungus can sprout several kilometres of strands in a few days

People who study mushrooms: Mycologists

People who fear mushrooms: Mycophobes

People who are addicted to mushrooms: Mycophagists

Edible-mushroom nutrients: Folic acid, vitamins D and B_7

Common poisonous mushrooms: Death angel, fly agaric, death cap. Most have spore gills on the underside of their caps

Mushroom sex: Strands of two fungi grow and fuse together, uniting nuclei of the opposite sex to create a reproductive, spore-producing organism

Fairy circles: Rings of dead grass, left in fields by mushrooms produced by a central underground fungus

Fairy steps: Long-lasting, woody bracket fungi on trees

Mycorrhizal mushrooms: Tan, brown, yellow, red or orange, with tubular pores beneath their fleshy caps, growing near tree trunks

T HE MUSHROOMS sprinkled throughout moist forests, especially after autumn rains, and the fungal shelves climbing up trees offer only hints of the incredible pervasiveness of fungi. Above-ground structures such as mushrooms are only the external, spore-producing, fruiting bodies of extensive fungal organisms. Fungi spread networks of threadlike fibres, called mycelia, through every nook and cranny of the upper soil, forming a mesh on the underside of decaying leaves, intertwining with roots and entering rotting logs, live trees, mosses, dead animals and droppings—literally tying the forest together. A thimbleful of soil can have two kilometres (1.2 miles) of microscopic fungal strands running through it.

Of known fungi, the world's biggest, in Washington state, has a network of fibres covering about six square kilometres (2.3 square miles), sporting mushrooms throughout. In a Michigan hardwood forest, the network of a single golden brown honey mushroom organism—an edible species that glows in the dark and also grows in Ontario—is estimated to weigh more than 100 tonnes (110 tons) and be at least 1,500 years old. Fungal networks are like veins and capillaries in the soil, keeping ecosystems alive. Fungi cannot produce chlorophyll, so must get their energy from plants. Latching on to dead vegetation to reclaim nutrients back into the life cycle, fungal strands secrete enzymes that dissolve the organic material into food molecules they can absorb. A succession of different fungus species is usually involved in breaking down the sugars, cellulose, lignins and hemicellulose that form leaves, wood and other organic material, like the processes of a pulp mill breaking down wood fibre.

Fungi engage in an interspecial chemical trading network that is essential for up to 90 percent of all trees, shrubs, herbs and grasses

---

About 90 percent of all dry vegetable material is consumed by decomposers rather than by herbivores, and 80 to 90 percent of the energy from decaying organic matter goes to fungi and bacteria. Fungi are of prime importance in central Ontario's coniferous forests, where the acidic soil and thick litter layer are inhospitable to many bacteria. Without fungi and bacteria, all the carbon required for life would become locked up in a growing layer of dead material that would never break down. Life would peter out within a few decades.

Mycorrhizal: From Latin *myco,* "fungus," and Greek *rhiza,* "root"

Spore dispersal: By wind, rain, insects and mushroom-eating animals

Most important animal dispersers of spores: Mites, both on their bodies and in their droppings

Smelly-fungi spore spreaders: Flies are attracted to the rancid-meat smell of slimy stinkhorn fungi. Northern flying squirrels sniff out and eat the underground fruiting bodies of some mycorrhizal fungi

Meat-eating fungi: Some species use looped strands to snare underground roundworms, or paralyze them with toxic drops, afterwards secreting enzymes to digest them

Amount of carbon returned to the air by microorganisms accounted for by fungi: 13%

First appearance of fungi in ancient oceans: Probably about 2.5 billion years ago

Number of mycorrhizal-fungi species in coniferous forests: Up to 5,000

Other forms of fungi: Yeasts, molds, mildew

Number of named fungi species worldwide: About 100,000

Estimated number of fungi species worldwide: More than 1.5 million

Also see: Humus, Lichens, Moccasin Flower, Soil

Some fungal strands or spores spread into the roots or into wounds in the trunks of living trees as well, weakening them and speeding their demise. Logging can sometimes help nourish such fungi with the dead roots and stumps left behind, resulting in more formidible parasites for new trees or those left standing.

Many species of fungi engage in an interspecial chemical trading network that is essential for up to 90 percent of all trees, shrubs, herbs and grasses. By entwining their fibres around rootlets, these "mycorrhizal" fungi transfer water and nutrients, most notably nitrogen and phosphorus, to trees and plants. In return, trees and plants pass about 10 percent of their high-energy sugars, created through photosynthesis, on to the fungi. In effect, the fungi are middlemen that connect all living things beneath the ground, even transporting important materials from one plant to another and producing chemicals that protect trees from microbial diseases and parasitic fungi species.

Fungi also manufacture a stew of other chemicals for their own protection and competition. Some produce antibiotics to make it difficult for bacteria and other fungi to grow near them. In 1929 Alexander Fleming isolated one of these substances from the Penicillium mould and produced the first modern medical antibiotic, penicillin.

Defence chemicals are probably the active ingredients in most poisonous mushrooms, known as toadstools. Ancient peoples often learned ways of taking small doses of toxic mushrooms to achieve a state of ecstasy. The Roman writer Seneca called such mushrooms "voluptuous poison." Fly agaric was used ritually throughout much of Asia and Europe. Soma, the sacred elixir of Indo-European peoples more than 4,000 years ago, is believed to have been made from a deadly mushroom that grew on the steppes of central Asia. It induced a battle rage among warriors that made them fearless and heedless of pain. Many of the rites involving wine in Christian Churches come from the soma ceremony, via Zoroastrianism in ancient Iran.

GOLDTHREAD
Staying Green Beneath the Snow

A MID THE CARPETS of oft-forgotten tiny green plants growing on the forest floor, goldthread is one of the most common. Goldthread gets its name from the thin, bright gold rootstocks it spreads out just beneath the surface to colonize an area, with clone plants growing up from the root ends. The Ojibway pulled the roots up to make a yellow dye for porcupine-quill embroidery and to tan hides. Red dyes were obtained from bloodroot and the inner bark of white birch, alder and cedar.

Although bitter tasting and even toxic in strong concentrations, goldthread root solutions were used to treat aching throats, gums and cold sores. Natives introduced the plant to European settlers, who also used it as a drink to cure scurvy and to soothe stomach problems.

Goldthread, a member of the dainty buttercup family, is a perennial, able to live for many years. Its thin roots, however, can't store nutrients like the thick rootstocks of trilliums, orchids and deciduous trees to get it through the winter.

Instead, it survives the cold by keeping its leaves, as do wintergreen and many herbs of forests farther to the north. Like coniferous trees, which don't have the thick, deep root system of broad-leaved trees either, their foliage possesses natural, sugary antifreeze that keeps them evergreen. As soon as the snow melts, and as long as temperatures remain above freezing in autumn, goldthread can collect extra energy from the sun, unavailable to its leafless deciduous neighbours.

Height: 5–12 cm (2–5 in)

Alias: Canker root, yellow root, mouth root, *coptide du Groenland, Coptis groenlandica*

Leaves: 3 tiny, shiny green leaflets, like frilly shamrocks, joined at the top of a thin stem; 2–4 groups of leaflets per plant

Flower: Single, star-shaped blossom, 1.3 cm (0.5 in) wide, with 5–7 petals, growing on a leafless stem; blooms in late May and June

Seeds: Long-stalked clusters of tiny pods, each with 4–8 seeds

Preferred habitat: Moist, mossy, coniferous forests, bogs, red maple and cedar swamps

Range: All of Ontario and across Canada

Also see: Red Maple

GRASSES
The Hair of Mother Earth

Word origin of *grass*: From ancient Germanic *gro*, meaning "thing that grows." Also the root of the words "grow" and "green"

Number of the world's 15 major food crops that are grasses: 10

Date grain first cultivated: About 10,000 B.C.

Date corn first cultivated in Central America: Before 2000 B.C.

Tallest wild grass species in Ontario: Giant reed, up to 3 m (10 ft)

Stems: Jointed, hollow

Leaves: Long, narrow

Flowers: Usually green, without petals, wind pollinated

Scientific family name: *Gramineae*

Lifespan: A few species less than a year; others have root systems that live for centuries

Age of earliest grass fossils: About 35 million years

Number of Ontario species: More than 600

Portion of Ontario species that are not native: About 25%

Number of species worldwide: About 7,500

World's most widespread species: Kentucky blue grass, used for lawns and common in wild; originally from northern Eurasia

World's tallest grass: Bamboo

Also see: Beaver, Cattail

FROM THE dawn of civilization, grasses have been of utmost importance to humans. All grain crops, including wheat, oats, barley, rice and even corn, are derived from wild grasses. Our main sweetener, sugarcane, is a grass. Most livestock, as well, subsist on hay and other grasses. As Isaiah noted in the Bible, "All flesh is grass."

Even in central Ontario, hunter-gatherer peoples harvested wild rice (illustrated), which is not true rice, but an aquatic grass. It grows in the clear shallows of some lakes in the Kawarthas and eastern Ontario, where from mid-August till October natives harvested it in canoes and hunted migrating waterfowl that were also attracted to the rice.

The Ojibway and other peoples braided and burned another species, called sweetgrass, to bring blessings. Growing in wet, sandy soil along shorelines, sweetgrass symbolized in their religion the hair of Mother Earth. It was woven into baskets and mats that retained a distinctive, sweet scent for years. It is abundant only around Lake Superior.

Grasses are most common in open areas because they economize their use of water under the full heat and light of the sun. On average, to create one gram (0.03 ounce) of tissue they use 250 to 300 grams (nine to 10.5 ounces) of water, only a quarter as much as many plants. They sprout green in spring earlier than almost all others. With up to 90 percent of their weight beneath the ground, in dense, fibrous root systems, grasses minimize water loss and are protected from fire and the elements. They also grow from the base of the stem, rather than from their tips like most other plants, making them amazingly resilient to grazing animals and lawnmowers.

HAWTHORNS
Well Defended from Nibblers

Maximum height: 10 m (32 ft)

Other names: Thornbush, thorns, haw, hawes, *l'aubépine*, *Crataegus* family

Thorn length: 1–7.5 cm (0.5–3 in)

Leaves: Vary greatly with each species, but generally tooth edged, often lobed, turn red in autumn

Flowers: In bunches, small, disc-shaped with 5 white or rarely pink petals, fragrant

Fruit: Usually red or yellow when ripe, looks like a small apple, 1–3 cm (0.4–1.3 in) wide, with 1–5 large, hard "carpets" containing seeds

Bark: Smooth, grey-brown or chestnut coloured on young trees; shaggy, in narrow shreds, grey to brownish on older trees

Wood: Hard, dense, heavy

Preferred habitat: Thickets, forest edges, meadows, hillsides, open forests, swamps, riverbanks

Companion plants: Beaked hazel, rosehip, raspberry, blackberry, goldenrod, aster

Common nesters: Cedar waxwings, catbirds, song sparrows, yellow warblers, goldfinches, indigo buntings, mourning doves

Lifespan: Few live more than 50–75 years; up to 200 years when cultivated

Range: Southern Ontario to the eastern edge of the Hudson Bay lowlands. Also found in all other provinces

Number of Ontario hawthorn species: About 40

Number of hawthorn species worldwide: More than 150

PASSING FROM THE WOODS into an open area when there is no path is often like fighting through a thick barbed-wire barrier strung around the forest edge. Sun-loving hawthorns, which grow as large bushes or small trees, thrive in such sites. Their sharp thorns ward off the many browsers that frequent high-forage open areas, giving hawthorns a competitive advantage over plant smoothies. If they are nibbled by deer or others with tough stomachs, hawthorns respond by growing ever-denser branches and twigs, creating an impenetrable tangle.

After flowering sometime from April to June, depending on species, latitude and temperature, hawthorn branches become heavily weighted with small fruits, called haws or hawthorn apples, which can be used in homemade pies and jellies. Haws are not very sweet, with little sugar and only one to two percent fat. Although some ripen by the end of August, most migrating birds pass them by, favouring instead fruits, nuts and seeds with more than 10 percent fat, which provide them with the energy they need for their long flights. But in the lean days of late fall and early winter, as other food sources disappear, birds and mammals that remain behind turn to haws and other low-quality seeds such as sumac.

COMMON JUNIPER
Berries That Pack a Punch

Average height: Under 1.5 m (5 ft)

Maximum height: 4.5 m (15 ft)

Alias: Gin berry, *le genièvre, Juniperus communis*

Needles: 8–20 mm (0.3–0.7 in) long, green with white streaks above, in bundles of 3

Flowers: Clusters of tiny male or female conelets, on separate shrubs, blooming in May or June

Cones: Called arils, look like berries, with a waxy coating, whitish or greenish ripening to blue or black-purple; woody inside, with a spicy, sweet taste; take 2 years to mature

Preferred habitat: Dry, rocky, open hilltops, limestone ridges, fields, burnt-over areas

Range: All of Ontario. Also found in all other provinces

Traditional juniper uses: Berries or tea treated rheumatism, bronchitis, digestive problems; assisted vision, memory, brain functions and childbirth; acted as an antidote to poison. Branches protected stables from demons and lightning. The Ojibway inhaled fumes of burning juniper to cure headaches and colds. Sailors rubbed ashes on their gums to prevent scurvy. Berries seasoned wild game and beef stew

Number of juniper species native to Ontario : 3

Number of juniper species worldwide: About 50

THOUGH IT USUALLY grows as a shrub about a metre (three feet) high, common juniper is officially designated as the most widespread "tree" in the world. Its many uses are similarly far-reaching. Native North Americans put the shrub to scores of tasks, including rubbing its resinous oil on the skin as insect repellant and using the smoke of its burning branches to purify their lodgings.

But it was juniper's powers as a diuretic (helping people to pee), known both to the Iroquois and Europeans for 3,000 years, that led to its most popular use today. In the 1600s, a Dutch doctor discovered how to distil juniper berries to create an alcoholic beverage as a cheap substitute for the medicinal juniper-berry oil. The drink *genever*, from the Latin *juniperus*, became known as *gin* in English. Its imbibers came to relish its benumbing side effects far more than its urinary utility. Distilling innovations in the late eighteenth century made cheap gin available on a wide scale in England, in time to become the popular opiate for the first generations of displaced agricultural workers pressed into the drudgery of sweathouse factories in the early industrial revolution. Gross national product and alcoholism rose hand in hand.

Juniper's gin-joint legacy is easily evoked by the pungent aroma of a few crushed ripe berries. Many birds feast on them and spread the seeds in their droppings.

LICHENS
Two Organisms in One

HARD, BRITTLE and dormant when dry, with a little rainfall lichens transform into a soft, spongy, glowing carpet, a delight to bare feet. A rocky open area can sport a riot of different lichen species, a veritable world unto itself. Deriving their sustenance from thin air, lichens are the hardiest of all plants, with some surviving more than a year without water. Others thrive around hot springs at temperatures above 200°C (392°F), while in Antarctica, 400 species flourish. Crustose lichens form a wafer-thin living layer over bare rock on the Canadian Shield, continuing a process of colonization that began hundreds of millions of years ago when plant life first edged its way from the sea onto sterile, barren land.

Lichens gained a foothold on dry ground through a unique symbiosis of two plants in one. All lichens are combinations of fungal threads entwined around cells of algae. The fungi provide shelter, shade and water-absorbant tissues for algae. The algae capture the sun's energy with their chlorophyll to photosynthesize and make carbohydrate food for both organisms from rainwater and carbon dioxide in the air. Although lichens have no roots, they stick to bare rock and produce acids that slowly break down stone, creating depressions to anchor themselves more securely. Mineral grains of broken

Average annual rate of growth of map lichen: Less than 1 mm (0.25 in)

Average annual rate of growth of other lichens: 2–4 mm (0.1–0.2 in)

Earth's land surface on which lichens are the dominant vegetation: 8%

Variety of colours: Green, grey, black, red, orange, brown, pink, white, yellow, lilac

Lichen eaters: Moose, deer, northern flying squirrels, snails, slugs, moth caterpillars, mites, termites

Number of North American birds that use lichens for nesting material: 46

Date first land plants emerged: 400–500 million years ago

Number of lichen species in Ontario: 700–800

Number of lichen species worldwide: 15,000–20,000

Also see: Algae, Fungi, Moss, Soil

183

rock gradually mix with past generations of decayed lichens, a process that created the world's first organic soil on land. As mosses and larger plants evolved, they took root in these pockets, expanding the soil base to eventually clothe the Earth in an ever-thickening mantle that sustains all terrestrial life.

Crustose lichens are the pioneers, clinging flat on rock, bark and soil and growing outwards in crusty rings. About half of Ontario's lichen species are in the crustose group. They grow very slowly. Some, such as the round

Round patches of light-green map lichens form colonies that are up to 5,000 years old

patches of light-green map lichens, form colonies that are up to 5,000 years old. Another type of crustose lichen grows at the waterline, leaving even black tracings that mark the high-water point of lakes and streams.

Foliose lichens are also flat, but are attached to surfaces by small filaments only at their centre. They often have curled edges and leaflike lobes. Rock tripe, which grows in black or dark brown clusters on granite, is one of the most common. Crispy when dry, it becomes rubbery in the rain, with its underside like velvet. A third group—fruticose, or shrubby, lichens—are three-dimensional, growing like miniature, scale-model bushes, such as the distinctly branched, silver-green reindeer moss, which grows on open ground or in light shade. Other fruticose lichens, including the pale

yellow-green old man's beard, hang in wispy strands from trees. Canadian naturalist-artist Aleta Karstad reports identifying 20 types of lichens on one climb up a white spruce, each occupying a different zone.

A lichen is named for the fungus rather than the alga in the pairing, because the fungal portion makes up about 95 percent of the lichen. More than one type of alga may also be present. Algae reproduce asexually, by cell division, within the lichen, while the fungus grows tube- or flask-shaped fruiting bodies (photo on p. 183) that spread spores in the wind. The spores must land where the right kind of alga is already present in order for a new lichen to develop. But most commonly, lichen reproduce by fragmentation, their broken-off pieces starting a new colony.

Instead of dying when there is no water, lichens simply go dormant, often appearing dead. When it does rain, some species can hold up to 30 times their dry weight in water, which in turn can be absorbed by other plants, along with the nutrients it contains. But because they are designed to maximize water retention and do not lose any tissue during the cold months, lichens can't filter out air pollutants. Accumulated toxins in their tissues soon kill them, which is the reason they seldom occur near urban areas.

Lichens' own natural, bitter acids make them unpalatable to humans. When food was scarce, however, native peoples and northern explorers sometimes resorted to eating rock tripe and various other species. Some of the acids and the negative effects on the digestive system were neutralized by boiling. Natives also found partially digested lichens from the stomachs of slain caribou much easier to eat. Many historians even believe that the manna that nourished the biblical Israelites in the Sinai may have been greyish white lichens that are sometimes blown from rocky areas into the desert lowlands. There are historical accounts of these lichens piling up to 15 centimetres (six inches) deep over wide areas and feeding large numbers of people and livestock.

Two species are still eaten by local Bedouins.

Lichens were also used in antiquity to produce soft-coloured dyes and medicine. The word *lichen* is taken from the Greek term for "leperous," both for its scaly appearance and because it was used to treat the disease. In North America, native peoples used reindeer moss to treat fevers, coughing, convulsions and jaundice. Natural antibiotics produced by lichens for protection against microscopic grazing organisms have been extracted and used by humans in modern times. Lichens also provide fibres used in clothing, unique chemicals for cosmetics and stabilizing perfumes and the dye used in litmus paper.

WILD MINT
That Cool, Refreshing Feeling

ALONG A SUNNY stream bank or beaver pond, the fresh scent of wild mint, with its invigorating kick, usually gives the plant away before it's seen. In its many varieties, mint has struck the nostrils of people around the world from the beginning of civilization. It was spread on the floors of temples and public buildings to sweeten the air and was used in burials to cover up the smell of death. The Greeks said the nymph Minthe was transformed into the first mint plant by the goddess Persephone after attracting the amorous attentions of her consort Hades, ruler of the underworld. Even well into Christian times, mint leaves placed with dead bodies were said to ward off Hades, or the devil, by reminding him of the incident.

Mint has also long been a common spice, medicinal herb and even aphrodisiac when mixed with vinegar. Menthol, a clear, crystalline alcohol distilled from the oil of peppermint leaves, has a mild anesthetic effect on nerves, while at the same time stimulating sensitivity to cold and creating a cooling, soothing feeling. The sensation in the mucous membranes makes menthol medicine effective for colds, while menthol oil dulls itching. For the same reason, candy mints are helpful for upset stomachs after eating.

Wild mint, the only mint native to North America, has qualities similar to peppermint—which was created by cross-breeding in Europe—but is not as strong. The juice of fresh, crumpled wild mint leaves can soothe the irritation of a mosquito bite. Both natives and Europeans brewed a tea from its leaves to relieve fevers, stomach- and headaches. Drinking the juice of its fresh leaves even helps to cool hot, overexerted bodies.

Relatives of mint: Catnip, sage, thyme, basil, rosemary, lavender, bergamot

Height: 15–60 cm (6 in–2 ft)

Alias: Canada mint, field mint, la menthe du Canada, Mentha arvensis

Leaves: 2–8 cm (0.8–3 in) long, serrated, pointed at the tip

Flowers: Tiny, tubular, white to purple-pink blossoms with 5 petals each, in dense clusters where leafstalks meet the main stem, appearing in summer

Seeds: 4 tiny seeds to each blossom, catapulted by stiff stems whipped by wind or passing animals

Stems: Distinctly 4-sided, usually hairy

Preferred habitat: Mint forms dense mats along stream banks, lakeshores, meadows and other moist, rich sites

MOCCASIN FLOWER
An Orchid That Plays the Odds

L IKE OTHER FOREST ORCHIDS, the moccasin flower is highly specialized, near the summit of high-tech wildflower development. During its three-week blooming period in June, the flower's beautiful lower petal curves inwards to form a large hollow chamber, like a slipper. It is called an insect-ambush design. Bumblebees are especially attracted to the flower's splash of pink and its slight scent. Pushing her way through the long slit where the two curled lips meet at the front of the flower, a bee is sadly surprised when she gets inside. There is little or no nectar to reward her efforts, and the front doors do not bend backwards to let her out. There is light, however, coming from an opening at the top of the flower, which the bee follows to escape. Precisely placed stamens deposit their pollen on the bee's back on her way out through the narrow passage.

Dependent on limited encounters with forgetful bees, only about two percent of moccasin flowers are successfully fertilized each year

Since the ungratified bee is not about to repeat the same mistake with nearby moccasin flowers, she leaves them alone. But the pollen remains stuck on a part of her back that she cannot clean with her legs. The bumblebee's memory not being perfect, the bee may be lured by a distant moccasin flower's deceptive beauty at a later point, again crawling through and cross-pollinating it.

The whole process is still a long shot, dependent on limited encounters with forgetful bees. Studies show that only

Alias: Pink lady's slipper, nerve root, squirrel's shoes, stemless lady's slipper, old goose, two-lips, Indian moccasin, *le sabot de la vierge, Cypripedium acaule*

Seeds: Up to millions produced by a single flower in a green capsule, about 4 cm (1.5 in) long, with three ribs, which split in autumn to release seeds to wind

Height: 30–40 cm (12–16 in)

Flower: Pink, with 2 narrow, inconspicuous upper petals and one large, specialized lower petal curling inward to form a hollow sack, about 5 cm (2 in) long

Leaves: 2 large, pointed leaves, 10–20 cm (4–8 in) long, attached near the base of the stem; shiny, dark green with parallel veins

Preferred habitat: Acidic soil in coniferous and mixed forests and bogs

Companion plants: Trailing arbutus, bearberry, violets, leatherleaf, bog orchids

Range: All of Ontario except far north. Also found in all other provinces except British Columbia

Designation of moccasin flowers in Iroquois lore: The whippoor-will's shoes

Folk-medicine applications: Roots used as a sedative, to calm nerves, relieve headaches, treat tremors, epilepsy, fever and hysteria

Origin of name: From *orkhis*, Greek for "testicle," referring to the shape of roots

Number of orchid species native to Ontario: 67

Number of orchid species worldwide: 20,000–35,000

Also see: Bees, Fungi, White Trillium

about two percent of moccasin flowers are successfully fertilized each year. They play the odds, by being very long-lived and by producing hundreds of thousands of seeds that spread like dust in the wind when their lucky number does come up. They also propagate themselves by spreading runners that send up more flowers.

Orchid seeds are much smaller than those of all other flowering plants, lacking any significant store of protein to nourish them. Instead, they form tiny sprouts beneath the ground that join with fungal threads to form a close symbiotic relationship. Extensive fungal networks collect nutrients and water for the orchid, while the plant transfers some of the sugars it produces through photosynthesis to the fungus. Growth is slow at first. It may take a dozen years for a moccasin-flower seed to produce a blossom.

All orchids are highly specialized for their own niche. Each forms a partnership with a different fungus species. A moccasin flower's needs are so specific that in less-diverse environments, such as regularly sprayed forest plantations, few survive with the disappearance of bumblebees. Charles Darwin, recognizing in orchid diversity an ideal model for explaining how natural selection works, wrote an entire book on them as the sequel to his earth-shaking *Origin of Species*. The multitude of ways orchids are pollinated by insects, he concluded, "transcend in an incomparable manner the contrivances and adaptions which the most fertile imagination of man could invent." Or as Shakespeare before him wrote, "There are more things in heaven and earth..."

MOSS
The Second Wave of Vegetation

MOSS OFTEN GROWS thickest on the north side of trees because, in the northern hemisphere, the north side receives less sunlight and doesn't dry out as much as a southern exposure. Having no true roots, only filaments called "rhizoids" for anchors, moss thrives in moist conditions, getting all its nutrients from rain, snow, humidity, dust or organic matter that collects on it. Ground moss often grows in rounded, furry clumps that minimize moisture loss.

The lack of roots allows moss to grow almost anywhere, without need of fertile soil. Some species grow only on moose droppings. Moss is often the second wave of vegetation established in rocky spots, latching on to pioneer lichens and taking advantage of the moisture and nutrients they hold. Sometimes moss comes in even before lichens, growing on bare granite rock. Over centuries, soft moss mats help build up a layer of organic soil as they decay, allowing more advanced plants to take root.

Though moss functions very much like lichen, it makes its own chlorophyll and has no need of an algae-fungi partnership. Deciduous-forest mosses, such as plush green mats of hairy cap moss, are like spring flowers, doing most of their growing after the snow melts and before forest leaves open and block off both rain and sunlight. Each hairy cap moss plant is either a male or female. Males have a cup-shaped structure at their tip. They transfer their sperm to the female plant tips through a film of moisture coating the moss bed, or with the splash of a raindrop. A fertilized egg develops into a new plant with a spore capsule at the end of a long

Average number of spores in the fruit head of hairy cap moss: 65 million

Height: 0.5 mm–70 cm (0.03 in–2.3 ft)

Age of oldest moss fossils: 320 million years old

Number of moss species in Ontario: About 450

Number of moss species worldwide: More than 15,000

Number of sphagnum moss
species worldwide: 350
Number of clubmoss species
in Ontario: 10
Also see: Lichens, Soil, Wetlands

stem rising above the green moss mass. When the capsule opens, the spores are spread by the wind.

Aquatic moss grows with long, green, serrated leaves, like wet shag rugs, on top of rocks in fast-flowing streams, waterfalls and headwaters. Water moss thrives on high levels of carbon dioxide, which in a fast-moving stream has not had a chance to escape into the air. Among the many minute lifeforms inhabiting water-moss mats are one-celled diatomaceous plants, which contain glassy silica and sparkle in the light.

Native peoples used dried sphagnum as diapers because of its superabsorbency

Sphagnum moss, on the other hand, colonizes and dominates the still, stagnant water of bogs, forming springy mats several feet thick across the surface. Sphagnum grows in long strands with small leaves only one cell thick. The leaf's small green, living cells are interspersed with much larger porous dead cells that balloon with water. Native peoples used dried sphagnum as diapers because of its superabsorbency. As sphagnum mats grow and thicken, the large dead cells of long-covered layers continue to absorb and transfer water up to the top living layer, like a giant sponge.

A further kind of common "moss" is actually not a moss at all, but a distant relative of ferns. Clubmosses, or running pines, are, like ferns, miniature descendants of large spore-bearing trees that flourished 300 million years ago. Some species, in fact, look like miniature evergreen trees, no more than two or three centimetres (about one inch) tall, attached to horizontal ground runners, often forming dense carpets. The fine, yellow dust of clubmoss spore cones was inhaled by natives to stop nose bleeds, creating, in effect, a nasal powder keg, since the highly inflammable spores were also once used in fireworks, photo flashes and theatrical explosions.

POISON IVY
'Leaves of Three, Let It Be'

THREE POINTED LEAVES, or leaflets, are always cited as the warning identification of poison ivy, a rare northern member of the tropical cashew group, but there are many plants, such as raspberry, that feature leaflets growing in threes. Further complicating the issue, poison ivy can take widely differing forms. It can grow as herblike ground cover, a low woody shrub or a vine on the ground, or up trees, with long rootlets clinging to bark crevices. The leaflets are usually shiny, waxy green, with a slight notch and/or a few irregular teeth along the edges. They may be wide or narrow, but one side of the leaflet is usually a little bigger than the other. They also tend to droop. In the cluster of three, the two lower leaflets meet close together, while the middle one is separated from them by a little space. In its shrub form, poison ivy often grows in dense patches, in which it spreads quickly by underground runners.

All of a poison-ivy plant's tissues contain a pernicious oil that can cause a painfully itchy rash, breaking out in bead-like blisters one or two days after contact. The rash usually lasts less than two weeks, disappearing as the affected skin is

Remedies for relieving itching: Soap and water, calamine lotion, wet compresses of equal parts whole milk and ice water, or baking soda in cold water, plain cold water, scented fern

Height: Shrub form 0.1–2 m (4 in–6.6 ft); vine form, either running along the ground or up trees, can be more than 15 m (49 ft)

Leaves: Branching into 3 slightly asymmetrical, pointed leaflets, 7–15 cm (3–6 in) long, sometimes with irregular, jagged edges, but can be smooth; reddish or purplish when they unfold in May or early June, shiny green in summer, turn bright red in early fall, yellow in shaded areas

Flowers: Tiny, waxy, greenish white, in small 5-cm (2-in)-long clusters branching from where leafstalks meet main stem beneath leaves, appearing June to Aug.

Berries: White or dull greenish yellow, about 5–6 mm (0.2 in) wide, in clusters on long stalk, begin appearing in mid-July, may remain on plant all winter

Roots: Long, woody, underground stems

Alias: Poison creeper, markweed, 3-leaved ivy, climbing sumac, picry, climath, l'herbe à la puce, Rhus radicans

Preferred habitat: Forest gaps and edges, along paths, stream banks, open woods, meadows, islands, swamps, rocky ridges

Closest Ontario relatives: Poison sumac and other sumacs that are not poisonous

Range: Southern Ontario to about Cochrane and Kenora. Also found in all other provinces except Newfoundland

lost in the normal process of shedding. Even in winter, when it has lost its leaves, the plant's blackened twigs and berries are hazardous. Sweet-smelling smoke and vapour from burning poison-ivy branches can also cause the rash. The oil can remain active on shoes or unwashed clothes or on pets for a week and sometimes even for years.

Depending on the dose, it can take minutes or hours for the resin to bond with the skin. It can be washed off with soap and water before that happens. Rubbing the juice of crushed jewelweed leaves and flowers—which often grow near poison ivy—immediately after contact is an Ojibway and folk remedy that seems to work for some people.

> *Even in winter, when it has lost its leaves, the plant's blackened twigs and berries are hazardous*

Not everyone is affected to the same degree. All humans are said to be immune after their first contact, but an estimated 70 percent develop allergic reaction after subsequent encounters. Some may acquire only a mild itch. Light-skinned people are more prone than those with dark complexions. But any one person's susceptibility may change with time, depending on her or his body chemistry, diet and exposure to the sun.

There is actually nothing toxic about poison ivy. Humans bring the trouble on themselves with a defence reaction by their immune systems. Most animals don't seem to be bothered at all by poison ivy. Rabbits, deer and mice eat the leaves and stems. Many species of birds and rodents gorge on the shrub's small berries with no ill effects, spreading its seeds in their droppings. Poison-ivy leaves exposed to sunlight turn bright red, like their close sumac relatives, literally waving a red flag to migrating birds that berries are available below to fuel their flights.

WHITE TRILLIUM
Seven Years to First Flowering

DURING THE FIRST World War, when the public longed for an official flower to mark the graves of soldiers, federal bureaucrat James Burns Spencer proposed the white trillium as a national emblem for Canada. He said the white petals bespoke purity, while their number represented the Holy Trinity and the foundations of the British Empire—England, Scotland and Ireland. Though a national flower was never named, Spencer's arguments, and the votes of thousands of high-school students, led Queen's Park in 1937 to name the trillium Ontario's floral emblem.

White trillium is one of the monarchs of the spring ephemerals. Like other early forest flowers, its reign is brief, taking over from the hepaticas, bloodroot and trout lilies in May, and lasting for two to four weeks, until deciduous tree leaves unfold and cut off the light overhead. Spring forest flowers take advantage of the time between the thawing of the soil and leafing out, when the sheltered woods are actually warmer than open fields, to grow very rapidly. Naturalists say dead leaves may be heard rustling on still nights as the flowers push their way up from the ground— the sound of plants growing. Meadow flowers, on the other hand, with the benefit of the sun all the time, bloom throughout summer to early autumn.

Being sheltered by trees, forest flowers must depend on insects rather than the wind for pollination. Spreading out tender, colourful petals to attract the six-legged pollinators, spring ephemerals are the essence of fleeting beauty. Trilliums are considered unspecialized flowers because, like

Name origin: From Latin *tres*, meaning "three," in reference to number of petals, leaves and sepals on each plant
Height: 30–45 cm (12–18 in)
Alias: Great white trillium, wake-robin, large-flowered trillium, trinity lily, bath flower, white lily, *le trille blanc, Trillium grandiflorum*
Flowers: 3 white, pointed petals, 2.5–8 cm (1–3 in) long, fading to pink before they die; yellow organs at centre; 3 narrow, sharply pointed, green sepals beneath petals

Berries: Dark red, hexagonal, appearing in mid- to late summer, about 9 or 10 seeds in each

Leaves: 3 wide, pointed, smooth-edged leaves, 3.5–16 cm (1.5–6 in) long, meeting together at stem below flower; wither by mid- to late summer

Roots: Thick, tuberlike rootstock; roots reach at least 12 cm (5 in) below surface

Pollinators: Bees, beetles, flies

Preferred habitat: Rich soil in mature deciduous forests

Companion trees: Sugar maple, beech

White trillium range: Southern Ontario to Sault Ste. Marie and Lake Nipissing. Also found in Quebec

Red trillium range: Southern Ontario to the southern boreal forest

Number of trillium species native to Ontario: 4

Number of trillium species world-wide: About 40

Also see: Bees, Lowbrush Blueberry, Sugar Maple

the world's first flowers, which appeared about 120 million years ago, their simple petals are on a horizonal plane, offering a broad landing pad for incoming insects. Herbivorous mammals tend to leave most flowers alone because many contain psychoactive chemicals that have a bitter taste.

Trillium seeds have nutritious green handles that ants grab and drag into their nests. Ants eat only the handles, leaving the seeds to sprout. Birds and small mammals probably eat trillium berries and spread the seeds in their droppings.

Reproduction requires great amounts of energy from plants. Trilliums, with the limited sunlight they receive in spring before the forest canopy unfurls, take about seven years from the time the seeds sprout until they produce their first flowers, all the while storing energy captured by their leaves in their thick roots. If the leaves are picked, the plant usually dies. When it's ready, a trillium takes about one month to produce a flower. Because its sunlight window of opportunity is much shorter than that, the plant actually pre-forms the flower in a tightly packed bundle at the tip of its root the year before it blooms, allowing it to sprout and inflate as soon as the soil thaws enough to water its roots the following spring.

Many native peoples brewed tea from trillium root for menstrual cramps, or made it into a poultice to be placed on sore eyes. The Ojibway innovated an early form of innoculation by spreading the juice of ground, boiled trillium roots on rheumatic joints and then puncturing the skin with thorns or bone needles.

Native peoples also ate red-trillium roots as an herb to help stop bleeding after childbirth and for many other ailments. Red trillium, which also blooms in May, is more tolerant of acidic soil than white trillium and becomes more common in rocky Canadian Shield, especially highland, areas. It is dark purple-red with straight-edged, sharply triangular petals, though it is also sometimes light yellow. Red trillium has no nectar, but is pollinated by carrion flies, attracted by its rotting-flesh smell. A similar strategy is used by skunk cabbage and jack-in-the-pulpit.

WATER LILY
Bloom of the Gods

THE LOTUS FLOWERS sacred to Buddhists, Hindus, ancient Egyptians and Mayans are tropical relatives of Ontario's water lily. Some water lilies are eaten in parts of Africa because of their hallucinogenic effects, which ethnobotanists speculate may have been at the root of the lotus's universal status as a sacred plant. The Buddha, Brahma and Ra are often portrayed seated on lotus flowers. In these cultures, the lotus represents the primal womb of Mother Earth. Because it floats, radiant and serene, in stagnant ponds, the flower symbolizes the powers of light and beauty emerging from darkness. Similarly, the floating leaves, which remain dry on top, represent the inner self unsullied by the temptations of the senses.

Lily pads are designed to remain dry on top because, unlike land plants, their upper surface rather than their underside has air-breathing pores. If a lily pad is blown over, the waxy, waterproof upper surface does not stick to the water as the underside does. The red pigment of the leaf's underside also increases its temperature slightly above that of water. The extra heat helps the leaf get rid of the excess water through transpiration from pores on the upper surface,

Flowers: Up to 15 cm (6 in) wide, with many white petals around yellow centre; strong fragrance similar to licorice; blooms in summer

Alias: Fragrant water lily, water nymph, sweet-scented water lily, water cabbage, toad-lily, lotus, *le nénuphar blanc*, *Nymphaea odorata*

Ojibway name: *Anung Pikobeesae,* "star fallen in the water." According to one legend, water lilies are the embodiment of a star maiden who chose to live on Earth close to people

Leaves: Up to 25 cm (10 in) wide, dark green, waxy on top, purple-red on underside, round or heart-shaped, with a V-shaped cut to the centre; floating separately from flowers

Seeds: 600–700 per flower, mature in late summer or early fall

Roots: Up to 1 m (3.3 ft) long and 6 cm (2.4 in); thick, heavy

Preferred habitat: Calm waters 15 cm–5.5 m (6 in–15 ft) deep in bays, ponds and slow streams

Range: Southern Ontario to midboreal forest. Also found in all eastern provinces and Manitoba

Average sodium content: 9,375 parts per million

Average sodium content of terrestrial plants: 9 parts per million

Number of native Ontario water lily species: 3

Number of water lily species worldwide: 35–40

Also see: Beaver, Moose, Porcupine

keeping the plant buoyant. Water-lily stems have air tubes that keep them afloat as well, enabling the leaves and flowers to reach the surface for light and air in water that is often low in oxygen and too murky for sunlight to penetrate far beyond the surface.

Water lilies survive winter by withdrawing all their nutrients into their deep, thick rootstocks in the mucky sediment. As soon as the ice is gone in spring, they send up new floating stems, with leaf and flower buds ready to sprout when they reach the surface. The flowers ensure cross-pollination by having their male, pollen-producing parts mature later than the female pistil. Nectar-feeding insects picking up pollen on older flowers cross-pollinate the younger ones as they check them out. The flowers open early in the morning, but close by midafternoon, possibly conserving the pollen to ensure overlap between young and old flowers.

After blooming for four or five days, a fertilized flower closes for good. At the same time, its stem begins to coil, gradually pulling the flower beneath the surface, where seeds develop for three to four weeks. Eventually, large, air-filled capsules with many seeds break off from the shrivelled stems in late summer and autumn and float away. As the slimy pod membrane dissolves, seeds sink to the bottom. A seed takes about three years to produce a flower. New plants are also started by spreading rootstocks and root fragments that break off and are carried away.

Because water lily rootstocks are so efficient at storing nutrients, they are a mainstay of beavers, moose and even fish-eating loons in warm months. The plant's high sodium levels make it an important salt source for many vegetarian animals, such as porcupines. Native women pulled up the rootstocks in spring and late fall, when their nutrients are most concentrated. The roots are high in sugar and starch, and can be eaten like potatoes after soaking and boiling to get rid of bitter tannins. Seeds can also be eaten raw or ground into flour, while leaf and flower buds are eaten in salads.

TREES

LOOKING OUT *from a hilltop over the seemingly endless expanse of forest in Ontario's interior, one may find it hard to imagine how loggers could ever have cleared such vast tracts of green. Yet much of the province, and almost all of central Ontario, have been visited by the axe and saw. Most of today's red and white pines have grown up since lumberjacks began felling the province's ancient towering forests 100 to 200 years ago.*

Luckily, central Ontario is blessed not only with the great pines, but also with many trees characteristic of two quite different forest zones to the north and south. Dominating hills in much of the region, sugar maples transform the countryside with rich hues of red, orange and yellow in autumn. At the same time, the boreal zone's wealth of birch and Christmas-tree forests of fragrant fir and spruce spill over into much of the central region.

Together these trees clothe the land and give it its character. They are the greatest expressions and storehouses of the life force in the wilderness. The lion's share of the sunlight is captured by tree leaves and needles and used to power phenomenal growth. Every day, each mature tree sucks up thousands of litres of water from the ground through its roots, releasing much of it in turn through pores in its leaves, moistening the forest air. Life is indeed at its richest inside a deep, dark forest.

SPECKLED ALDER
Little Tree with Special Powers

courtesy of Friends of Algonquin

BEING SMALL SHRUBBY trees, alders weren't given a second glance by the first lumberjacks hacking their way through Ontario's forests. Finnish loggers, though, seemed to have some intuition about these trees' special powers. When they introduced the Swede saw—which cut trees twice as fast as the old one-person crosscut saw—into Ontario's lumber camps in the 1920s, they used alder wood for their homemade saw frames, saying it had a spirit that kept lumberjacks from cutting themselves.

Before the saw-happy Finns came along, native peoples boiled alder bark to treat rheumatism and to make a poultice for wounds. Like willow and trembling aspen, the bark contains salicin, the active ingredient of aspirin.

Perhaps more than anyone else, Canadian beavers know the value of alder. Thriving in fast-growing, dense curtains along shorelines, it is their most common dam-building material. Alder's water-tolerant branches are particularly durable in beaver constructions.

In fact, speckled alder's unique qualities make it vitally important as a nourisher of all life in the forest—plant and animal, terrestrial and aquatic. Because its abundant cone clusters begin forming in late summer and don't release nutlets until autumn of the following year, alder feeds high-energy seeds or flowers throughout the year to a large variety of wood warblers and other birds. Its dangling catkin flowers, among the first to open in spring, attract hordes of bees. Thick, extensive lakefront or swampside alder tangles also provide shelter for both birds and mammals. Its roots, which

Average mature height: Up to 9 m (30 ft)

Width of trunk: Less than 15 cm (6 in)

Alias: Tag alder, grey alder, hoary alder, *l'aune commun, Alnus rugosa*

Bark: Reddish brown, smooth surface densely speckled with small, horizontal, pale marks

Leaves: 5–10 cm (2–4 in) long oval, pointed, dull green, with serrated edges and straight, distinct veins that feel like ribs on the underside; wrinkled above. Fall while still green in autumn

reach into streams and lakes to get oxygen from running water, help stabilize banks and provide shade and cover for aquatic creatures.

Unlike other trees, alder can also fix nitrogen from the air. Though it constitutes about 80 percent of the atmosphere, nitrogen is one nutrient most plants cannot absorb in its gaseous form. But it is needed to make proteins and enzymes in all life-forms. Alder, along with legumes such as clover and beans, has clusters of knobby chambers, called nodules, on its rootlets, containing bacteria that take nitrogen from the air and transform it into ammonia, a form plants can absorb. This ability promotes extremely rapid growth in alders.

Alder leaves contain three or four times as much nitrogen as the leaves and needles of most trees. When they are shed, they provide about 160 kilograms of nitrogen per hectare (140 pounds per acre). In the water, they feed aquatic insect larvae, injecting precious nitrogen into the entire aquatic food chain. On the ground, nitrogen compounds from fallen alder leaves are absorbed by other trees and plants. The high nitrogen content also causes the leaves to decay more quickly than most others, in about a year. Although it cannot grow in shade, alder has soil-enriching powers that make it an important pioneer species in burnt or cut-over areas. If logging companies, spraying to destroy "weed trees," kill too many alders, they may impoverish the soil and decrease the long-term chances of success for commercially grown trees.

Sex: Bunches of 3–5 dangling, cylindrical male catkins, 2 cm (0.8 in) long, appear in late summer and open in April, before leaves unfold, along with clusters of 2 or 3 tiny, oval female flowers

Seeds: 1.5 cm (0.6 in) long oval, woody cones open in fall to release winged seeds; cone may remain on tree for several more years

Buds: Dark red-brown, on a distinct stalk

Roots: Shallow, with clusters of coral-like nodules

Wood: Light, soft, pale brown, not very strong

Preferred habitat: Shorelines, swamp thickets, creeks, wet meadows

Companion trees: White cedar, red maple, black ash, balsam, poplar, willow, chokecherry

Companion plants and shrubs: Elder, jewelweed, red osier dogwood, sweetflag, stinging nettle, winterberry

Common nesters: Hummingbirds, alder flycatchers, golden-winged warblers, woodcocks

Common visitors: Ruffed grouse, goldfinches, redpolls, siskins

Range: All of Ontario to the tree line. Also found in all other provinces and territories

Number of alder species native to Ontario: 3

Number of alder species worldwide: About 30

Also see: Beaver, Fungi

BLACK ASH
Fabled Tree in Many Cultures

Average mature height:
12–18 m (40–60 ft)

Maximum height: 27 m (90 ft)

Average mature width of trunk:
20–60 cm (8 in–2 ft)

Alias: Swamp ash, basket ash, brown ash, *le frêne noir*, *Fraxinus nigra*

Leaves: Composites of 7–11 opposite, narrowly pointed, dark green leaflets, each 10–13 cm (4–5 in) long, with fine teeth on edges. Pale yellow turning rust early in autumn

Bark: Soft, light grey, corky with flaky ridges

Sex: Clusters of tiny, shaggy, greenish yellow, petal-less male flowers and smaller raggedy females, usually on separate trees

Seeds: 2.5–4 cm (1–1.5 in) long, green, flat, paddle-shaped and winged

Wood: Dark greyish brown with coarse grain, not strong, 641 kg/m³ (40 lb/cu. ft)

Preferred habitat: Rich loam or organic soil in swamp forests and other low, moist sites

Range: Southern Ontario into midboreal forest. Also found in eastern Manitoba, Quebec and the Maritimes

White-ash range: Rare north of Muskoka. Also in Quebec, New Brunswick and Nova Scotia

Number of hockey sticks made in Canada annually: Nearly 5 million

ASH TREES OCCUPY an important place in early mystical beliefs on both sides of the Atlantic. A common story among Algonkian-speaking peoples tells of the first humans emerging from a hole made in an ash by an arrow shot by the legendary Glooscap. Similarly, the Romans, Greeks, Vikings and others all had legends of the first people coming from an ash or other tree. The Norse world tree, Yggdrasil, which held Heaven and Earth, was a European ash, similar to the black ash.

Though a member of the southern olive family, the slender, straight-trunked black ash is common in swampy areas in Ontario, often in pure stands. It moves into the edges of swamps as they begin to dry up, though it may be surrounded by shallow water in spring and early summer. In its wet habitat, it usually grows slowly, and cannot live at all in shade. Black ash is easy to pick out because it is one of central Ontario's only trees with oval leaflets and twigs spreading out in pairs opposite each other.

Though black ash wood is weak, its upland cousin, white ash, holds a hallowed place in Canadian culture as the source of hockey sticks. Its strong elastic boughs, along with those of maple, were also used by natives to make bows, spear shafts, lacrosse sticks, axe handles and canoe ribs.

TREMBLING ASPEN
Stirred in the Slightest Breeze

MURMURING AND shimmering in the slightest breeze, the trembling aspen has a name that fits. The trembling is due to long, flat leaf stems that are more easily swayed by the wind than if they were round. According to certain European legends, aspens shake because the wood of Christ's cross was made from one. North American natives called the tree "noisy leaf" or "noisy tree," while in several European languages it is referred to, at least by the men, as "woman's tongue."

The forestry industry tends to look down on aspen because its wood is of little use except as pulp, largely for magazine stock. Along with white birch—which it resembles, though aspen bark is not papery and peeling or as white—it is considered a "weed tree" because it springs up so quickly after fires or clear-cutting on moist, well-drained sites. It can swiftly take advantage of new forest openings because its tiny, light seeds, borne on tufts of fluff, are carried for kilometres by the wind. Most aspens are clones of a successful tree, growing up around it from roots capable of starting new trees. Often after logging or a fire that is not too hot, surviving roots quickly reestablish a stand, sending up as many as 50,000 new shoots per hectare (2.5 acres). A hectare or more can be covered by clones of a few trees.

Portion of Ontario's forest made up of trembling aspen and other poplars: 19%

Average mature height: 12–18 m (40–65 ft)

Maximum height: 27 m (90 ft)

Average width of mature trunk: 20–25 cm (8–10 in)

Maximum width: 60 cm (2 ft)

Alias: Quaking aspen, golden aspen, mountain aspen, trembling poplar, popple, *le peuplier faux-tremble*, *Populus tremuloides*

Number of seeds per kilogram (2.2 lb): 6.5 million

Bark: Smooth, glossy, silver grey or light green, lightest on south side, with rough black patches; grey and furrowed with age

Leaves: Squat and rounded, with small pointed tip, 4–5 cm (1.5–2 in) wide, finely toothed edge, green above, silvery pale below

Sex: When 15–20 years old,

TREMBLING ASPEN

begins producing 4–5 cm (1.5–2 in) long, hanging strands of yellowish green flowers, called catkins, either all male or all female on a tree. Flowers open before leaves in Apr. or May for efficient wind pollination. Big seed crops every 4–5 years

Wood: Greyish white, close-grained, soft, brittle, not very strong, 400 kg/m³ (25 lb/cu. ft), but much heavier when green because it holds a lot of water

Roots: Shallow, very widespread

Preferred habitat: Moist, well-drained sand, loam or gravel soils, from bottomlands to upper slopes, where previous forest cleared by fire or other disturbances

Companion trees: White birch, white spruce, balsam fir, black spruce, jack pine, red maple, white cedar, speckled alder, other poplars

Companion plants and shrubs: Chokecherry, red osier dogwood, beaked hazel, bracken fern, mountain maple, raspberry, sedges, bunchberry, starflower, fragrant bedstraw

Range: All of Ontario to the tree line. Also found in all other provinces and territories

Number of species in the poplar family native to Ontario: 4

Number of species in the poplar family worldwide: 35

Photosynthesis: The production of sugars, starches and other materials from water, minerals, carbon dioxide and sunlight in green plant cells

Also see: Black Bear, Beaver, Red Pine, Ruffed Grouse

Despite all the bad press aspen receives in the human kingdom, it is actually a crucial forest tree. The sun-fed vitality that makes it grow by more than a metre (a yard) a year in its early youth packs an abundant store of energy for other life-forms. Its bark is the beaver's favourite winter food, while newly sprouted aspen leaves are the usual main course for bears in late May and June. Moose and deer feed heavily on freshly sprouted twigs and catkins. Aspen catkins contain about 20 percent crude protein, more than cereal crops. Porcupines, hares and mice prize its bark, which is a living layer that photosynthesizes like leaves. In winter, ruffed grouse depend heavily on aspen buds. Whole aspen trees are even ground into chips for an animal feed called "muka."

Young trees and fresh spring shoots, which have not yet built up chemical defences of phenols against browsers and insects, are preferred as food. Older leaves can double their phenolic concentration within three days after an insect attack on nearby branches begins. Such chemicals may have been responsible for the extremely bitter taste of the medicine pioneers and lumberjacks brewed from boiling the inner bark of aspen in water.

Among the nutrients packed into aspen leaves, and most plants, are beta-carotenes, molecules that trap and transfer the sun's energy for photosynthesis in chlorophyll. They are a vital link for all animal life, because when leaves are eaten, each beta-carotene breaks into two vitamin A molecules. Beta-carotenes give carrots, oranges, squash and egg yolks their colours. A related molecule, xanthophyll, which protects chlorophyll from burning up in the sun's rays, gives trembling aspen its pale yellow colour in autumn. Largetooth aspen, with its bigger leaves and fuller crown, turns a more brilliant gold about a week earlier. The yellow pigments are uncovered after trees withdraw nurtrients from leaves (to be stored in branches during winter), stopping the production of chlorophyll, which normally colours leaves by reflecting green light while absorbing the other colours of the spectrum in the sun's rays.

BEECH
Signpost of the Ages

Or shall I rather the sad verse repeat
Which on the beech's bark I lately writ

VIRGIL, ca. 1st century B.C.

A STAND OF BEECH TREES can have an almost surreal, storybook presence, its silvery smooth, curvaceous trunks like the gnarled limbs of sentient giants. The thin, seamless bark of beech trees is more like living skin than the bark of most other trees. On oaks, maples and conifers, dead bark cells gradually build up, crack open and form deep ridges or plates. Dead beech bark cells are soon shed like powder from the tree's surface.

Like skin, beech bark scars permanently, forming wound cork that rises up like a bump along the scar. These qualities have made beech a favourite signpost for lovers' initials and other graffiti since before Shakespeare's day. In fact, the word "book" is believed to be derived from the old Germanic word for beech, *boko*, because ancient runic inscriptions were carved on beechwood tablets.

According to one story, the tree actually triggered the greatest revolution of the written word ever, after Johannes Gutenberg, one day in the fifteenth century, idly carved

Average mature height:
18–25 m (60–82 ft)

Tallest known beech: 49 m
(160 ft) in Michigan

Average width of mature trunk:
60–100 cm (3–3.3 ft)

Maximum width of mature trunk:
120 cm (4 ft)

Alias: American beech, *le hêtre
à grandes feuilles, Fagus
grandifolia*

Average lifespan:
200–300 years

Maximum lifespan: More than
400 years

Bark: Smooth, light bluish grey,
thin

Leaves: 5–13 cm (2–5 in) long,
shiny green, oval-shaped and
pointed at end, serrated, with
straight, prominent veins,
papery texture

Sex: Tiny male flowers hang in
round, greenish yellow clusters

on long stalks, females with 2–4 petals on short stalks near branch tips; open after leaves; wind pollinated

Nuts: 2 13 mm (0.5 in) long, 3-sided, pointed nuts contained in round, reddish brown, bristled casings, 22% protein, 42% fat. Fall with frosts of late Oct. and Nov.; big crops every 2–8 years

Buds: 20–25 cm (8–10 in) long, thin and pointy

Roots: Shallow, widespread

Wood: Pale to reddish brown, hard, strong, 705 kg/m³ (44 lb/cu. ft), close-grained

Preferred habitat: Well-drained, sandy loam soil on hills

Companion trees: Sugar maple, yellow birch, hemlock, basswood, white pine, red maple

Companion plants and shrubs: White trillium, beaked hazel, wild ginger, Blue cohosh

Damaging agents: Thin bark makes it susceptible to frost cracks, sucking insects and even small ground fires

Parasites: Beechdrops, beech scale

Range: Southern Ontario to northwestern limits of Muskoka and Algonquin Park. Also found in Quebec, New Brunswick, Nova Scotia and Prince Edward Island

Number of beech species native to Ontario: 1

Number of beech species worldwide: 10

Also see: Black Bear, Sugar Maple

some letters in beech bark, then wrapped the letter shavings up in paper while still damp and carried them home. When he later discovered that they left impressions on the paper, a light bulb went on and the printing press was born.

Its thin skin does not allow beech trees to survive winters much farther north than Algonquin Park, or to withstand fires. Wounds also allow wood-rotting fungi into the tree, a common cause of demise for many beeches. But in the right conditions, the tree can be long-lived. It does not even start producing nuts until it is 40 to 60 years old. Black bears often cause beech wounds, clawing their way up the trunks to get at big nut crops. More damaging still, bears often leave "bear nests" in the crotch of a tree, where they sit and pull in branches while gorging, breaking limbs and twigs as they munch.

The nutritious nuts are edible to humans as well, as noted by the tree's scientific name, *Fagus*, from the Greek word for "eat." The original Indo-European word for "beech," *bhagos*, may have meant the same thing.

Beechnuts, like maple seeds, sprout fairly big, strong seedlings, whose roots can penetrate the forest's thick litter layer. Like maples, they are content in the shade, growing very slowly until a mature tree falls and brings the sun's light down on them. Eventually they come to dominate the canopy. In more open areas, older beech trees often propagate themselves by spreading out sucker roots, resulting in clumps of beeches around a mature tree.

In contrast to sugar maples, beeches tend to turn a dull yellow or bronze in the autumn. On lower branches and saplings, these leaves often don't fall, because their stem bases do not fully form the corky abscission layer that on most trees separates autumn leaves from the twig. Instead, they remain on the branch, becoming bleached by the winter sun, until they are pushed off by new leaves in the spring. Early settlers often stuffed dry beech leaves into their mattresses because they are springier than straw.

WHITE BIRCH

Invaluable to Woodland Peoples

BIRCHBARK HAS A SPECIAL quality that makes it famous: it resists water and decomposition. It can last for years on the moist forest floor and still burn long after the wood it surrounds turns to mush. Fossilized birch has been found in Siberia with bark still in its original state, while elsewhere birchbark provides some of the world's oldest manuscripts. This characteristic was of inestimable importance to woodland peoples, such as the Ojibway, who depended on the bark for their wigwams, canoes, containers, moose-calling cones, as a quick fire starter even when wet and to wrap their dead for burial.

Birchbark was an ideal material for the perfect design that is the canoe. It took two people about two weeks to make one, with men usually supervising and women doing most of the work. Bark was most easily stripped in early summer, whole tree lengths being used. Seams were stitched together with pliable spruce, cedar or tamarack roots and sealed with conifer resin. Ribs were made from strong, flexible spruce or cedar boughs. The canoes were swift, light to portage and easy to fix, their materials abundant everywhere without recourse to Canadian Tire. European explorers and fur traders quickly adopted birchbark canoes as the best means of travelling in the interior. Birch was also used to make boats in the boreal forests of Russia, but the true *canoe*—one of the first native words Columbus learned—is a New World perfection.

Perhaps because of its beauty, the birch was considered a magical tree in northern Europe. Brooms were made out of its twigs to sweep away evil, and the Maypole of pagan spring rites was a birch. The Ojibway said the white birch was a living reminder to abide by the word of their magician-deity Nanabush. In their legend, Nanabush thrashed a

Maximum height: 25 m (82 ft)

Width of trunk: 30–60 cm (1–2 ft)

Leaves: Light green, about 9 cm (3.5 in) long, spade-shaped, serrated, amber or yellow in fall

Alias: Paper birch, canoe birch, *le bouleau à papier*, *Betula papyrifera*

Sex: 7–10 cm (3–4 in) long, hanging greenish tan male flowers at twig tips and smaller, upright green female flowers farther back on branch; open before leaves for wind pollination, develop 10–12.5 cm (4–5 in) long brown, woody seed cones

Seeds: Tiny, 3.3 million to a kilogram, with 2 thin wings, released from 4 cm (1.6 in) long, hanging, caterpillarlike cones in early fall

Buds: Greenish brown, gummy

Wood: Pale brown, strong, hard, 625 km/m³ (39 lb/cu. ft), very warm burning

Pests: Bronze birch borer

Maximum lifespan: 150 years

Average age of reaching majority: 60–70 years

Portion of Ontario's forest made up of white birch: 7%

Preferred habitat: Sandy or silt loam bottomlands to upper slopes and ridges of disturbed sites, forest openings or lakeshores

Companion trees: Trembling aspen, red maple, white spruce, balsam fir, balsam poplar, pin cherry, willow

Companion plants and shrubs: Beaked hazelnut, red osier dogwood, chokecherry, strawberry, bracken fern, starflower, bunchberry, violets, fragrant bedstraw, wild black currant, bluebead

Frequent visitors: Common redpolls, pine siskins

Range: All of Ontario, except for extreme south, to tree line. Also found in all other provinces and territories

Number of birch species native to Ontario: 5

Number of birch species worldwide: About 50

Also see: Beaver, Black-capped Chickadee, Canadian Shield, Black Spruce, Trembling Aspen, Lakes

drowsy birch with a pine branch for allowing birds to steal his meat, which the birch was supposed to be guarding. The pine needles that stuck to the sap of the birch's oozing wounds are still evidenced by the numerous narrow, black marks in birchbark.

Fossilized birch has been found in Siberia with bark still in its original state

Though its thin, flammable bark makes white birch an unlikely fire survivor, flames are actually its salvation. The tree cannot grow in shade, but newly burnt-over areas provide sunlight for birch to take root and thrive, sometimes in pure stands. Birch can also resprout from a stump and its surrounding roots. After very fast initial growth, however, birch becomes susceptible to heart-rot, fungi and wood-boring insects. At about 60 years old, they often begin to decline rapidly. The rotting trees provide ideal sites for cavity-nesting birds and animals.

The more scattered yellow birch leads a far different life than its cousin. It can tolerate shade. But to take root, its delicate seeds must find an old rotted stump or other spot not covered by fallen sugar-maple leaves or hemlock needles typical in the forests where it grows. Stiltlike yellow-birch roots are often visible where the original seed-bed stump has disintegrated. Once established, yellow birch can live for up to 300 years and reach more than 30 metres (100 feet) into the sky. The orangish bronze bark gradually transforms on the trunks of older trees into thick, dark plates and furrows. Deer love yellow-birch seedlings because of their wintergreen taste, not shared by white birch.

WHITE CEDAR
The Tree of Life

Photo by Bill Ivy

CEDAR WAS REVERED by native peoples. To many, it represented the east, one of the four sacred directional elements (north, west and south were sweetgrass, tobacco and sage respectively). The sweet scent and smoke of its crackling, burning foliage was used to purify a person, place or thing, or to make offerings of thanks to the Creator. Even today, cedar leaf oil is used in perfumes and medicines, and as a deodorizer and insect repellent.

The tree's sacred status may have sprung from its powers to heal a vast array of ailments. Among cedar's many medicinal uses, an effective poultice was made from its fibres and placed on the eyes to cure snow blindness. Tea was also brewed from its foliage for headaches, congestion and scurvy. Like the needles of many other evergreens, cedar contains more vitamin C than oranges. Natives saved Jacques Cartier and his crew from the ravages of scurvy during their first winter in Canada, in 1536, with cedar tea. Cartier brought seedlings of the wonder tree back to France, where the king promptly named it *arbor vitae*, the "tree of life." Cedar (pictured above with a luna moth) is believed to have been the first North American tree planted in Europe.

Average mature height: About 14 m (46 ft)

Maximum height: 25 m (80 ft)

Average width of mature trunk: 30 cm (1 ft)

Maximum width of mature trunk: 1.5 m (4.8 ft)

Lifespan: Usually up to 300 years

Oldest in Ontario: 1,032 years

Alias: Northern white cedar, *arbor vitae*, swamp cedar, *le thuya de l'est, Thuja occidentalis*

Foliage: Light green, flat, waxy, scalelike splays

Bark: Light grey to reddish brown, stringy

Sex: Tiny male conelets on tips of leaves, female conelets usually on separate branches

Cones: 8–13 mm (0.3–0.5 in) long, in dense bunches at tips of branches, especially in top branches, pale green at first,

207

turning brown as they ripen by end of summer, fall off the following year

Seeds: Light chestnut brown, encased in two wings

Roots: Shallow, extensive

Wood: Light brown, soft, weak, 304 kg/m³ (19 lb/cu. ft), non-resinous, aromatic, snaps, crackles and pops when burned

Preferred habitat: Wet, organic soil along lakeshores, in lowlands, or thin, sandy loam soils on top of limestone on hill slopes and upland plains

Companion trees: Fir, black ash, white spruce, tamarack, black spruce, and red maple in wetter areas and swamps; yellow birch, hemlock, white birch, white aspens and poplar on drier upland sites

Companion plants and shrubs: Ferns, fragrant bedstraw, raspberry, black currant, violets, sedges, wild lily-of-the-valley

Frequent visitors: Pileated woodpeckers, pine siskins, crossbills, finches, white-throated sparrows, kinglets, warblers

Frequent nesters: Black-throated green warblers

Principal pests: Carpenter ants, leaf miners

Range: All of Ontario, except upper half of northwestern section. Also found in Manitoba, Quebec, New Brunswick, Nova Scotia and Prince Edward Island

Number of similar species worldwide: 6

Also see: Canadian Shield, Limestone, White-tailed Deer

The tree of life is also an apt name given cedar's amazing tenacity, as well as its ability to lean, bend, twist and turn to find the sunlight it must have to grow. Roots, similarly, snake through rocks and cliffs to wedge themselves into the narrowest crevices and tiniest pockets of soil. Branches of uprooted cedars can shoot up to become the trunks of new trees or can burrow into moist soil to form roots.

Communities of the cliff-side dwarfs probably form the most ancient old-growth forests in Ontario

In recent years, dendrochronologists—people who study tree rings—have discovered scraggly cedars growing in extremely harsh conditions, on the cliff faces of Mazinaw Rock in Bon Echo Provincial Park, and along the Niagara Escarpment, that are 400 to 1,000 years old. Most are only a few metres tall. Some, with annual growth rings only one cell thick, are considered the slowest-growing trees in the world. Protected in their inaccessible locations from wildfire and lumberjacks, communities of the cliff-side dwarfs probably form the most ancient old-growth forests in Ontario.

Cedar lives long on steep cliffs and wetlands because it is both drought and rot resistent. Its durability makes it highly favoured for hedges, fence posts and shingles. Having the lightest wood of any tree in Ontario, much less than half the density of oak, it has always been popular for canoe and boat frames.

Acidic soil is anathema to cedar. In the Canadian Shield, cedar is restricted mostly to lakeshores and bog edges, where moving groundwater can provide nutrients not available in the rocky, acidic ground. Farther south, cedar thrives in dense stands on thin soil over limestone bedrock and in wetlands. Deer, which love browsing on cedar foliage, often yard up in the shelter of such stands during winter.

BALSAM FIR
The Fragrance of the Forest

BALSAM IS DERIVED from an ancient Hebrew word for aromatic tree resins used for balms—soothing ointments or salves. In Ontario, it is the rich, sweet essence of the forest. The balsam fir's thick, sticky resin literally bubbles up beneath its bark, oozing from old knots and wounds and caking its buds and cones, making them difficult for squirrels and crossbills to eat. When fungus attacks, a fir increases sap production, laying it on thick where invading fungal strands seek to penetrate the tree's soft wood. Natives and lumberjacks took their cue from the trees and squeezed fir "gum" from the blisters to use as an effective antiseptic seal for cuts and wounds. Today the resin is used for Canada balsam, a glue for mounting specimens on microscope slides.

The gooey sap common to all northern conifers is, in fact, the key to their survival through winters too harsh for the watery sap of most deciduous trees. It acts as a sugar-rich natural antifreeze in the roots and branches, allowing the tree to hang on to its dormant waxy needles through the winter. As soon as temperatures rise above freezing, the needles can start photosynthesizing, allowing them to be productive through the entire short growing season. From spring thaw till June, the energy they capture goes to the season's new sprouting growth. Afterwards, as in other trees, most of the energy is used in forming new buds containing all the tissue for the following spring's shoots.

In pagan times, Germans celebrated the winter solstice Yule festival by bringing evergreen boughs, holding the promise of spring and providing shelter for visiting elves, into their homes. Hundreds of years later, they brought the

Average mature height:
  12–19 m (40–62 ft)

Average width of mature trunk:
  30–60 cm (1–2 ft)

Average lifespan: 60–70 years

Alias: Blister fir, white fir, balm of Gilead, church steeple, silver pine, *le sapin baumier*, *Abies balsamea*

Number of Christmas trees grown and sold in Ontario annually: 1 million

Bark: Grey and smooth, with horizontal specks and raised blisters filled with resin when young. Brownish scales form on older trees

209

BALSAM FIR

Needles: 2–3 cm (0.8–1.2 ft) long, blunt, dark green on top, white lines on underside; curving upwards in flat, horizontal rows on lower branches; remain on branch 3–4 years

Sex: Reaches puberty after about 20 years; very tiny purple-red male flower conelets clustered at base of needles along twig; much larger, dark female cones stand erect; wind pollinated

Cones: 5–10 cm (2–4 in) long, dark purplish, erect; mature in one season, then disintegrate on the branch, leaving behind pointy spindles; big crops every 2–4 years

Seeds: 130,000/kg, (60,000 per lb) fall from Aug. to late Sept.

Wood: White, soft, weak, fairly brittle, with coarse grain, 417 kg/m³ (26 lb/cu. ft)

Preferred habitat: Moist lowlands of silt loam soil, but also found in dry, sandy uplands

Average number of fir saplings in a healthy fir-spruce forest: 4,000/ ha (2.5 acres)

Average number of spruce saplings in a healthy fir-spruce forest: 500

Range: All of province, except extreme southwestern Ontario and far northern boreal forest. Also found in all other provinces except British Columbia

Number of fir species native to Ontario: 1

Number of fir species worldwide: About 40

Also see: Cedar, Humus, White Spruce

tradition with them to North America. It really caught on in Canada in the late 1800s after Queen Victoria, herself of not-distant German lineage, was pictured with her family gathered around a tabletop Christmas tree in the *London Illustrated News*. Balsam fir, along with white spruce and Scotch pine, continues to be the most popular choice for Christmas trees everywhere today.

In a forest of Christmas trees, firs can be distinguished from spruce at a distance by the way they taper more narrowly to a perfect point. Up close, fir can be seen to have flat needles, unlike four-sided spruce needles, which are easily rolled between the thumb and forefinger.

Because fir is more tolerant of moist soil and shade than white spruce, it forms pure stands much more often, its seedlings dominating the forest floor even where spruce tower above. Fir, however, is shorter-lived and more prone to many stresses. With a lower cellulose content, its wood is not as dense as spruce, allowing rot to set in when some trees are as young as 40 years old. Weakened firs, anchored by shallow roots, are easily toppled by the wind.

Fir forests can also be especially volatile tinderboxes. Spruce budworms love balsam fir above all other trees, creating huge tracts of soft, dry, dead and dying wood during outbreaks. The thick layer of needle litter on the ground also makes coniferous forests more prone to fires than deciduous trees. When humidity levels drop below 30 percent—as they often do in May and June in boreal forests—the fire hazard becomes extreme. Trees dry out, trying to keep their needles moist, and lose billions of gallons of water to the air through transpiration. Such conditions led to one of the worst infernoes in Canadian history, the Chapleau-Mississagi fire of 1948. Though no one was killed, it burnt for a month, covering 2,660 square kilometres (1,000 square miles), and blackening the skies with smoke clouds that necessitated street lights as far away as Texas to be turned on during the day.

HEMLOCK
Creating Clear, Sheltered Havens

EASTERN HEMLOCK IS not the poisonous herb Socrates was obliged to sample by the leading citizens of Athens in 399 B.C. The Old World toxic plant lent its name to our broad, graceful evergreen because European settlers fancied the scent of its burning needles was similar to that of poison hemlock. They eagerly learned the native practice of brewing teas from its twigs and needles.

Hemlocks have it made in the shade. They love moist, cool, rocky ground near lakeshores, ridge tops and north-facing hillsides in mixed forests. Where lower branches on other evergreens die and drop off as the shade above grows too great, densely needled hemlock limbs stretch out and flourish. Little sunlight penetrates through to nourish undergrowth on the forest floor, making for clear, sheltered campsites. A thick mat of constantly falling needles pro-

vides a soft bed while making the ground too acidic for most plants, save for the occasional yellow birch taking root in a dead log or stump.

Deer make themselves comfy in hemlock stands in the winter, when the tree's dense, flat needles and flexible horizontal boughs keep out deep snow. They create wintering yards below, nibbling on delectable hemlock and yellow-birch twigs. At the northern limit of the deer's range, Algonquin Park's once-thriving population depended heavily on hemlock yards for its survival. Logging in the nineteenth century created vast areas of new browse for deer, while largely sparing hemlock because the knots of its abundant branches render the lumber of little economic value. But vast numbers of park hemlock were cut in the 1950s and 1960s to provide shoring timbers for tunnels during the con-

Average mature height:
20–25 m (63–82 ft)

Average width of mature trunk:
50–120 cm (1.7–4 ft)

Alias: Eastern Hemlock, Canada hemlock, common hemlock, hemlock gum tree, hemlock spruce, white hemlock, weeping spruce, *la pruche de l'est*, *Tsuga canadensis*

Preferred habitat: Cool, moist, shady, often rocky locations in mixed hardwood forests, often near shorelines on north-facing slopes and in ravines

Bark: Scaly and orange-brown on a young tree, becoming deeply furrowed with broad ridges of purplish grey-brown bark as it matures

Needles: Flat, 1–2 cm (0.4–0.8 in) long, dark green on top, two white lines below

Sex: Each tree a hermaphrodite, with tiny yellow male flower cones and larger, pale green female flower cones appearing in May once every 2–3 years

Cones: 1–2 cm long, pale green ripening to red brown

Companion trees: Yellow birch, white pine, white spruce, sugar maple

Frequent visitors: White-winged crossbills, red-backed voles

Frequent nesters: Golden crowned kinglets, black-throated green warblers, black-burnian warblers

Oldest known tree: 988 years

Tallest known tree: 49 m (164 ft)

Wood: Harder than most softwoods, 416 kg/m³ (26 lb/cu. ft)

Lifespan of average needle: Several years

Companion plants and shrubs: Labrador tea, ferns, wild lily-of-the-valley

Range: Southern Ontario to just north of Lake Nipissing and the North Channel of Lake Huron. Also found between Lake Superior and Lake of the Woods, in southern Quebec, New Brunswick, Nova Scotia and Prince Edward Island

Number of hemlock species worldwide: 10–14

See also: White Birch, White-tailed Deer

struction of Toronto's subway. Already hard-pressed for food in a maturing forest, deer numbers plummeted with the loss of habitat. Several heavy winters in the late 1960s and early 1970s also contributed to their decline.

At the northern limit of the white-tails' range, Algonquin Park's once-thriving deer population depended heavily on hemlock yards for its survival

Once gone, hemlocks are not easily replaced. Direct sunlight dries out their seedlings, while other trees thrive. Instead, rooted in the shade, hemlock roots grow slowly, patiently awaiting their opportunity. A 200-year-old hemlock can look like a sapling and suddenly shoot dozens of centimetres up in a single growing season when an opening appears in the canopy above. Eventually, the deep green centuries-old trees come to dwarf their neighbours in mature forests.

RED MAPLE
Flowering Early for a Head Start

RED MAPLE IS NAMED for its bright purple-red shoots, buds, flowers, seeds and unfolding leaves in spring. Early settlers made red ink and dye by boiling its bark. In fall, however, its leaves are not simply red. Unlike most other trees, red maples most often feature either all-male or all-female flowers on one tree. Come autumn, the female trees change various shades of yellow or orange, while males range from orange-red to scarlet.

Because it is not as shade-tolerant as sugar maple, red maple is not as common. It's not as fussy as its cousin, however, about soil. Red maple often wins out in areas that are wetter for longer periods of the year or on dry, sandy sites. It also springs up on disturbed sites that previously held conifers, or on the forest fringe. A red maple's seeds are smaller and lighter than a sugar maple's, so can travel farther to find those sites. They also get a head start because red maples flower earlier in spring than most other trees and release seeds in late June.

The deeply notched silver maple—said to have inspired Toronto schoolteacher Alexander Muir to write "The Maple Leaf Forever" in 1867—also grows in swamps and on floodplains, but rarely anywhere else. The striped maple is a common understory shrub, with huge three-pointed leaves and distinctive vertical white stripes on its green bark. Another shrub, mountain maple, is abundant in Temagami's pine forests, where other maples are extremely rare.

Average mature height: 20–27 m (65–90 ft)

Tallest known red maple: 37.6 m (125 ft), in North Carolina

Width of mature trunk: 40–130 cm (16 in–4.3 ft)

Lifespan: Well over 100 years

Alias: Swamp maple, scarlet maple, soft maple, water maple, curled maple, *l'érable rouge, Acer rubrum*

Bark: Smooth, silvery grey on young trees, darker and ridged when older

Sex: Clusters of tiny bright red flowers, females on long stems, males in short bunches

Seeds: 2 cm (¾ in) long, in pairs with long wings

Wood: Light brown, moderately strong, hard, 609 kg/m³ (38 lb/cu. ft)

Leaves: 7–13 cm (3–5 in) long, with right-angled notches, toothed edges

Preferred habitat: Wet sites around swamps, sandy loam bottomlands, bogs and beaver ponds or dry, sandy soils

Most common companion trees: Black ash, white elm, red oak, white pine

Range: Southern Ontario to the southern boreal forest. Also found from Thunder Bay to Lake of the Woods and in all other eastern provinces

Number of maple species native to Ontario: 7

Number of maple species worldwide: About 150

Also see: Sugar Maple

SUGAR MAPLE
Sweetness, Colour and Pride

Average number of buckets of sap to make one bucket of maple syrup: 40

Average sugar content of sugar-maple sap: 3%

Average sugar content of maple syrup: 66%

Average height of a mature sugar maple: 24–27 m (80–90 ft)

Maximum height: 40 m (130 ft)

Average width of mature trunk: 60–90 cm (2–3 ft)

Maximum width: 1.5 m (5 ft)

Average lifespan: 200–300 years

Maximum lifespan: 400 years

Alias: Hard maple, rock maple, sweet maple, black maple, sugar tree, curly maple, bird's eye maple, *l'érable à sucre, Acer saccharum*

Average number of maples in a 15-year-old 1-ha (2.5-acre) stand: 50,000

Average number of mature sugar maples in a 1-ha (2.5-acre) stand: 38

Leaves: 7.5–13 cm (3–7 in) long, with wide, curving lobes, smooth edges

Bark: Dark grey, long, flat ridges curling out on one side

Buds: Reddish brown, pointed

Sex: Clusters of tiny greenish yellow flower catkins hanging from long stems at branch tips; sprout with leaves in May

Seeds: 4 cm (1.5 in) long, green, winged, joined in pairs, maturing in fall

A SUGAR-MAPLE LEAF graces the Canadian flag. In central Ontario's upland forests, sugar maple is the most common tree, though it is rare north of Algonquin Park. The tree's abundance is due to many qualities that might figuratively be attributed to the nation itself, among them strength, tenacity and the ability to grow in the shade of others.

Tough, early-sprouting sugar-maple seedlings are very shade-tolerant, sometimes covering the forest floor with up to 140,000 seedlings per hectare (2.5 acres). Many, however, live only five to 15 years in the limited light, while others may last 30 years. But if a space opens in the canopy above, the lucky seedling directly below wins the lottery and shoots upward. Once there, it hogs all the sunshine. A maple branch, with its large, abundant leaves, captures or reflects 90 percent of the sunlight hitting it. Beneath the eight to 12 leaf layers of the deep, solid canopy of a mature maple, few plants other than its own offspring can grow in the summer.

> *The wider and deeper the crown of a sugar maple, the more light it captures and the more abundant and sweeter its sap*

The amount of sunlight sugar maples receive is critical for both autumn colours and maple-syrup production in spring. Warm, sunny fall days spur the production of sugars in leaves. But cool nights below 7°C (45°F) cause a waterproof abscission layer to form at the end of leaf stems, trapping the sugars in the leaves. With the stem sealed, chlorophyll production stops and the leaf's green pigment fades. Red antho-

cyanin pigments are then formed, owing to the accumulation of sugars—the same pigments that colour cherries, grapes, beets, radishes and many other vegetables and flowers. The sunnier the autumn, the brighter the colours, with the best oranges and scarlets appearing on the most exposed or southern side of trees. The acidic soils of the Canadian Shield make for the deepest reds.

Sugar maples are among the first trees to change colour in September, having withdrawn much of the nutrients from their leaves back into their branches in preparation for winter. Eventually, as anthocyanins that remain break down, red and orange leaves join those in shadier parts of the tree in fading to yellow. Jack Frost is not responsible for painting leaves. He shrivels and oxidizes them, turning them brown.

In Ojibway legend, a stand of bright autumn maples near a waterfall hid Nokomis, grandmother of the fabled magician Nanabush, from a band of evil windigo spirits chasing her. Through the mist of the waterfall, the windigos were convinced they were staring at a blazing fire in which Nokomis must have died. Nanabush rewarded the sugar maples by giving them sweet, strong-flowing sap.

Illustration: Sugar-maple leaf (top) and red-maple leaf

Number of seeds produced per ha (2.5 acres) in sugar-maple stands: 500,000–10 million

Wood: Light yellow-brown, close-grained and often wavy, hard, heavy, strong and durable, 705 kg/m³ (44 lb/cu. ft)

Roots: Deep, widespread

Preferred habitat: Rich, deep, moist, well-drained sandy loam soil on glacial-till hills

Companion trees: Beech, yellow birch, hemlock, white elm, white cedar

Companion plants and shrubs: White trillium, juneberry, violets, beaked hazel, ferns, blue cohosh, wild ginger, wild lily-of-the-valley

Pests: Tent caterpillars, sugar-maple borers

Parasites: Maple trumpet skele-
tonizers, honey fungus, yellow
cap fungus, stereum fungus,
spongy rot fungus, mossy top
fungus

Secrets of maple resilience:
Glassy crystals in leaf tissues
and hard veins wear down
caterpillars' teeth. Tannins in
leaves taste raunchy to
mammals

Range: Southern Ontario to lower
rim of the boreal forest. Also
found in Quebec, New
Brunswick, Nova Scotia and
Prince Edward Island

Peak annual emissions of sulphur
dioxide (SO_2) from Ontario's 4
biggest acid-rain contributors
(Ontario Hydro; Inco and
Falconbridge in Sudbury;
Algoma Steel in Wawa) in past
years: More than 2 million
tonnes

SO_2 from Ontario's 4 biggest
acid-rain contributors in 1991:
862,000 tonnes

Legal limit of SO_2 emissions by
Ontario's 4 biggest contributors
in 1994: 575,000 tonnes

Ontario SO_2 emissions produced
by the 4 biggest contributors:
80–85%

Average annual decrease in
sulphite precipitation in Ontario
in recent years: 1%

Also see: Beech, Big Dipper, Deer
Mouse, Lakes, Red Maple

Both the Ojibway and Iroquois collected sugar-maple sap by placing a flat stick or reed in a gash in the bark and collecting the drips in birchbark containers or hollow logs. The first run of sap, during the time of greatest privation at the end of winter, was greeted with ceremonies of thanksgiving. The sap was boiled, then was strained or dried in the sun on sheets of birchbark. Much of the maple sugar produced was stored for use during the following winter. Until about the 1840s, this was the main source of sugar for pioneers as well.

Temperatures above 5°C (41°F) during March days and nights below freezing increase pressure within the tree, which stores sugars during winter in the dead-wood tissues of the trunk. Sap only flows if there is a tap hole or natural wound in the tree, providing an outlet for the pressurized, melted sugar-water solution. Once the tree's buds start opening, they create a continuous draw on the sap and quickly suck up the winter's store of sugars from it, making the sap no longer sweet.

The wider and deeper the crown of a sugar maple, the more light it captures and the more abundant and sweeter its sap. Over the past two decades, the crowns of many sugar maples in central Ontario have withered under the combined assault of acid rain, invading gypsy moths from Europe, low snowfalls and higher temperatures. Because soil nutrients dissolve into acidic water solutions more readily than usual, they are washed away in acid rain runoff more quickly than they can be replenished by decaying vegetation. At the same time, acid precipitation frees up 10 to 30 times as much aluminum into soil solutions as is normal. Aluminum is toxic to trees. To avoid absorbing it, roots diminish their uptake, further starving themselves of nutrients in the process. Once undernourished, trees fall easy prey to root- or heart-rot fungi and other natural afflictions.

RED OAK

'Beware of an oak, It draws the stroke'

THE TALL, WIDE CROWN of oak trees makes them particularly susceptible to being struck by lightning. Even in predominantly beech forests, oak is estimated to be hit by lightning 10 to 20 times as often as beech. When hit, oak often bursts into flame. The ancient Europeans saw in this spectacular phenomenon a direct connection with the gods, and the thunder tree was venerated above all others.

The most ancient Greek traditions depicted Zeus, the thunder god, as an oak or at least living in one. Oaks were sacred to Thor and Jehovah, both thunder-and-lightning deities. Oak was similarily the supreme god of the Gauls, and the name of the Finnish thunder god was Ukko, meaning "oak." Sacred oak groves were the scenes of oracles by Greek priestesses, ceremonies by the druids and Roman women beseeching oak nymphs for safe births. Roman poets wrote that acorns were the first food to sustain newborn humans. Even the oak tree's parasite, mistletoe, was deified

Average height: 18–24 m (60–80 ft)

Maximum height: 40 m (133 ft)

Average width of trunk: 30–90 cm (1–3 ft)

Maximum width: More than 120 cm (4 ft)

Lifespan: 200–300 years

Alias: Northern red oak, black oak, grey oak, champion oak, le chêne rouge, Quercus rubra

Leaves: Average 19 cm (7.7 in) long, 7–10 cm (3–4 in) wide, with 7–9 pointed lobes between V-shaped notches, unfold later than maple and beech in spring

Bark: Smooth and grey when young, flat ridges on older trees

217

Sex: Greenish yellow male flowers hang in long strands, tiny female flowers with 2–4 petals at the junction of twigs near the edge of canopy, open with or after leaves

Acorns: 2–3 cm (0.8–1.2 in) long, woody, brown, with reddish brown cap of scales; take 2 years to ripen; taste bitter and contain 8% protein and 37% fat

Buds: About 6 mm (0.2 in) long, pointy, shiny reddish brown

Roots: Deep, often with taproot

Wood: Reddish brown to pink, course-grained, very strong, hard, 665 kg/m³ (41 lb/cu. ft)

Preferred habitat: Rocky ridge tops and other dry uplands

Companion trees: White pine, trembling aspen, red maple

Companion plants: Beaked hazel, snowberry, bush honeysuckle

Frequent visitors: Scarlet tanagers, blue jays, ruffed grouse, cedar waxwings, nuthatches and many mammals in autumn

Pests: Gypsy-moth caterpillars, tent caterpillars, oak-leaf shredders, gall wasps, acorn weevils, wood-boring beetles, oak-leaf rollers, filbert worm moth, sap beetles

Range: Southern Ontario to hinterlands of Lake Huron's North Channel and Lake Timiskaming. Also found in a thin band from Thunder Bay to Quetico Provincial Park, and in southern Quebec, New Brunswick, Nova Scotia and Prince Edward Island

Number of oak species native to Ontario: 7

and is still hung at Christmas. Unable to shake pagan reverence for sites of sacred oaks, where sacrifices were made to older dieties, the Christian Church eventually took their sites by blessing them and erecting crucifixes and images of Mary.

Even the oak tree's parasite, mistletoe, was deified and is still hung at Christmas

In central Ontario, red-oak groves are most often found on dry, rocky ridge tops and south-facing slopes, where deep roots and tough, waxy leaves give the trees an advantage in finding and retaining scarce groundwater. Elsewhere, red oak is usually crowded and shaded out by much faster-growing, more shade-tolerant maples and beech. Oak also cannot withstand prolonged periods of extreme cold, and become increasingly rare north and west of Algonquin Park. Even where it is rare, red oak is very noticeable from a distance in the spring because its high levels of tannin—a bitter-tasting, acidic defence chemical against animal browsing—makes newly unfolding leaves bright red. Later, chlorophyll production kicks in to turn them green. When the green fades in October, the tannin pigment reemerges to colour hilltop oaks rusty brown. The leaves remain long after maples and other trees drop theirs. Tannin is also the compound, released by slowly rotting vegetation, that turns swamp water brown.

As autumn draws near, red-oak stands become the centre of attraction for a wide variety of wildlife. Deer, raccoons, chipmunks, ruffed grouse, wood ducks and nuthatches come from far and wide to munch on acorns, one of the most nutritious of woodland foods. Bears fatten up for hibernation by climbing up oaks and pulling limbs towards them to get at the acorns, often leaving conspicuous "bear nests" of broken branches behind. Squirrels, blue jays and white-footed mice help spread the seeds by storing acorns in various locations. Those they fail to retrieve have a high germination rate. Squirrel and blue-jay populations in some areas rise and fall from year to year with acorn-crop cycles. Millions of migrating passenger pigeons, which once blackened the skies over Ontario, were dependent on acorn and beechnut crops. Their extinction is believed to have greatly limited the oak's ability to spread.

Oaks are also a major attraction for many species of wasps, which lay eggs on leaves, twigs, acorns and roots. When the eggs hatch in spring, the wasp larvae eat burrows into the vegetation. In response, the tree starts building up dense tissue that gradually hardens around the cavity, forming a tumourlike gall. Oak leaves can have up to 100 tiny galls each. Other galls on branches may be five centimetres (two inches) long. Although beetles, moths, butterflies, aphids and flies cause galls on a wide variety of trees, they most commonly use oaks. A key chemical called purpurogallin, produced in nutgalls on oak trees, was recently discovered by researchers at the University of Toronto to prevent cell damage in labratory animals. It may eventually be used to treat arthritis, stroke and cancer.

The bur oak, with its large tapered leaves and burred acorns, also grows in central Ontario, but it is rare, restricted mainly to clay bottomlands. The great white oak, with its round-lobed leaves, is common south of the Canadian Shield. Bearing the best-quality wood of any oak, vast stands of white oak in eastern Ontario ranked next to white pine in importance to the loggers of the early 1800s. Because white oak wood is so dense and heavy, early river drivers had to lash timbers of pine to it to keep it from sinking. Red oak is also used for floors, furniture and trimmings.

Number of oak species worldwide: More than 200

Also see: Blue Jay, Red Squirrel, Thunder & Lightning

JACK PINE
Fire Frees Seeds to Sprout

Photo by Bill Ivy

Most famous jack pine: Subject of Tom Thomson's 1916 *Jack Pine*, painted, some say, on the shore of Grand Lake in Algonquin Park

Average frequency of fires in jack-pine forests: Every 125–180 years

Average mature height: 12–18 m (40–60 ft)

Average width of trunk: 20–30 cm (8–12 in)

Maximum width: 60 cm (2 ft)

Alias: Scrub pine, grey pine, banksian pine, pine princess, princy, *le pin gris*, *Pinus banksiana*

Needles: 2–5 cm (0.8–2 in) long, thick, stiff,rough, pointy, curved, in bunches of 2

Bark: Reddish brown to grey when young, turning with age to dark brown or grey, in large furrowed flakes

Sex: Tiny, dark, purplish female flowers near branch tips, light brown males in clusters at base of shoots in May

Cones: 2.5–7.5 cm (1–3 in) long, curved, in pairs, green at first, turning grey with age, sometimes fused into branch

Preferred habitat: Dry, sandy or rocky sites, especially in open

Range: Southern edge of Canadian Shield to northern boreal forest. Also found in tree plantations in southern Ontario and growing naturally in all other provinces except British Columbia, Newfoundland and Prince Edward Island

JACK PINE IS LIKE the poor cousin of the majestic taller pines. Though on ideal sites it can be straight, it is usually twisted, knotty and scruffy looking, with its small tufts of needles on downward-bending branches. Early settlers thought they poisoned the ground and futilely tried to clear them, only to find more sprouting up.

The truth is that jack pine is one of the few trees that will grow on very poor ground. It takes root in dry, sandy, rocky sites, often on steep, south-facing hillsides, where even hardy red pines have trouble. Its flexible, contorted limbs are wind resistent and it clings tenaciously to exposed sites. Being specially adapted for such conditons, jack pine is also ideally suited for growing in burnt-over or logged areas, particularly if damage to the soil has been severe and competing pioneer species such as aspen can't be supported. Unable to live in the shade of other trees, jack pines usually mark the spot of such a disturbance, growing in pure, relatively open stands.

Having little chance of success without their specific site requirements, jack pines do not even bother to release their seeds at regular intervals like other trees. Instead, most cones remain on the tree for up to 25 years, tightly closed, sealed in resin, until fire or temperatures above 47°C (116°F) in direct sunlight open them. Fires also release minerals from burnt vegetation into the soil to nourish the new seedlings growing up from the ashes. If no new fires come along in their lifespan, jack pines are eventually replaced by shade-tolerant species growing beneath them, such as fir, white spruce and red maple.

18. *Putting needles and cones (first closed, then open) in perspective. L-R: white spruce, white cedar, jack pine, red pine and white pine. The red and jack pine needles also bear clusters of male "flowers." See "Trees" section.*

19. *Easily recognizable by their splotchy tufts of needles, red pines are super-tough giants that can withstand the wind, disease, infestations and fires that cause the demise of lesser trees.* *See page 221.*

20. Wispy cirrus clouds, 8-12 km high and composed of ice crystals, carry a message in their delicate beauty: rotten weather is probably a day or two away. See "Clouds" page 231.

21. A bank of altostratus clouds, like this one advancing over a Shield lake and emaciated white pine, may also presage rainy weather. They float 2-6 km high.

22. Zeus is nearby when foreboding cumulonimbus clouds darken the horizon. Lightning from these huge thunderheads sparks 35 percent of all forest fires. See page 243.

23. Altocumulus clouds, which often result from the break-up of altostratus, are one of the ten main clouds types in the classification system developed by pharmacist Luke Howard.

24. Camel? Weasel? Whale? What shape yonder cloud? Cumulus clouds, the cloud watchers' favourites, derive their name from the Latin word for "heap."

25. Ground-hugging stratus clouds soften the sharp lines of the horizon around a hushed lake. The spindly pine on the left is also seen in photo 21, from another angle.

26. *Polaris, the North Star or The Star That Does Not Walk Around, is the bright dot around which all the other stars seem to rotate in this 45-minute time exposure. The camera also reveals the stars' colours, which are largely indistinguishable to the naked eye. See page 268.*

27. *Towering above a fir and pine forest a stunning cathedral of northern lights is powered by electrical energy created by the sun. Spires of rare magenta fringe the more common greenish-yellow hues that shimmer about 110 km high. See page 266.*
Photo by Terence Dickinson

28. A late-afternoon double rainbow, formed by sunlight reflecting twice off raindrops, arches across an Algonquin lake. It signals clear skies for the next day and symbolizes God's Biblical promise never to flood Earth again. *See page 236.*

29. Marble, a metamorphic form of limestone, has been the preference of stone carvers around the world. Hundreds of years ago, artists engraved images of the guiding spirits of native cosmology into the marble rockface at Petroglyphs Provincial Park. *See page 301.*

30. Thrusting up from the Canadian Shield's thin soil, granite bedrock offers a glimpse of the foundation of the continent. See page 295.

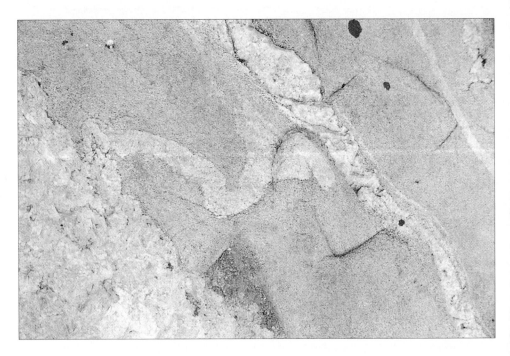

31. Varying bands and compositions of granite, like an imperfectly blended cake, reveal how molten rock solidified beneath the earth's surface more than a billion years ago.

32. Though resembling sedimentary rock, the fine layers of metamorphic gneiss are squeezed into alignments by the pressure-cooker effect of deep-Earth forces. See page 296.

33. Although stagnant and nutrient poor, many bogs are alive with pickerel frogs, salamanders, foxes and red-belly snakes. They ring with the music of white-throated sparrows by day and, perhaps, of wolves by night. See page 308.

34. White plugs of quartz may lead to riches: gold and other precious metals are most commonly found with veins of "milky quartz." See page 303.

35. Beneath the dry, sun-bleached, newly fallen leaves, older litter is black and slimy with bacteria. It eventually falls apart to form a rich, organic humus. See page 297.

RED PINE
Drawing Strength from Adversity

Average mature height: 18–25 m (60–80 ft)

Maximum height: 38 m (125 ft)

Average width of mature trunk: 30–60 cm (1–2 ft)

Maximum width: 1 m (3.3 ft)

Alias: Canadian red pine, hard pine, bull pine, Norway pine, *le pin rouge, Pinus resinosa*

Lifespan: Up to 350 years

Needles: 10–16 cm (4–6.5 in) long, dark green, coarse, thick, stiff, two to a stalk, sharp points and finely toothed edges

Bark: Flaky and reddish pinkish brown, furrowing into long, platelike, flat ridges on older trees

Sex: Tiny, purplish male flower conelets in bunches at base of spring shoots; purple or scarlet female flower conelets partly hidden by tufts of needles at branch tips

Cones: 4–7 cm (1.5–2.7 in) long, squat, dark at first, fading to tan-brown; opening in autumn and remaining on tree for a year after dropping seeds

Seeds: Winged, about 1.3 cm (0.5 in) long

Buds: 1–2 cm (0.4–0.8 in) long, pointy, resinous

Roots: Widespread, moderately deep

Wood: Light to reddish brown, straight-grained, harder than white pine, 529 kg/m³ (33 lb/cu. ft), very resinous

Preferred habitat: Usually sandy, dry, acidic soils, outwash plains, rocky lakeshores, islands, ridges

RED PINE IS A TOUGH, resilent, almost invincible giant of the forest, springing from underdog seeds that stand little chance of success in competition on fertile ground. The tree grows poorly in shade, but along rocky lakeshores and burnt-over areas with soil too sandy, dry and poor for many other trees, it thrives. With its strong roots set in these harsh niches, red pine can endure for hundreds of years, withstanding disasters that claim most trees.

More saturated with thick, protective resin than the other pines, red pine is resistant to most harmful insects and fungi, and can live through cold snaps of more than -50°C (-58°F). It often survives forest fires because its thick bark scorches

221

Companion trees: White pine,
jack pine

Frequent visitors: Red squirrels,
common yellowthroats, white-
winged crossbills

Pests and parasites: European
pine-shoot moth, pine weevil,
scleroderris pine-canker
fungus, blister rust

Range: North shore of Lake
Ontario to the midboreal
forest. Also found in all eastern
provinces and Manitoba

Name origin of *pine*: From
proto-Indo-European *pit*,
meaning "resin"

Number of pine species native
to Ontario: 4

Number of pine species worldwide: 80–90

Also see: Red Squirrel, White Pine

but doesn't readily burn, while its buds are protected within thick bunches of long, slow-burning needles. These qualities have long made the red pine a favoured species for tree plantations.

Red pine can endure for hundreds of years, withstanding disasters that claim most trees

Red-pine cones are not immune from the attentions of squirrels and birds such as crossbills. To ensure some seeds survive, the species follows the strategy of most conifers and many other trees. In most years, only a small number of pine cones are produced, with few escaping the hungry jaws of seed-eaters. But every three to seven years, red pines over a large area produce extraordinarily bountiful cone crops. So many seeds are suddenly available that squirrels and cross-bills cannot possibly eat or store them all, allowing some seedlings to get started. Any population rise in seed-eaters that results from the bounty is reversed when only a few cones are forthcoming the following year.

With distinctive tufts of long needles on relatively short, snaking branches, red pine has a splotchy appearance in silhouette. The shape is quite different from the more sweeping, layered white pine. Though less common than its taller cousin, red pine, with three-quarters of its trunk often clear of knots and branches, it was also prized for ships' masts in the early days of logging. It was loaded at the bottom of the holds of timber ships sailing to Britain because red pine is heavier than white.

WHITE PINE
Towering Above All Others

Average mature height:
30–35 m (100–115 ft)

Maximum height: 70 m (240 ft)

Average width of mature trunk:
60–100 cm (2–3.3 ft)

Maximum width: 1.5 m (5 ft)

Age of maturity: About 250
years old

Lifespan: Up to 450 years

Age of second-growth trees cut
by logging industry: 60–100
years

Portion of Ontario's forest
that is white pine: About 2%

Tree weight: Can be more than
60 tonnes

White-pine wood density:
400 kg/m³ (25 lb/cu. ft)

Sugar-maple wood density:
705 kg/m³ (44 lb/cu. ft)

Alias: Yellow pine, Quebec pine,
Weymouth pine, majestic pine,
cork pine, pattern pine, pump-
kin pine, *le pin blanc, Pinus
strobus*

Average age of a Temagami pine
when it reaches the height of
an 80-year-old Algonquin Park
pine: 120 years old

Growth rate: 100-year-old trees
up to 25 m (82 ft) high

Needles: Soft, 6–13 cm (2.3–5
in) long, in clusters of 5, finely
toothed edges

Ontario's largest remaining
old-growth white-pine stand:
Obabika, Temagami, 12,400
ha (6,000 acres)

Bark: Smooth grey-green on a
young tree, turning rough,
deeply furrowed and grey-
brown as it ages

AMONG HIS MANY FEATS, Napoleon
Bonaparte had a profound and lasting influence on
the forests of Ontario. In November 1806, after
defeating Prussia and becoming master of northern Europe,
he closed the Baltic seaports, cutting off Britain's biggest
source of lumber. With supplies dwindling, the huge British
Baltic trading fleet sailed to Canada in 1809, sparking a logging boom that quickly spread up the Ottawa Valley and
through rich green veins of white pine deep in the interior.
Within a year, wood surpassed furs as Canada's biggest
export, with tens of thousands of pines cut annually.

White pine, with its layers of long, sweeping, wind-sculpt-
ed branches, was the focus of logging for almost 100 years.

223

WHITE PINE

Sex: Small, light green, male flower cones appear in bunches near branch tips in spring and disintegrate after they release their pollen

Cones: 7.5–20 cm (3–8 in), light green at first, turning woody and tan-brown as they mature over 2 years, opening in Sept. to release seeds, then falling off during winter; big seed crops every 3–7 years

Seeds: Winged, about 2 cm (0.8 in) long, 60,000 weigh 1 kg (2.2 lb)

Roots: Widespread and moderately deep

Wood: Soft, clear, light, creamy white to yellow, with an even texture

Preferred habitat: Along lakeshores and points, islands, hillcrests, moist, sandy outwash plains, in pure stands or mixed with hardwoods and other conifers

Companion trees: Red pine, hemlock, sugar maple, white spruce, balsam fir, trembling aspen

Companion plants and shrubs: Beaked hazel, red osier dogwood, strawberry, wild lily-of-the-valley, juneberry, chokecherry

Frequent nesters: Pine warblers

Pests and diseases: White-pine weevil beetle, gypsy moth caterpillar, bark beetles, blister rust fungus

Range: Southern Ontario to midboreal forest. Also found in all other eastern provinces and a tiny portion of Manitoba

Central Ontario's virgin forests were dominated by ancient pines that towered more than 10 storeys high, making surrounding hardwoods look like shrubs. Its size and grace, and the many medicines it yielded, made the white pine the Iroquois tree of peace. But its thick, straight trunk, tapering very gradually and often free of branches for 25 metres (82 feet) or more, made it ideal for the masts of Britain's world-dominating naval and merchant fleets. Masts had to be 23 to 30 metres (75 to 100 feet) long and 60 to 100 centimetres (two to three feet) wide at the base. An even larger number of pines were cut into 12- to 18-metre- (40- to 60-foot-) long square timbers, tied together and floated down the Ottawa and St. Lawrence rivers in huge rafts, bound for the saw pits of Britain. Protected by high tariffs on non-Empire imports, Canadian lumber provided 75 percent of Britain's lumber needs by the 1820s.

The lumberjacks followed the tributaries of the Ottawa and Trent rivers far into the headlands of Haliburton and what is now Algonquin Park in the 1830s and 1840s. They spawned legends, such as those of Joe Montferrand—"Joe Mufferaw" of the Stompin' Tom Connors classic. Montferrand was a real person, the champion of Québécois *bûcherons* against the Irish in the Shinners' War brawls around the swampy little logging settlement called Bytown—later redubbed Ottawa.

As the lumberjacks pushed farther into the interior, the rapidly expanding U.S. construction market gradually replaced Britain as the major destination for Ontario pine. As logging reached Muskoka and the east shore of Georgian Bay in the 1870s, the large-toothed, two-man crosscut saw began to replace the axe, doubling the cutting speed of two axemen. Logging continued up the North Channel of Lake Huron, finally reaching Temagami in the 1920s and the Chapleau-Mississagi River region in the 1940s.

Though most of the great stands of white pine were gone by the Second World War, the mechanization of the logging industry has since allowed companies to get at many of the remnants. Bulldozers, trucks and logging roads replaced horses and rivers for transporting logs out of previously inaccessible high country. Chainsaws and giant cutting machines replaced the crosscut. Today, there are only 10 known stands exceeding 500 hectares (1,235 acres) of old-growth white pine left in Ontario. The logging industry wants those too, labelling them "overmature" or "decadent."

Many scientists counter industry claims that old pine forests need catastrophic disturbances such as cutting or fire to bring in enough sunlight and prepare the soil for regeneration. Some mature pine stands have gone 1,000 to 2,000 years without major disturbances. Instead, new trees sprout up when an old one dies, or a small fire has burned, opening up space in the canopy and on the forest floor. Young white pines can grow in as little as 20 percent of full sunlight. In fact, if white-pine seedlings are subjected to more than 40 to 50 percent full sunlight, the likelihood of being preyed on by pine weevils—beetles that eat new shoots—increases significantly.

Origin of word *lumber:* From "lumber room" for odds and ends, originally "lombard room," where the bankers of Lombardy, Italy, stored unredeemed pledges

Also see: Fungi, Humus, Red Pine, Soil

Its size and grace, and the many medicines it yielded, made the white pine the Iroquois tree of peace

Ancient pine forests with natural gaps are very complex, with greater biological diversity than even-aged forests. The gaps provide a varied habitat for many plants and animals. Naturalists hold that modern science can never hope to fully know or recreate the immensity and minutia of vital interrelationships that have been developed and fine-tuned over thousands of years in such a forest. There is even great genetic diversity within the pines of a single stand, unlike the homogeneity of replanted trees, which are more vulnerable to the spread of disease and insects. Diversity supports ecosystem stability with a complex web of interactions.

BLACK SPRUCE

The Hardy Bog Dweller

Average mature height: 10–15 m (33–50 ft)

Average width of mature trunk: 15–25 cm (6–10 in)

Maximum height: 30 m (100 ft)

Maximum width: 90 cm (3 ft)

Alias: Bog spruce, swamp spruce, l'épinette noire, *Picea mariana*

Needles: About 1 cm (0.4 in) long, dark green, not prickly

Bark: Dark grey-brown, thin and very flaky

Cones: About 2.5 cm (1 in) long, brown to purplish, with thin, dense scales that open in stages to release very tiny black winged seeds over several years

Sex: Small crimson male flower conelets, deep red female conelets in dense clusters in crown

Roots: Very shallow, extensive and intricate, making trees prone to being blown down

Usual habitat: Bogs, swamps, moist ground or dry uplands

Companion trees: Tamarack, white spruce, white birch, trembling aspen

Companion plants and shrubs: Feather moss, sphagnum moss, lichens, Labrador tea, leather-leaf, bog orchids, bog laurel

Frequent visitors: Spruce grouse, boreal chickadees, white-winged crossbills, kinglets

Frequent nesters: Red squirrels, olive-sided flycatchers, grey jays, northern parula warblers

Range: All of Ontario, except extreme south and Hudson Bay fringe. Also found in all other provinces and territories

DARK, spindly stands of black spruce, with little moss-draped branches hanging down like shriv-elled, dropping arms of ghouls, give some people the heebee-jeebees as they drive into northern Ontario's boreal for-est. Yet to others, the trees evoke a sombre, sublime solitute, hauntingly reproduced in the works of the Group of Seven. Black spruce is also the most important commercial tree in the province, feeding northern pulp and paper mills in untold numbers.

Though not as common in central Ontario, black spruce usually fringe remote bogs and swamps, where difficult grow-ing conditions mimic the north. Bogs maintain a micro-climate that is cooler than the surrounding forests. Black spruce, one of the first cold-resistant trees to follow the retreat of the glaciers back into Ontario, remained clustered around bogs in the south long after more temperate trees took over higher ground.

Black spruce are the best bog dwellers because they can make do with less better than all the trees that crowd them out elsewhere. Their stringy roots—used by native peoples to sew the seams of birchbark canoes and containers—spread and intertwine through the bog's spongy moss mat. Spruce gets by on a minimum of nutrients in the acidic wet-land, growing slowly, managing to sprout only tiny branches.

WHITE SPRUCE
Dense Boughs Shield Against Winter

THE DENSE, SWEEPING boughs that give white spruce its beauty were long used by natives, trappers, lumberjacks and campers as comfortable and springy wilderness bedding. The same qualities that make it a great mattress suit spruce to northern environments that few other trees could survive. Flexible, curving branches bend under the weight of heavy snow, which is held in place by dense, thickly needled layers of twigs, insulating the tree from cold winds. Spruce and fir trees, in fact, brace for the weight of heavy snows by contracting—closing the space between their branches—when the atmospheric pressure drops. In Switzerland, cut, Y-shaped fir branches are used as barometers, the two ends drawing close before rain or snow.

White spruce can hold its own in moderate climates as well. It is the most widespread tree in Canada and North America. Logging, however, has made white spruce less common in many areas, often replaced by fir. As the red- and white-pine forests fell to the axe in the late 1800s, loggers turned to white spruce, with its tall, thick trunk and strong, durable wood, to supply the sawmills feeding a great building boom across North America.

The discovery of efficient techniques for making paper from wood fibre in the 1860s redoubled the economic value of spruce. Paper, invented by the Chinese 1,900 years ago,

---

Portion of Ontario's forest that is spruce: 40%

Name origin of *spruce*: From Old English *Pruse*, meaning "Prussia"

Maximum lifespan: More than 200 years

Average mature height: 20–25 m (66–82 ft)

Maximum height: 37 m (123 ft)

Average width of mature trunk: 30–60 cm (1–2 ft)

Maximum width: 120 cm (4 ft)

Alias: Cat spruce, *l'épinette blanche, Picea glauca*

Needles: 2–3 cm (0.8–1.2 in) long, dark green, often with a bluish tint, four-sided, curved towards tip of branch. Remain on branch for at least 5 years

Bark: Scaly or flaky, thin, light grey

Sex: Tiny yellow male conelet flowers and larger purple-pink females flowers open high on trees in mid-May; wind pollinated

Cones: About 5 cm (2 in) long, flexible, with thin, light orange-brown scales, open in late summer and autumn and drop off through winter and spring. Big cone crops every 4–6 years

Seeds: About 2 mm (0.1 in) long, winged, about 130 per cone, 530,000/kg (240,000 per lb)

Roots: Shallow

Wood: White or yellow, with a straight grain, soft, 400 kg/m³ (25 lb/cu. ft), durable

Preferred habitat: Wide range of soils and landscape

Companion trees: Balsam fir, trembling aspen, large-toothed aspen, white birch, white pine, red maple, cedar, red pine, jack pine

Companion plants and shrubs: Chokecherry, red osier dogwood, beaked hazel, feather moss, raspberry, strawberry, buckthorn, poison ivy, fragrant bedstraw, violets, juneberry, bracken fern

Frequent nesters: Yellow-rumped, blackburnian, Cape May, bay-breasted and black-throated green warblers

Frequent visitors: Red squirrels, red-breasted nuthatches, white-winged crossbills, kinglets, olive-sided fly catchers, pine siskins

Range: Most of province, except parts of southwestern Ontario and far northern fringe. Also found in all other provinces and territories

Size of Ontario's commercially productive forest: 377,000 km³ (226,000 sq. mi), 75% of province

Portion of Ontario's productive forest that is publicly owned: 85%

Earth's land mass covered by forest: 30%

Average time between outbreaks of spruce budworm over a large area: 20–60 years

Age of oldest spruce fossils: 55–65 million years

Number of spruce species native to Ontario: 3

Number of spruce species worldwide: About 40

Also see: Balsam Fir, Humus, Soil, White Pine

was previously made from straw or rags. Spruce, even spindly black spruce, was ideally suited to the new process because its wood is long fibred, light coloured and less resinous than other conifers. As supplies of prime lumber trees dwindled around the turn of the century, the lumber barons gradually sold their cutting rights to the new pulp and paper companies, which thrived on smaller trees. By the 1930s they were penetrating deep into the boreal forest, and today an area three times the size of Metro Toronto is cut every year in Ontario, the majority for pulp and paper.

White spruce is the most widespread tree in Canada and North America

Large tracts of forest are also eaten up each year by tiny brown caterpillars called spruce budworms. Forest-industry efforts to poison them with pesticides may ultimately be counterproductive. Budworms actually prefer balsam fir to spruce needles, but the pulp mills and sawmills favour spruce. Fir, being the more shade-tolerant of the two species, tends to grow faster and crowd out young spruce in the forest understory. With prolonged budworm outbreaks—which can last seven to 10 years—fir dominance in the understory can be drastically cut back. The budworms, by providing nutrients to spruce seedlings in their droppings and decaying fir trees, act as intermediaries in what scientist Alan Gordon, at Ontario's natural resources ministry, calls an "energy transfer pulse" from fir to spruce.

TAMARACK
The Deciduous Conifer

THE lacy, dangling limbs of tamaracks are unique among Ontario's coniferous trees in that they shed their soft needles every fall. Tamarack needles are soft because they do not need the waxy coating and strong cells that allow other conifer needles to survive winter. Before dropping, the needles turn a bright yellow, enlivening the dark environs of the bogs and swamps where they're found.

Tamaracks can afford to shed their needles because they usually grow close to running water and draw new nutrients from it each spring. They are also fed by many species of fungi (some found only around tamarack), which wrap their threads around tamarack rootlets and transfer nutrients.

Moving water also provides tamarack roots with the oxygen they must have to live in soggy, acidic soils. Tamarack is often the first tree to colonize a new bog, though it is usually mixed with other species and widely spaced apart. Willowy branches allow lots of light through for other plants to grow beneath it. Its seedlings, however, must have full sunlight to grow. More shade-tolerant black spruce eventually takes over throughout much of the bog, leaving tamarack only along the open edges.

Average mature height: 10–20 m (33–66 ft)

Maximum height: 25 m (82 ft)

Average width of mature trunk: 30–60 cm (1–2 ft)

Lifespan: More than 150 years

Alias: Eastern larch, American larch, takmahak, hackmatack, red larch, black larch, *le mélèze laricin, Larix laricina*

Needles: About 2.5 cm (1 in) long, soft, bluish green, growing in clusters of 10–20 from round knobs, or singly near branch tips

Sex: Tiny, round, brownish male conelets and slightly larger, bright purple female conelets, growing from round twig knobs

Cones: 1.3–2 cm (0.5–0.8 in) long, light brown, with thin scales opening in fall, remains on tree for almost a year

Number of seeds produced annually: Up to 300,000

Bark: Smooth and grey when young; flaky, pinkish brown on older trees

Wood: Yellowish brown, often spiral grained, fairly hard, strong, oily, rot resistant, 609 kg/m³ (38 lb/cu. ft)

Preferred habitat: Bogs, swamps or drier, rocky, open sites

Companion trees: Black spruce, balsam fir, white spruce, trembling aspen, white birch

Range: All of Ontario, except extreme southwest. Also found in all other provinces and territories

Also see: Black Spruce, Fungi

229

HEAVENS

DAY SKY

MALLS, OFFICES, CARS and subways have all but made weather irrelevant to city living. But in the outdoors, weather is everything. It regulates the ebb and flow of life, from the sex lives of all animals to the date of the local regatta.

After a while, those living outdoors become, like animals and plants, attuned to every change in the day sky: shifting wind, falling or rising temperature, varying cloud cover that announces the arrival of a new weather system. A fun game is to try to guess the time by the position of the sun. It doesn't take long to become good at it.

Like the starry night sky, the day sky is a repository of human myths and legends. Sun gods, thunder gods and wind gods all made their home in the sky. As the habitat of such seemingly supernatural forces, the sky is an obvious place for heaven.

In a way, though, we have hell to thank for heaven. Ancient volcanoes spewed gases from deep inside the planet to form the early atmosphere. Later, plant life provided the oxygen necessary for life as we know it.

The weather does its thing at night as well as during the day, of course. But for simplicity, we've grouped all the weather-related topics in this section.

CLOUDS
Exploring the Skyscape

Hamlet. *Do you see yonder cloud that's almost in shape of a camel?*

Polonius. *By th' mass and 'tis, like a camel indeed.*

Hamlet. *Methinks it is like a weasel.*

Polonius. *It is backed like a weasel.*

Hamlet. *Or like a whale?*

Polonius. *Very like a whale.*

— HAMLET, III, 2

Cloud: The Old English word *clud* also meant "rocky mass, or hill." It was first used to mean "clouds" in the 13th century. An earlier Old English word for cloud, *weolcen*, still exists as *welkin* in English and *Wolke* in German.

Amount of water in a cloud: A cloud the size of a typical two-storey house may contain up to half a sink full of water

Famous cumulonimbus cloud: God appeared as a "pillar of cloud" to lead the Israelites out of Egypt and across the Red Sea

Also see: Groundhog, Mist, Rain, Thunder & Lightning, Wind

CLOUD WATCHING IS an old pastime that even Shakespeare obviously enjoyed. While his Hamlet took up the activity as a device to feign madness, cloud watching can't be beaten as a salve for modern stress. Up north, the ideal perch for cloud watching is a warm slab of rock jutting into a lake on the Canadian Shield. Not only is it fun to anticipate the changing shape of clouds, but nature always entertains with other diversions. A merganser mom and her obedient brood may paddle by only metres away. A tiny song sparrow may land in nearby bushes and boom out its distinctive gurgled call. An osprey halfway down the lake may dive into the water for a bass snack. Perhaps a nosy mink will drop by to watch the cloud watcher.

The main attraction on days like this are cumulus clouds, the familiar giant cotton balls with flat bases that metamorphose into camels and weasels and whales. *Cumulus*, Latin for "heap," is one of 10 main cloud types described in 1803 by English pharmacist Luke Howard, a part-time naturalist who spent many hours flat on his back looking at the sky. Before his time there was no specific system for classifying cloud types. He figured there had to be a way to do so and came up with one, and it remains in use

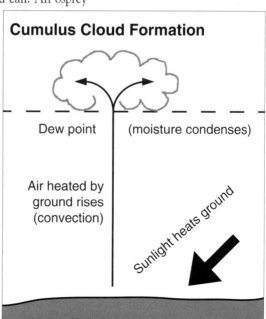

Cumulus Cloud Formation

Dew point (moisture condenses)

Air heated by ground rises (convection)

Sunlight heats ground

CLOUDS

HOWARD CLOUD CHART		
CLOUD NAME	DESCRIPTION	AVG. HEIGHT
Cirrus	Wispy, feathery. Very high	8–12 km
Cirrocumulus	Blotchy cirrus clouds, may be rippled	8–12 km
Cirrostratus	Thin veil, doesn't block out sun, may cause halo	7–9 km
Altostratus	Thicker than cirrostratus. Midlevel. Partially blocks sun	2–6 km
Altocumulus	Puffy midlevel clouds. Small puffs	2–6 km
Cumulonimbus	Giant cumulus clouds. Thunderheads, maybe anvil top	450 m–15 km
Stratocumulus	Expansive, puffy clouds.	150 m–2 km
Cumulus	Low puffy clouds, detached, flat bases	450 m–2 km
Nimbostratus	Grey layer of solid or almost solid cloud. Rain	1–2 km
Stratus	Low-lying dull clouds. May drizzle	0–450 m

moisture-laden exhaust from the jet engines cools, the water vapour condenses into ice crystals.

The presence of certain cloud types in the sky is useful for predicting weather.

today. The German poet Goethe was so impressed with Howard's system that he wrote four poems to the man.

Clouds are airborne reservoirs of water. All air carries water in an invisible form called water vapour. For a cloud to form, there must be enough water in the air, and the air must cool past a certain relative temperature, called the dew point. At this point, tiny water droplets condense around bits of dust in the air. Billions upon billions of these droplets form visible clouds. When it's cold enough, the water droplets freeze into small, six-sided ice crystals.

Cumulus clouds are created when air, heated near the ground, rises and then cools again at higher altitudes. Moisture-laden air moving over mountains also cools as it rises, and clouds may result. Large cloud banks occur along weather fronts, where a parcel of warm air meets a parcel of cold. Exhaling on a cold day produces a minicloud as warm, moist breath heated by the lungs hits the cold air outside. Contrails from high-flying jet aircraft are artifical cirrus clouds. As hot,

Wispy cirrus clouds, including the type known as "mares' tails," often precede a storm front by a day or so. Veil-like cirrostratus clouds also usually mean poor weather is on the way. When these clouds obscure the sun or the moon, they may produce faint halos around the heavenly bodies, leading to the old saying "a ring around the sun or moon brings rain or snow upon you soon." Sky-covering altostratus clouds are another sign of rainy weather.

Cumulus clouds usually don't appear in winter, because snow reflects sunlight that would otherwise heat the land and cause air to rise. That's why winter days often have clear blue skies, and why summer is supposed to arrive early when it's cloudy on Groundhog Day.

The most depressing clouds are unbroken, low-lying nimbostratus clouds associated with weather fronts. When they roll in, it usually means a day or two of rain and dreariness. Cloud watching then is an exercise in hope.

MIST, DEW & FOG
Variations on a Theme

I T'S EARLY MORNING. Down by the lake the air is still. Golden sunlight bathes the scene in a bright, purifying glow. A lone duck disappears into the soft white mist that lingers peacefully over the mirror-smooth water.

There's a good reason why mist is associated with such tranquil moments: it usually appears when the weather is calm and clear. The process begins at night, when the darkened Earth cools. As any night swimmer knows, the air cools faster than water. When water vapour from the warm lake rises into the cool air, it soon condenses into tiny water droplets, forming the mist that hangs just above the surface. Mist vanishes when the morning sun heats the air and vaporizes the water again. If it's overcast at night, mist will usually not occur, because the air doesn't cool enough. Similarly, wind turbulence disrupts the steady cooling process.

Fog is the same thing as mist, although meteorologists define fog as any bank of mist that reduces visibility to less than one kilometre (3,100 feet). Fog that rolls in off large lakes or the sea is created in a slightly different manner than mist over small lakes. In summer, water vapour in the warm air over land tends to condense as it hits cooler air over water. A fog bank appears. In winter, water vapour in warm sea air condenses when it moves across the cool land.

Dew is simply water vapour that condenses along surfaces that cool overnight. Sometimes, usually during the summer, only grass will be dewy, while nearby objects such as stones will not be. Dew forms more easily on grass because the plant's large surface area, relative to its mass, gives up heat quickly. Stones retain much of their heat overnight, so the air surrounding them doesn't cool as much.

Because dew, like mist, occurs when the weather is good, the following old saying is fairly accurate:

"When the dew is on the grass
Rain will never come to pass."

Mist: The ancient Indo-European word *migh* or *meigh*, meaning "mist," has evolved into our modern English word. Similar in other Indo-European languages, including *migla* in Lithuanian and Latvian, *mgla* in Russian, *omíkhlé* in Greek and, like the English, *mist* in Dutch and Swedish

Dew: Also Indo-European roots, from *dheu*

Frost: Old English word, from the root *freusan*, for freeze

Fog: No clear origin for the English word, but may come from the Danish *fog*, for spray or shower

Water vapour: Air is composed of up to 4% invisible water vapour at any given time. Warm air can contain more vapour. When air cools, excess water vapour condenses into visible water droplets.

Also see: Clouds, Rain

RAIN
Step on a Spider and It Will Rain

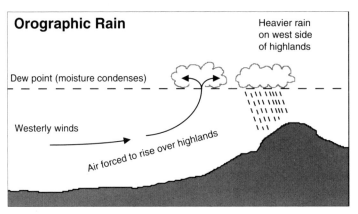

Orographic Rain

Dew point (moisture condenses)

Westerly winds

Air forced to rise over highlands

Heavier rain on west side of highlands

WELL, not exactly. Much of our old weather lore is about as accurate as a weather forecaster on a bad day. Long-range forecasts, especially those that predict next year's or next season's weather, are pure superstition.

Rain: From Old English and Old Norse *regn*; Old High German, *Regen*

Maximum falling speed: 30 km (18 mi) per hour. Air friction prevents faster velocities.

Raindrop size: 0.5–5 mm ($\frac{1}{32}$–$\frac{1}{5}$ in) in diameter Average 2 mm ($\frac{1}{12}$ in)

Cloud droplet size: About 0.01 mm ($\frac{1}{1000}$ in)

Number of droplets to make a raindrop: Estimated 30,000 to one million

Average Canadian precipitation that falls as snow: 36%

Average worldwide precipitation that falls as snow: 5%

The walk-or-run debate: Scientists have proven that a runner stays drier (or, more accurately, less wet) than a walker while getting to shelter during a rainstorm. Although a runner does run into more raindrops than a walker in the same unit of time, the greater time a walker is out in the rain means a worse soaking. The only exception is when rain is

But like the home remedies that scientists later discover have a basis in fact, some rhymes and sayings about short-term weather—especially rain—have good reason to be true. The Roman poet Virgil noted that "when swallows fly low there will soon be rain," or Latin words to that effect. This happens to be the case, because certain insects the swallows eat hang low just before a storm. One of the characteristics of a storm front is that the air is more humid higher up. Water vapour tends to condense on the little bugs and make them less airworthy. So they stick closer to the ground.

Many other animals and plants react to subtle atmospheric changes before rainfalls. Ants may be more active just before it rains because the relatively warmer temperature of a low-pressure rain system heats up their blood. Likewise, spiders pick up the pace in fixing and reinforcing their webs just before poor weather. Pine cones, as they absorb the moisture of an oncoming rain front, close up and become more supple. And the leaves of some deciduous trees, such as poplars, often turn bottom side up just before rain. Moisture-laden air softens the stems, and strong updrafts associated with thunderstorms rustle the leaves. "When the leaves show their undersides, be very certain that rain betides," as one saying goes.

Most rain betides when heated air rises and then cools at higher altitudes. Water vapour in the air condenses into microscopic water droplets around dust, soot and organic particles always present in the sky. As these droplets are tossed about in the cloud, they may collide and grow bigger. Eventually, the raindrop becomes heavy enough to fall to the ground. Contrary to popular depiction, they are not shaped like teardrops. "Instead, they are shaped like tiny hamburger buns, with the flat side down," Terence Dickinson, a noted Ontario skywatcher, has observed.

Average annual number of wet days, from Environment Canada				
LOCATION	RAIN	SNOW	THUNDERSTORMS	FREEZING PRECIPITATION
Toronto	99	47	26	10
Muskoka	106	77	27	12
North Bay	105	85	23	19
Ottawa	107	62	24	16
Kingston	109	46	27	12
Timmins	94	96	17	14
Thunder Bay	88	61	26	8
Sault Ste. Marie	98	79	22	9

Often temperatures inside a cloud are cold enough for the water droplets to freeze into six-sided ice crystals, even in summer. These form the nuclei of snowflakes, which grow as other water droplets condense along their sides. If the air beneath the cloud is warm, the snowflakes will melt and fall as rain. If it's Canada, they'll fall as snow.

An average 700 to 1,000 millimetres (28 to 39 inches) of rain and snow falls across Ontario each year, a layer of life-giving rain about equal to the depth of the shallow end of a swimming pool. (The B.C. coast gets the most rainfall in Canada, more than 2,500 millimetres, or 100 inches.) The west sides of highlands receive greater amounts of precipitation because the prevailing winds force air up over them. Water vapour is then more likely to condense and fall as rain. This is called "orographic precipitation," from the Greek root *oros*, or "mountain" (orography is the study of mountains). The west side of the Algonquin highlands receives more than 1,000 millimetres (39 inches) of rain and snow. Burk's Falls, located in this zone between Huntsville and North Bay, holds the Ontario record for having the most wet days in a year: 232 days, in 1980. The east side of the highlands lies in a rain shadow and thus receives less precipitation, averaging about 700 millimetres (28 inches).

falling on a slant in a tailwind. If this is the case, running faster than the wind would mean catching up to raindrops that would otherwise fall in front of the runner. But one mathematician has calculated that if the rain were falling at a 45° slant, this would entail running faster than the 4-minute mile

How radar tracks rainstorms: Radar waves are sensitive enough to bounce off raindrops

Also see: Clouds, Granite, Humus, Lakes, Mist, Thunder & Lightning, Wind

RAINBOWS
Covenant with Humanity

Rainbow: From the Old English, *regnboga*. In French, *arc-en-ciel*

Why rainbows are semicircular: Rainbows are actually circles, which can sometimes be seen from airplanes. From the ground, only the top portion of the circle is visible because of the angle of view. The bottom portion is below the horizon. A low sun produces taller rainbows, and vice versa

Why rainbows appear in only late afternoon or early morning: Sunlight reflects off each raindrop at angles between 42° (red) and 40° (violet). When the sun is higher than 42° in the sky, the colours from a rainbow pass over an observer's head and are not visible. Generally, rainbows appear in a 3-hour period before sunset or after sunrise

Moonbows: The light from a full moon can sometimes produce a dim rainbow, if the same conditions that create a normal rainbow are in place

Iris: The name for the coloured circular ring around the pupil of an eye comes from the Greek word for rainbow. Iris was also the Greek rainbow goddess

Also see: Clouds, Rain

IF THE MILKY WAY is the nighttime path of souls travelling from Earth to the heavens, rainbows serve the same function in daytime. To the Babylonians, the rainbow was a bridge formed by the necklace of the goddess Ishtar, linking Heaven and Earth. Similar descriptions exist in Norse, Persian and Japanese mythologies, and in Buddhist scriptures. In Turkic languages, the word for rainbow is the same word for bridge.

The rainbow is rich in other meanings for humans. Perhaps the most famous rainbow in history is the one that appeared to Noah after the Great Flood had cleansed the world of sin—and pretty well everything else. God, who was feeling kind of sorry for what he had done, sent the rainbow as a promise that "never again will the waters become a flood to destroy all creation."

In a Cree story, rainbows were said to be made of flowers. A young girl who loved rainbows was carried up to one by a Thunderbird, and she sent some of the flowers back to Earth to beautify the land. In Ireland, leprechauns liked to bury their pots of gold at the end of rainbows, probably because it is impossible for a mortal to get there. The ancient Greeks were among the few to look upon rainbows with trepidation. Iris, the rainbow goddess, was a messenger of the gods. But she was usually dispatched when the news was bad: impending war, or perhaps the death of a loved one.

Though rainbows don't lead to gold, they usually signify improved fortunes, at least as far as the weather is concerned. A rainbow needs two ingredients, sunlight and raindrops. The sun must be located low in the sky and behind the rainbow-watcher. The raindrops must be in the air in front of the observer. Late-afternoon rainbows may foretell good weather because it means the sun is unobstructed in the west. Since weather systems generally come from the west, clear skies are probably on the way. And since the rain in the east is moving away, the bad weather has probably passed. For the same reasons, the opposite is true of an early-morning rainbow. The clear skies have already passed to the east, and the rain in the west is bearing down

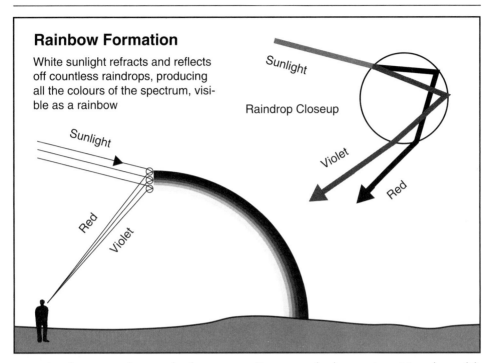

Rainbow Formation

White sunlight refracts and reflects off countless raindrops, producing all the colours of the spectrum, visible as a rainbow

Sunlight

Raindrop Closeup

Violet

Red

Sunlight

Red

Violet

upon the observer, to dampen the day.

Rainbows are created by sunlight penetrating billions of falling raindrops. Most of the light passes straight through the drop; however, a small amount of light is bent as it enters the drop, and refracts into the seven main colours that make up the visible spectrum: red, orange, yellow, green, blue, indigo and violet. The back of the raindrop acts like a mirror to reflect these colours out the front of the drop, towards the observer.

A rainbow watcher sees only one colour from each raindrop. But because the sunlight is refracting and reflecting off countless raindrops, the full spectrum is visible in the beautiful arc of a rainbow. Red is always the outside colour, and violet the inside.

Because each observer is positioned at a different angle to the raindrops, each sees his or her own rainbow.

The most brilliant rainbows usually appear after a thunderstorm, because the large raindrops of that type of storm reflect more light. But rainbows can appear through the mist of a waterfall or the spray of a lawn sprinkler. All it takes are water droplets and the sun at the right angle. Sometimes double rainbows are visible, with the secondary rainbow much fainter. This occurs when sunlight reflects off the interior of raindrops twice. Each reflection dims the intensity of the light. The order of colours in the secondary rainbow are reversed.

SKY

Thank Goodness for Algae

Composition of atmosphere: 79% nitrogen, 20% oxygen, 1% other gases including carbon dioxide, ozone, hydrogen, methane and helium

Indian Summer: The brief respite from autumn cold, usually in late Oct. or early Nov. after the first major frost. The warm, calm and sunny weather is caused by an air mass from the Caribbean or Gulf of Mexico moving north and lingering for a few days. American settlers coined the name, though there are several theories for its origin. It is said to be the time when aboriginals would gather supplies for winter, or carry out late-season raids. Another story recounts that natives told settlers to expect such weather before winter

Why the is sky blue: Air is transparent, which is why we can see the stars at night. The daytime colour comes from the complex interaction of sunlight striking gas molecules and particles of dust and moisture. White sunlight is actually composed of the seven main colours of the spectrum. During the day, all these colours except blue travel directly to the Earth's surface. The blue light is scattered by gas molecules throughout the sky. The sun, which is white when viewed from outer space, appears yellow from the Earth's surface—all the colours of the spectrum minus blue

THE SKY IS a security blanket that protects all life from the deadly vacuum of space. But it's a fragile blanket. For one thing, it's not very thick. If Earth were the size of a beachball, our sustaining layer of air would be about as thick as a paper towel. Breathable air ends eight kilometres (5.9 miles) above sea level—two kilometres (1.2 miles) below the cruising height of an airliner.

The sky's composition is also precarious. The ozone layer is thinning and permitting increased amounts of dangerous ultraviolet radiation to strike the Earth's surface. Also, increasing amounts of carbon dioxide pumped into the atmosphere by industrialized nations are blamed for the greenhouse effect, a gradual warming caused by heat trapped underneath a thickening layer of the gas.

It seems almost inconceivable that the sky could change so much that it would endanger our lives. But there was a time when the atmosphere wouldn't have supported human life at all. In ancient times it was composed mostly of carbon dioxide, water vapour and ammonia spewed out of volcanoes. Only in the past 40 percent of the history of the planet has the atmosphere been oxygenated. For this we must thank blue-green algae and other primitive plants, which converted carbon dioxide into oxygen through photosynthesis. They also provided ozone, a type of oxygen that absorbs the sun's deadly ultraviolet radiation. Our modern atmosphere, of 79 percent nitrogen, 20 percent oxygen, and other trace gases, remains relatively stable because of the ongoing exchange of oxygen and carbon dioxide via photosynthesis. But the sky is increasingly at peril from human activity.

Long before the age of TV forecasts, our ancestors watched the sky for clues to tomorrow's weather. Behaviour of plants and animals also helped them predict the weather. Memorable ditties or sayings that pertained to long-range forecasts were more superstition than science, but short-range predictions were often quite accurate, for sound reasons:

- "Red sky at night, sailors delight.
  Red sky in the morning, sailors take warning."

If the sun is shining in the west at sunset, this means it is not obscured by clouds. Since weather systems generally move from west to east in Ontario, it's a good bet that the following day will be clear. If the sun is shining in the morning, that means good weather is far to the east. It may not be long before bad weather arrives.

- "If there's enough blue in the sky to make a sailor a pair of pants, the weather will improve."

Low-pressure systems associated with bad weather have many layers of clouds. If large patches of blue sky are present, it means there are fewer levels of clouds, and the storm system is probably moving on. This is especially true if the blue is in the west.

- "If the maple sap runs faster, it is going to rain."

Low pressure enables the sap to run more freely. Low pressure means bad weather.

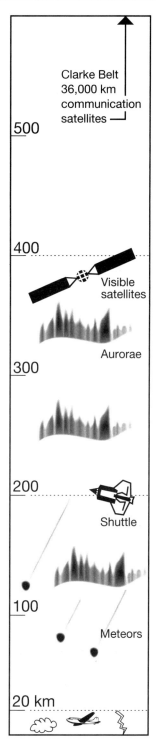

APPROXIMATE LENGTH OF TWILIGHT			
Early Jan.	1 h 45 min	Early July	2 h 21 min
Mid-Jan.	1 h 42 min	Mid-July	2 h 12 min
Early Feb.	1 h 39 min	Early Aug.	1 h 56 min
Mid-Feb.	1 h 36 min	Mid-Aug.	1 h 57 min
Early Mar.	1 h 35 min	Early Sept.	1 h 43 min
Mid-Mar.	1 h 39 min	Mid-Sept.	1 h 37 min
Early Apr.	1 h 44 min	Early Oct.	1 h 34 min
Mid-Apr.	1 h 47 min	Mid-Oct.	1 h 38 min
Early May	2 h 00 min	Early Nov.	1 h 39 min
Mid-May	2 h 10 min	Mid-Nov.	1 h 39 min
Early June	2 h 25 min	Early Dec.	1 h 44 min
Mid-June	2 h 27 min	Mid-Dec.	1 h 44 min

SUN
The 0.7 Percent Solution

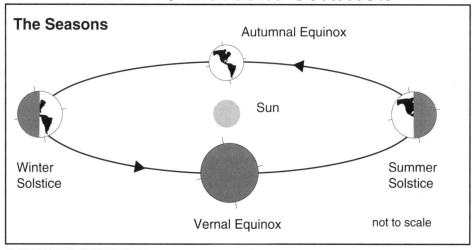

The Seasons

Autumnal Equinox

Sun

Winter Solstice

Summer Solstice

Vernal Equinox

not to scale

Historic expedition: In 1768, the English dispatched astronomer Charles Green and Captain James Cook—the latter of whom had distinguished himself in the Gulf of St. Lawrence during the English conquest of Canada—to Tahiti to record the transit of Venus across the face of the sun. The measurements were to be used to determine the distance of the sun from Earth. On his way back from Tahiti, in 1770, Cook became the first European to encounter eastern Australia. His ship sailed into Botany Bay and changed the history of that continent forever

Period of rotation (the sun's "day"): 25 Earth days at the equator

Diameter: 1,400,000 km (840,000 mi), or 109 times Earth's diameter

Mass: 333,000 times Earth's

THE SOURCE OF all life on Earth begins with a slim surplus of mass deep inside the sun. Under pressure 250 billion times greater than the atmospheric pressure on the Earth's surface, and in 15 million°C heat, four hydrogen atoms fuse into one helium atom. But the helium does not equal the mass of the hydrogen parents; a tiny amount, 0.7 percent, is left over. This missing mass is converted into energy that ultimately becomes the heat and light that bathes our planet and all the other worlds in the solar system.

Science has uncovered many of the secrets of nuclear fusion, as this process is called. But most ancient cultures understood that the sun is the giver of life, and had a sun deity or being who played a prominent role in their mythology. Shamash was the sun god of Babylonia; he was responsible for justice. The Egyptian Ra was the great creator and defender of goodness. Helios of ancient Greece rode his sun-chariot across the sky and lived in a magnificent palace where darkness never fell. Apollo was also identified as a Greek sun god, although more properly he was the god of light and truth. The sun in Ojibway stories was a symbol of the Great Spirit or Kitche Manitou; sometimes it was referred to as the Great Spirit's wigwam. An Inuit fable describes the sun and the moon as brother and sister who committed incest while they were humans. In the sky they were to be forever parted. Nearly all cultures identify the sun with the masculine or fatherhood, perhaps because Earth and the moon are so closely associated with the feminine, and sunlight is the agent that fertilizes life.

Great festivals, such as the rowdy Roman Saturnalia, often marked significant solar events. Saturnalia was held around the winter solstice in December. At that time, the north pole is tilted away from the sun because of the Earth's 23.5° axial tilt to its orbital plane around the sun. At the summer solstice in June, after the Earth has travelled halfway around its orbit, the north pole is tilted towards the sun. The northern hemisphere thus receives the sun's warming rays at a more direct angle in summer. In December, when shadows are longest because the sun is low, the northern hemisphere receives the rays at an oblique angle. In other words, the same amount of sunlight has to heat a far greater area of land in the winter than it does in the summer. The seasons are reversed in the southern hemisphere.

On summer solstice the sun rises at its most northerly point along the northeastern horizon, and traces its highest arc of the year across the sky. It is the longest day of the year. The opposite occurs on the winter solstice, when the sun rises in the southeast and loops low across the southern sky. On the vernal and autumnal equinoxes, the sun rises and sets midway between the points demarcated by the solstices. This happens to be due east and due west. On the equinoxes, the hours of the day are split into roughly equal amounts of light and darkness, hence the name.

Approximate sunrise and sunset times for the Muskoka, Haliburton, North Bay regions of Ontario. For other locations and dates, see notes below

DATE	SUNRISE	SUNSET
Jan. 1	7:49 a.m. EST	4:52 p.m. EST
Jan. 15	7:47	5:08
Feb. 1	7:37	5:28
Feb. 15	7:15	5:50
Mar. 1	6:57	6:05
Mar. 15	6:30	6:24
Apr. 1	6:00	6:45
Apr. 15	6:34 a.m. DST	8:02 p.m. DST
May 1	6:08	8:23
May 15	5:50	8:39
June 1	5:35	8:56
June 15	5:30	9:07
July 1	5:43	9:01
July 15	5:52	8:56
Aug. 1	6:08	8:39
Aug. 15	6:22	8:22
Sep. 1	6:38	7:50
Sep. 15	6:57	7:28
Oct. 1	7:16	6:59
Oct. 15	7:32	6:36
Nov. 1	6:56 a.m. EST	5:07 p.m. EST
Nov. 15	7:15	4:50
Dec. 1	7:36	4:38
Dec. 15	7:50	4:36

For dates between the chart dates, take an average. For other locations, add or subtract the number of minutes as indicated: Kapuskasing: +12, Kingston: -12, Ottawa: -15, Peterborough: -5, Sudbury: +6, Thunder Bay: +39, Timmins: +8. Daylight Saving Time starts on the first Sunday in April and ends on the last Sunday in October. This chart has been adjusted to account for DST.

Temperature: 15,000,000°C
(27,000,000°F) at core,
5,500°C (9,900°F) at surface

Age: 4.6 billion years

Composition by number of
atoms: 92% hydrogen, almost
8% helium, heavier elements
the remainder

Magnitude: -27

Closest distance between the
Earth and sun: 147 million km
(88 million mi) at perihelion,
early January

Farthest distance: 152 million km
(91 million mi) at aphelion,
early July

Vernal (Spring) Equinox: Mar.
20–22 (exact date changes
from year to year)

Summer Solstice: June 20–22

Autumnal Equinox: Sept. 21–23

Winter Solstice: Dec. 20–22

Time it takes for sunlight to reach
Earth: 8.3 minutes

Speed of light: 299,792 km
(186,282 mi) per second

Solar radiation reaching Earth
that is absorbed into the
ground and converted into
heat: About 50%. Half the radiation reflects off clouds and the
Earth, or is absorbed by the
atmosphere

Sun: From ancient Indo-European
sau or *su*. Some groups of sun-
related words adopted an "l"
suffix, including *soleil* in
French, *solar* in English and
helios in Greek. Others adopted the "n" suffix, including
sun, sonne in German and *zon*
in Dutch

Also see: Milky Way, Moon,
Northern Lights, Stars, Planets
& Comets, Zodiac

Although the sun is a great benefactor, it does emit ultraviolet radiation. Most is absorbed by ozone, a form of oxygen, in the atmosphere.

Ultraviolet Index (sunburn time for fair-skinned person)		
INDEX	RISK	TIME TO SUNBURN
9+	Extreme	15 minutes
7–8.9	High	20 minutes
4–6.9	Moderate	30 minutes
0–3.9	Low	1 hour +

But man-made chemicals have eaten away at the ozone layer in recent decades, allowing more UV radiation to reach the surface. This radiation causes sunburns and in the long term may lead to skin cancer in humans. In 1992, Environment Canada began issuing an ultraviolet radiation index that rates UV exposure on a scale of 1 to 10. The higher the number, the greater the danger.

Our sun is in comfortable middle age. Now and then the photosphere, the sun's roiling surface, erupts with violent flares and enormous gas prominences, but that's normal for a Class G2 V nuclear-fusion reactor, as astronomers categorize our star. The flares are associated with sunspots, which are cooler areas of the photosphere caused by fluctuations in the sun's powerful magnetic field. These fluctuations have an 11-year cycle, so that every 11 years solar flares seem more pronounced.

But like all living things, the sun's time will come. In another five billion years or so, the engine of our solar system will be running on empty. Shortly afterwards, the sun will swell into a "red giant" that will engulf Mercury, Venus and Earth. Immense gravitational forces will then cause the sun's matter to contract into a small, dense star called a white dwarf. The stored-up heat from its previous processes will radiate away, and our sun will die.

THUNDER & LIGHTNING
Flashes Hotter than the Sun

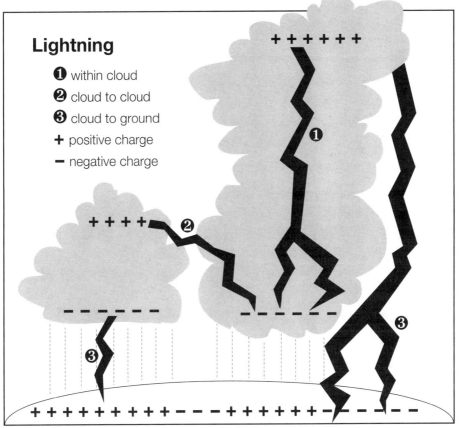

Lightning

❶ within cloud
❷ cloud to cloud
❸ cloud to ground
+ positive charge
– negative charge

A NYONE WHO HAS experienced the full fury of a thunderstorm, especially from inside a tent, has an idea of how our ancestors must have felt during one of nature's most awesome shows. The howling winds, the crashing thunder and the alien lightning bolts seem like a backdrop to the end of time. Perhaps that's why the thunder gods of many ancient civilizations were supreme beings, even more than sun deities. Zeus of Olympus and Thor of Valhalla hurled thunderbolts with impunity. Marduk, the supernatural hero of ancient Babylon, was also a thunder god. One of the manifestations of the Semitic god Baal was a storm god with an arsenal of thunderbolts. Maybe they're

Temperature of lightning bolt:
10,000–40,000°C
(18,000–72,000°F)

Temperature of sun's surface:
About 5,500°C (9,900°F)

Average current of a lightning bolt: 20,000 amperes

Typical speed of a lightning bolt:
150,000 km (90,000 mi) per second

Speed of light: 299,792 km
(186,282 mi) per second

Speed of sound: 0.332 km (1085 ft) per second

Typical width of a lightning bolt: 2 cm (¾ in) at point of strongest current

Maximum height of a thundercloud: 20 km (12 mi)

Height of Mt. Everest: 8.8 km (5.3 mi)

Height of Maple Mountain, the highest point in Ontario, in the Temiskaming area: 683 m (2,240 ft)

How far away the lightning is: Determine the distance to a lightning bolt by counting the number of seconds between a lightning flash and its resulting thunder. Each second is about 300 m (1,000 ft)

Maximum distance thunder travels: About 40 km (24 mi)

Estimated number of thunder storms occurring at this moment: 18,000 around the world

Estimated number of lightning bolts striking the ground every second: 100

Average number of times the CN Tower gets hit every year: 75

Tennyson's description of lightning: "Flying flame"

Ben Franklin's kite: In 1752, Benjamin Franklin flew a kite in a thunderstorm to prove that lightning was caused by electricity. He invented lightning rods

Speed of falling hail: 160 km/h (96 mph)

all the same god—one story passed down and altered through the millennia.

Native peoples of Canada also respect thunderstorms. To the Ojibway and many other nations, mythic Thunderbirds, or *pinesi*—important beings who played roles in many old stories—brought thunderstorms. When storms were raging, the Thunderbirds were said to be hunting. Thunder came from the flap of their wings, lightning from the flash of their eyes. Although *pinesi* had no definite shape, they are generally associated with hawks, undoubtedly based on the observation that hawks and thunderstorms appear about the same time each year, in April, and fade away at the same time, in October.

Another Ojibway conception of thunderstorms linked them to grandfathers. Because grandmothers were traditionally closer to their children and grandchildren than granddads, they were given a more regular, symbolic presence in Grandmother Moon. Grandfathers, angry at this lack of attention, returned as thunder, or Grandfather Thunder. Families offered tobacco in thunderstorms to appease the grouchy old man.

The classic thunderstorm occurs on hot, humid summer afternoons, when massive amounts of heated air rise to form huge cumulonimbus clouds. Within the thunderheads, powerful down drafts ionize the air by stripping molecules of electrons, similar to the way rubbing a balloon gives it an electrical charge. The top of a thunderhead is thus positively charged, while the base is negatively charged. The ground immediately below a thunderhead is positively charged, too. Nature seeks to correct the electrical imbalance by transferring electrons from the positive ground or positive cloud-top to the negative cloud base. Most lightning occurs within a cloud or between clouds. Only 20 percent is cloud-to-ground lightning.

Lightning forms along a route called a tunnel. In cloud-to-ground lightning, one end of the tunnel starts at the cloud base and moves downwards, while the other starts on the ground—generally from a tall point such as a tower or tree—and moves upwards. The two meet, usually at a spot close to the ground, and the circuit is completed. The visible lightning bolt emanates from this point, moving up and down the tunnel in about 1/10,000 of a second. The explosive bolt heats the air instantly, up to seven times the temperature of the surface of the sun, and the resulting air expansion vibrates as thunder.

Sheet lightning is not another form of lightning, but simply the glow of lightning bolts that occur within a cloud. Contrary to popular belief, lightning often hits the same place twice, especially tall towers.

Buildings and hard-top cars are the safest places to wait out thunderstorms. Appliances should be unplugged because electrical charges can sometimes surge down power lines. Standing under tall trees, in the middle of open fields or atop hills or ridges is dangerous. Swimmers and boaters should head for shore as soon as they hear thunder. Woods are relatively safe, but don't set up a tent beneath the tallest tree. If you're caught in the open, the "golfer's crouch" can prevent serious injury or death: kneel on the ground with hands on knees and bend forward. If a lightning bolt strikes nearby, the charge should pass under you without striking vital organs. Don't lie flat. Lightning strikes are lethal about 20 percent to 30 percent of the time, when the charge passes through the heart or spinal cord.

Another hazard associated with thunderstorms is hail. These ice balls can kill animals, damage cars and wipe out fields of crops in seconds. Usually they are the size of peas, but grapefruit-sized monsters have been recorded in Canada. Hail occurs when ice crystals in a thunderhead are carried up and down by violent air currents. The crystals grow along the way as more moisture condenses and freezes on their surface. When they are too heavy to be supported by air currents, they fall explosively out of the bottom of the cloud.

Tornadoes may also accompany the biggest thunderstorms, and are usually preceded by heavy hail. Tornado winds can reach 500 km/h (300 mph), about twice as fast as the worst hurricane winds. Waterspouts are similar to tornadoes but not as violent, with winds approaching 80 km/h (48 mph). Both are rare in hilly Shield country, but relatively common in southwestern Ontario, where about 25 tornadoes are reported each year.

Thunderstorms occurring in winter: Yes. The flash of lightning in a snowstorm can be spectacular. But winter thunderstorms are rare, because there is not as much heating of air (convection) in winter as in summer.

Forest fires caused by lightning: About 35%

Forest fires caused by human activity: About 65%

Maximum length of a thunderstorm: About 2 hours

Also see: Clouds, Rain, Red Oak, Sapsucker

WIND & WEATHER SYSTEMS
A Blow-by-Blow Account

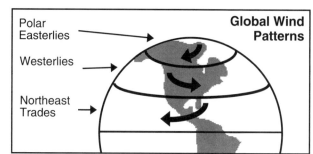

Global Wind Patterns

Polar Easterlies

Westerlies

Northeast Trades

WIND IS ESSENTIAL for life on Earth. Trees and plants owe their existence to winds that carry pollen and distribute seeds. Wind transports moisture around the world, bringing life-sustaining rains. Tailwinds and vertical air currents called thermals enable birds to migrate thousands of miles. Worldwide wind patterns distribute heat more evenly across the planet. The profound importance of wind was not lost on the ancients: wind is one of the four elements of antiquity, along with fire, water and earth.

The science of wind is complex. Many questions about its behaviour still stump researchers, not to mention novice sailboarders. But the basics are well understood. Put simply, wind occurs when air rushes from a high-pressure zone to a low-pressure zone, answering nature's call for equilibrium. A vacuum cleaner uses the same principle. In the machine, a powerful fan creates an artificial low-pressure zone. Air outside the vacuum cleaner, now suddenly under higher pressure, swooshes up the nozzle towards the low-pressure area, carrying dust, dirt and lost subway tokens along with it. The greater the difference in pressure, the faster the wind. Hurricanes and tornadoes are like enormous vacuum cleaners: both are extreme low-pressure systems, sucking deadly winds towards their centres and picking up everything in their paths.

Typical low-pressure systems aren't as violent, but they generally bring bad weather. In a low, the inward-rushing air is warm and moves upward as it converges towards the centre. As the warm, moisture-laden air ascends, it cools. Water vapour condenses into cloud banks, and it often rains.

High-pressure zones are characterized by heavy, cooler air that sinks as it moves outwards. Cool air contains less moisture; therefore, the air is sometimes cloudless. A high-pressure system in the winter brings cold, clear air. In summer, the air in a high-pressure system doesn't

	BEAUFORT WIND SCALE		
Named after Francis Beaufort, a British admiral, who invented the scale in 1805			
NUMBER	WINDSPEED KM/H	DESIGNATION	CHARACTERISTIC
0	up to 1	Calm	Smoke rises vertically
1	1–5	Light air	Smoke drifts, leaves rustle
2	6–11	Light breeze	Wind on face, small wavelets
3	12–19	Gentle breeze	Flags flutter
4	20–29	Mod. breeze	Dust blows, branches move
5	30–38	Fresh breeze	Flags stretched, trees sway
6	39–50	Strong breeze	Wires hum, wind whistles
7	51–61	Moderate gale	Walking impeded
8	62–74	Fresh gale	Twigs break off, high waves
9	75–86	Strong gale	Branches break, tiles blown
10	87–101	Whole gale	Trees uprooted, damage
11	102–120	Storm	Widespread damage
12	over 120	Hurricane	Major destruction

seem so cool because it heats up during the day as intense sunlight warms the ground. Both high-pressure and low-pressure systems generally move westward across the continent because of prevailing westerly winds.

Boaters use a system called "the crossed-winds rules" to help predict weather, at least for the short term. They observe which direction the lower wind is travelling by watching the low clouds. They face that direction. Then they observe which direction the upper wind is travelling by carefully watching the high clouds (obviously, this only works if there are low and high clouds in the sky). If the upper wind is coming from the left, this means a low-pressure system is approaching and the weather will usually get worse. If the upper wind is coming from the right, the weather should improve. If the lower and upper winds are travelling parallel to each other, either in the same or opposite directions, then the weather probably won't change. These forecasts are generally good for the following few hours or half day.

In the summer, gentle winds die down at night because their creator—the sun—disappears. During the day, the sun heats the ground, which then warms the air. As the warm air rises, other air rushes in to take its place, creating wind. Once the sun is gone the process stops.

Why wind feels cool or cold against skin: Wind evaporates moisture in the skin, a process that removes heat energy. Thus, in the summer, a gentle breeze will cool us down. In the winter, a breeze freezes, and reminds us of our northern heritage

Wind and canoe routes: Avoid adversity by taking prevailing westerlies into consideration when planning circuitous canoe routes. Plan eastward sections of the trip along lakes to take advantage of tailwinds. Plan westward sections along narrower bodies of water and rivers, which are more protected from the wind

Also see: Clouds, Broad-winged Hawk, Mist & Fog, Mosquitoes, Rain, Sky, Thunder & Lightning

NIGHT SKY

"If the grandeur of a planetary world in which the earth, as a grain of sand, is scarcely perceived, fills the understanding with wonder; with what astonishment are we transported when we behold the infinite multitude of worlds and systems which fill the extension of the Milky Way!"—German philosopher and part-time astronomer Immanuel Kant, 1755 (translated by W. Hastie)

I N KANT'S TIME, *before the invention of urban streetlights, the experience of beholding the night sky must have been more regular and intense than it is today. Now, most people are transported with astonishment only during those infrequent forays up north, where the sky is crisp and clear and studded with thousands of stars.*

Gazing at the universe is an ancient pastime. Some scholars believe that civilization itself was born when humans acquired time-factoring skills through observations of the heavens. The invention of Western philosophy is said to stem from the ponderings of the Greek astronomer Thales in the sixth century B.C. No doubt he asked the question of every stargazer, "What is the meaning of life?"

If not the answer to the meaning of life, the stars contain the stories of cultures around the world. Myths and legends are played out every night as the constellations, planets and moon parade across the celestial dome. This section of Up North contains several of those stories, as well as star maps to aid the novice stargazer, and practical information about other heavenly phenomena, including the times of meteor showers.

Learning about the night sky and its stories connects us with the past and the future in a way that Kant and all humans have understood, deep within our souls.

BIG DIPPER
The Universal Bear

THROUGH the millennia, people in the northern hemisphere have gazed into the night sky and connected the same starry dots to form what we now call the Big Dipper. It's the constellation we learn first because it's easy to pick out, it's prominent in the sky on warm summer nights and two of its stars conveniently point to the North Star, Polaris.

In fact, long before the Golden Arches came to exist, the Big Dipper was one thing many ancient civilizations had in common. A surprising number of myths from Europe, Asia and North America refer to the Big Dipper as a bear. It's thought the bear story originated in prehistoric Asia, and travelled both eastward and westward with various human migrations.

The Micmacs of Nova Scotia have just such a story, in which the four stars making up the cup of the Big Dipper represent a bear. The three stars of the handle, plus other nearby stars, represent birds. When spring came, the hungry birds hunted the bear. From high in the sky, they chased it closer to Earth. In autumn, the lead bird, Robin, shot an arrow at the bear. Blood splashed Robin, giving the bird its red breast. Blood also dripped onto the leaves below, giving them autumn colour. The hunt's cycle is repeated every year, with the position of the constellation serving as a calendar to record the seasons. The motion of the bear through the sky during the night also serves as a clock.

The Greeks, as always, saw in the Dipper constellations a star opera of love and jealousy. In one version of the legend,

Latin and Greek names: *Ursus* is the Latin word for "bear," evident in such modern words as *ursine*, meaning "bearlike." The Greek word for bear, *arkitos*, is the root for Arcas, son of Callisto; Arcturus, the bright star in the constellation Boötes; and even King Arthur, who was sometimes called Arturus. Because the stars associated with the bear stories lie in the northern sky, things relating to the north often contain the *arkitos* root— e.g., "arctic"

Closest star in Big Dipper to Earth: Megrez, 53 light-years away

Travel time to Megrez in our fastest spacecraft: 1.8 million years

Farthest star in Big Dipper: Alkaid, 140 light-years away

249

BIG DIPPER

Brightest stars: Alioth and Dubhe, both magnitude 1.8

Double-star names: Mizar (larger star) and Alcor. This pair is called an optical double, because they are close to each other only by virtue of our line of sight from Earth. They are not gravitationally linked to each other like a true double-star system. Mizar itself appears as a double star in telescopes

Also see: Bear, Boötes, Corona Borealis, Muskrat, North Star & Little Dipper, Robin, Star Charts, Stars, Weasel

Zeus seduces the nymph Callisto. Zeus's betrayed wife, Hera, retaliates by turning Callisto into a bear. Out of compassion, Zeus transforms Callisto's son Arcas into a bear, too, to keep her company, placing both of them in the heavens to protect them from hunters. There they are known by their Latin names Ursa Major, the greater bear, and Ursa Minor, the lesser bear. Zeus's manner of delivering both bears to the heavens—a cosmic heave—explains their stretched tails.

Another story also refers to the tail or handle of the Dipper, though it doesn't involve a bear. In an Ojibway legend, the Big Dipper is a fisher, a member of the weasel family. One year, the story goes, summer did not arrive. A certain hunter, named Fisher after the animal spirit that inhabited him, concluded that someone had captured the migratory birds that brought good weather. The culprit was Fisher's selfish cousin, Cruel-Face. After a skirmish, Fisher was able to release the birds of summer. Cruel-Face chased Fisher up a tree, where the hero's only escape was to follow the advice of the stars and leap into Sky Country. He did, forming the constellation. But as Fisher leapt, Cruel-Face fired off his last arrow, wounding Fisher in the tail. To this day, Fisher's injured tail—the crooked handle of the Big Dipper—attests to Cruel-Face's desperate shot. And to this day, the freed birds bring summer every year.

Like the Ojibway, other cultures saw unique shapes in the Dipper configuration. The Saxons called it a wagon, as did the Babylonians. In Britain it is still sometimes called the Plough. Ancient Egyptians looked up in the sky and saw a bull's thigh.

The official constellation Ursa Major, as defined by the International Astronomical Union, actually includes many more stars than just those in the Big Dipper. For this reason, the Big Dipper portion is technically called an asterism. It includes some notable astronomical features. The star at the crook of the Big Dipper's handle appears as a double star, for example. It is barely perceptible with the naked eye, which is why it was used as an eye test by many peoples, including native North Americans, before wall charts were invented. One of the stars in the double star is itself a double star, the first ever discovered through a telescope, in 1650.

250

BOÖTES

Ice-Cream Cone in the Sky

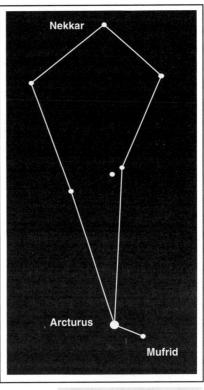

THE CONSTELLATION BOÖTES contains the brightest star of the summer sky, Arcturus. This giant nuclear furnace is about 120 times more luminous than our own sun and 25 times wider. The only star to outshine Arcturus in the northern hemisphere is brilliant Sirius, the "dog star" of winter that burns low in the southern sky.

Arcturus has great significance for northern peoples. It is the harbinger of spring, a signal to start thinking about planting crops or opening up the cottage. Arcturus climbs over the horizon into the early evening sky around the time of the spring equinox in late March.

Arcturus means "guardian of the bear" in Greek. The star was thought to herd Ursa Major, the Great Bear or Big Dipper, around the North Star. At some point in history, this notion was extended to include the entire constellation of Boötes, which means "plowman" or "herdsman." In the Micmac myth of the Big Dipper, Arcturus was an owl in the group of birds hunting the celestial bear, while for thousands of years the Chinese have thought of Arcturus as one of the horns on a great sidereal dragon.

To find Arcturus and Boötes (pronounced *bow-OW-tays*), follow the curve of the handle of the Big Dipper to the next bright star—the famous "arc to Arcturus." Boötes extends out from Arcturus in the shape of a giant ice-cream cone; some people prefer to think of it as a kite. Continue the arc through Arcturus to find another bright star, Spica. Spica is the other horn on the Chinese sky-dragon. As summer progresses, Arcturus moves high across the night sky. It is almost directly overhead as darkness descends in late June and early July.

How Arcturus lit up Chicago: At the 1933 world's fair in Chicago, organizers used the star's light to turn on the fair's floodlights. The starbeam was focused through a telescope onto a photoelectric cell, which generated the voltage to flip the switch. The starlight hitting the cell would have begun its journey to Earth in 1899, since Arcturus is 34 light-years away

Brightest star in Boötes: Arcturus, magnitude -0.04

Star closest to Earth in Boötes: Mufrid, 31 light-years away

Star farthest from Earth: Nekkar, 230 light-years away

Also see: Big Dipper, North Star, Star Charts, Stars

CASSIOPEIA
Stairway to Heaven

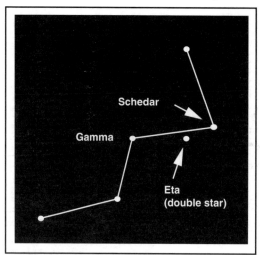

C ASSIOPEIA, QUEEN of Aethiopia in Greek mythology, easily calls attention to herself from her heavenly perch. For many stargazers the Cassiopeia constellation is the one they learn right after the Big Dipper. Like the Dipper, it is circumpolar, revolving around Polaris and never setting below the horizon.

Northern cultures gave various meanings to Cassiopeia's distinctive shape. When it is low in the sky it looks like a giant W. As it moves higher it turns upside-down to become an M. To the Inuit this outline reflected the pattern of stairs cut in snow, an astral stairway connecting Earth to the sky country. The ancient Egyptians called it the Leg; to the Chinese it was the charioteer Wang Liang.

But it is the Greco-Roman tale that gives us the name Cassiopeia. The Queen of Aethiopia, married to King Cepheus, was an unpleasant woman, apparently. She bragged that she was more beautiful than the sea nymphs— not a smart move, since the nymphs were the offspring of the mighty sea god Poseidon. The enraged god dispatched the monster Cetus to attack Aethiopia's coast. An oracle advised Cepheus that the only way to save his citizens was to sacrifice his daughter Andromeda to the briny beast. This he reluctantly did, although Andromeda was rescued by Perseus before Cetus could get his flippers on her. As punishment for her boastfulness, Cassiopeia was strapped to a chair and placed in the heavens. The other characters in this myth, including Cepheus, Andromeda, Cetus and Perseus, have nearby constellations named after them.

The Sea Monster: Cetus, sent by Poseidon to terrorize Cassiopeia's subjects, took its name from the Greek word for whale, *ketos*. The modern word *cetacean* refers to the order of animals that includes whales, dolphins and porpoises; *cetology* is the study of whales

Closest star in Cassiopeia to Earth: Eta Cassiopeiae, 18 light-years away

Farthest star from Earth: Gamma Cassiopeiae, 730 light-years away

Brightest star: Schedar, magnitude 2.2

Double star: Even small telescopes reveal Eta Cassiopeiae, which lies between Schedar and Gamma Cassiopeiae, as a double star

Also see: Milky Way, Pegasus, Star Charts, Stars

CORONA BOREALIS
A Love Message to Ariadne

CORONA BOREALIS IS one of those constellations that actually looks like the thing it is named after. The delicate Northern Crown is a small half circle of stars lying between Boötes and Hercules. Not bright enough to compete with city lights, it glitters conspicuously in the night sky of wilderness areas.

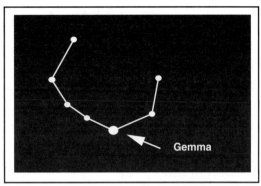

Gemma

Its Greek origins are traced to the story of Ariadne, the daughter of King Minos of Crete. In return for a promise of marriage, the lovestruck Ariadne helped the Athenian prince Theseus to enter the Labyrinth safely and kill its evil tenant, the Minotaur. Ariadne slipped Theseus a ball of thread, which he deployed as he searched for the grotesque half man, half bull. Theseus slew the Minotaur and followed the thread back to safety. Ariadne was supposed to return to Athens with her new husband, but the boat stopped first at Naxos, where it seems Theseus dumped her. But the god Dionysus came upon the heartbroken Ariadne and fell in love with her. As a show of affection, Dionysus placed his crown in the heavens in her name.

In the mythology of several North American native groups, including the Ojibway in Ontario, the stars of Corona Borealis were dancing maidens. The young women liked to descend to Earth each night to dance and play. One night a hunter spotted them and fell in love with the most beautiful dancer, while the others returned to the night sky.

The shape of Corona Borealis suggested other meanings to other cultures. In the Micmac myth Corona Borealis represented the den from which the bear—the Big Dipper—emerged each spring. To the Arabs, the constellation was a bowl or platter. The Australian aborigines saw a celestial boomerang they called Woomera.

Ariadne, the opera: In 1912 the German composer Richard Strauss wrote *Ariadne auf Naxos*. It was an opera-within-an-opera that told the story of lovesick Ariadne on the Greek island of Naxos

Dionysus: God of wine and fertility; Bacchus to the Romans. Festivals celebrating his death and resurrection gave rise to the dramatic arts

Theseus's other wives: After Ariadne, Theseus married the Amazon queen Hippolyta (also named Antiope), and after her death, Phaedra, Ariadne's sister. The hero of Athens became unpopular in his old age and was eventually murdered

Gemma: Latin for "jewel" and root of the word *gem*

Do-si-do: Gemma is an eclipsing double star or eclipsing binary. The two stars orbit each other every 17 years, and from our line of sight, one star eclipses the other as they pirouette about the sky. The system is too far away to see with a backyard telescope

Also see: Big Dipper, Hercules, Star Charts, Stars

DRACO
Dragon of the Cosmos

DRACO, ACCORDING TO American astronomy writer and lecturer Mark Chartrand, "has stood for all the dragons of mythology..." The word *Draco* comes from the Greek *drakon*, meaning "snake." But its origins slither back long before the Greeks. Draco is a direct link to creation.

In many cosmogonies, creation is the moment of "separation" in the primitive chaos, whether it be night and day ("Let there be light") or Heaven and Earth. In Babylonian mythology, the genesis story is told in *Enuma Elish*, an ancient composition dating to about 1500 B.C. In this story, the sea is called Tiamat, one of the elements of the watery chaos, and is identified with the female. Apsu is another element, representing the fresh waters, and is identified with the male. Together they begat other gods, including Enki, the Earth. Scholars link the story to the observation that earth in Mesopotamia is literally formed from the alluvial action of the Tigris and Euphrates rivers (Apsu, the fresh waters) depositing silt in the Persian Gulf (Tiamat).

Once the basic components of the universe were created, they had to be organized. This part of the story began when the children/gods of Tiamat and Apsu rebelled against their parents. In defence, Tiamat raised a powerful army of fire-breathing dragons, and herself assumed the shape of a serpent. The younger gods crowned Marduk as their king and champion, and he led them into battle. Marduk captured Tiamat and, since he was a storm god, blew a fierce wind down her gullet. Tiamat split in two, and Marduk lifted up half her body to form the sky, represented by Draco. The moment of Marduk's victory—action over chaos—was the moment of creation.

Similar elements of the story are contained in the Greek chronicle of the Titans versus the young gods of Olympus. Zeus, like Marduk, was a storm god, for example. In one battle against the Titans, the goddess Athena hurled an attacking serpent into the heavens, where it wrapped around the celestial north pole. Four thousand years ago, the star Thuban in Draco was the pole star. (Because Earth wobbles on its axis while the stars stay fixed, the pole star changes over the millennia.)

Draco appears in many other legends—protecting the golden fleece snatched by Jason, guarding the golden apples of Hesperides, stolen by Hercules as one of his twelve labours. In Spenser's *Faerie Queene*, the Knight of the Red Cross slew a dragon in his mission to rescue the parents of truth—an allegory for the story of St. George, the patron saint of England. Draco is also associated with the dragon in the German epic *Nibelungenlied*; the story is partly retold in Wagner's famous opera cycle *Der Ring des Nibelungen*.

There are three other drag-

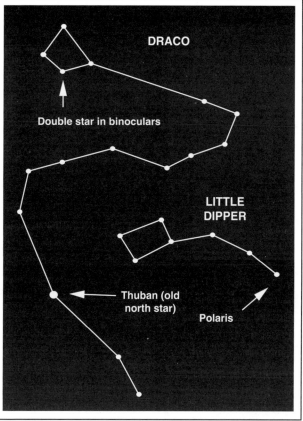

ons or serpents in the night sky: Cetus, Hydra and Serpens. Cetus appears low in the southern sky in autumn; it is the monster in the myth of Andromeda. Hydra, the many-headed serpent slain by Hercules, is the largest constellation in the heavens and skims the southern horizon in spring. Serpens is a dim but important constellation lying south of Hercules in the summer. It is the only constellation found in two parts: Serpens Caput, the head, and Serpens Cauda, the tail. They are joined by the constellation Ophiuchus, the Serpent Bearer. The legend goes that Ophiuchus killed a snake and watched in amazement as another snake came along to revive its companion with herbs. This led to the medicinal use of

plants and Ophiuchus's future as a healer. He was placed in the sky, with a serpent, in honour of his achievements. The modern symbol of medicine, the caduceus, depicting snakes wrapped around a staff, has its origins in this story.

The squarish head of Draco lies near the feet of Hercules, and its long body winds between the Big and Little Dippers. Urban lights obscure the dim stars of Draco, but in the darkness of wilderness the constellation writhes to life.

FALLING STARS
Anything to Worry About?

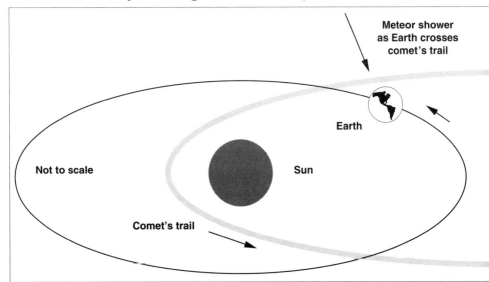

Meteor shower as Earth crosses comet's trail

Earth

Not to scale

Sun

Comet's trail

Favourite target of meteorites: Wethersfield, Connecticut. Two meteorites smashed into homes in this town, one in 1971 and the second in 1982

Close calls: An Alaskan woman suffered injuries to her arm when a meteorite slammed through the roof of her house in 1954. In 1991, a meteorite crashed into Arthur Pettifor's garden in England. He was quietly planting onions about 18 m (59 ft) away. A dog in Egypt was struck dead by a meteorite in 1912

Meteor: From the Greek *meta*, "beyond," and *eora*, "suspension"

Estimated number of meteorites heavier than 100 g (3.5 oz) landing on Earth's landmass each year: 5,800

Estimated weight of space dust that floats to Earth each day: About 20 tons

A PADDLE DIPS LANGUIDLY into the ink black water. A loon laughs. The night sky is a treasure chest of sparkling stars, reflected on the still lake. Every few minutes, high overhead, blue-green light streaks across the heavens. Sometimes there is a trail of sparks, like fireworks.

In mid-August, to a human lying back in a canoe in the middle of a dark lake, the Perseid meteor shower entertains like no other show on Earth.

Meteors are reminders that the space between the stars and planets is not completely empty. "Falling stars" are caused when rocky particles called meteoroids enter Earth's atmosphere. Nearly all meteoroids are the size of a grain of sand or smaller. But every once in a while a big sucker gets through. Imagine how surprised the grazing dinosaurs of ancient Mexico must have been when a boulder 20 kilometres (12 miles) wide came out of nowhere and wiped out the neighbourhood. The collision, which scientists believe occurred 65 million years ago in the Yucatán (then under a shallow sea), would have thrown up an enormous cloud of dust, blocking out the sunlight for years. It seems certain this is what killed off the dinosaurs. Chicken Little has run scared ever since.

In fact, the fate of the dinosaurs has led some scientists and leaders to wonder if a giant asteroid has the name "homo sapiens" written on it. In 1989, an asteroid about one kilometre (0.6 mile) wide crossed a spot in the Earth's orbit about six hours before the planet was there. NASA has proposed setting up a worldwide network of telescopes to spot an incoming apocalypse. The world would also need an asteroid-blaster rocket. But so far, preventing death from space has ranked low on political agendas.

The term *meteor* refers to the actual flare in the sky. The meteoroid vaporizes in about a second, 65 to 160 kilometres (40 to 100 miles) above the Earth's surface. A meteorite is a meteoroid large enough to survive the scorching descent to Earth. Anything bigger than an apple will make it to the ground, although a meteoroid's survival also depends on the speed it hits the atmosphere, the angle of entry and the integrity of its structure.

Where does all this space gravel come from? Some of it is debris that has wandered from the asteroid belt between Mars and Jupiter, destined to evaporate in a blaze of glory. Meteorites that hit Mars and the moon blow fragments into space that may also head our way—a meteoroid domino effect. Stray meteors appear at an average rate of about three to 12 an hour, and cannot be predicted. But look for them after midnight, because by then Spaceship Earth has spun so that we are looking "forward" into our orbit. The planet is now motoring into the path of any nearby meteoroids, so more meteors occur. Astronomers often compare this effect to a car travelling through a snowstorm: it collects more snow on the front windshield than the rear.

Regular meteor showers are a different phenomenon. Most occur when Earth intersects the path of a comet that's gone by. As a comet rushes towards the sun, it slowly disintegrates, leaving behind a concentrated trail of dirt. Because the trail is located along a specific line in space, a meteor shower occurs each time Earth crosses it; in other words, at the same time each year. The trail of the comet Swift-Tuttle causes the Perseid meteor shower. The rate of observable meteors may vary from year to year, sometimes wildly. Most years the Leonids in November produce about 15 meteors an

Number of meteorite craters on Earth: About 130

Number of craters on the Canadian Shield: 24

Notable craters: The Brent Crater in northern Algonquin Park was discovered by aerial photography in 1951. It is a circular depression 4 km (2.4 mi) wide that now contains lakes Gilmour and Tecumseh. The crater was gouged into the Canadian Shield 450 million years ago by a meteorite about 150 m (492 ft) in diameter. Some scientists think Hudson Bay may have been formed by a massive meteorite. The mineral-rich Sudbury Basin is also thought to be the legacy of a meteorite that hit Precambrian Ontario 1.7 billion years ago. Other impact sites include the Slate Islands in Lake Superior, Lake Wanapitei northeast of Sudbury, and Holleford, north of Kingston

Force of meteorite that created the Brent Crater: Estimated 250 megatons

Largest nuclear explosion ever set off: 60 megatons

Why the moon has more impact craters: The moon has no atmosphere to burn up incoming meteoroids. Also, geophysical forces on Earth erode crater features. No such forces exist on the moon

Age of meteorites: About 4.6 billion years old

Age of solar system: About 4.6 billion years old

"Go and catch a falling star": The famous first line of John Donne's poem "Song," written

MAJOR METEOR SHOWERS				
SHOWER	DATE (PEAK)	RADIANT	RATE/HOUR*	SPEED HITTING EARTH
Quadrantids	Jan. 4	Draco	40	41 km/s
Lyrids	Apr. 21	Lyra	15	48
Eta Aquarids	May 4	Aquarius	20	65
S. Delta Aquarids	July 28	Aquarius	20	41
N. Aquarids	Aug. 12	Aquarius	20	42
Perseids	Aug. 12	Perseus	50	60
Orionids	Oct. 21	Orion	25	66
S. Taurids	Nov. 2 or 3	Taurus	15	28
Leonids	Nov. 17 or 16	Leo	15	71
Geminids	Dec. 13	Gemini	50	35
Ursids	Dec. 22	Ursa Minor	15	34

* Single observer under exceptional conditions. Most observers will see far fewer.

hour under the best conditions. But every 33 years or so a spectacular Leonid shower may occur, with tens of thousands of meteors falling each hour. The next Leonid blast is expected in 1998, 1999 or 2000.

Keeners will note that each meteor in a shower emanates from approximately the same point in space, called the radiant. Meteor showers are named after the constellation in which the radiant is located, the radiant of the Perseids being the constellation Perseus, for example. The Perseids is one of the best showers to enjoy because of the high intensity—about 50 an hour—and the fact that it's not –40° outside.

In the old days, people came up with all sorts of explanations for meteors. In Islamic folklore, meteors were missiles hurled by angels at evil spirits lurking around the gates of Heaven. English peasants in the Middle Ages believed a falling star was a soul passing from Heaven to Earth at the birth or conception of a new person—the reason they were wished upon. An Ojibway story describes meteors as demons sent to Earth by an idle sky spirit who wished to perplex the people living in the meteor's target zone; another tale says falling stars represent gifts of Kitche Manitou, the Creator, to someone on Earth. Pliny the Elder, a Roman philosopher and naturalist, thought a falling star marked someone's death, as every person had his or her own star in the sky. That raises the question: Did a meteor appear the day Pliny died? There should have been thousands, because the poor man went to Pompeii to study the eruptions of Mt. Vesuvius in 79 A.D., and got caught in the most famous eruption ever. There were no reports of unusual meteor showers at the time.

in 1633, in which he suggests that fantastic feats such as catching a falling star are all easier than finding "a woman true, and fair"

Also see: Canadian Shield, Fireflies, Limestone, Planets & Comets, Sky

HERCULES
The Strongman and the Star Cluster

HERCULES seems an incongruous constellation. It's one of the dimmer formations in the summer sky, yet one of the oldest star patterns known to humanity. Behind this set of stars lies a story of heroism and foolishness, hope and suffering, the redeeming power of love versus the terrible fury of jealousy, and the best way to flush mountains of cow poop out of a barn.

Hercules was a Roman strongman, but his roots go deeper into Western mythology. Some scholars say he is descended from the Sumerian king Gilgamesh, who also led an epic life and left a trail of dead monsters behind him. More directly, *Hercules* is Latin for Heracles, the Greek hero. Heracles was the son of Zeus and one of Zeus's many mistresses, Alcmene, the lonely wife of a general. When Zeus's own wife, Hera, learned of the love child, she placed two serpents in the youngster's crib to kill him. Little Heracles got to them first, and the legend was born. Later, Hera's jealousy caused her to cast a spell of temporary madness on Heracles, during which he killed his wife and children. To purge himself of guilt for this act, he became a slave to King Eurystheus, who set out the famous "Twelve Labours of Hercules" as penance. Heracles completed each one (despite more of Hera's meddling), and went on to perform many more feats of strength.

Because the stars in this constellation are dim, Hercules is best viewed on dark nights away from city lights. It is located roughly halfway between the bright stars Vega and Arcturus. The constellation is often depicted on star maps as the "butterfly," which could be said to outline Hercules's knees, waist and shoulders. The figure is actually upside-down; imagine him kneeling on his right knee and stepping on the head of nearby Draco with his left foot. Other stars in the constellation mark his arms and head. Old illustrations sometimes show him wielding a club in his right hand and grasping the multiheaded Hydra in the other. One of the brightest stars in Hercules, Ras Algethi, is Arabic for "the kneeler's head." It is actually a double star, observable in a small telescope.

Another notable astronomical feature of Hercules is the

The Pillars of Hercules: The rock of Gibraltar, on the coast of Spain, and Jebel Musa, Morocco, the gateposts to the Mediterranean

Hercules's great-great-grandparents: Perseus and Andromeda

Closest star in Hercules to Earth: Mu Herculis, 25 light-years away

Farthest Star: Alpha Herculis, also called Ras Algethi, 630 light-years away

Distance of globular cluster M13 from Earth: 22,000 light-years away

The M in M13: Charles Messier, an 18th-century astronomer, catalogued many faint, hazy objects to make sure they weren't mistaken for comets.

The 12 Labours of Hercules:

1. Kill the Nemean Lion. Its soul became the constellation Leo

2. Kill the Hydra, a monster that grew 2 heads when 1 was chopped off. Hydra is also a constellation, located next to Leo

3. Bring back alive the golden-horned stag from the Cerynitian forests

4. Capture the great boar on Mount Erymanthus

5. Clean the Augean stables— which had been without janitorial services for years—in one day. This he did by diverting 2 rivers through the stables

6. Eradicate the enormous flock of birds that was getting in the hair of the people of Stymphalus

259

7. Capture and present to Eurystheus the savage bull of Crete that Poseidon had given Minos. This bull was the father of the Minotaur, the half-man, half-bull monster

8. Capture the man-eating mares of Diomedes

9. Snatch the girdle from Hippolyta, Queen of the Amazons

10. Rustle the cattle of a 3-bodied monster named Geryon

11. Fetch the Golden Apples of Hesperides. In one version of this story, the apples were guarded by the serpent Ladon, who is sometimes represented by the constellation Draco

12. Retrieve the three-headed dog Cerebus from Hades

Other significant feats: Hercules freed Prometheus by killing the eagle that each day ate out his liver. That broke the cycle of torture that was Prometheus's punishment for giving fire to mankind. He had been bound to a rock, and each night, after the eagle's feast, his liver would grow back

Also see: Corona Borealis, Milky Way, Pegasus & Andromeda, Star Charts, Stars

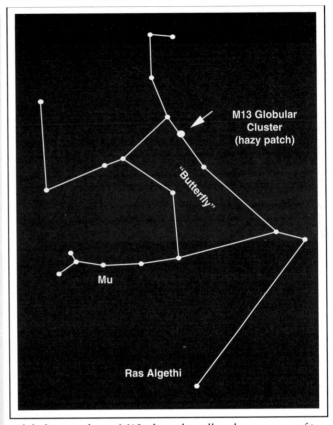

globular star cluster M13, the only stellar phenomenon of its type visible to the naked eye in the northern hemisphere. A globular star cluster may contain millions of stars grouped together by gravity. They travel around the Milky Way outside the main galactic disc in a region called the halo. M13 appears to the unaided eye as a faint hazy patch on a line between the stars Eta Herculis and Zeta Herculis. Binoculars give a better view of this fuzzy structure, although a telescope is necessary to discern individual stars.

Neither optical instrument, however, matches the best viewing aid of all for looking at Hercules: the imagination. To gaze upon this ancient figure is to peer into a deep reservoir of mythology.

MILKY WAY
The Path of Souls

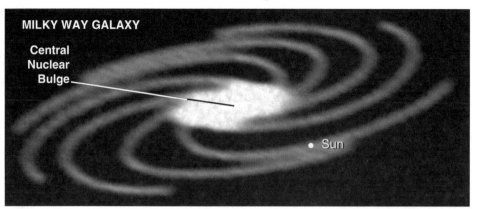

MILKY WAY GALAXY

Central Nuclear Bulge

Sun

T HE MILKY WAY, obliterated by city lights, glows to life in the dark night sky of the countryside and wilderness. Its horizon-to-horizon span suggests a pathway to the stars, a notion that ancient cultures fixed upon. In many mythologies, humans and their spirits ascended this path to the heavens, or gods and sky creatures descended it to join mortals on the ground. The Ojibway called the Milky Way the Path of Souls. As part of the Ojibway burial ritual, a campfire is lit near the death-post marking a grave. The fire is kept burning for four days to light the way for the soul-spirit, which must travel the Path of Souls to reach the Land of Souls.

In classical Greek mythology, the whitish band is said to represent a stream of milk from Rhea's breast as she suckled her son Zeus. Another story says the milk came from Hera, Zeus's wife. (The word *galaxy* comes from the Greek word for "milk," *gala* or *galaktos*.) An account is also found in the myth of Phaeton, son of Apollo. One day Phaeton persuaded his dad to let him take the sun chariot for a spin. Apollo, wary as any father lending his car to his young son would be, told Phaeton to steer a middle course between Heaven and Earth. But Phaeton ended up an insurance statistic. The young driver lost control of the chariot, flew too high and scorched the sky, creating the Milky Way. Then he swerved back to Earth and burned the vegetation off the Sahara. Zeus ended the joyride with a fatal thunderbolt.

Pythagoras and other scientific Greeks theorized that the

Diameter: About 100,000 light-years

Thickness: About 13,000 light-years

Travel time to leave the Milky Way galaxy in our fastest spacecraft: About 570 million years

Age: Uncertain, but probably 10 to 15 billion years old

Number of stars: Uncertain; probably 300 billion, maybe one trillion

Closest large neighbour: Andromeda Galaxy, 2.2 million light-years away

Number of galaxies in the universe: Uncertain, but likely 50 to 100 billion

Time it takes for our solar system to orbit the Milky Way: About 220 million years

Speed of our solar system as it orbits the Milky Way: 250 km/sec (150 mi/sec)

Number of dry vodka martinis in the Milky Way: There are enough vodka molecules — composed of water, ammonia and ethyl alcohol — in interstellar gases to fill 10,000 glasses the size of Earth, according to some thirsty scientists. But because the water content is so high, the vodka is only 0.002 proof. Also, a Milky Way martini would be spiked with hydrogen cyanide

Other names for the Milky Way: Many peoples from India to Scandinavia thought of the Milky Way as milk from the moon-cow goddess. Worlds and creatures were created from the curdled milk, including a moon of green cheese. Celts called the Milky Way *Bothar-Bo-Finne* or Track of the White Cow—the source of the story about the cow jumping over the moon. The Egyptians called it the Nile of the Sky, which flowed from the udder of the moon-cow Hathor-Isis. Other names include Irmin's Way, Anglo-Saxon; *Hiddagal* or River of the Divine Lady, Akkadian; *Umm al sama* or Mother of the Sky, Arab; *Manavegr* or Moon Way, Norse; Silver Stream of Heaven, Chinese

Galileo: Florentine astronomer and physicist, 1564–1642. Condemned by the Roman Inquisition for his support of Copernican theories, which placed the sun, not the Earth, at the centre of the Solar System. The Vatican acknowledged its error 359 years later, in 1992

Also see: Moon, Pegasus & Andromeda, Star Charts, Stars, Summer Triangle, Yellow-rumped Warbler

glow from the Milky Way came from a multitude of stars. But it took Galileo and his telescope to prove this conclusively. Modern science has shown that galaxies are the basic building blocks of the universe. Colossal agglomerations of stars, they come in four basic shapes: elliptical, spiral, barred spiral and irregular. The Milky Way, our own galaxy, is a relatively large spiral galaxy with several arms of super-bright and many less-bright stars. Our solar system is located in the Orion Arm, towards the edge of town, cosmically speaking.

For people of the northern hemisphere, the Milky Way is more prominent in summer than winter. This is because of the solar system's position about two-thirds out from the centre of the galaxy. On summer nights (winter in the southern hemisphere), the Earth is positioned so that we look into the dense middle of the galactic disc. In winter, all we see is the final one-third of the galaxy and the dark, deep space beyond. The vast swath of the Milky Way arcs across the celestial dome from north to south on early-summer evenings. It twists in the sky as summer progresses, until in mid-November it reaches from the eastern to western horizon.

The spout of the famous "teapot" constellation, Sagittarius, which appears low over the southern horizon in the summer, points to the hub of the Milky Way. This is where the Milky Way is at its widest and most luminous. But the galaxy's central nuclear bulge, a region where older stars are densely packed, is not clearly visible. Vast clouds of interstellar dust and gas block the view. These same clouds are responsible for visible rifts in the Milky Way. One of these dark patches cuts through the Summer Triangle.

Several constellations are located along the Milky Way, including Cassiopeia, Cepheus, Cygnus and Aquila. Both Cygnus the swan and Aquila the eagle fly in the direction of the astral belt. Ornithologists speculate, and natives traditionally believe, that migrating birds use the glimmer of the Milky Way as a navigational aid—making it truly a path in the heavens.

MOON
The Original Timepiece

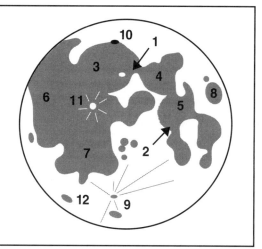

IF THE SUN STANDS for permanence, the moon is transience. Our nighttime companion transforms itself every night; it appears and disappears, dies and is resurrected. For this reason the moon is powerfully connected with the rhythms and mysteries of life and the passage of time.

The first calendars were based on the phases of the moon. There is evidence that cave dwellers in France recorded the lunar cycle with notches in animal bones and antlers, 25,000 years before the first writing in Mesopotamia. It would have taken a few years, but eventually cavemen or cavewomen must have figured out that the seasons repeated themselves every 12 full moons or so.

In Europe the year was based on a lunar calendar until 45 B.C.—an imperfect system because 12 lunar months do not add up to a solar year of 365 days. Julius Caesar, with the help of an Egyptian astronomer, resolved the problem when he ditched the idea of lunar months and divided the year into 12 independent calendar months, with a leap year every four years. The month of July is named after him. Later, in 1532, Pope Gregory XIII refined the Julian calendar because it was coming up short one day every 128 years. Gregory artificially shortened October that year— October 5 to 14, 1532, do not exist in history—and made

Number of one-way trips between Toronto and North Bay it would take to travel the mean distance between Earth and the moon: 1,148

Distance from Earth: 356,400 km (213,840 mi) at closest (perigee); 406,700 km (244,020 mi) at farthest (apogee)

Diameter: 3,476 km (2,085 mi)

Moon gravity: About one-sixth Earth's gravity

Age: 4.6 billion years old

First lunar probe to land on the surface: The Soviets' *Luna 2*, crashed Sept. 13, 1959

First man on the moon: Neil Armstrong, *Apollo 11*, July 20, 1969

Last man on the moon: Eugene Cernan, *Apollo 17*, Dec. 11, 1972

Magnitude: -12.7 at full moon

Why we see only one side of the moon: Just as the moon causes tides on Earth, the Earth's gravity causes "tides" on the moon. There is no sea, of course, but the landmass does shift. Over time, friction caused by the shifting land has slowed down the moon, so that the period of rotation on its axis—its "day"—exactly matches the 27.3 days it takes to orbit Earth. In other words, Earth's gravity has locked on to the moon so that only one side ever presents itself to us. Tides on Earth are also slowing down our planet. The day is getting longer by one second every 60,000 years. When Earth was first formed, a day used to be 22 hours long

Tides on lakes: Even a cup of tea is affected by the moon's gravity. But the lake tides are imperceptible to all but the most sophisticated equipment

Once in a blue moon: There are two explanations for this expression. The second full moon in a month with two full moons (it happens twice every five years or so) is said to be a blue moon. Also, the full moon sometimes appears blue because of atmospheric conditions created by high dust content after volcanic eruptions or large forest fires. Huge fires in Canada in September 1950 created stunning blue moons

Harvest moon: The full moon closest to the autumnal equinox, occurring either in Sept. or Oct. Owing to the alignment of Earth, moon and sun at this time of year, the bright moon before, after and during the Harvest Moon stays in the night sky longer than at other times of the year—ideal

other changes, so that the calendar is now accurate to within one day every 3,200 years.

Although the Julian/Gregorian calendar has been adopted almost worldwide, some cultures retain the lunar calendar for religious, festive and day-to-day use. Moslem countries use a lunar calendar that began the day Mohammed was chased out of Mecca by unruly citizens enraged by his preachings (on July 16, 622, by the Gregorian calendar). The Moslem year of 12 lunar months makes no provision for the solar year. Every year the seasons begin earlier, until, in $32\frac{1}{2}$ years, the cycle starts repeating. The Jewish calendar is also based on the lunar month, beginning with the biblical moment of creation (3761 B.C. Gregorian time). It is adjusted for the solar year, however, with the addition of a thirteenth month every three to four years. Another lunar calendar, the Chinese, has been abandoned for civil use, but important Buddhist and Taoist festivals are still held around new and full moons.

The lunar cycle was of great importance to native peoples in Ontario, who also used it as a calendar. Full moons were often named after natural events occurring around the same time, and were sometimes associated with human activities such as hunting, fishing or food-gathering. The Ojibway call the full moon in May the Sucker Moon. That is the month suckers spawn up Ontario streams. June is the Blooming Moon, July the Berry Moon, August the Grain Moon and September the Leaves-Turning Moon. The Ojibway in more southern latitudes have given the moon names related to other natural events.

The rhythms of the moon are also deeply linked to fertility. The $29\frac{1}{2}$-day period between full moons closely matches the average female menstrual cycle. The word *menstruation* comes from the Latin word for "monthly." Charles Darwin suggested that since humans ultimately evolved from the sea, it followed that menstrual periods were a distant echo of the tides. Whether the female and lunar cycles have a rational connection is a matter of debate. The menstrual cycles of other mammals, for example, do not match the average 28-day human one. But the fact that the lunar and human periods do coincide may have had a profound impact on the development of civilization. Some feminist scholars believe the earliest timekeeping evolved through the need of women to know the season of birth of their children, which would have required a knowledge of the link between menstrual and moon phases, and the nine-month or nine-moon gestation period. This could have led to the first calendars, perhaps those same cave calendars of France.

Symbolically, the fact the moon is "reborn" each month has led to its deep association with women since ancient times. Many mythologies and religions have moon goddesses; the most famous is probably Artemis, the Greek goddess of hunting, whose Roman equivalent is Diana. The Ojibway think of the moon as Grandmother Moon, the first mother in the creation myth, who still keeps watch over her offspring. The Sioux call it the Old Woman Who Never Dies.

The moon is related to another aspect of the human condition: madness. Lunacy, from the Latin *luna*, or "moon," has been attributed to a mysterious connection between the full moon and our mental state. It is traditionally thought that lunar gravity—the same force that causes the tides and probably earthquakes—somehow pulls our psyche out of kilter, perhaps in the same way it starts the menstrual flow. There is little proof for this, although there is no doubting the fact that 200 years ago, inmates in English lunatic asylums were flogged just before the full moon to deter violent behaviour. Who was actually mad in this case is another question.

One moon mystery remains unsolved even after visits to the silvery orb by several well-educated, middle-aged American men: how was it that Earth came to have a companion in the first place? Scientists have a few theories. The moon may have formed close to Earth at the same time Earth condensed out of the cloud of dust and gas that became our solar system. Alternatively, the moon may have formed elsewhere in the solar system, but was somehow captured by Earth's gravitational field. A more recent theory proposes that a huge asteroid smashed into Earth early in the planet's evolution, and threw up debris that eventually coalesced into the moon. No one knows for sure.

for farmers harvesting their crops at night

Why the moon seems bigger when it's close to the horizon: The best explanation for this illusion is that the full moon seems large near the horizon because the eye can easily compare its size with other objects, such as buildings. To check the illusion, hold an Aspirin tablet at arm's length and place it over the moon. It covers the moon whether it's near the horizon or higher up

Moon goddesses: Artemis, the Greek goddess of hunting; Selene, a Greek Titan sometimes associated with Artemis (*selenology* is the study of the moon); Hecate, the Greek goddess of the new moon (and thus darkness); Diana, the Roman goddess of hunting; Mama Qilla, the Inca moon goddess; Isis, the mother of Egypt; Galata, the Celtic moon goddess; Hina, of Polynesia

How to tell if the moon is waxing or waning: If the right-hand side of the moon is illuminated, the moon is waxing—heading towards full moon. If the left-hand side is illuminated, it is waning—past full moon and heading into new moon

Also see: Milky Way, Planets & Comets, Sun

NORTHERN LIGHTS
Ghostly Illuminations from Solar Wind

THE INUIT CALL them the Dance of the Dead. Poet Robert Frost likened them to "tingling nerves." Astronomers describe them as ionospheric gaseous luminations triggered by precipitating energetic particles. But to most people they are the northern lights, among nature's most stunning creations.

Northern lights are usually seen as a shimmering white or greenish glow just above the northern horizon. At first they may be mistaken for the haze of city lights, or even the glow of a gibbous moon before it rises over the horizon. But dark-adjusted eyes soon detect the telltale pulses of vertical shafts of light, which intensify, then fade seconds later in a wavy, ethereal curtain. Sometimes a ray will shoot high into the sky, then dissolve into the blackness. In an intense display, the curtain rises higher, until it appears directly overhead like a surreal tunnel of light reaching to the zenith. This is called the aurora's corona. Magnificent streams of light cascade up and down the crown, accompanied by eerie pulses of white light unlike anything concocted in a sci-fi movie.

More prosaically, northern lights are the result of solar wind entering Earth's magnetic field. Solar wind comprises millions of tons of electrons and protons emitted by the sun every minute. When these atomic particles enter the magnetic field surrounding Earth, they are separated, creating a vast store of electrical potential high above the ground. The magnetic field, in effect, becomes a 20,000- to 150,000-volt battery of static electricity. For reasons not yet fully understood, an occasional disturbance will send a burst of this energy along the lines of Earth's magnetic field, towards the north or south magnetic poles. The energy excites oxygen and nitrogen molecules, at altitudes of 100 to 400 kilometres (60 to 240 miles), into a gaseous glow: the northern lights, or aurora borealis.

Although it's almost impossible to predict exactly when northern lights will occur, or their intensity, some things are known about their behaviour. In years when the solar wind blows stronger, the northern lights are more intense. "Gusts" of solar wind are caused by sunspots and solar flares, which

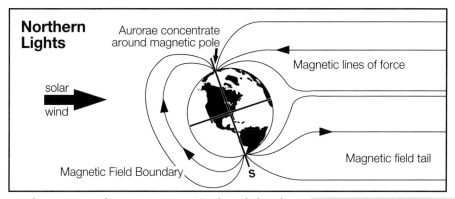

Northern Lights

Aurorae concentrate around magnetic pole

Magnetic lines of force

solar wind

Magnetic field tail

Magnetic Field Boundary

S

intensify approximately every 11 years. Northern lights thus tend to put on greater displays every 11 years or so, according to this solar cycle. The peak may last for two or three years. On March 13, 1989, at the beginning of the most recent peak period, a spectacular and rare display of red northern lights was seen as far south as the Caribbean. The energy storm was so powerful that it knocked out the Hydro-Québec power grid, putting six million people in the dark.

Green, the most common auroral colour, is produced by excited oxygen atoms about 110 kilometres (66 miles) above Earth's surface. Blue comes from nitrogen molecules at approximately the same height. Red light, a special treat, is produced by traces of oxygen between 200 and 400 kilometres (120 and 240 miles) up. Because the gas is so thin at that altitude, red light is rare and occurs only when great quantities of energy flow along the magnetic-field lines. Another type of red aurora, sometimes seen fringing other colours, occurs through a slightly different interaction lower in the atmosphere. Common white aurorae are simply northern lights of such low intensity that the eye cannot discern colours.

Some people claim they hear northern lights as a soft crackling. Sceptical scientists tend to discount this possibility, because the aurora occurs far above Earth in the thin atmosphere. But so many people have reported hearing the "murmurings of the spirits" that the jury is still out.

Central Ontario gets an average of 20 displays a year.

Best viewing time: Between 11:00 p.m. and 2:00 a.m.

Aurora australis: The southern lights are rarely seen except by penguins. Of the populated continents, only the tip of South America extends into the prime viewing zone

Also see: Sky, Sun

NORTH STAR &
LITTLE DIPPER
The Peg That Fastens the Universe

Cynosure: The Greeks also called Polaris the Dog's Tail, or *Kynosoura*. This is the root of the word *cynosure*, meaning "a centre of attraction."

Distance of Polaris from Earth: 820 light-years away

How to determine latitude: At the North Pole, Polaris is directly overhead, or 90° straight up. The star is at a 45° angle to a viewer at 45° latitude, and so on. A sextant measures the angle. Early navigators who sailed below the equator got lost because Polaris disappeared over the the the horizon.

Precession: Gravitational forces of the moon and sun affect the spinning of the Earth, causing our planet to wobble on its axis like a spinning top as it slows down. Called precession, this wobble has a cycle of about 26,000 years. Because of precession, the star marking the celestial north pole changes over the milennia. The Babylonians observed the phenomenon 5,000 years ago; the Greek astronomer Hipparchus recorded this effect in the 2nd century B.C. Hipparchus also invented the system of magnitude for classifying the brightness of stars.

Is there a south pole star? No. The spot in the sky marking the south celestial pole is not occupied by a convenient star.

Also see: Big Dipper, Draco, Milk Snake, Star Charts, Stars, Zodiac & Ecliptic

THE NORTH STAR, Polaris, is the most important star in all the heavens. It is not the brightest star in the night sky, but by dint of its fixed location almost exactly over Earth's north pole, it has assumed a prominent role in civilization. It was the star by which early mariners navigated their way about the treacherous seas. It was central to the cosmology of many cultures. It remains a powerful metaphor for the constant, the truth. As Hitler was consolidating his forces and war broke out in Spain, the American poet Archibald MacLeish wrote in his poem "Pole Star for This Year:"

We too turn now to that star:
We too in whose trustless hearts
All truth alters and the lights
Of earth are out now turn to that star...

Because of the rotation of the Earth, all the northern constellations appear to revolve counterclockwise around Polaris. The observation of this movement as well as the cycles of the moon, sun and planets gave the ancients their sense of time. People of many old cultures believed the appearance of specific stars at certain times of the year actually caused events, such as the flooding of the Nile—hence the origin of astrology.

The North Star appears in all mythologies. Its apparent immobility in the whirling procession of the stars must have been observed by the earliest cave dwellers. The Moguls called it the Golden Peg that fastened the universe together. In Scandinavia's violent mythology it was the World Spike, the *Veralder Nagli*. (The Norse gods constructed their sky out of the chopped-up bits of adversaries; the nail in the centre of the universe finished off the job.) In an Arab myth, the Big Dipper was a coffin that held the body of a great warrior killed by the evil North Star. The stars that revolve around the North Star, including the Big Dipper, formed a funeral procession. Chinese stories about the North Star relate it to T'ai Chi, the great Absolute or Unity; it was the perfect union of the yin and yang principles. The North Star was also a symbol for the emperor, representing permanence in a transient world. The Pawnee called it the Star That Does Not Walk Around.

An Ojibway story of two male cousins describes the origins of the North Star and the echo phenomenon. The cousins were great friends and hunters. One day their grandmother introduced them to two women who were to be their companions. But the cousins were suspicious and thought the women might form a wedge in their friendship. Sure enough, one cousin fell in love with his chosen mate and neglected his buddy, who remained the better hunter because his mind was not distracted. The hunter left his friend and ascended into the stars to become the North Star, *Ke-wa-den-ah-mung*, where he still pursues the bear. His love-struck cousin stayed on Earth and cried in the forest for his lost friend. He became known as *Bah-swa-way*, or Echo.

The pole star has actually changed over the millennia because the Earth wobbles slightly on its axis, a phenomenon known as precession. Four thousand years ago the pole

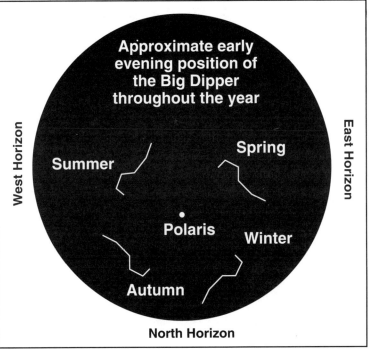

Approximate early evening position of the Big Dipper throughout the year

West Horizon

East Horizon

Summer

Spring

Polaris

Winter

Autumn

North Horizon

star was Thuban, in the constellation Draco. Archeologists have discovered that Egyptian pyramids were built to align with Thuban. Polaris will be nearest the spot that is the true celestial north in the year 2100.

In modern astronomy, Polaris is placed at the end of the constellation Ursa Minor, the lesser bear, commonly called the Little Dipper. Ursa Minor is a dim constellation, several of whose stars are at the limits of naked-eye visibility. Polaris is usually the only star visible from a city. Ursa Minor is, of course, related to Ursa Major, the great bear hauled into the heavens by Zeus in the Greek myth. One way to remember the arrangement of the two Dippers in the night sky is to think of them pouring their contents into each other.

PEGASUS & ANDROMEDA
The Steed and the Princess

Plot of 1971 B-movie
Andromeda Strain: A lethal
virus from deep space arrives
in the U.S. Scientists race
against time to save the world

Number of stars in Andromeda
galaxy: Uncertain, perhaps
300 to 500 billion

Distance of Alpheratz, the
shared star in Andromeda and
Pegasus, to Earth: 100 light-
years away

Medusa: The only mortal Gorgon,
3 mythical monsters with hair
of serpents. Medusa's counte-
nance was so horrible to
behold that viewers were
immediately turned to stone.
Perseus, in killing Medusa,
avoided this fate by using his
bronze shield as a mirror.
Shortly afterwards he used
Medusa's head to help save
Andromeda from Cetus.
Perseus waved the head in
front of Cetus, and the sea
monster fossilized instantly

Chimera (pronounced *kuh-MIR-ah*): This monster's name
entered the English language
with several related meanings.
Chimera is an absurd creation
of the imagination, or any
grotesque, fantastical creature;
it is a hybrid organism with
mixed characteristics; it is the
genus of fishes that includes
sharks and rays

LATE-NIGHT COTTAGE or campfire gatherings are ideal occasions to watch the grand procession of constellations across the night sky. One of the greatest sights is the flight of the legendary winged horse, Pegasus. In mid-July this majestic constellation soars above the eastern horizon at about 10:00 p.m. and by 4:00 a.m. it is high in the southern sky. (The later in the year, the earlier it rises; add about one hour for every two weeks.) Pegasus's most famous feature, the Great Square, is like a huge window into the inky depths of the universe.

In Western culture, the ancient Mesopotamians first construed these stars as a heavenly horse. Its form, like Hercules, is upside-down: the head and neck are the suite of stars along the bottom, while the two prongs coming from the top right of the Great Square are the horse's forequarters. The hindquarters are missing; one theory is that the nearby constellation Aries was formed with stars that may have been, in ancient times, Pegasus's rear end.

Greek poets wrote various episodes in the story of Pegasus. He was born when drops of blood from the head of the Gorgon Medusa fell into the sea foam. Medusa had been decapitated by Perseus, who used the head as a novel wedding present for his mother, Danaë, and her lover, King Polydectes. The sea foam accounts for Pegasus's whiteness.

Another story concerns Bellerophon, a young man whose greatest desire was to tame and ride Pegasus. As a pair, their most famous adventure was the slaying of the Chimera, a ferocious monster with the head of a lion, the body of a goat and the tail of a serpent. Bellerophon was actually sent on the mission under false pretences. He had spurned the love of Queen Anteia, and in her bitterness she set in motion a chain of events that was supposed to lead to the death of Bellerophon by the Chimera. But astride Pegasus, Bellerophon was invincible.

Almost. Success went to his head, and Bellerophon decided to ride up to Olympus to join the gods. Pegasus thought

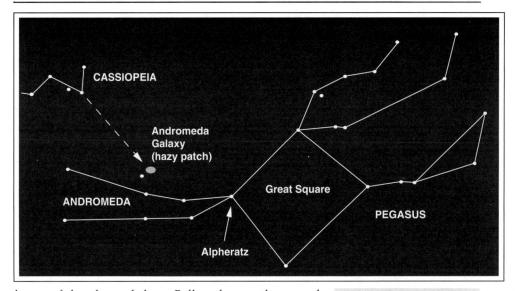

better of the idea and threw Bellerophon to the ground below. (In another version, Zeus sent a horsefly to sting Pegasus, causing the steed to buck his rider.) Pegasus ascended with the permission of the gods, to become a member of the Olympian stalls—and a constellation in the heavens.

Alpheratz, the top-left star in the Great Square, is officially a member of the constellation Andromeda. The two constellations are connected in mythology as well as in form. It was during his journey home after slaying the Medusa that Perseus spotted Andromeda chained to rocks in the sea off ancient Aethiopia. Perseus rescued Andromeda before she was assaulted by the sea monster Cetus, and later the two were married. Perseus also lies next to Andromeda in the night sky.

The famous Andromeda galaxy is so named because it is found in the vicinity of the constellation. The galaxy is the farthest object from Earth detectable with the naked eye, 2.2 million light-years away. The light we see today left the Andromeda galaxy just as our species was evolving in Africa. On a dark night the galaxy is visible as an oval smudge; through binoculars it's possible to see a brightening in the middle that is the galaxy's central nuclear bulge. To find the Andromeda galaxy, imagine that the brightest star in Cassiopeia, Schedar, is the point of an arrow aimed directly at our galactic neighbour.

Homer: Scholars aren't sure whether a person named Homer actually existed, but the *Iliad* and the *Odyssey* are traditionally attributed to him. Part of Pegasus's story is contained in the *Iliad*. Homer, if he lived, probably wrote in the 9th century B.C.

Hesiod: Greek poet of the 8th century B.C. who told the story of the Chimera

Also see: Cassiopeia, Deer Flies & Horse Flies, Star Charts, Stars

PLANETS & COMETS
Wanderers of the Night Sky

Planetary and night-sky updates: The McLaughlin Planetarium in Toronto offers a regularly updated taped phone service with information about current night-sky sights.
Call 416-586-5736

Also see: Falling Stars, Milky Way, Moon, Northern Lights, Sun, Zodiac

MERCURY ☿

Distance from sun:
58 million km (35 million mi)

Diameter: 4,880 km
(2,928 mi)

Day: 59 Earth days

Year: 88 days

Surface temperature: 430°C (806°F) day-side, -180°C (-292°F) night-side

Moons: 0

Magnitude: +1 to +2

Successful probes: *Mariner 10*, 1974

Day of the week: Wednesday, from *Woden*, Norse for Mercury; *mercredi* in French

Notable: Craters on Mercury are named after men and women of the arts, including Rubens, Dickens and Beethoven. Mercury has a highly elliptical orbit

VENUS ♀

Distance from sun: 108 million km (65 million mi)

Diameter: 12,100 km (7,260 mi)

Day: 243 Earth days

Year: 225 days

FOUR-AND-A-HALF billion years ago, in this particular corner of the universe, there was no sun, no Earth, no solar system at all. But there was matter—a vast, churning cloud of gas and dust. Gravity caused this cloud to begin contracting, until internal heat from the great inward pressure ignited a powerful nuclear fusion reaction in the centre of the nebula. The sun was born.

Leftover material was blown away from the solar furnace, but remained trapped in the sun's gravitational grasp. Over eons, this rotating matter coalesced into asteroids and comets, and eventually into the nine planets that today make up our cosmic neighbourhood.

As the planets move along their orbits around the sun, they appear in different positions against our night sky. Hence, the word *planet* comes from *planetes*, Greek for "wanderer." All the planets rotate around the sun in the same direction and on a rough plane called the ecliptic.

MERCURY, the Messenger

The naked eye can detect Mercury, Venus, Mars, Jupiter and Saturn, the planets (plus Earth) known to the ancients. Mercury is the most difficult to observe, because of its small size and its orbit close to the sun. However, it can be seen skimming the western horizon at dusk or the eastern horizon at dawn at certain times of the year. This scorched, cratered planet has virtually no atmosphere, owing to the sun's blazing heat. It is named after the Roman god Mercury, the messenger with winged sandals, winged hat and winged magic wand who faithfully delivered Jupiter's memos. The planet is appropriately named: Mercury has the fastest orbit, taking only 88 days to circumnavigate the sun.

VENUS, the Goddess of Love and Beauty

Venus, in contrast with Mercury, is the easiest planet to observe. After the sun and the moon, it is the brightest object in the sky, a radiant jewel in the early evening or early-morning darkness. It is observable for about six months out of every 18, and travels closer to Earth than any other planet. Venus shines brilliantly because three-quarters of the sunlight hitting the sphere reflects off the dense, white, carbon-dioxide atmosphere that enshrouds the planet. Lovely from a distance, Venus is in fact a greenhouse hell, with a surface temperature of 480°C (896°F). Had they known the astronomical truth about this nightmarish world, the Romans might have been disappointed. Venus, after all, was their goddess of love and beauty. The Greeks called her Aphrodite. But in Mesoamerican societies of the central U.S. and Mexico, the planet Venus played a major role in rituals of war and sacrifice. Scholars believe the appearance of Venus regulated the timing of military raids and wars.

MOTHER EARTH

Nearly Venus's twin in size, but in all other respects completely different, is our own world. Earth is the only planet to support life, thanks to miraculous circumstances such as its distance from the sun and the 23.5° tilt that produces the seasons. These conditions give Earth its ability to produce and hold water, which covers 70 percent of the planet.

The Earth's surface is divided into six or seven major crustal plates and many smaller plates that move about on the slippery mantle. Plate movement is caused when convection currents formed deep within the planet rise to the surface along

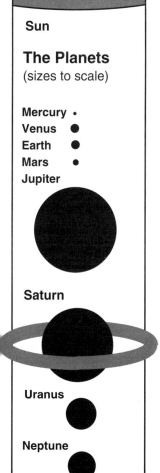

Sun

The Planets
(sizes to scale)

Mercury ·
Venus ●
Earth ●
Mars ●
Jupiter

Saturn

Uranus

Neptune

Pluto ·

Surface temperature: 480°C (896°F)

Moons: 0

Magnitude: -4.0 to -4.1

Successful probes: *Mariner 2*, 1962; *Venera 7* (landed), 1970; *Venera 9* (landed), 1975; *Magellan*, 1990–92

Day of the week: Friday, from Old English *Frigg* or Norse goddess *Freya*, translation of Latin Venus; *vendredi* in French

Notable: The Venuvian day is longer than its year. The planet spins in the opposite direction from Earth and most other planets. Venereal diseases are "diseases of Venus." Surface features are named after famous women, both real and fictional

EARTH ⊕

Distance from sun: 150 million km (90 million mi)

Diameter: 12,756 km (7,654 mi)

Day: 23.9 hours

Year: 365.2 days

Spinning speed: 38,400 km/h (23,040 mph)

Orbital speed: 105,600 km/h (63,360 mph)

Surface temperature: Avg. 15°C (59°F)

Moons: 1

Atmosphere: 77% nitrogen, 21% oxygen, traces of carbon dioxide, methane, neon and other gases

Notable: Earth was the centre of the universe until 1543, when Polish astronomer Nicholas Copernicus pointed out that we circle the sun, not vice versa

PLANETS & COMETS

(Some early Greek astronomers also thought this, but like Copernicus, they had a hard time convincing people.) Earth is considered a double planet, like Pluto, because of its relatively large single satellite. Its name comes from the Old English *oerthe*, meaning "dry land." It is the only planet with a name not derived from Greco-Roman mythology

MARS ♂

Distance from sun: 228 million km (137 million mi)

Diameter: 6,787 km (4,072 mi)

Day: 24.6 hours

Year: 687 days

Surface temperature: Avg. -50°C (-58°F)

Moons: 2, Phobos ("Fear") and Deimos ("Panic"), Mars's dogs in Roman mythology

Magnitude: +1.1 to +1.4

Successful probes: *Mariner 4*, 1965; *Mariners 6 & 7*, 1969; *Vikings 1 & 2* (landed), 1976; *Mars Observer*, 1993

Day of the week: Tuesday, from Old English *Tiw*, equated with the Roman Mars; *mardi* in French

Notable: Mars has polar caps like Earth, but they are composed of frozen carbon dioxide and water. They advance and recede with the planet's long seasons

JUPITER ♃

Distance from Sun: 778 million km (467 million mi)

Diameter: 142,800 km (85,680 mi)

midocean ridges. This upwelling of hot magma pushes the ridges apart, creating new crust and shoving the plates outward; Europe and North America are moving about one inch farther apart each year. At the other edge of the plates, such as in California, old crust descends back into the interior under overlapping fault lines. Earthquakes and volcanoes occur along midocean ridges and faults. Mountain ranges may be formed where continents collide; the Himalayas are the result of the Indian subcontinent crashing into Asia.

This idea of moving plates was first considered when Europeans noticed that the shapes of the two sides of the Atlantic seemed to fit together. At the time, Europeans thought Earth was only 6,000 years old, according to biblical reckoning. Recent scientific inquiry, dating only from the 1960s and including advances made by Canadian J. Tuzo Wilson, proved the theory of plate tectonics. Plates have been moving about on the surface of the Earth for at least 2.5 billion years, and as little as 200 million years ago all the continents were attached in a supercontinent called Pangaea. Old granitic rock such as that forming the Canadian Shield is less dense than the new rock on ocean floors, and thus remains atop plates as a sort of "granitic scum," as Wilson has called it. Earth is very much alive.

MARS, the God of War

Until recently, hopeful (or fearful) humans thought there was intelligent life on Mars, our closest neighbour after Venus. Evidence was supposedly found in 1877, when Italian astronomer Giovanni Schiaparelli reported seeing channels on the planet's surface, and others mistook this to mean artificial canals were present. Reputable scientists dreamed up various schemes for communicating with Martians, including a giant mirror to engrave words on the Martian desert with the focused rays of the sun. On Halloween in 1938, Orson Welles caused widespread panic in the United States when his "Mercury Theatre of the Air" broadcast an adaption of H.G. Wells's *War of the Worlds*, a story about an invasion of Earth by Martians. The fanciful idea of life on Mars was finally put to rest in 1976, when two *Viking* landers failed to meet any welcoming committees.

Primitive life may have once existed on the planet—there are formations that look like riverbeds—but Mars today is sterile. Its thin atmosphere of mostly carbon dioxide has less than one percent the barometric pressure of Earth's, and the surface is covered in red, iron-oxide dust that is sometimes blown into huge dust storms. The red dust accounts for Mars's appearance from Earth. Mars's bloodlike colour explains how the planet got its name. Mars was revered as the Roman god of war. The Greeks called him Ares. The red star Antares in the constellation Scorpius looks a lot like Mars. *Antares* is Arabic for "rival of Mars."

ASTEROIDS, the Minor Planets

There is a vast gap in space between Mars and the next planet, Jupiter. In 1800 a German astronomer, Johann Schröter, formed a group called the Celestial Police to find what was thought to be a missing planet in this gap. The group, along with other astronomers, soon found instead the asteriod belt. There are more than 3,000 identified asteroids in the belt, but millions more smaller ones, down to the size of a pebble. But why didn't Schröter and gang find a major planet in the asteroid belt? Astronomers theorize that the disruptive gravitational forces of nearby Jupiter prevent the space gravel from agglomerating into a planet.

JUPITER, the King

Jupiter is immense. It contains 70 percent of the mass of the entire solar system, excluding the sun. Though not as brilliant from Earth as Venus (because of its great distance), through binoculars Jupiter appears as a distinct white disc against the starry dots in the blackness. Some of those dots are Jupiter's moons. Four of its 16 satellites—Io, Europa, Ganymede and Callisto—are easily visible through a small telescope or binoculars mounted on a tripod. Viewing Jupiter and its moons is one of the most thrilling nighttime pastimes for a cottager or camper. Each night the moons are in a different position. More powerful backyard telescopes can detect Jupiter's famous Great Red Spot, a 300-year-old

---

Day: 9.9 hours

Year: 11.9 Earth years

Temperature at cloud tops: -130°C (-202°F)

Moons: 16; largest Ganymede

Magnitude: -2.1 to -2.3

Successful probes: *Pioneer 10,* 1973; *Pioneer 11,* 1974; *Voyagers 1 & 2,* 1979; *Galileo,* planned to arrive 1995

Day of the week: Thursday, from the Norse god Thor, equated with the Roman Jupiter; *jeudi* in French

Notable: The surface area of the Great Red Spot is larger than Earth's. The Chinese studied Jupiter at least as far back as 1000 B.C., when the 12-year orbit was observed

SATURN ♄

Distance from sun: 1,427 million km (856 million mi)

Diameter: 120,600 km (72,360 mi)

Day: 10.7 hours

Year: 29.5 Earth years

Temperature at cloud tops: -185°C (-300°F)

Moons: 18 (maybe more); largest Titan

Magnitude: +0.7 to +0.6

Successful probes: *Pioneer 11,* 1979; *Voyager 1,* 1980; *Voyager 2,* 1981

Day of the week: Saturday

Notable: Saturn's moon Titan is bigger than Mercury and Pluto and has a dense nitrogen atmosphere. It can be seen with a backyard telescope

URANUS ♅

Distance from sun: 2,870 million km (1,722 million mi)

Diameter: 51,300 km (30,780 mi)

Day: 17.2 hours

Year: 84 Earth years

Temperature at cloud tops: -200°C (-328°F)

Moons: 15; largest Titania

Magnitude: +5.7

Successful probes: *Voyager 2,* 1986

Notable: Uranus spins "horizontally" on a 98° tilt, while all other planets spin more or less "upright." Scientists speculate that a gigantic passing object may have knocked Uranus on its side

NEPTUNE ♆

Distance from sun: 4,497 million km (2,698 million mi)

Diameter: 49,100 km (29,460 mi)

Day: 16.1 hours

Year: 165 Earth years

Temperature at cloud tops: -200°C (-328°F)

Moons: 8; largest Triton

Magnitude: +7.9

Successful probes: *Voyager 2,* 1989

Notable: Neptune's moon Triton has nitrogen geysers and revolves around the planet in the "wrong" direction. *Voyager 2* passed only 4,900 km (3,063 mi) above Neptune's north pole, a cosmic pool shot of unbelievable accuracy

storm in the planet's swirling hydrogen-rich atmosphere.

As befitting its size, Jupiter is named after Rome's supreme god, who was fashioned after Zeus, the chief Olympian in ancient Greece.

SATURN, the God of Agriculture

Spacecraft have determined that Jupiter has faint rings, perhaps fed by sulphuric material ejected by volcanoes on Io. But they are nothing like the great rings of Saturn. The first sight of Saturn's rings through a backyard telescope is unforgettable. Suddenly, the solar system seems tangible.

The rings themselves are composed of billions upon billions of icy particles, ranging in size from dust flakes to garages. There are thousands of separate rings. The whole system, about a mile thick, revolves precisely around Saturn's equator. No one knows why Saturn alone has rings so pronounced.

Not only is Saturn beautiful, but for the ancients it had certain pleasant associations. Saturn was the Roman god of agriculture, and every December a great festival called the Saturnalia was held to mark the solstice. Businesses and public institutions were closed, citizens exchanged presents, wars were interrupted and slaves were freed. In other words, the people partied.

URANUS, NEPTUNE, PLUTO, the Distant Planets

Of the final three planets in the solar system, only Uranus can be seen with the unaided eye. But it is extremely dim, and an observer needs to know its exact location in order to spot it. The planet was discovered in 1781 by English astronomer William

Orbits of the Planets

(distances to scale)

● SUN
● MERCURY
● VENUS
● EARTH
● MARS

● JUPITER

● SATURN

● URANUS

FOR PLUTO, DOUBLE THE DISTANCE FROM SUN TO URANUS

● NEPTUNE

Herschel, and was named Uranus after the Greek father of heaven, king of the Titans.

Neptune, the last of the gas giants, was mathematically predicted before it was finally seen from the Berlin Observatory in 1845. It was named after Jupiter's brother, the god of the sea. To the Greeks he was Poseidon.

Distant Pluto, first seen in 1930 by American Clyde Tombaugh, is the last planet in the solar system. It is smaller than the moon, and is actually considered a double planet because its own moon, Charon, is about half Pluto's size. Pluto is thought to be an old comet, or perhaps an escaped moon from Neptune. Pluto was the Roman god of the underworld, who rarely left his dark kingdom. Charon was the boatman who ferried the dead across the river Styx.

THE OORT CLOUD, Birthplace of the Comets

Pluto's mean distance from the sun is 5.9 billion kilometres. But our solar system may extend out as far as 18.8 trillion kilometres. This is estimated to be the edge of the Oort Cloud, named after Dutch astronomer Jan Oort, who proposed in 1950 that comets are born in a distant ring of primordial matter that encircles the sun. Every once in a while a gravitational bump knocks a comet out of the cloud. The comet then begins its long trek towards the sun.

The average comet is composed of a rocky nucleus about a kilometre or two (3,300 to 6,600 feet) in diameter. An icy layer around the nucleus is warmed as the comet approaches the sun. The ice vaporizes into a cloud called the coma. Solar radiation blows some of the material away, creating a tail that can be hundreds of thousands of kilometres long. The tail gets bigger as the comet approaches the sun (the word *comet* comes from the Greek *kometes*, "long haired").

Some comets have such huge orbits that they are seen once and never again. Others develop orbits within the inner solar system and return regularly, such as Comet Encke every three years and Comet Halley every 76 years.

PLUTO ♇

Distance from sun: 5,900 million km (3,540 million mi)

Diameter: 2,300 km (1,380 mi)

Day: 6.4 Earth days

Year: 248 Earth years

Surface temperature: -230°C

Moons: 1; Charon

Successful probes: none sent

Notable: Pluto has an exaggerated elliptical orbit. From 1979 to 1999, it is actually closer to the sun than Neptune is

OORT COMET CLOUD

Distance from sun: About 9,600,000 to 18,800,000 million km (1–2 light-years, or 6–12 trillion mi)

Estimated number of comets in cloud: billions

Probes: *Voyager 2* should pass through the Oort Cloud around 60,000 A.D. On board is Chuck Berry's record "Johnny B. Goode," among other artifacts of human achievement.

Comet Halley: Named after English astronomer Edmond Halley, who in 1682 noticed its regular return. It was last seen in 1985–86, and will reappear in 2061. The Chinese have records of Comet Halley dating before the birth of Christ

SATELLITES
Smile! They're Taking Pictures

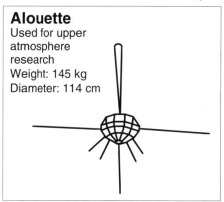

Alouette
Used for upper
atmosphere
research
Weight: 145 kg
Diameter: 114 cm

First Canadian satellite: *Alouette*, launched Sept. 29, 1962, making Canada the third country in space after the U.S.S.R. and U.S. Canada was the first country to have a domestic satellite-communications system, with the launch of the *Anik* satellites in the early 1970s

Pieces of man-made space junk orbiting Earth: More than a million, but 7,700 pieces larger than 10 cm (4 in) in diameter are tracked by Earth stations

Satellite sizes: *Sputnik* was about the size of a basketball. The cargo bay of the space shuttle is large enough to hold a bus

Also see: Sky, Stars

THE WORLD ENTERED a new era on October 4, 1957. On that date the Soviet Union launched *Sputnik*, the first successful spacecraft. Now nearly every industrialized country has a satellite orbiting the planet.

It's usually possible to spot a satellite within minutes of gazing into the early-evening sky, even from urban areas. Although the sky appears black, sunlight is still streaming high overhead for a few hours after sunset (and a few hours before dawn). Satellites soaring through space as they orbit Earth reflect these sunbeams. The artificial stars travel in all directions. They don't blink like aircraft, but some satellites seem to pulsate slowly. This is caused by a satellite's spin: as it revolves, it may present more surface area—such as the large solar "wings" that generate electrical power—towards the sun. Visible satellites orbit Earth at altitudes of 200 to 500 kilometres (120 to 300 miles). The space shuttle, which is also visible, flies about 200 kilometres (120 miles) high.

Smile as a satellite passes overhead: it could be taking pictures. The low-flying birds are either spying, mapping, collecting weather information or performing scientific experiments. Navigation satellites in the Global Positioning System, used for military and commercial purposes, circle Earth almost 18,000 kilometres (10,800 miles) above the surface and are not visible. Farther out at 36,000 kilometres (21,600 miles) are communications satellites. At that altitude, a satellite's orbital speed precisely matches the speed of the rotating Earth, about 38,400 kilometres (23,040 miles) per hour. This is called geosynchronous orbit, because a satellite appears fixed over one spot on Earth. Arthur C. Clarke, the British science-fiction author who wrote *2001: A Space Odyssey*, first conceived the notion of geosynchronous orbit in 1945. Satellites parked 36,000 kilometres high are said to be in the Clarke Belt. Satellite dishes in backyards and atop taverns point towards distant spacecraft in Earth's artificial ring system.

STARS
Just How Many Are There?

ON A DARK, clear night, from the end of a dock or the seat of a canoe, the celestial sphere seems composed of countless stars. With the unaided eye an observer can actually see about 4,000. Yet, combined, they are barely a mote in the universe. All the visible stars occupy only one minuscule area of our galaxy. The Milky Way, in total, contains at least 300 billion stars. And astronomers reckon there are another 50 to 100 billion galaxies in the universe. Terence Dickinson, the dean of Canadian astronomical writing, has figured out that in the space of sky occupied by the area of a thumbnail held at arm's length, there are some 50,000 galaxies.

The size of a star determines its life cycle. Small, modest stars live long, stable lives; most stars are in this category. Massive, ostentatious stars burn brightly but quickly. Our sun is roughly average in the universe overall (though in the top 10 percent of stars by size and luminosity in the Milky Way) and is about halfway through its "main sequence" or fusion stage. After the main sequence, a star cools and swells to become a "red giant" or supergiant. Then it contracts to form a "white dwarf," an extremely dense star that radiates away the stored-up heat from its previous life. A bottle cap full of matter from a white dwarf would weigh tons. Some massive stars explode in violent supernovas after the supergiant phase, because the collapse of matter is too great to sustain stability.

In the second century B.C., the Greek astronomer Hipparchus ranked the brightness of stars according to a system that remains in use today, with some refinements. He divided his magnitude scale into six levels, 1 being the brightest and 6 the dimmest. The naked eye can see to

Constellations
Line-of-sight effect

Range of star sizes: About $1/10$ mass of sun to 100 times mass of sun

Closest star to sun: Alpha Centauri Proxima, one of three stars in the Alpha Centauri triple-star system, 4.2 light-years away

Travel time to Alpha Centauri Proxima in our fastest space-craft: About 143,000 years

Farthest "star" from sun: Quasars, fantastically bright and dense light sources thought to occur primarily in young galaxies, are the farthest objects observable from Earth. They may be up to 13 billion light-years away. Quasars are thought to be about the size of our solar system, yet emit the equivalent light of 1,000 galaxies with 100 billion stars each. The Algonquin Radio Observatory in Algonquin Park was employed in part to study quasars. The huge dish, of excellent quality, is now the centre of the Algonquin Space

Campus, which takes part in international space experiments and runs an education program during the summer

Star ages: The sun is a relatively old star at 4.6 billion years (its lifetime is about 10 billion years). The Big Dipper stars are only about 200 million years old. They were born as the dinosaur age began on Earth

STAR WORDS:

Influence, influenza, influx: all from the Latin root *influentia*, meaning "an emanation of ethereal fluid from the stars affecting mankind"

Disaster: from the Latin, bad or evil star

Consider: from the Latin, to observe a star thoroughly for an omen. Astrological roots

Lucid: from Latin, to shine (like a star). The brightest star in a constellation is called the "lucida"

Lucifer: from Latin *lucis*, light, and *ferre*, to bear

Asterisk: from Greek, little star

Sidereal: of or pertaining to the stars, from Latin *sideris*, star

Also see: Milky Way, North Star & Little Dipper, Sun, Star Charts

The ten brightest stars visible from up north, in order:			
NAME	MAGNITUDE	DISTANCE IN LIGHT-YEARS	LOCATION (PROMINENT)
Sun	-27	8 light-min.	Sky (day)
Sirius	-1.5	8.6	Canis Major (winter)
Arcturus	-0.04	34	Boötes (summer)
Vega	+0.03	25	Lyra (summer)
Capella	+0.08	41	Auriga (winter)
Rigel	+0.12	1,400±	Orion (winter)
Procyon	+0.37	11.4	Canis Minor (winter)
Altair	+0.77	16	Aquila (summer)
Betelgeuse	+0.5	310	Orion (winter)
Aldebaran	+0.9	60	Taurus (winter)

about magnitude 6 on an exceptionally clear night away from urban lights. Each increment represents a star 2.5 times brighter or dimmer than the last.

A star's colour reflects its temperature. Blue stars are the hottest, red stars the coolest, with white, yellow and orange in between. Most stars appear white to an observer, however, because colour is not discernible at low levels of light. The twinkling of stars is caused by turbulence in the Earth's atmosphere.

Most stars are actually double or triple stars, although they are generally too close together to differentiate with the naked eye. Our sun is in the minority as a solitary star.

To ensure a standard roadmap of the heavens for professional astronomers, the International Astronomical Union, headquartered in Paris, in 1930 set out official names and boundaries for the 88 modern constellations. Most of these were based on the original 48 classical constellations catalogued by the Egyptian astronomer Ptolemy in the second century A.D. Many southern constellations were added to Ptolemy's collection in the sixteenth century when European explorers sailed across the equator. They tend not to have colourful stories attached to them. Several were named after technological breakthroughs of the day, including Microscopium, Telescopium and even Antlia, the humble air pump.

STAR CHARTS
Seasonal Roadmaps of the Heavens

THE FIRST PRINTED STAR MAP was produced by German painter and engraver Albrecht Dürer in 1515, a few decades after the invention of the printing press. But humans had been charting the night sky for millennia before that, bringing order to the heavenly confusion by grouping stars into constellations. The star patterns provided a home to mythological characters and served as navigational aids.

The modern constellations are descended from the *Almagest*, a star catalogue hand-produced by the famous Alexandrian astronomer Claudius Ptolemy around 150 A.D. Most of his constellations, in turn, were derived from traditions going back to at least 2000 B.C. Until modern times, most star maps were works of art, depicting heroes, heroines, villains

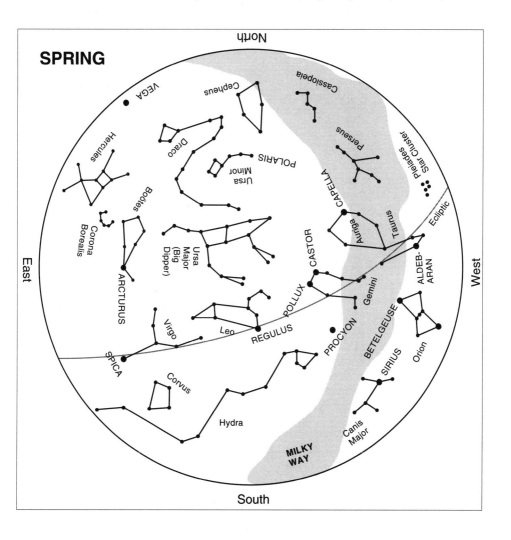

and other mythological figures in their places in the sky; however simpler star charts showing just the stars and other main astronomical features are easier to use.

Many bright stars have their own names that have been handed down over the centuries. Most are Arabic, because the Arabs preserved and translated the classic works of Greco-Roman civilization while the barbarians cast Europe into the Dark Ages. In 1603, the German astronomer Johan Bayer took a scientific approach to naming stars. He named the brightest star of each constellation *alpha*, after the first letter of the Greek alphabet. The second-brightest star was named *beta*, and so on. (There are a few exceptions to this scheme.) Thus, astronomers refer to the brightest star in Lyra as Alpha Lyrae, although it also has an ancient Arabic name, Vega.

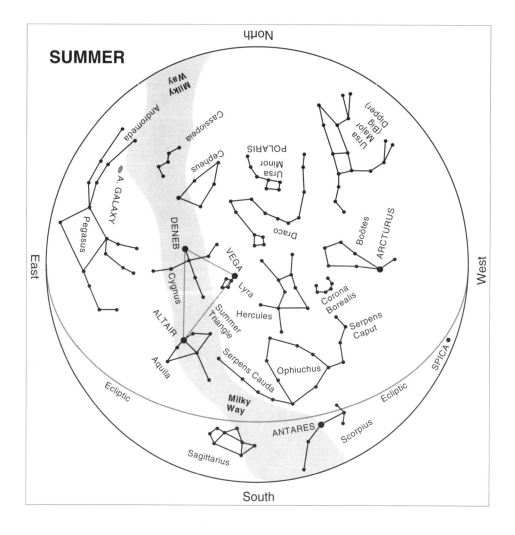

The rotation of the Earth makes it appear as if all the stars are circling Polaris, the north star, in a counterclockwise direction (see colour plate 26). Because of this motion, the star charts below are not exact for every time of night, every night of the year, or every location in the northern hemisphere. But they are good guides to the heavens shortly after nightfall in the middle of each season in central Ontario.

To use a chart, hold this book upside-down, place it over your head and face north. The position of the constellations in the night sky should roughly match those in the chart. Find the most prominent features first—the Big Dipper, Summer Triangle, or Orion in winter— and use them as guideposts to the other constellations. Star names are printed in UPPER CASE, while constellations are printed in Upper and Lower Case.

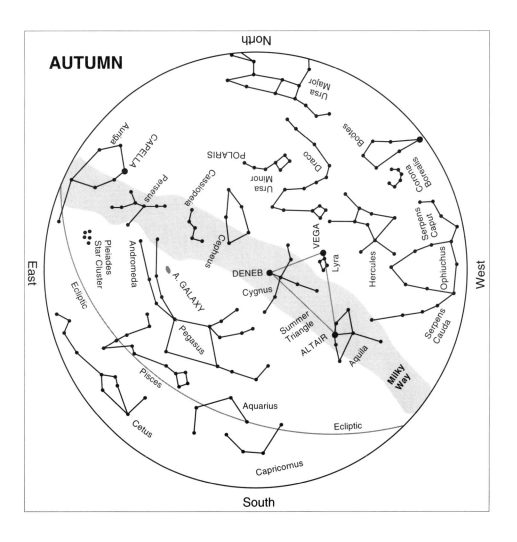

To find planets, look for what appear to be bright stars along the ecliptic. (Planets travel along this imaginary line in space.)

Most of the summer constellations have their own entries and star maps in this book. Some have interesting astronomical features, such as double stars and star clusters. A good pair of binoculars is an excellent viewing aid.

To help your eyes adjust to the dark, use a flashlight with red cloth or red paper wrapped around the light.

After a while, you will become familiar with the night sky, and will be able to follow the march of the seasons by simply gazing into the starry depths—repeating a habit formed by our earliest ancestors.

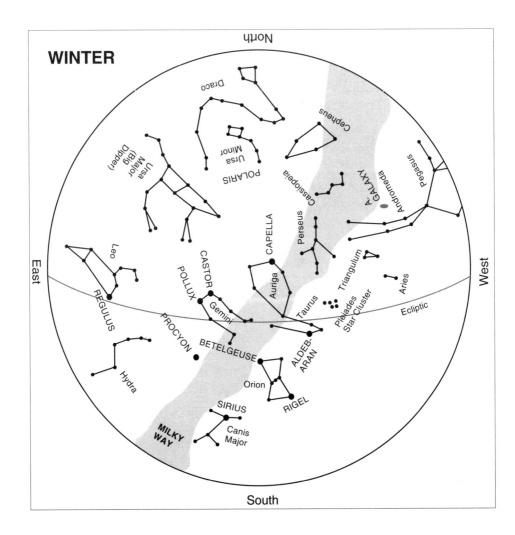

SUMMER TRIANGLE
The Swan, the Eagle and the Vulture

THREE BRILLIANT STARS dominate the heavens from June to September. They are Vega, Deneb and Altair, and together they form the unmistakable Summer Triangle. Over the course of a summer night, the Triangle flies high across the sky like an enormous celestial kite, passing almost directly overhead. The formation is called an asterism because it is not an official constellation. But its prominence makes it one of the first groupings of stars introduced to novice stargazers.

Vega, Deneb and Altair are, however, members of their own constellations. Vega, the brightest of the three, is the lucida of the constellation Lyra. It is named after the lyre the Greek musician Orpheus used to enchant listeners during his various adventures. The most famous story concerns his attempt to rescue his wife, Eurydice, from the underworld of Hades. Orpheus took his lyre and entered the gates of hell to bring her back to life. His beautiful music so charmed Hades that the god granted Orpheus's wish, but with one condition: he must not look back as his wife followed him to the land of the living. Orpheus obeyed until, just as he stepped out into the sunlight, he could resist no longer and glanced back. It was too soon, and Eurydice disappeared. Orpheus was later reunited in death with his wife, and Zeus placed the lyre in the heavens to commemorate the musician's sweet melodies.

Asians also have a well-known myth for Vega, which the Chinese call Chih Nu, the Spinning Damsel or Weaving Sister. In one version of the story, Chih Nu was sent to Earth by her father, the Lord of Heaven, to marry and look after a poor servant. The servant did not have any paper money to place in the grave of his dead father, as required by ritual and still practised today. But the devoted Chih Nu wove her husband beautiful tapestries that brought him great wealth. Before her powers on Earth expired, the Lord of Heaven returned Chih Nu to the skies.

Vega is an Arabic word meaning "the stooping one," or "vulture"—the ancient conception of the constellation before the Greeks. The other two constellations of the

Scan zone: The Summer Triangle is one of the best areas of the sky to scan with binoculars. One of the thickest parts of the Milky Way runs through this part of the skydome, and hundreds of stars invisible to the naked eye materialize

Look for: Delta and Epsilon Lyrae are double stars visible through binoculars. Epsilon Lyrae is actually a double-double, visible through telescopes. Beta Lyrae is an eclipsing double star: 2 orbiting stars that eclipse each other from our vantage point, producing what seems to be a star of variable brightness. Its luminosity changes over a period of about 13 days. The 2 stars in Beta Lyrae are so close to each other that astronomers believe superheated gas is flowing between them at a rate of 1.6 million km/h (1 million mph)

Distance of Vega from Earth: 25 light-years away

Distance of Altair from Earth: 16 light-years away

Distance of Deneb from Earth: 1,500 light years away

Magnitude of Vega: 0.0

Magnitude of Altair: 0.8

Magnitude of Deneb: 1.3

Lucida: The brightest star in a constellation, from which we get the word *lucid*

Also see: Milky Way, Star Charts, Stars

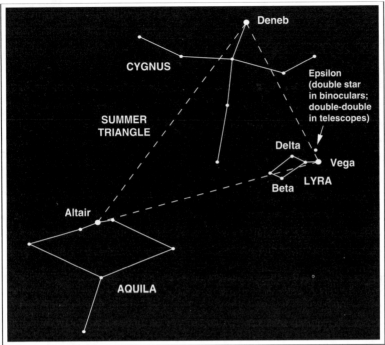

songs of grief along the river-bank, the gods took pity on him and placed him in the heavens as a swan. Thus was born, supposedly, the superstition that swans sing sad songs before they die.

Aquila, the constellation that includes Altair, was another bird of Greek mytholo-gy—the eagle that transported Zeus's thunderbolts. *Aquila* is Latin for "eagle," and the modern word *aquiline* means "of or like an eagle." *Altair* is Arabic for "the flying one." In Hindu mythology, Altair and the two bright stars nearby were thought of as the footprints of Vishnu, the preserver spirit.

Summer Triangle, Cygnus and Aquila, represent birds to this day. Cygnus looks much like its namesake, the swan. It is easy to imagine the outline of the great white swan as it flies along the shimmering path of the Milky Way. Deneb marks the tail of Cygnus; the word is Arabic for "tail of the hen." Christians also gave their own name, the Northern Cross, to Cygnus.

One of the Greek myths for Cygnus is said to explain the origin of the expression "swan song." Phaeton, the young man who created the Milky Way during a wild ride in his dad's sun chariot, had a close friend named Cycnus. When Zeus struck Phaeton dead with a thunderbolt, the mortal fell into a river. Cycnus tried several times to retrieve the body of his friend for burial, but his dives were unsuccessful. As he sang

A comparison of Deneb and Vega gives a good idea of how difficult it is to judge the size of stars and their distance from Earth. To the naked eye, Vega is slightly brighter than Deneb. Yet Deneb is, by astronomical reckoning, almost 60,000 times more luminous than Vega. The explanation, of course, is distance. Vega is only about 25 light-years from Earth, while Deneb, a colossal star 60 times wider than our sun, is about 1,500 light-years away.

ZODIAC & ECLIPTIC
Highway in the Sky

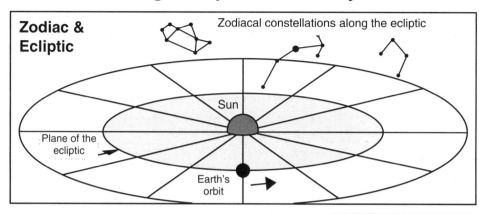

Zodiac & Ecliptic

Zodiacal constellations along the ecliptic

Sun

Plane of the ecliptic

Earth's orbit

P ICO DELLA MIRANDOLA was one of the first to scoff at the science of astrology. The Renaissance scholar declared in 1487 that the positions of the sun, moon and planets, in relation to the background constellations, had diddly-squat to do with human behaviour, as the ancients believed. Today, astrology has more implications for the science of newspaper publishing than anything else.

But the zodiac remains a vital feature of the sky. First conceived by the Mesopotamians about 5,000 years ago, the constellations of the zodiac lie along an imaginary line in the heavens called the ecliptic. Think of it as a highway in the sky. The sun, moon and planets all travel along this highway, more or less, as they cross the starry expanse. When astronomers say, "Saturn is in Sagittarius," they mean Saturn, from our point of view on Earth, is positioned along the ecliptic somewhere within the boundaries of the zodiacal constellation Sagittarius. It's a convenient way to describe the location of the wandering spheres.

The first full-time astrologers were priests who nightly scrutinized the sky to keep track of the stars, moon and planets. The position of the celestial spheres became associated with certain events, such as the annual flooding of rivers. It was an easy leap for the ancient Mesopotamian mind to believe that the stars actually caused events when they reappeared. What other explanation was there? Astronomer-priests thus commanded the people when to hold seasonal festivals or when to plant. Astrology was part

Horoscope: From the Greek *horoskopos,* meaning "observer of the hour of nativity." From *hora,* "hour," and *skopos,* "watcher"

Ecliptic: The plane defined by Earth's orbit around the sun. The orbits of other planets are also roughly along this plane. To an observer positioned on the north side or "above" the ecliptic, all the planets would orbit the sun in a counter-clockwise direction. The plane is called the ecliptic because when the moon crosses it, eclipses occur. If the moon is between Earth and the sun, there is a solar eclipse. If Earth is between the sun and the moon, there is a lunar eclipse

Time span for zodiac to shift one full sign at equinox, owing to Earth's "wobble": 2,160 years

Retrograding: Planets move eastward, night after night, against the backdrop of stars. But occasionally they change direction, a phenomenon called "retrograding." It's exactly the same effect one notices when passing a car on the highway. For a

THE ZODIAC

CONSTELLATION SIGN	REPRESENTATION	ASTROLOGICAL PERIOD	SAID BY THE ANCIENTS TO RULE THE:
Aries	Ram	Mar. 21–Apr. 19	Head and face
Taurus	Bull	Apr. 20–May 20	Neck
Gemini	The Twins	May 21–June 20	Breast
Cancer	Crab	June 21–July 22	Arms
Leo	Lion	July 23–Aug. 22	Heart
Virgo	Maiden (Virgin)	Aug. 23–Sept. 22	Bowels
Libra	Scales	Sept. 23–Oct. 22	Reins (wrist)
Scorpius	Scorpion	Oct. 23–Nov. 21	Secrets (genitals)
Sagittarius	Archer	Nov. 22–Dec. 21	Thighs
Capricorn	Goat or Sea Goat	Dec. 22–Jan. 19	Knees
Aquarius	The Water Carrier	Jan. 20–Feb. 18	Legs (shins)
Pisces	Fish	Feb. 19–Mar. 20	Feet

moment it looks as if the other car is moving backwards. Of course, it is only moving slower. The visible outer planets—Mars, Jupiter and Saturn—retrograde when Earth overtakes them. Mercury and Venus, the inner planets, retrograde when they overtake Earth

Also see: Moon, North Star & Little Dipper, Planets & Comets, Star Charts, Stars, Sun

of everyday life.

The ecliptic was divided into 12 constellations, and the signs of the zodiac were named after them. The word zodiac is Greek for "circle of animals." Some constellations are bigger than others, but the zodiacal circle was divided into 12 equal sections of 30° each to equal 360°. The astrologers probably chose 12 divisions because it takes Jupiter—well known to the ancients because of its brightness—12 years to complete one journey around the ecliptic.

Each zodiac sign was associated with the time of year the sun was located "in" it. The sun was in Libra, for instance, around the time of the autumnal equinox (the stars couldn't be seen during the day, of course, but astronomer-priests could figure out the sun's location based on their knowledge of the ecliptic). But because the Earth wobbles slightly on its axis, an effect called precession, the zodiac has actually shifted two signs since its invention. Thus, the sun is no longer in Libra when the astrological period called Libra begins on September 23. The astrological signs no longer match astronomical facts.

Most of the signs have Greek or Roman stories attached to them. Scorpius, which appears low in the south during the summer, is said to be the scorpion that Hera sent to kill the great hunter Orion. The unfortunate woodsman claimed that no animal was his match. Hera despised such hubris. To keep Orion and Scorpius safe from each other in the heavens, the gods placed them at opposite ends of the sky. By the time Scorpius appears, Orion is gone. The famous bright red star Antares is the "heart" of Scorpius.

MOTHER EARTH

THE GEOLOGICAL DRAMA *takes place over such a long period of time that it is almost impossible to comprehend. If the history of our planet were condensed into one year, the entire evolution of our species would have taken place over the last four hours. The rocks of the Canadian Shield, meanwhile, would be as old as 314 days. Indeed, there's a good chance that the rocks around your campfire are older than many of the stars overhead.*

Though it's slow moving, the drama is very real. The Earth is constantly changing, evolving, alive with transformation. The signs of this continuous metamorphosis are all around us, from devastating earthquakes in faraway lands to the erosion of rock into sand down at the lakeshore. Some think of Earth as a single living organism called Gaia, the ancient Greek name for Mother Earth, who with Father Heaven begat the first creatures.

In central Ontario, the Canadian Shield is never far beneath the soil, influencing everything on it. The hard rock outcroppings are the remnants of ancient granitic intrusions, exposed by glacial erosion. Shield outcrops are the visible portions of the basement of the North American continent. The Earth's all-powerful forces can be seen in the lines, layers and shapes of the bedrock breaking the surface.

CANADIAN SHIELD
The Basement of the Continent

Total area of Shield: 4.6 million km² (1.84 million sq. mi)

Total area of Canada: 10 million km² (4 million sq. mi)

Age of oldest Shield rocks: 3.96 billion years (Acasta gneiss from Northwest Territories)

Age of Earth: 4.6 billion years

Shield: Austrian geologist Eduard Suess coined the word *Shield* in 1892 to describe the bedrock that seemed to form the foundation of each continent. Other continents have Shields, too, but they are mostly buried under younger rock

Precambrian: *Cambria* was the Roman word for Wales. Sedimentary rock from the area, about 600 million years old, seemed to contain the oldest-known fossils. Older rock didn't appear to have fossils and thus was called "Precambrian." Precambrian fossils were found later

Valuable metals found in the Shield: Gold, silver, nickel, zinc, uranium, copper, iron, platinum, selenium, cobalt, lead

Igneous rock: Molten rock, called magma, under the Earth's crust, forces its way to the surface along cracks and weak points. Some escapes to the surface as lava. Some, such as granite, hardens before it reaches the surface. Both are called igneous rock, from the Latin word for" fire," *ignis*

Sedimentary rock: Composed of particles of eroded rock, and chemicals from the skeletal remains of marine animals

A BUSH PLANE dips and soars above the rich expanse of pungent green forests and clear blue lakes. Highways carve their way through magnificent pink granite outcrops. The female loon ululates longingly across a moon-drenched lake. A lonely white pine clings tenaciously to the tip of a windblown island.

This is the Canadian Shield, an ancient expanse of land that has shaped our national identity as solidly as the glaciers shaped the primal bedrock. "Like the sea, some landforms have a metaphysical force…" wrote journalist Barbara Moon in 1970. "There are a number of people who believe that the Canadian Shield is such a landform. Certainly something in the country's geography has a grip on the subliminal consciousness of all its citizens…"

The Shield derives much of its mystic power from sheer age. It contains the oldest rocks in the world, almost four billion years old. These rocks were formed when the hot young Earth, covered in roiling molten magma, began to cool in space. A hard crust developed, like the scum that forms on thick soup when it has been removed from heat and left standing. Ancient volcanoes poked through the crust and spewed lava and ash, concentrating valuable metals that would enrich Bay Street mining barons aeons hence.

This was just the beginning of the Canadian Shield. Over the following billions of years, the land that is now a mecca for peace-seeking urbanites was subjected to powerful geological forces. Cottage country as we know it today was once a mountain range as high as the Rockies. Later the area was repeatedly submerged under vast seas. Long after the seas retreated, wave after wave of glaciers, some of them four kilometres (2.5 miles) thick, bulldozed the land. Only when the last glacier retreated, about 10,000 years ago, did the first humans battle the traffic to spend a weekend in the area.

Today the oldest volcanic rock is found in a region geologists call the Superior Province. Ancient rivers and glaciers eroded the Superior Province and dropped

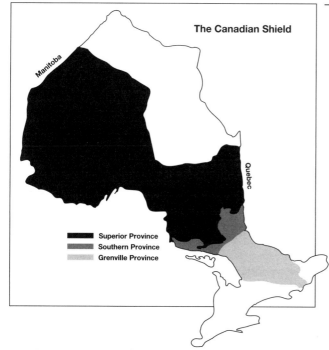

The Canadian Shield

Manitoba

Quebec

Superior Province
Southern Province
Grenville Province

and from plant matter. Laid down at the bottom of seas

Metamorphic rock: Originally igneous or sedimentary rock that has been altered by heat and pressure. Gneiss, a metamorphic rock, comprises a large portion of the Shield

First appearance of humans in Shield country: About 10,000 years ago, as the last glacier retreated

Invention of birch-bark canoe for traversing Shield lakes: At least 7,000 years ago

Ancient Shield life: Woolly mammoths, mastodons and giant beavers weighing 200 kg (440 lb) once roamed cottage country. They all died out by the end of the last ice age, about 10,000 years ago. Changing climate and, in the case of woolly mammoths, human predation, sealed their fate

Main years of CPR construction across the Shield: 1882–84

Number of men needed to build the CPR across the Shield: Almost 15,000

Number of horses: 4,000

Number of dogsled teams: 300

Number of dynamite factories built for railway construction across the Shield: 3

Also see: Birch, Eskers & Moraines, Falling Stars, Granite, Lakes, Painted Turtle, Planets & Comets

sediments around its fringes, forming the Southern Province. The Grenville Province comprises the 1.4 to 1.8 billion-year-old Central Gneiss Belt underlying Algonquin Park and Muskoka, and the 1.2 to 1.3 billion-year-old Metasedimentary Belt, stretching from Haliburton to Kingston.

After the Precambrian Era, when all this activity took place, seas advanced over the land and completely submerged the proto-North American continent. Sediments deposited at the bottom of the sea developed into a thick rock cover over the Precambrian Shield. When the waters retreated, the forces of erosion took over again. During the ice ages, glaciers scraped away the softer sedimentary rock, exposing the Shield in the contours we see today. Where the sedimentary rock was too thick to be removed entirely (such as in southwestern Ontario), or where glaciers didn't reach, the Shield remains hidden. It actually extends underneath most of North America, lying at the bottom of the Grand Canyon in Arizona. The Colorado River has cut through the sedimentary rock there just as the glaciers in Canada cut through to the Precambrian basement throughout much of Ontario.

CLAY, SHALE & SLATE
How Rock Gives Birth to Rock

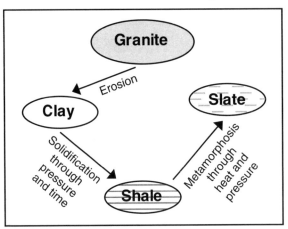

Principal component: Feldspar

Trace components: Microscopic quartz grains and bits of mica

Hardness of shale and slate on the Mohs scale of 1–10: 5.5

Colour: Clay and shale are usually dark grey, almost bluish, though iron oxides can sometimes colour them red or brown. Slate is usually darker, sometimes black

Earth's sedimentary rock that is shale: 79%

Sedimentary rock at the Earth's surface that is shale: 50%

Earth's surface rock that is sedimentary: 70–75%

Sedimentary rock in the Earth's crust: 5%

Also see: Canadian Shield, Granite, Soil

HUMAN HANDS began forming clay into figures of primitive art at least 13,000 years ago. The oldest clay pottery so far found in Ontario is about 3,000 years old. Nature, however, has been creating enormous sheets of ceramics for hundreds of millions of years. Shale is essentially time-hardened clay. It, in turn, under heat and pressure, recrystallizes as metamorphic slate.

Large clay beds in central Ontario were formed by sediments settling at the bottom of the giant post-glacial Lake Algonquin 14,000 to 5,000 years ago. The beds cover many areas of Manitoulin Island, the Bruce Peninsula and Muskoka, reaching as far north as Sudbury and North Bay. All of Ontario's clay, shale and slate originated ultimately from the solid, slowly weathering granite masses of the Shield. Clay's microscopic particles are primarily bits of feldspar, the grey or pink aluminum silicates of granite.

Shale is usually arranged in the same very thin layers originally laid down by clay. It is especially common in southern Ontario, including the Bruce Peninsula and Manitoulin Island, and is exposed in many layers along the Niagara Escarpment. Thick deposits of clay built up and hardened through the entire area for hundreds of millions of years, under the seas that lapped at the foot of the ancient continent that is now the Canadian Shield.

When shale recrystallizes into slate, flakes of mica form and line up in horizontal planes, causing the slate to break easily into flat, thin sheets that have long been used for roofing tiles, flagstones and chalk boards. Carbon or graphite content turns some slate black. In Ontario, native peoples often used its sharp fragments for tools and weapons.

ESKERS, MORAINES &
OTHER GLACIAL FEATURES
Landscaping on a Grand Scale

WINTERS TODAY can get pretty cold up north, but they're nothing compared to 14,000 years ago. At that time Ontario was frozen solid all year round. The land that would become the province sat under a gigantic ice sheet up to four kilometres (2.5 miles) thick.

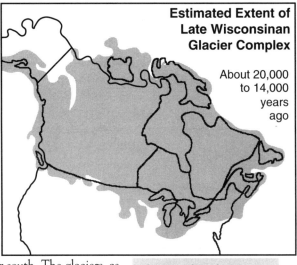

Estimated Extent of Late Wisconsinan Glacier Complex

About 20,000 to 14,000 years ago

But over the next 4,000 years, the world heated up, the ice receded, plant and animal life began to flourish and humans moved into the area from the warmer south. The glaciers, as they melted, left behind vast lakes, millions of tons of rubble and the exposed bedrock that underlies the modern Ontario landscape.

The rubble, or glacial till, is composed of clay, sand, gravel and boulders, and is found in several types of formations across the province. Eskers are sinuous ridges typically a few kilometres or miles long and 10 to 45 metres (33 to 150 feet) high. They are the deposits left by ancient glacial streams. These meltwater streams ran along the top of glaciers, in crevasses, or through tunnels in or under the ice. The streams usually ran in the same direction the ice flowed.

Moraines are much larger formations, some of them hundreds of kilometres long and up to 250 metres (825 feet) high. A moraine contains massive amounts of till, released from a glacier as it melted or bulldozed by the front or side walls of a glacier as it ploughed forward. A terminal moraine marks the farthest advance of a glacier. The Oak Ridges Moraine north of Toronto is an unusual type called an interlobate kame moraine, formed between the margins of two ice lobes, one moving southwest and the other, south of it, moving northwest.

Esker: From the Irish *eiscir*, "ridge"

Some eskers in Ontario: Balsam Lake Provincial Park (near Kirkfield), Esker Lakes Provincial Park (Kirkland Lake), south of Deux-Rivières (Mattawa), Madawaska (8 km [4.9 mi] west of town, on Highway 60), White (Lanark County)

Current extent of glacial coverage over world's land surface: 10%, mostly in Antarctica and Greenland

Maximum extent of glacial coverage over entire planet at height of ice age: 30%

Maximum extent of glacial coverage over Canada: 97%

Maximum extent of glacial coverage over Ontario: 100%

Recent ice ages: Began up to 2.5 million years ago. Four main glaciations are recorded in Ontario, called (from oldest to most recent) the Nebraskan, Kansan, Illinoian and Wisconsinan. Each glaciation lasted about 100,000 years, with warm periods in between. Many scientists believe we are currently experiencing an interglacial period

What causes ice ages? The exact sequence of events is unknown, but Earth's 26,000-year "wobble" on its axis, volcanic activity and other factors are believed to interact to cause ice ages. Volcanic ash spewed into the atmosphere can dramatically cool the planet in a relatively short period of time. The location of large masses of land in polar and temperate regions is a prerequisite for continental glaciation

Oldest glacial till found in Ontario: 120,000 years, in Toronto's Don Valley and the Moose River basin

Last time Ontario was completely covered by glaciers: About 14,000 years ago

Last remnant of ice age in Canada: Barnes Ice Cap, Baffin Island, 9,300 km² (3,720 sq. mi)

Speed of advancing ice flow: Varies greatly, depending on climatic conditions and terrain. Mountain glaciers in cold climates may move as slowly as 1–4 m (3.2–13 ft) a year. Warmer climates speed up this rate to about 300 m (984 ft) a year. But some "outlet" glaciers may temporarily surge at rates up to 7 km (4.3 mi) a year

Far from being pristinely white, glaciers consist of dirty ice packed full of debris. The embedded debris causes glaciers to act like enormous sheets of sandpaper scraping the underlying rock. Evidence for this is seen in scratches across polished rock faces, or in smoothly gouged or furrowed rocks. The direction of the markings generally indicate the direction of the ice flow.

Other glacial features include drumlins, kames, kettles and erratics. Drumlins are humpy hills sometimes called "whalebacks," which tend to occur in groups. The steeper side of a drumlin faces the glacial advance, while a gentler slope points in the direction the glacier travelled. A large drumlin field is found in the Peterborough area; they also occur along the south shore of Georgian Bay. Cone-shaped kames mark the bases of old waterfalls. Kames are made of debris carried over the edge of a glacier, or a crevasse in the ice, by a meltwater stream. They may also be formed of debris that accumulated in a depression in the ice. There is a kame field in the Tim River area of Algonquin Park. Kettles are small, round depressions usually occupied by a lake or a bog. They are formed when a block of ice is trapped underneath till and later melts. The collapse of the covering layer creates the depression. Erratics are boulders moved far from their place of origin by the Herculean forces of an ice sheet, some carried as far as 1,000 kilometres (600 miles), though usually no more than 100 kilometres (60 miles), and deposited randomly as the ice melted. Sometimes erratics assume bizarre perches atop smaller rocks.

Glacial deposits are enormously important to modern humans, because they provide the sand and gravel used in construction and road building. Gravel pits are often dug into the sides of kames or eskers. Many old eskers also form natural pathways. Portages, hiking trails, roads and railways sometimes run along the tops of eskers, which nature so conveniently placed thousands of years ago.

GRANITE

Rock of Ages

Granite Intrusion

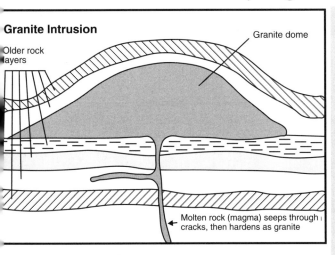

Granite dome

Older rock layers

Molten rock (magma) seeps through cracks, then hardens as granite

Muskoka: The word *Muskoka* may be derived from a combination of two Huron words, *musquash,* "it is red" and *ooka,* "large rocks." Thus, *Musquash ooka* meant "large red rocks," or granite slabs. The more likely origin is the name of two local Ojibway chiefs, father and son, spelled variously as Musquedo, Misquuckky, Mesqua Ukie or Mesquakie. Both fought in the War of 1812 for the British, and they oversaw the cession to the British of land to the south and west of Muskoka

Feldspar content of granite: 50–72%

Quartz content of granite: 25–40%

Mica and other dark mineral content of granite: 3–10%

Content of silicon dioxide, contained in feldspar and quartz, in most granite: 64–76%

Proportion of the Earth's crust made of silicon, oxygen and aluminum: 82%

Average hardness of granite on the Mohs scale of 1 to 10: 5.5

Size of granite crystal grains: 1.6 to more than 13 cm (0.6–5 in)

Aluminum content of granite: 8–16%

Potassium content of granite: 2.7–6.5%

Sodium content of granite: 2–6%

Calcium content of granite: 0.1–3%

S OUTH-CENTRAL ONTARIO'S granite reveals the molten, creative forces of the Earth, for they crystallized deep beneath huge mountains 1.1 to 2.2 billion years ago—when single-cell bacteria and algae ruled the world. Time, wind, water and ice eventually swept the mountains away, leaving the Canadian Shield's harder, weather-resistant granite domes. When a canoe lands on the granitic shore of a lake in Shield country, it scrapes along the ancient foundation of the continent.

Granite is an easy rock to read. Its three main minerals can be picked out among the grains. The black specks are usually mica or hornblende, while about a third of the crystals are transparent or white quartz—pure silicon dioxide. The rest, more than half, is feldspar—silicon dioxide with a dash of aluminum. A topping of potassium produces the familiar red or pink feldspar, while sodium or calcium yields grey or white granites.

Wherever it occurs, granite holds clues to countless ages. Varying coloured bands reflect the direction its parental magma oozed into place, often in successive waves, with different minerals hardening at different temperatures. The result is like an imperfectly blended cake, with the most compatible elements crystallizing together first and the heavier contents settling to the bottom. The deeper beneath

Other trace elements present: Iron, magnesium (about 2%, with oxides)

Main ingredients of pegmatite: Potassium feldspar, quartz, mica

Other minerals found in pegmatite: Calcite, garnet, pyrite, hornblende, chlorite, sericite, tourmaline

Size of pegmatite crystals: At least 5 cm (2 in) wide

Average length of a pegmatite dike: 30–300 m (100–1,000 ft)

Average width of a pegmatite dike: 1.5–30 m (5–100 ft)

Longest pegmatite dikes: More than 2 km (1.2 mi)

Hardness of pegmatite on the Mohs scale: Average of 6

Temperature at which pegmatite crystallizes: 500–900°C (932–1,652°F)

Meaning of Greek root words for pegmatite: Solid mass

Estimated portion of Canadian Shield made up of gneiss: Up to 80%

Gneiss: From the Slavic word for "rotted" or "decomposed"

Metamorphic: From the Greek *meta*, "beyond," and *morphe*, "form"

Also see: Canadian Shield, Lichens, Quartz, Soil

the Earth's surface the granite forms, the more slowly it cools, producing larger grains.

The largest crystals are in pegmatites, veins that contrast strongly in colour, texture and grain with the rock they run through. These veins, formed as the finishing touches of igneous-rock creation, are an amalgam of leftover, often volatile, ingredients that crystallized only after the more compatible elements of cooling magmas bonded and solidified. Squeezed into crevices created by the contraction and splitting of the host rock as it cooled, miscellaneous magmas, gases and water combined very slowly to form large, imperfect, but often spectacular crystals.

At the other end of the scale, gneiss (pronounced "nice") often looks like granite but has smaller crystals in much finer, more distinct bands, sometimes in patterns that curl and loop like the fine lines of a fingerprint. At first glance the bands in gneiss may be mistaken for familiar sedimentary layering. But gneiss is a metamorphic rock. Under unimaginable heat and pressure, older rock deep below the surface becomes plastic. Different minerals in the rock align themselves into fine, thin layers, typically a few millimetres wide, that bend and swirl according to the pressures acting upon them. The patterns are fixed as the rock cools. Gneiss may be metamorphosed granite or sedimentary rock, and comes in many varieties. Zircon, a trace mineral that contains uranium and is sometimes found in gneiss, allows geologists to date the rock by measuring its radioactive decay.

The rock has often folded, buckled and slid along fissures in the moving crust. Most recently, a million years of advancing and retreating glaciers sculpted and polished the granite and gneiss surface and deposited a thin granitic soil from the constant grinding. Granite yields acidic soil, making it largely unsuitable for farming even where it is thick. The countless lakes filling granite depressions, left by melting glacial ice 10,000 years ago, are also more acidic and harbour less vegetation than those farther south, making them especially susceptible to acid rain. From these conditions, all things in the ecosystem spring forth.

HUMUS
The Drama of Decomposition

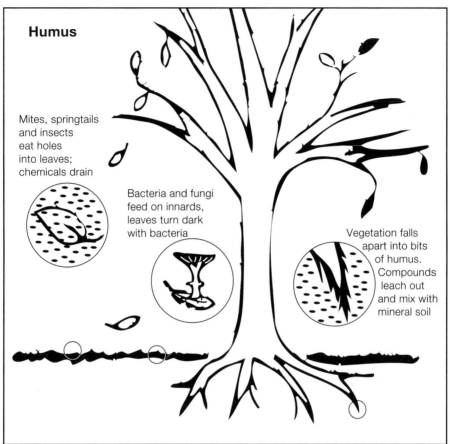

Humus

Mites, springtails and insects eat holes into leaves; chemicals drain

Bacteria and fungi feed on innards, leaves turn dark with bacteria

Vegetation falls apart into bits of humus. Compounds leach out and mix with mineral soil

HUMUS CONTAINS the past and the future life of a forest. Virtually every living thing eventually ends up in the organic humus layer— the return of dust to dust. Plant-eating animals capture and pass on through the food chain only a small fraction of the ecosystem's energy and nutrients. But underfoot, on the forest floor, lies a seething mass of fungi, bacteria, insects and other agents of decomposition that dines on 90 percent of all plant matter. Humus also acts like a giant sponge, absorbing up to five times its weight in water, allowing rain and meltwater to percolate into the soil for plant use, rather than running off quickly and causing erosion.

Minuscule springtails, mites and insects are the shock

Decomposer organisms in soil: Fungi, bacteria, springtails, earthworms, snails, slugs, potworms, rodworms, mites, fly larvae, beetles and their larvae, millipedes, protozoa

Amount of leaves and branches that falls on the floors of hardwood forests annually: 2.5–5 tonnes/ha

Most numerous soil animals: Springtails, roundworms, mites

297

HUMUS

Portion of carbon returned
to the atmosphere annually
that is expired by decomposer
organisms: 80%

Ratio of carbon to nitrogen in
sugar-maple leaves: 20 to 1

Ratio of carbon to nitrogen in
pine needles: 66 to 1

Ratio of carbon to nitrogen in
animal flesh: Between 3 and
5 to 1

Time it takes sugar-maple and
alder leaves to decompose:
1–1.5 years

Time it takes pine needles to
decompose: 3–9 years

Lignin (the hardest material in
wood to break down) content
of vegetation: 10–30%

Lignin content of humus:
30–60%

Also see: Fungi, Soil, Spiders,
Springtails

troops of decomposition. They chew holes into leaves, conifer needles and other dead plant parts falling on the forest litter. By breaking through the waxy outer layers, the tiny animals drain a plant's defensive chemicals and start the breakdown of tough cellulose and lignin structures. Bacteria and fungal threads can then invade and feed on the plant's tender innards, capturing 80 to 90 percent of the energy in dead plant matter. Hordes of bacteria and other microorganisims cover dead leaves and turn them black and slimy by the time they reach the bottom of the litter layer. Deeper still, decaying vegetation falls apart into small bits of moist humus. Chemical compounds leach into and mix with the mineral soil, eventually to be reabsorbed and incorporated into new life by tree and plant roots.

Compared with areas to the south, decomposition is slower and the litter layers thicker in Ontario, because soil organisms are active only during the growing season. Litter layers are especially thick in evergreen forests because conifer needles are acidic, discouraging bacteria, with fungi becoming the main decomposer. Evergreen needles also contain high levels of resilient defensive chemicals—but low nitrogen levels. Nitrogen is common in easy-to-decompose chemicals such as proteins, making the flesh of dead animals especially simple to strip away from bone. Carbon, which forms cellulose and other structures, is much more difficult to break down.

Dead twigs, branches and tree trunks also eventually contribute to the humus layer, though more slowly. Bark- and wood-boring beetles, mites and other animals eat tunnels into the wood, allowing other insects, fungal strands and the roots of living plants to follow. Termites digest wood by harbouring fibre-eating protozoa in their stomachs. The wood is processed and fertilized by the droppings and bodies of the animals eating into it. There is so much activity by decomposers that a dead tree contains more living cells than a living one. As it rots, it also soaks up water, acting as a reservoir for roots and soil animals. A fallen tree can take hundreds of years to decay, ultimately influencing its surroundings far longer than the duration of its life.

LAKES

A Fragile Abundance

A CROSS THE FACE of the Canadian Shield, deep, rugged depressions in the Earth's bedrock crust have been filled with cool, fresh, clear, dark water. Rock and water, together with climate, determine the nature of all life in the ecosystem. Even humans, consisting of about 70 percent water, become part of whatever lake they drink.

Most of the lakes puddling the Shield were formed by huge blocks of glacial ice that as they melted filled up the pockmarks and gouges in the eroded surface. Because there are so many lakes, especially in headwater areas such as the Algonquin and Temagami highlands, many have small drainage basins around them, with short, fast-running streams. The abundance of lakes and connecting rivers has long provided ideal, often circular transportation routes, with relatively short portages, for the Shield's first peoples, followed later by European explorers, trappers and modern canoe campers.

With their often-small watersheds of thin soil and hard, acidic rock, most Shield lakes do not receive nearly as much nutrient as those farther south. Much of the plant debris that does wash into them sinks to the cold, deep bottom where bacterial decay is very slow and circulation is limited to spring and fall, locking up their nutrients for much of the year. Low nutrient levels curtail algae growth, the base of the aquatic food chain.

Circulation within lakes is limited because cold water is heavier than warm water. During the summer a warm layer, three to six metres (10 to 20 feet) deep, floats on top of a much colder transition zone of a few metres. After that, all the way to the bottom, the lake is about 5° or 6°C (41° to 43°F) all summer and never mixes with the top layer. In autumn, however, the upper layer cools till it reaches the same temperature as the lower, cold zone, eliminating the barrier and allowing water, oxygen and nutrients to circulate through the entire lake body. Though vital to the health of the aqueous system, the fall turnover, as well as that of early spring, can be a dangerous time to canoe, since the free flow

Number of lakes in Ontario: About 250,000

Average time taken by water flowing into upper Lake Superior to reach the St. Lawrence River: 329 years

Deepest lake in southern and central Ontario: Mazinaw Lake, north of Kingston—more than 100 m (330 ft) deep

Maximum depth of Lake Superior: 410 m (1,323 ft)

Maximum depth of Lake Huron: 229 m (750 ft)

Largest freshwater lake (by surface area) in the world: Lake Superior

World's largest island within a lake: Manitoulin Island, 2,800 km² (1,068 sq. mi)

Largest lake-within-a-lake in the world: Manitou Lake, on Manitoulin Island, 103 km² (41 sq. mi)

Origin of *Ontario*: Iroquoian for "beautiful lake" or "beautiful water"

Most popular sport-fishing lake in Ontario: Lake Simcoe

Average production of trout per hectare (2.5 acres) in Algonquin Park lakes: 560 g (1.25 lb)

Average production of trout per ha (2.5 acres) in the Kawartha lakes: 10,000 g (22 lb)

Sunlight that reaches 5 m (16.5 ft) below the surface of a clear lake: 20%

Temperature at which water is heaviest: 4°C (39°F)

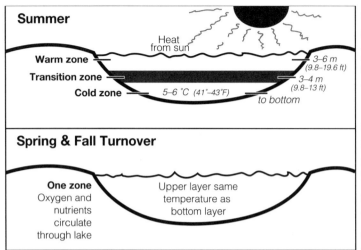

Summer

Heat from sun

Warm zone

Transition zone

Cold zone — 5–6 °C (41°–43°F)

3–6 m (9.8–19.6 ft)

3–4 m (9.8–13 ft)

to bottom

Spring & Fall Turnover

One zone
Oxygen and
nutrients
circulate
through lake

Upper layer same
temperature as
bottom layer

of water allows winds to stir the whole lake, not just the top five metres, creating much bigger waves.

Ice in winter cuts the entire lake off from its oxygen supply, which is captured from the air by wave action. With spring breakup, the whole reservoir again circulates until the upper layer warms and reestablishes the temperature barrier, first in the shallows, then radiating to the centre of the lake.

Unfortunately, with the oxygen and nutrients that come in the spring, lakes can also receive an acid shock from the runoff of melting snow. Precipitation is naturally more acidic than lake or ground water because it reacts with nitrogen in the air. Rain or snow contaminated with sulphur dioxide and nitrogen oxides from industrial emissions is four to 400 times more acidic than normal precipitation. Canadian Shield lakes are especially vulnerable because the region's granite-based soils and coniferous forests make them more acidic than southern lakes, and they have few nutrients to neutralize acid rain.

Massive acid loading in spring runoff can push many organisms over the edge, especially those near the base of the aquatic food chain such as freshwater shrimp and stonefly larvae. It can also strike early-spawning fish, including pike, pickerel, minnows and white suckers, that congregate near inlets, where the acid infusion is greatest. In highly acidic conditions, some die in 24 to 36 hours. The eggs of fish and amphibians, especially spring peepers and salamanders, can also be severely affected. Compounding the damage, acidic runoff may leach natural toxic metals such as mercury, zinc and aluminum out of the soil.

Number of Ontario lakes in which fish reproduction is affected by acid rain: 19,000

Number of Ontario lakes threatened by acid rain: 48,000

pH (potential hydrogen) of distilled water: 7

pH of rain unaffected by pollution: 5.2

Average pH of rain falling on Ontario: 3.5–5

Natural pH of a Canadian Shield lake: 6.5

pH of highly acidic lakes (30–40% above normal): 4.7

pH of lemon juice: 2

People who study lakes, ponds and streams: Limnologists

Reason water feels warm to humans swimming in the rain: The body has already adjusted to coolness caused by rain, so blood vessels do not suddenly constrict upon submersion in lake water, as they do on a hot day

Also see: Algae, Brook Trout, Granite, Limestone, Soil

LIMESTONE

Ashes to Ashes, Life to Limestone

A STEEP, TOWERING, limestone cliff can be seen as a monument to life on Earth. All limestone is formed from accumulating layers of marine plants and animals, combining and solidifying with calcium, or lime, on shallow sea floors. Together with the world's deposits of petroleum and coal, which form in deeper seas or on land, limestone stores much of the carbon that made past life possible.

Carbon is the material of all life because its atoms have unique abilities to form extensive and varied stable chains, which can build living tissue and store energy chemically. The first living cells, three billion years ago, probably obtained carbon from the Earth's then-poisonous atmosphere. While carbon atoms have been continuously recycled from dead plants or animals back into the air ever since, time has frozen beneath the Earth's surface huge stores that have escaped decomposition.

But limestone erodes more quickly than most rocks and, after perhaps hundreds of millions of years, eventually does return to the carbon cycle. Much limestone once covering the Canadian Shield—built up on top of the ancient, eroded continent while it was submerged 450 to 250 million years ago—has since been washed away. To the south, limestone forms the backbone of Manitoulin Island and the Bruce Peninsula. The spine is part of the 2,300-kilometre- (1,400-mile-) long Niagara Escarpment, which runs in an arch from near Rochester, New York, to central Wisconsin. The escarpment exposes the outer rim of an 800-kilometre-wide (480-mile-wide) expanse of sedimentary bedrock called the Michigan Basin, with the state of Michigan at its centre. Some 600 million years ago, the basin was the broad bay of a shallow, tropical sea lapping the southern shores of the continent of Laurentia, today's Canadian Shield. There was no life on dry land at the time. The first multicellular marine organisms were just beginning to appear.

Over the next 300 million years, layers of sand, mud, algae, coral and primitive life-forms accumulated in the Michigan Basin, up to 12,000 metres (7.2 miles) thick at its centre. Gradually, as the sediments collected, the centre of the basin began to sink, creating a saucer shape. Then, over the next 200 million years, deep-Earth forces pushed the entire basin upwards out of the water, like a raised bowl, until the rim finally broke free of the surrounding land, forming a continuous, rocky cliff. The escarpment's edge has since eroded steadily inwards, 80 kilometres (48 miles) from the original cleavage, around Port Hope and Madoc in Ontario, towards the centre of the basin. The fallen rock has dissolved, crumbled or been carried away by glaciers.

Limestone also slowly dissolves into any lakes that rest upon it, releasing bicarbonate, which neutralizes acid rain. This buffering capacity has been a life-saver for many sport-fishing lakes, especially on Manitoulin Island, while Shield lakes have suffered. Two exceptions in the Shield are lakes Gilmour and Tecumseh, which lie in a four-kilometre- (two-and-a-half-mile-) wide crater gouged into the ground by a meteorite that struck the northern Algonquin Park area 450 million years ago. Limestone subsequently accumulated within the crater while later seas covered the Shield.

Some areas, especially near the edge of the Shield, also feature limestone that has been recrystallized through heat and pressure beneath the Earth's surface to become the rock's metamorphic form, marble. Native peoples carved numerous mythologic figures in the marble rockface at Petroglyphs Provincial Park, near Peterborough, more than 500 years ago. After finishing his or her work, each carver would cover it with leaves, preserving the site from weathering and from outsiders until its discovery by non-natives in 1954.

QUARTZ
Crystals Harder Than Steel

THE CANADIAN Shield is a treasure trove of one of the oldest, most valuable gemlike stones known to humans. Quartz in its many forms and colours has been used to make tools throughout the world for more than 100,000 years. Coloured, banded quartz called agate was used to make beads and other jewellery in Mesopotamia and Egypt. Long before people of Near Eastern cultures learned to mould or blow glass, they were painstakingly chipping and polishing plates up to 70 centimetres (27 inches) wide and cups and urns as much as 25 centimetres (10 inches) deep out of solid pieces of quartz, sometimes from a single giant crystal. Glass itself was—and still is—made mainly from quartz sand grains melted into liquid and cooled too quickly to allow crystals to re-form, essentially freezing the liquid configuration.

There is an abundance of quartz in sand and granite, and in its pure state around the world, because it is composed of the two elements that make up three-quarters of the Earth's crust. Some 90 percent of all rocks contain both oxygen and silicon. Quartz is pure silicon dioxide, known as silica. Most pure quartz rocks are thought to form from groundwater that becomes supersaturated with silica it picks up from rocks as it moves deep into the increasingly hot nether regions of the Earth. A change in temperature, or else evaporation, causes the solution to crystallize in subterranean cavities to form quartz, later exposed on the surface as it is pushed up with the surrounding igneous rock.

Because oxygen and silicon form such a stable bond, quartz is harder than steel. Flint, a type of quartz tinted dark

Alias: Silica, silicon dioxide, SiO_2

Hardness on the Mohs scale of 1 to 10: 7

Hardness of diamond: 10

Hardness of gold: 2

Portion of the Earth's crust composed of silica: About 60%

Portion of the Earth's crust composed of quartz uncombined with other rocks: 12%

Crystal shape: Hexagonal

Number of varieties of quartz: More than 200

Ontario's official mineral: Amethyst, a purple quartz, coloured by a rare alignment of iron atoms, mined around Bancroft, Lake Nipissing and Lake Superior

Other semi-precious forms of quartz: Rose quartz, smoky quartz, opal, onyx, tiger eye, citrine. Variously formed by

QUARTZ

characteristics of temperature, pressure and trace impurities at the time of crystallization

Quartzlite: Sandstone composed of at least 95% white quartz that has recrystallized and hardened through heat and pressure beneath the surface

Famous quartzite formations: The white ridges of Killarney Provincial Park, which were quarried by natives up to 10,000 years ago, when the crests were islands innundated by the meltwaters of a receding glacier then only 150 km (90 mi) to the north

Melting temperature: 1,723°C (3,133°F)

Minimum temperature oxygen needs to combine with silicon: 400°C (752°F)

Temperature at which quartz usually forms: Less than 800°C (1,472°F)

Temperature at which amethyst forms: 90–250°C (194–482°F)

Largest quartz crystals ever found: 2 m (6.5 ft) long, 45 cm (17.7 in) wide, 350 kg (770 lb), in New England. Another in Russia 750 kg (1,650 lb)

Percentage of quartz in sand used to make glass: 95–99%

Date of oldest-known human-made glass: About 2500 B.C.

Date of oldest-known moulded glass: About 1500 B.C.

Date of oldest-known blown glass: About 200 B.C.

Also see: Canadian Shield, Granite, Sandstone

by fossilized marine microorganisms, is so hard and brittle that Stone Age humans shattered it to make tools and weapons from its shards. By hitting it together, they produced sparks to start fires. The word *silica* is derived from the Latin *silex*, meaning "flint." Living things also incorporate silica to give strength to their tissues, such as in tree trunks. The abrasiveness of a grass blade's sharp edge, which can in certain species cut a finger, is due to tiny bits of quartz in the plant.

Clear, colourless quartz, known as rock crystal, is common in Ontario. The word *crystal* comes from the Greek *krustallos*, meaning "ice," because the ancients believed quartz was ice frozen at such a low temperature that it could not melt. The belief persisted even into the eighteenth century, when Carl Linnaeus, Swedish father of the modern scientific system of classifying species, wrote that sand was caused by raindrops that had fused and permanently solidified. The ancients used rock-crystal lenses as magnifying glasses to start fires, especially ceremonial blazes. Large crystal balls of transparent quartz, which would take many months to make, have been used by seers in India and Europe for thousands of years. In Rome and Japan, the rich rolled the cool surfaces of small, sculpted crystal spheres over their skin for refreshment on hot, sweaty days.

Another form of silica rock that is especially abundant in the Canadian Shield is called milky, or white, quartz. Numerous microscopic cavities filled with liquid carbon dioxide or water within the rock cause its whiteness. Milky quartz is the most common rock appearing in seams that shoot through other igneous or metamorphic bedrocks. Most gold and other precious metal deposits in Ontario are contained within milky-quartz veins. Native peoples commonly used this quartz for spear- and arrowheads, since flint and chert (another form of quartz) were rare in Ontario and usually had to be obtained from elsewhere through trade.

SANDSTONE
From Beaches to Buildings

LIKE SAND itself, most sandstone is composed mainly of quartz grains. It forms where sand has collected and been pressed together for ages on ancient beaches, riverbeds, dunes and sandbars, spreading out as those landforms gradually shift position.

Sandstone usually retains tiny air spaces between the grains, taking up five to 30 percent of the rock and making it quite porous. Vast sandstone shelves far underground are important reservoirs of water and hold the world's largest deposits of oil and natural gas.

Unlike other sedimentary rock, sandstone can be resistent to erosion and is found even among the most ancient rocks, as well as the youngest. In north-central Ontario, it began to accumulate 2.5 billion years ago at the edges of the lifeless Laurentian continent, today the Canadian Shield. Many large areas of ancient sandstone, such as the Temagami Plateau, were transformed into metamorphic rock by heat and pressure while buried deep beneath later sedimentary deposits.

Some of the most prized sandstones, like those around Sault Ste. Marie, are cemented with iron oxides, colouring them brown, orange, yellow or reddish. They can be cut into big, attractive blocks that are both easy to carve and weather resistant. Canada's Parliament Buildings in Ottawa and the Ontario legislature at Queen's Park are built of 400- to 500-million-year-old brown sandstone from southern Ontario, as were many brownstone houses at the turn of the century.

Thickness of sandstone deposits in central Ontario: Up to 11,000 m (36,000 ft)

Portion of sandstone that is quartz: 80%

Other common minerals found in sandstone: Feldspar, mica, hornblende, garnet, zircon, magnetite, gypsum, pyrite, chert, barite, opal

Colours: Grey, red, white, salt-and-pepper

Graywacke: Grey sandstone with more than 10% feldspar

Arkose: Sometimes pink sandstone composed of 25% or more feldspar

Quartzite: Hardest sandstone, at least 95% pure white quartz, metamorphosed so that quartz crystals fill all pores

Portion of Earth's surface sedimentary rock that is sandstone: 30%

Portion of Earth's total sedimentary rock that is sandstone: About 13%

Also see: Canadian Shield, Granite, Quartz, Soil

SOIL
The Skin of the Earth

Maximum depth of glacial till on southern Canadian Shield: 50 m (165 ft)

Number of roundworms per cubic metre of soil: Up to 20 million

Content of the Earth's outer core: Primarily molten iron and nickel

Thickness of the inner core: 2,440 km (1,514 mi)

Podzol: Acidic soil with low nutrients

Possible organisms found in 1 m³ of soil: More than 1,000 species, including tens of millions of springtails, mites, protozoa, roundworms and bacteria, with most living in the top 3 cm (1.2 in). Earthworms, ants, termites and other insects also aid plants and the soil by burrowing channels for air, water and nutrients, as well as by acting as a check on fungi and other organisms harmful to plants

Possible hazards to the soil of clearcutting forests: Soil compaction by large tree-cutting vehicles and bulldozers, erosion, flooding or drying out, loss of nutrients from removal or vapourizing of slash in too-intensive burnings, loss of beneficial fungi

Also see: Canadian Shield, Fungi, Humus, Lichens, Thunder & Lightning, Worms & Leeches

PEOPLE OF ALMOST every culture, from native North Americans to ancient Egyptians and Chinese, conceived of the earth, the soil, as the primal womb of life, Mother Earth. Their observation of the endless cycles of decay and regeneration probably inspired early beliefs in reincarnation. The more that soil is understood in modern times, the more the original concept of it as a living layer, the water-moistened skin of the planet, seems to ring true. Growing and thickening with the weathering of rock and with each year's dead vegetation, soil reclaims and recycles the materials of life via a vast network of roots and fungal threads that run through it. Soil teems with unimaginable quantities of living things. Echoing the ageless attachment people and nations have had to their soil, one forester astutely describes it as the most fundamental form of wealth.

While carbon (the principal building material of living organisms), oxygen and nitrogen are taken ultimately from air or water, another 16 basic chemical elements needed for life come from soil. The proportions of those elements occurring in the soil, together with precipitation, dictate the types of life in each ecosystem. Calcium, potassium, sodium, phosphorus, iron and magnesium, among the most important, react with water at varying temperatures to give the soil its colour. Most Canadian Shield topsoils are red, from the leaching of iron and aluminum oxides from decomposing vegetation in the humus layer above. Shield subsoils are naturally grey.

The Shield's predominantly podzolic soils are high in potassium, aluminum and iron, derived from granite bedrock. But they are low in the calcium and magnesium common to the deeper, limestone-based soils of southern Ontario. Because silicates, the primary material of granite and quartz, are acidic minerals, granitic soils are not very fertile.

The world's first soil formed on dry land began to build up more than 400 million years ago, when terrestrial plants began to appear. As they proliferated and evolved, plants mixed their accumulated organic debris with the particles of mineral soil the plants helped weather. The extremely ancient, eroded Canadian Shield, however, had most of its remaining soil scraped away during the last ice age. Its present soil layer, except for thick sand and gravel till deposits dumped by the glaciers, has had only 10,000 years to build up again since the ice retreated. Unlike farther south, where the soil builds up at a rate of about 0.5 centimetres (0.2 inches) every 300 years, Shield granite is very hard, yielding mineral particles to erosion much more slowly.

Sand grains are the largest particles in soil, followed by microscopic bits of clay and silt. Fertile loam soils contain a mixture of all three, which make up about half the volume of richer soils. About a quarter of the space is filled with films of water around the particles, and another quarter is larger air-filled spaces, providing oxygen for roots and soil animals. Trees and plants themselves send 50 to 80 percent of their energy into their roots, which, along with fungal fibres, break up rocks and hold the soil down. Some kinds of fungi and microbes also produce extracellular polysaccharids, or ELPs, which glue soil particles into clumps that are not dissolved by water.

Making the whole system work, there are greater numbers of creatures within the soil than exist anywhere else. Bacteria feed away at dead vegetable matter, while one-celled protozoa and microscopic roundworms swim within the film of water around soil particles, eating bacteria and each other. Mites and springtails in turn wade through the film to eat the roundworms and the strands of fungi.

WETLANDS
Mother Nature's Kidneys

THE VAPOURS AND GASES that sometimes rise from swamps and other still bodies of water were once believed to be the cause of many of the contagions that long plagued humanity. Even after the discovery of microbial pathogens in the past century, the popular bias against wetlands generally held sway. Only now are wetlands coming to be recognized by the public for the vital roles they play, including actually purifying water and providing hatcheries, food and habitat for a vast array of species.

Ontario's wetlands can be divided into four main categories: swamps, marshes, bogs and fens.

Swamps, often located along the edges of rivers, are wetlands specifically featuring trees. Usually sitting on top of clay or other nonporous material, swamps are flooded or wet all year long, though standing water sometimes dries up in summer. Because swamps are undefined collecting basins, their water levels may fluctuate significantly. They slow down the flow of water, helping prevent flooding and erosion. During dry spells, they are reservoirs, their soaked soils keeping the water table close to the surface, while releasing water slowly into outflowing streams. The abundant dead trees in swamps are mined by woodpeckers, which in turn provide cavities for many songbirds. The relative inaccessibility of swamps also makes them favoured locations for heron rookeries (see photo opposite) and wolf dens.

In more open areas near the mouths of rivers, in shallow bays and around ponds, marshes form. Marshes are the richest of all habitats, forming where silty, organic sediments collect in calm water. They teem with life. The still water, filled with insects, pollen, algae and bits of organic matter, allows cattails and other water plants to sink roots and take advantage of the superconcentration of nutrients in the muck. Fast-growing marsh plants are far more efficient than most others at capturing nutrients and quickly turning them into living tissue. The rich plant life in turn supports high densities of insects, snails, fish, frogs, birds and mammals.

With their absorbent plants, marshes effectively filter silt and other contaminants. They have been dubbed "Mother Nature's kidneys." Creating marshes, which use less land than municipal water-treatment lagoons, has been suggested as the best means of cleaning up water pollutants, including sewage.

At the opposite end of the scale, bogs are the most nutrient-poor wetlands. With no drainage outlets, their water becomes stagnant. Many were formed 10,000 years ago by chunks of glacial ice that left depressions when they melted. Bogs maintain cold microhabitats because cold air settles in low pockets of land in summer. Dead vegetation tends to accumulate in bogs rather than decompose, because the cold, acidic, low-oxygen conditions are inhospitable to bacteria and most fungi. Sphagnum moss, which thrives in bogs, intensifies the condition by drawing atoms of calcium, magnesium and other mineral nutrients from the water in exchange for hydrogen ions, making the bog even more acidic.

Compressed, unrotted vegetation piled up over the centuries in bogs, called peat, can be used as a long-burning fuel. The species succession of plant life after the retreat of the glaciers can be traced and dated from well-preserved pollen grains extracted from peat-bog layers. Intact prehistoric animals and 3,000-year-old human bodies have been unearthed from bogs in various parts of the world.

Fens are somewhat like bogs, though they are not as acidic and are dominated by sedges, grasslike plants with unjointed, three-sided stems. Peat builds up at the bottom of fens, also. Large areas of bogs and fens, called muskeg, cover much of northern Ontario.

Marsh dwellers: Red-winged blackbirds, swamp sparrows, marsh wrens, herons, bitterns, ducks, rails, osprey, muskrat, water snakes, snapping turtles, painted turtles, frogs, minnows, large-mouthed bass

Bog vegetation: Sphagnum moss, black spruce, tamarack, insect-eating sundew, pitcher plants, orchids, Labrador tea, bog laurel, leatherleaf, crowberry, cranberry, bog rosemary

Bog dwellers: White-throated sparrows, Wilson's warblers, hawks, foxes, weasels, lynx, bobcats, pickerel frogs

Fen vegetation: Sedge, grasses, reeds, shrubs, tamarack, cedar

Also see: Black Ash, Beaver, Cattail, Black Spruce, Tamarack, Red Maple, Moss

RECOMMENDED READING

*For those interested in delving in more detail into
various subjects we have touched upon in this guide,
we recommend the following books:*

The Audubon Society Field Guide to North American Rocks and Minerals *(Alfred A. Knopf)
provides colour photos and good thumbnail accounts of just about any chunk of geological curiosity you can
stumble upon.*

The Audubon Society Field Guide to North American Weather *(Alfred A. Knopf) is a
comprehensive and useful guide to observing and forecasting the weather, with a large section of sometimes
spectacular colour photographs.*

Familiar Amphibians and Reptiles of Ontario *(Natural History/Natural Heritage), by Bob Johnson,
provides good accounts of all of the province's frogs, salamanders, turtles and snakes, along with illustrations
and range maps.*

*The Friends of Algonquin organization publishes a series of excellent booklets on the trees, flowers,
mammals, birds, fish, reptiles and amphibians found in Algonquin Park, available at Park gate stations and
outfitting centres or from the Ministry of Natural Resources.*

Legacy *(McClelland & Stewart), edited by John Theberge, is a thick, comprehensive compendium of the
natural history of Ontario, written by the province's leading naturalists and featuring some of the best colour
nature photography.*

The Mammals of Eastern Canada *(Oxford), by Randolph Peterson, though academic in tone, is one of
the best texts on the wildlife found in Ontario.*

Native Trees of Canada *(Fitzhenry & Whiteside), by R.C. Hosie, is the definitive text on identifying
Canadian trees, featuring photos of leaves, seeds, flowers, buds and bark for each species. An updated
version is soon to be published.*

A Natural History of Trees *(Houghton Mifflin), by Donald Peattie, though written in 1950, is one of the
most informative and beautifully written books about North American trees.*

Nightwatch, An Equinox Guide to Viewing the Universe *(Camden House Publishing), by Terence
Dickinson, is an excellent guide to observing the night sky, with everything from superb star maps to advice
on how to take pictures of the heavens.*

The Observer's Handbook, *an annual publication of The Royal Astronomical Society of Canada,
contains a huge amount of information about stars, planets, eclipses, sunrises and sunsets, meteor showers
and so on, most of which is accessible to the average reader.*

Peterson's Field Guide to Eastern Forests *(Houghton Mifflin), by John Kricher, is an excellent text that
explains the interrelationships among the many aspects of woodland habitats.*

Peterson's Field Guide to the Birds of Eastern and Central North America *(Houghton Mifflin), by
Roger Tory Peterson, is perhaps the best field guide for Ontario birds, complete with detailed colour
illustrations, brief descriptions and range maps.*

Seasons, *the magazine of the Federation of Ontario Naturalists, Equinox, Canadian Geographic, Nature
Canada and Cottage Life magazines are also excellent sources of ongoing information on nature in Ontario.*

Shrubs of Ontario *(Royal Ontario Museum), by Herb Hammond, offers the most comprehensive look at
much of the province's plant life, from bunchberry to hawthorn trees.*

310

RESOURCE GUIDE

Boy Scouts Canada, 9 Jackes Ave., Toronto, Ont. M4T 1E2, (416) 923-2461

Bruce Trail Association, P.O. Box 857, Hamilton, Ont. L8N 3N9, (416) 592-6821 (area code 905 after Oct. 4, 1993)

Canadian Parks and Wilderness Society, 160 Bloor St. East, Suite 1335, Toronto, Ont. M4W 1B9, (416) 972-0868

Canadian Recreation and Canoeing Association, 1029 Hyde Park Rd., Suite 5, Hyde Park, Ont. N0M 1Z0, (519) 473-2109

Earthroots, 401 Richmond St. West, Suite 251, Toronto, Ont. M5V 3A8, (416) 599-0152

Federation of Ontario Cottagers' Association, 215 Morrish Rd., Suite 101, Scarborough, Ont. M1C 1E9, (416) 284-2305

Federation of Ontario Naturalists, 355 Lesmill Rd., Don Mills, Ont. M3B 2W8, (416) 444-8419

Friends of Algonquin, P.O. Box 248, Whitney, Ont. K0J 2M0, (613) 637-2828

Girl Guides of Canada, 50 Merton St., Toronto, Ont. M4S 1A3, (416) 487-5281

Ministry of Culture, Tourism and Recreation, 77 Bloor St. West, 9th Floor, Toronto, Ont. M7A 2R9, (416) 314-7365

Ontario Heritage Foundation, 10 Adelaide St. East, Toronto, Ont. M5C 1J3, (416) 325-5000

Ontario Provincial Parks and Natural Heritage Areas Branch, Ministry of Natural Resources, 90 Sheppard Ave. East, 6th Floor, North York, Ont. M2N 3A1, (416) 314-1717

The Royal Astronomical Society of Canada, 136 Dupont St., Toronto, Ont. M5R 1V2, (416) 924-7973

Wildlands League, 160 Bloor St. East, Suite 1335, Toronto, Ont. M4W 1B9, (416) 324-9760

World Wildlife Fund (Canada), 90 Eglinton Ave. East, Toronto, Ont. M4P 2Z7, (416) 489-8800

Acknowledgments

We would like to sincerely thank the following people
for their advice and help in writing this book:

Jack Alex • Allen Alsop • Mark Bacro • Ken Barbour • Spencer Barrett • Jim Bendell • G. Bennett • Michael Berrill • T. J. Blake • Jim Bogart • George Boyko • Ron Brooks • Judy Brunsek • Ron Burrows • Michael Cadman • Rob Cannings • John Carnio • Charles Churcher • Nancy Clark • William J. Crins • Geoff Cutten • Nancy Dengler • Jim Dick • Terence Dickinson • Bruce Duncan • R. Michael Easton • J. E. Eckenwalder • Ken Elliott • J. B. Falls • M. B. Fenton • W. G. Friend • Fuzz • David L. Gibo • Alan G. Gordon • Karen Graham • Premek Hamr • John Harcus • David J. Hawke • Robert Hawkes • Anne Houtman • Brad Hubbly • Don Huff • David J. T. Hussell • Robert R. Ireland • Ross James • George Kolenosky • John Krug • Basil Johnston • Kathleen Kemp • Ellie Kirzner • Doug Larson • Anna Leggatt • Harry G. Lumsden • G. L. Mackie • David Malloch • Tom Mason • Chris McCall • Jon McCracken • Margaret McLaren • Nora McLoughlin • Don McNicol • Jack Millar • Ted Mosquin • Philip Mozel • Ted Mumford • Milan Novak • Ike Osmani • John Percy • Larry Petrie • Andrew Podgorski • Michael J. Power • James S. Pringle • Peter Quinby • George Rason • Pete Read • John W. Reynolds • Mike Rosen • Ann Shier • Howard Smith • Mark Stabb • Jocelyne St. Onge • Dan Stuckey • Gary Teeter • Victor Timmer • Tim Timmerman • Ron Tozer • Nick Tzovolos • Caren Watkins • Allan Wainio • Patrick Weatherhead • Ron Weir • Wayne F. Weller • D. V. Weseloh • Terry A. Wheeler • Jan Whitford • Jane Young, and Soonki Schaub, Ben Schaub and Nik Sheehan, who were on that fateful canoe trip.

INDEX

Page numbers in *bold-italic* indicate illustrations. "CP" refers to colour plates.

INDEX

INDEX